THE DIAMOND WORLD

◆

By the same author

THE MELLONS
JOSEPH P. KENNEDY

THE DIAMOND WORLD

◆

DAVID E. KOSKOFF

1817

HARPER & ROW, PUBLISHERS, New York
Cambridge, Philadelphia, San Francisco,
London, Mexico City, São Paulo, Sydney

THE DIAMOND WORLD. Copyright © 1981 by David E. Koskoff. All rights reserved. Printed in the United States of America. No part of this book may be used or reproduced in any manner whatsoever without written permission except in the case of brief quotations embodied in critical articles and reviews. For information address Harper & Row, Publishers, Inc., 10 East 53rd Street, New York, N.Y. 10022. Published simultaneously in Canada by Fitzhenry & Whiteside Limited, Toronto.

FIRST EDITION

Designer: Abigail Moseley

Library of Congress Cataloging in Publication Data
Koskoff, David E., 1939–
    The diamond world.

    Includes bibliographical references and index.
    1. Diamond industry and trade.   I. Title.
HD9677.A2K67   1981b   338.2'782   81–47357
ISBN 0–06–038005–5   AACR2

---

81 82 83 84 85 10 9 8 7 6 5 4 3 2 1

For Charlotte,
my love and my friend

CONTENTS

◆

Photographs follow pages 118 and 246.

When Randolph Churchill, father of Winston, peered down into the vastness of the Big Hole of Kimberley, the great worked-out diamond mine, and contemplated what it represented in human terms, he mused, "All for the vanity of woman." To which one of the women in the party added, "And the depravity of man."

INTRODUCTION

THE DIAMOND WORLD

◆

"Get the coat! Get the coat!" Harry Samuelson's father yelled from the ship's railing to his son on the wharf. "Go back to the hotel, pay the bill, and *get my coat!*"

Harry suspected what was afoot. The ship, from Vigo, Spain, to Cuba, was fully booked; the Samuelsons had appreciated that they would have to wait for the next boat to freedom. They had gone to the docks only to say good-by to some luckier friends, other Jewish refugees from Hitler, who had obtained the last berths available. Once aboard, though, the friends warned Harry's father: Spain might change its tolerant policy toward the Jews; there might not be a "next" boat. This might be the Samuelsons' last chance to escape. The friends were willing to help. At length Harry's father made the determination: They would stow away. Standing on the wharf, Harry, fifteen years old, pieced that much together.

But why the coat? What of their luggage, their important belongings? Why had his father neglected to mention these things of value? In Cuba it would be warm; his father would not even need an overcoat.

Harry rushed back to the hotel, threw the family's most valuable possessions into a suitcase, and with a mine-is-not-to-reason-why sigh, put the useless overcoat on his own back and returned to the dock. With a surreptitiously obtained pass, he boarded ship, and when it embarked for Cuba and freedom, the Samuelsons—seven in all—were aboard, secreted in their friend's cabin.

When the ship was well at sea, the Samuelsons confided in a Catholic priest, who brought young Harry to see the ship's purser to make the family's explanations and try to smooth things over. The purser was outraged to learn that there were stowaways on his ship and was not to be mollified by a mere boy. He demanded to see Harry's father immediately.

Harry was terrified. Would they order that the ship be turned around, and hand the family over to the authorities as common criminals?

Or worse, deport them from Spain across the border to Vichy France, where the Nazis were in firm control? He returned to the family's hiding place where his father calmly heard what had occurred.

No, the father would not go to see the purser. Instead, he said, Harry must return to see the purser—this time alone, without the priest. He was to tell the purser that they were honest people, that they would pay for their passage, that they were grateful for his understanding and for his assistance, and—fumbling about in the lining of his old overcoat— that they wanted the purser to have a token of their appreciation. The father removed his hand from within the coat and dropped something into Harry's palm: one shiny pebble.

Today Harry Samuelson is an important diamond dealer in Antwerp, Belgium, the capital of the world diamond trade. He has forgotten much in a full life, but he will always remember the look on the purser's face when Harry gave him the diamond: "You can't imagine how his face lit up; I saw a smile like I've never seen in my whole life." And he remembers the wonderful trip to Cuba—everything was first class all the way. He remembers, too, the coat, the old overcoat, and what was sewn into its lining, the family's passport to freedom.

Samuelson told me the story over a drink in Bombay, India, export center of the important Indian diamond-processing industry. He was one of some two hundred diamond people that I interviewed in fifteen diamond countries. I was to find that his was a common story, not peculiar to the Nazi era.

Today, Jews are coming out of Russia carrying diamonds that they have removed from pieces of heirloom jewelry. The stones that they carry are generally of unimpressive quality, and many of the refugees are bitterly disappointed to learn the current market value of their treasures. Still, it is better than nothing.

Diamonds are the world's hardest known substance, though they are brittle, fracture easily, and will burn. They are relatively scarce, though not as rare as rubies and many other less costly substances. When properly cut, diamonds are pleasant to look at. More important to the refugee or prospective refugee—the Southeast Asian refugee from communism, the mafioso refugee from justice, the banana-republic dictator, or maybe you—diamonds can easily and secretly be taken in flight and they can be converted into money. They represent the most compact form of wealth, optimally portable and infinitely smuggleable.

Diamonds are bought and sold by the "carat," which has no relationship to the "karat" that signifies the proportion of gold in an alloy. Traditionally, one carat was the weight of one of the remarkably uniform seeds of the carob tree, but the carat has now been regularized at 200 milligrams, 5 carats to the gram, 142 carats to the avoirdupois (kitchen-scale) ounce, or 156 carats per troy ounce.

As of June 1, 1981, "D-flawless" diamonds, the finest and rarest of the more than two hundred grades of gem diamonds, were trading at $40,000 per one-carat stone at the most wholesale market, the New York Diamond Dealers Club. If one could round up 156 of them, one troy ounce of one-carat D-flawlesses, they would fit in a king-sized cigarette package and represent a cool $6,240,000, as against gold's $483 per troy ounce. In short, one-carat D-flawlesses are worth thirteen thousand times as much as gold. No other medium of trade packs their value per volume.

Most diamonds, of course, are very far from D-flawless; indeed, most are so highly flawed and discolored that they are usable only for industrial purposes. As the hardest substance, diamond makes the very best possible cutting edge and has innumerable industrial applications. However, even the lowest-quality "industrials" are worth upward of $300 a troy ounce.

A parcel of even medium-quality stones the size of this book would be worth more than Shah Reza Pahlavi of Iran owned, and could have been taken with him when he left Tehran. Curiously, soon after the Shah went into exile a surprising lot of fine stones turned up on the Swiss market. For the Shah to have moved any substantial amount of wealth in gold bullion would have required a small boxcar, which would surely have been inspected by unfriendly eyes somewhere along his route. If the typical reader of this book were to convert all of his (or her) worldly possessions into good-trade diamonds, they would rattle around too much in a hollowed-out book or even in a cigarette package. A matchbox should do—at least for a few million dollars.

It is probably the portability of diamonds and the ease with which they can be hidden that has made the diamond an instrument of corruption and illegalities throughout history. The diamond, the symbol of purity, makes a market that functions both above and below ground, in which the licit and the illicit mingle freely and comfortably, the line between them almost imperceptible, usually irrelevant. Diamonds bring out the worst in men—and women.

Portability makes the diamond business ungovernable, or governable only with the freely given consent of the diamond community. Governments in most "diamond" countries must seek a modus vivendi with the diamond community, and it is the diamond men who hold the upper hand. In Belgium and Israel, the great diamond-cutting and -trading countries, the taxes actually extracted from the diamond people cannot be too onerous or the diamond people, as portable as their wares, will pick up and move away. Government people understand as much. The tax collectors there accept a thin slice of the loaf as better than none.

In the diamond-producing countries of Central and West Africa, countries with many small diamond-mining enterprises, the governments have had to exempt the miners and diamond traders from national income taxes. Otherwise all of the diamonds would be smuggled out. Export duties on "rough" (diamonds as they come from the earth, before cutting and processing) are set there, as a practical matter, by the exporters: They cannot be higher than the exporters are willing to pay. Otherwise, again, all the diamonds would be smuggled out. Even so, the diamond people customarily rob the producing countries. In the diamond control office of one producing country, the lead weight labeled "500 carats" used on its balance scale in weighing shipments to be exported was a gift to the country from one of its diamond traders. It actually weighs 750 carats, with the result that every shipment out of the country is underweighed by the tax collector, and leaves with an underassessment of the export duty.

The situation is much the same with those countries that import polished diamonds: import duties are set, as a practical matter, by the importers. The typical international diamond dealer will cost out duties, will ask himself, "How much will it cost me to pay the duty, and how much will it cost me not to pay the duty?" When the United States had a 20 percent levy of duties and excise taxes on the import of polished diamonds, the total revenues collected came to a little over zero. When the charges were halved, revenues soared. At 10 percent it paid to pay the duty—the professional smugglers were charging 12 percent—but at 20 percent it was cheaper to smuggle.

Diamonds make excellent bribes, whether for bribing Nazi border guards (which every civilized man applauds) or bribing the finance minister of France (which every civilized person condemns). Cash is blunt, too crass. Cash is ugly, while diamonds have romance and myth; they flatter the recipient. And they can more easily be rationalized as simple gifts if things go wrong. The late Pierre Arpels, partner in the celebrated firm of jewelers Van Cleef & Arpels, shook his head in dismay when asked in 1978 to comment on his brother Claude's conviction for having given an IRS examiner a diamond brooch and other jewels: "I think it's very difficult in our modern world to know where to draw the line between spontaneous human relationships and administrative must-nots." Jean-Bédel Bokassa, former emperor of the former Central African Empire, used diamonds freely in his spontaneous human relationships with the French government officials who kept his dictatorship afloat. Even French President Valery Giscard d'Estaing accepted thirty carats of spontaneity from the emperor while serving as French finance minister in 1973.

If money makes the world go round, the diamond world revolves around "black money," unrecorded, untaxed money that finds good refuge as well as diversion in diamonds. I asked a Singapore diamond dealer which nations Singapore's diamond customers came from, and he replied, "Any place that your great American corporations are bribing government officials or paying off buyers, we are selling diamonds!" Industry spokesmen in Antwerp estimate that in busy periods almost half the business is conducted outside official records. The large quantities of diamonds that are bought with black money generate more of it, which filters down in varying degrees and amounts throughout the diamond trade and the diamond-processing industry.

Because so much of their trade is in cash and unrecorded currency, the "diamantaires," the businessmen involved in one or more aspects of the diamond trade, are in the happy position of being able to create whatever books they wish, to file pretty much whatever tax returns they want to file, limited only by the requirement that they declare sufficient income to support their apparent life-styles. They are ideally situated to confront a world in which the economic problem for the private entrepreneur is often not so much how to earn money, but rather how to protect it (or hide it) from the tax collector.

There are historical reasons why tax evasion became part of the warp and woof of the diamantaires' culture, but by now it is respectable in the diamond world principally because it is venerable. One old Amsterdam diamond man told me, "To cheat a government is a *mitzva!*"—a meritorious act in accord with God's will. It would be unfair to say that all diamond people are cheating their governments' taxing authorities, but only a little unfair.

The diamond corrupts nations as well as individuals. Liberia, the People's Republic of the Congo (formerly French Congo, with its capital at Brazzaville), and Burundi, a steamy snip of a country in Central Africa, operate in the diamond world for the most part as "fencing" nations, which launder diamonds smuggled in from other nations in order to collect the modest duties they receive for their role as accomplices. Belgium and Israel more or less openly permit their diamantaires to perpetrate invoicing frauds against the taxing authorities of other nations in exchange for their own small takes. Much of the profits of the diamond world get funneled off to Switzerland (corrupted not alone by the diamond people), where the banking laws make the Swiss coconspirators in most of the world's most substantial tax frauds.

Diamonds corrupt Marxism whenever Marxists can get their hands on them. Communist China is now inviting foreign diamond firms to establish diamond-polishing factories on the mainland as joint ventures with the government. Peking hopes to have a cutting industry of large proportions by the mid-1980s, to turn out doodads to bring joy to the ladies of the oppressor class, as part of its great leap forward. China is learning from the bear to its north. The Soviet Union is now one of the world's most important diamond-mining and diamond-polishing countries. In the diamond world the USSR operates like the most arch capitalist. It willingly plays its part in the operation of the world's tightest commodity cartel, the cartel that controls the world's production and distribution of diamond rough, which is in turn controlled by De Beers Consolidated Mines, Ltd.

An institutional advertisement in a trade publication carries a photograph of a diamond and only seven words: at the top of the page, "Diamonds is a world" and at the bottom, "led by De Beers." De Beers, the great South African diamond-mining enterprise, owes its control of the diamond world not so much to the stones it mines (it mines only 30 percent of the world's total caratage) but rather to the fact that it is the selling vehicle for all of the world's other major diamond producers, together accounting for upwards of 80 percent of the output of gem-quality diamonds.

De Beers feeds out the goods at such rate as it determines, at whatever price it dictates, to whichever of the thousands of diamond-cutting enterprises it favors. It decides the fate of the diamond-processing industry in every country in which there is one, and whether any other countries will have significant processing industries. It indirectly controls the destinies of sometimes as many as 350,000 diamond polishers in the State of Gujarat in western India; it determines the future of Antwerp; and it has the power to wreak havoc on the economies of Israel and of several African countries.

In its role as a mining entity, the giant calls itself De Beers; in its merchandising roles it operates through one of its number of avatars—the Central Selling Organisation, the Diamond Corporation, the Diamond Trading Company, the Diamond Purchasing and Trading Company, Industrial Distributors, Diatrada, or Throgmorton. In all of its roles, De Beers is a kid-gloved operation characterized by fine tailoring, English accents, and ways as polished as a diamond. Yet it has the power to move nations and a grim willingness to use it. Much of this book is about the ways in which De Beers has attained and maintained control, the geopolitics of its power, and the benevolent and malevolent faces of its power.

De Beers is not a pacesetter in corruption. It really does prefer to have things "legitimate." It directly participates only in such corruptions as are culturally acceptable and necessary in the various societies in which it must operate. It is virtually impossible to do business in Liberia, Tanzania, or Sierra Leone without bribing officials, and it is completely impossible to do business in Zaire without paying off government leaders. It is not necessary to bribe in India, but it helps a lot. When one considers that the company's position is strong and stable in all of the above, it becomes inconceivable that it refuses to acknowledge local ways of life as do most other multinational corporations.

As for the conduct of those with whom it deals, De Beers minds its own business. Only one picture hangs in the waiting room of the company diamond-buying office in the inland town of Kenema, Sierra Leone, in West Africa: a lithograph depicts the three wise monkeys. The picture capsulates the company's ethic: see no evil, hear no evil, speak no evil.

There is no villain in this book. De Beers is definitely not one. The corporation is a decidedly positive force for racial progress in its troubled homeland, and a socially progressive factor in other countries in which it operates. De Beers claims that its control and direction of the diamond market operates in the best interests of everyone, including the consumer. It may be right. I believe that its own tax strategies are confined to legitimate tax-avoidance techniques as opposed to the illegal evasions usually practiced by the diamantaires, and De Beers does not cheat on duties. The diamond industries of South Africa and Namibia are 95 percent corruption-free, because De Beers accounts for 95 percent of their production.

S. N. Sharma, chairman of the Hindustan Diamond Company, India's leading dealer in rough diamonds, says, "The diamond has fifty-eight facets and the diamond trade a hundred sixteen—but some places, more." It is a business with a common sense all its own, in which sellers are periodically pleased to be able to say that they are not making any sales; in which buyers may ask the seller to raise his prices; in which the "monopolist," De Beers, as often as not, is holding down prices and minimizing its profits.

Diamonds is a multibillion dollar business revolving around an attractive pebble that has an intrinsic value of from $2 to $30 a carat— its value for industrial applications. Its higher value in the marketplace is principally an artificial one, attributable mostly to the strong hand of De Beers that keeps up the price. It is a business of strange bedfellows, in which Angola and other radical anti-apartheid countries call for a boycott of everything South African while they snuggle up happily with a South African–based company. It is a business in which things are often not what they seem.

For the layman, the terminology is baffling enough when it is not misleading. For example, diamonds can be mined in yellow ground, which is rarely yellow, or in blue ground, which is not often blue. The rough diamond is prepared for market by a diamond polisher, who does not polish the diamond in any sense that would be recognizable to an average consumer. If it is a small stone, he may make it into an eight-cut, which will have seventeen or eighteen cuts, but never eight. Very small stones become one-cuts, which are not to be confused with single-cuts. A single-cut is the same as an eight-cut, whereas a one-cut usually has two cuts. All of this is done on behest of a diamond manufacturer, who is not in the business of "making" diamonds. When it is done, it emerges as a "blue-white" diamond, the "blue-white" telling you substantially nothing about a diamond that is worth knowing. It may in fact be "perfect," which is usually misleading terminology meaning little other, perhaps, than that it is free of carbon spots (which are usually not spots of carbon). Anyway, the end product is, as everyone knows, "forever." But not really. Certainly the raw material—the diamond—is not eternal, but is relatively fragile, and insurance company actuaries working from divorce statistics could chart the probable sentimental life span of the "forever" gem. It is best, therefore, if the reader will wipe away whatever he knows about diamonds, and start over fresh with what follows.

PART I

THE DIAMOND PRODUCERS

◆

I've shivered through a thousand winter mornings. I've sifted through a hundred tons of earth. I've walked from Kimberley to Keetmanshoop, looking for bloody stones. Once I found a diamond as big as the nail on my thumb. That was in the year that the old queen died. That was the luckiest year of my life.

—*Anonymous diamond digger*
Vereeniging, South Africa

1

MAHARAJAS AND RHODES

◆

Diamond is a form of carbon, like pencil lead or charcoal but with a much denser, more compact crystalline structure. Diamonds were almost certainly created by nature as a transformation of common carbon hundreds of millions of years ago, before the configuration of today's earth had stabilized.

Though the process as performed by nature is not well understood, geologists are agreed in general terms. The transformation process required such tremendous heat and pressure that it must have begun at depths of more than a hundred kilometers beneath the earth's surface. Volcanic action then moved molten, pressurized, carbon-bearing magma upward, and in those very rare instances in which the conditions of the eruption were precisely right, the transformation from carbon into diamond was completed during the journey to the surface. In the circumstances suitable for the formation of diamond, a core of igneous rock was left behind plugging the volcanic channel.

Because it came from deep within the earth, this "plug hole," when and where it survives today, will be a different stone than that of the surrounding rock and also different from the usual volcanic lava. It is called kimberlite (after Kimberley, the South African diamond city), and the diamond-bearing volcanic plug hole is known as a kimberlite pipe.

Kimberlite pipes are the natural matrix of diamonds. They can be quite large at the surface, some covering much more than a hundred surface acres, but underground a kimberlite pipe will be carrot-shaped. The diamonds are trapped within the kimberlite, but distinct from it and easily liberated if the rocky mass should be eroded by nature or crushed mechanically.

Kimberlite pipes are scattered throughout the world, from northern Siberia to southern Africa, from China in the east to Arkansas in the west; they are found under frozen tundra and blazing deserts; on mountaintops; and probably they will be found one day on ocean bottoms too. They are, however, relatively rare, and diamondiferous kimberlite pipes are rarer still. Only one in two hundred kimberlite pipes contains enough diamonds to make mining economically feasible.

Mining a kimberlite pipe consists essentially of digging the kimberlite out of the surrounding country rock and then processing the diamonds out of the kimberlite matrix. In 1979 the plant at De Beers' Premier Mine, one of the great mines in diamond history, processed 7,535,100 metric tons of kimberlite, yielding 2,080,805 carats (916 pounds) of diamond—a quarter of a carat for every metric ton of stone, or about one part diamond to every eighteen million parts kimberlite. Some pipe mines have higher yields, some smaller.

Diamonds are found not only in pipes; indeed fewer are retrieved from pipes than from "alluvial deposits." In the millions of years that have passed since the kimberlite pipes were extruded, the upper reaches of most of them have been eroded by extremes of temperature and climate, by winds and waters, their diamonds released and carried away amidst quantities of sands and lesser gravels by rivers and other watercourses. A diamond's final resting place may be quite distant from its point of origin. Some geologists believe that the diamonds found in alluvial deposits in Brazil originated in pipes in West Africa before the South American and African continents drifted apart to form the Atlantic Ocean.

Alluvial searches sometimes yield incredible bonanzas. A well-placed pothole in the bedrock of a river bottom can make a fine drop-off place to catch the river's diamonds, and every few decades some lucky alluvial prospector will find a pothole brimming with diamonds. Almost always, however, the diamonds will be mixed in with vast quantities of other material, and will be indistinguishable to the naked eye until the sands and the gravels have been separated, and the gravels carefully picked over. At the rich alluvial tracts being worked by De Beers in Namaqualand on the west coast of South Africa in 1979, the company processed about two-thirds as much material as it did from the pipe at Premier Mine, and about two-thirds as many diamonds were recovered.

The first finds of diamonds were almost certainly made in alluvial deposits, probably in India, sometime in the first millenium BC. Ancient literature does not give many clues. The earliest undeniable mention of diamonds dates only from the third or fourth century BC, when the Indian scholar Kautilya, or his students, wrote the *Arthasâstra* (literally, *The Science of Profit*), which told the ancient Hindu jeweler how to profit from the diamond boom. The diamond had already become established as an article of trade and taxation in much of Asia Minor and the Near East and had begun to filter both to China and to the Hellenist world.

In the India of Kautilya's day, diamonds were mined by closely guarded, mysterious techniques. Finally the secret was revealed to the western world by the great Roman naturalist Pliny the Elder (AD 23–

79), in his thirty-seven-volume *Historia Naturalis*. As Pliny reported it, all diamonds came from a single deep pit which was guarded by poisonous snakes. The miners threw pieces of rotting flesh into the pit. These morsels landed on and about the diamonds. Vultures swooped down to carry off the flesh, and the miners had only to follow the birds to their resting places to retrieve the diamonds. At least that is how Pliny explained it. More likely, the diamonds were found in alluvial deposits scattered throughout south-central India, principally in the region between the Krishna and Penner rivers.

The rulers of India kept the best diamonds. Most of the rest ended up on the European markets, where, until the discovery of ways of polishing the diamond, they were prized for qualities other than their beauty. Rough diamonds are not generally beautiful. Some few are eight-sided octahedrons (diamond-shaped), glassy, clear-colored pieces of rock that might look something like a diamond, but more often a piece of rough is scarcely more attractive than any other pebble.

Instead, diamonds were prized for their supposed magical qualities. Diamonds could ward off evil spirits or help in visiting them upon one's enemies—like any other amulet, only better because diamonds were harder and also cost more. They were found to be effective in curing all kinds of ailments, especially lunacy, if held in the hand while making the sign of the cross. But mostly diamond's value lay in its hardness, which by the simple and familiar process of sympathetic magic might transfer itself to its wearer, making him more nearly invincible, more manly, and harder on the battlefield—and off the battlefield too. Naturally, diamonds were worn only by men—that is, until Agnès Sorel, the first to hold the distinguished position of official mistress to the king of France.

It was at about the time of Agnès Sorel (1422–50) that diamond "polishing," the process of grinding the surface of the rough diamond into flat planes or facets, became sufficiently advanced to transform unattractive raw diamonds into objects of relative beauty that a woman might find decorative for personal adornment. Agnès did rather like them.

According to the Eleventh Edition of the *Encyclopaedia Britannica* (1910), King Charles VII of France was chaste until he met Agnès Sorel, but not for very long thereafter. So brazen was she that she took to wearing diamonds, the amulets reserved by custom for males. She did not become more manly, but she did die young at twenty-eight. Notwithstanding her early death, Agnès helped establish the diamond as a courtesan's best friend.

Mistresses got diamonds before affianceds. Maximilian of Austria is said to have been the first, in 1477, to give his betrothed, Mary of Burgundy, a ring set with diamonds, thereby transforming the diamond from a symbol of the sinfulness of Charles and Agnès to an honorable token of esteem. Diamond publicists point to Maximilian as establishing the "engagement ring tradition." The diamond brought Maximilian not only Mary of Burgundy's love (well, at least her hand), but also the duchy's political support. Meanwhile, lots of Indians were making pots of money.

The diamond trade became centered at Golconda, the first capital of the diamond world, a great fortress-city now in ruins some five miles east of current-day Hyderabad, India. Many of the elements of the diamond business that are with us today were already operative. The rulers of Golconda appreciated that the value of the diamond turned upon its rarity, and imposed production controls to keep the diamond rare and its value high. They also did much to spread word of the "magical" properties of the diamond, thereby helping to keep up demand. So successful were they that diamond prices rose, notwithstanding increased supply. The government was largely dependent upon revenues generated by diamond digging and the diamond trade for public operating expenses, just as Botswana, Namibia, and Sierra Leone are running today on diamond-generated money. One firm, the Dutch East India Company, came to dominate the international trade, generating profits—well in excess of 100 percent—that would make the directors of today's De Beers envious. The company brought the stones to London, as De Beers now does, and there sold them to a select group of merchants, most of them Jewish. Most of the stones then were carried to the Lowlands for processing and further sale. The diamond world hasn't changed much in the last few hundred years.

Intense workings of the Indian diamond fields left them largely depleted by the late 1600s; by the beginning of the eighteenth century, the world was about out of diamonds. Diamond scholars estimate that by then India had yielded some twelve million carats—two and a half tons of diamonds.

In 1725 relief came for Europe's diamond-starved monarchs when a fresh find was made in unlikely Brazil. Brazil had gold, lots of it, and it was gold that had led Bernardino de Fonseca Lobo to abandon the Portuguese enclave of Goa on the western shores of India for the gold fields of Minas Gerais. After panning gold one day, he sat down to join in a game of cards and immediately recognized the funny pebbles that the players used as counters as the diamonds that he had known in India. The miners had picked them out of their gold pans as mere curiosities near the town of Tejuco, 250 miles inland from the Atlantic coast.

When word reached Lisbon that diamonds had been discovered in Portugal's colony, the news was celebrated with parades and numerous High Masses, and a stream of diamond rushers descended on Tejuco, later renamed Diamantina. Diamond prices tumbled as supply outpaced demand. The government soon ordered that the area be cleared of prospectors to preserve it for systematic exploitation by the state itself and for production control that might restore the value of the treasure.

Brazilian diamonds were greeted first with skepticism and then with scorn on the European market. Brazil, it was thought, could not have diamonds because none had ever been known there, or if it did, they must be very poor diamonds when compared with the Indian product. Or at least that's what the Indians said. So enterprising diamantaires shipped their stones from Brazil to Goa, from where they were then shipped to Europe as "Indian goods," or sent them to Venice for finishing "in the Indian manner." Diamond men have been camouflaging the origin of their stones ever since. (Today stones polished in India are sometimes sent to Israel for sale as "Israeli goods.")

By the end of the 1860s, the world's diamond-cutting industry came to a virtual halt in another diamond famine. All of a sudden the richest Brazilian areas had ceased to be profitable. More diamonds were there, but not in sufficient quantities to make it worth mining them by the techniques then known.

The depletion of rough sources came at a time of "democratization of luxuries." Rapid industrialization, especially in the United States, was creating large numbers of multimillionaires and a new class of haute bourgeoise, eager to establish their socioeconomic status by the purchase and display of bibelots. New finds came none too soon, as the focus of world diamond production switched to another unlikely place, South Africa—where the focus has since remained.

Erasmus Stephanus Jacobs was a boy of fifteen in 1866, the child of an unsuccessful Boer farmer, when he picked up a shiny stone by the banks of the Orange River in Hopetown, Cape Province, South Africa. It had no value to him or to his family other than as a marker in a child's game.

The Jacobs' neighbor, Schlak van Niekerk, saw it and suspected that it might be worth something, and offered to buy it. Mrs. Jacobs would not hear of selling such a worthless thing to a neighbor; she gave it to him. It passed through several hands before reaching a competent South African mineralogist, Dr. W. G. Atherstone, who pronounced the find to be "a veritable diamond," 21.25 carats, worth £500. It was sold at that price to the governor of the colony, but Erasmus Stephanus Jacobs saw not a shilling of the money. In 1927 the Johannesburg *Star* interviewed Jacobs, the man whose find led to the development of modern South Africa, and reported that he was living "in very indigent circumstances."

South Africa and the world barely took notice of the new diamond, or of several others that filtered onto the market from the Hopetown region in the next couple of years. The eminent British geologist James R. Gregory came to investigate in 1868 and concluded that the finds reported from South Africa were hoaxes or, at best, were stones that had been carried in from parts unknown by migrating ostriches.

In the spring of 1869, the same Schlak van Niekerk came upon an 83.25-carat stone in the possession of a native named Zwartbooi. Van Niekerk was certain that this was a diamond and a fine one—and so was Zwartbooi. He sold it to the white man for five hundred sheep, ten oxen, and a horse. Van Niekerk sold the stone, now known as the Star of South Africa, for a staggering (at that time) £11,200 (then $55,000).

At last the diamond rush to South Africa was on. By the end of 1869 there were perhaps ten thousand adventurers from all kinds of backgrounds digging diamonds on the banks of the Orange and Vaal rivers in central South Africa.

Not a year after the rush began, in August of 1870, a strange find was made. A large diamond was found "inland," not on the riverbanks but at the Jagersfontein farm a hundred miles south of the river diggings. This find was followed by others much closer to the Vaal River, at Dutoitspan and at Bultfontein. Early in 1871 a diamond was found on the farm owned by the de Beer brothers (whose name would be immortalized if misspelled as De Beers) and another was found at a different section of their farm. The throng of diggers scurried from the rivers to the "dry diggings," and overnight a town sprang up, New Rush, between the two digging areas on the de Beer farm. Within a year New Rush was Cape Colony's second largest city, with a population of fifty thousand. When British Colonial Secretary John W. Kimberley complained about the settlement's name it was changed—to Kimberley.

Possibly none of the diggers appreciated the geological significance of the new more-or-less-round diamondiferous areas: that they were the remains of the tops of the volcanic (kimberlite) pipes that were the natural matrix of diamond; that possibly no one before had ever dug for diamonds in the matrix itself. All they knew was that the crumbly yellowish ground in which they dug was yielding diamonds, and each man dug his claim as feverishly as he and his handful of black laborers could work. In a matter of months the main dry-digging areas—Dutoitspan, Bultfontein, and the two pipes on the de Beer farm—had been dug to considerable depth and become recognizable as mines.

As each miner proceeded at a different rate of speed, some of the small square claims lay much farther below surface level than others. Problems of hauling the "yellow ground" up and out of the hole, and across other claims, for processing on the surface, became confusing and technically complex. Cave-ins from one claim to another began to occur.

Then the yellow ground became exhausted. Beneath it lay a harder rocklike stuff, a bluish material that some believed spelled the end of the diamonds. Dr. Atherstone and others correctly surmised that the blue ground was merely a continuation of the yellow, only different in color and hardness because it had not weathered as had the upper levels. Mining continued, but the blue was much more difficult to work than the yellow. Finally the country rock, the nonkimberlitic stone that surrounded the pipe holes, began to break off and fall into the mines.

Only bigger, better organized, and much better capitalized production units could consider continuing operations. Everyone in the industry appreciated that the day of the independent digger was over; that diggers had to join together, to consolidate, in order to mine rationally and at the same time restore the "rarity" and the price of their product. And everyone with imagination and resources connived to centralize the control in his own hands. Among those was one bizarre, driven giant.

It was symptomatic of Cecil Rhodes's power lust that the diamonds which were to make him the colossus of Africa never really appealed to him. He told a friend:

> When I am in Kimberley and I have nothing much to do, I often go and sit at the edge of the De Beers mine, and I look at the blue diamondiferous ground, reaching from the surface a thousand feet down the open workings of the mine, and I reckon up the value of the diamonds in the blue and the power conferred by them. In fact, every foot of blue ground means so much power.

For good or bad the most significant person in the history of southern Africa, Rhodes was profound in nothing, generally inarticulate, unimaginative, probably not of unusual intelligence; a limited and predatory man with an element of ruthlessness, even brutality, in his character. His forte was the force of his personality, his instinct for control, and his appreciation of power and the uses to which it might be put. His great admirer Rudyard Kipling described him as an "immense and brooding spirit," which among other things meant that Rhodes was difficult and moody, often remote, possessive and tempestuous. When enraged his face became alarmingly contorted and his voice broke into a high falsetto. A charlatan with the unlikely name of Princess Radziwill claimed to have been his mistress, but nobody believed her, for Rhodes was an extreme misogynist. His emotional involvements were instead with a series of nice-looking younger men, "private secretaries" uniformly unsuited for roles as private secretaries, with some of whom he had intense, affectionate relationships. In today's world, in which a "man's man" and emotional involvements between men are suspect, his more recent biographers have tended to portray him as a repressed homosexual.

Rhodes was born in 1853 in Hertfordshire, England, one of twelve children of a clergyman father who succeeded in little other than paternity. His youth was plagued by ill health, which prompted his family to send him in 1870 to join his older brother Herbert in the healthier climate of South Africa.

Cecil tried a brief and unsuccessful stint at farming, after which he staked claims at the dry diggings and did well. His winnings made him financially independent by the age of nineteen. His health temporarily restored, he began "commuting" between South Africa and Oxford, where he studied for a degree finally awarded in 1881. It was probably in his first term at Oxford that he determined to dedicate his life to the cause of spreading British civilization—and especially British rule—throughout the world.

Diamonds meant power to fulfill his dreams of empire, not for himself but for the inseparable causes of Britain and civilization. Though thoughts of personal grandeur had much to do with it, Rhodes was essentially an unselfish visionary and idealist. The same could be said of others of the brigands of history.

Throughout the 1870s, Rhodes was buying up more and more claims in the "De Beers Mine," the earlier and smaller of the two mines on the de Beer farm, and in 1880 he and two other large holders combined interests to form De Beers Mining Company Ltd., controlling virtually the whole of the mine.

On the other side of town, Barney Barnato was doing pretty much the same thing at the Kimberley Mine, as the richer of the two pipes of the de Beers' farm was known. Barney Barnato was the other important personality of the early diamond world, born one year to the day before Rhodes. Son of a Petticoat Lane shopkeeper in London's East End Jewish ghetto, Barnato's real name was Barnett Isaacs; he took the other in his teens during a brief fling at the London stage as backup man for his brother Harry, a comic/magician. Had a nice sound to it, Barney Barnato, something like his father's name, Isaac Isaacs, or his brother-in-law's name, Joel Joel.

Harry Barnato (as his brother came to be known) had gone to seek his fortune on the South African diamond fields in 1872, and Barney joined him there a year later, with an armload of boxes of low-grade cigars which he hoped to peddle as Havana's finest. The Barnatos were good-natured fakers, roustabouts who lived from hand to mouth. Barney's buoyant spirit made him a popular fellow around town; his onetime partner Louis Cohen was to describe him as "a decidedly unscrupulous character, who had, nevertheless, a grain of gold in his nature." Barney was a regular at the taverns—where he sometimes ran into the hard-drinking Cecil Rhodes—and a regular at the brothels, which Rhodes avoided.

Barnato began buying up claims in the Kimberley Mine in 1879, just as Rhodes was doing at the De Beers Mine. By amalgamating his interests with those of other large claim holders, Barnato's Kimberley Central Mining Company became the biggest claim holder in the mine;

only the strategically located claims owned by the French Company stood in the way of his practical control of the entire mine.

Then Barney's interests at Kimberley came under attack. In 1887 Rhodes, with backing from the Rothschild family, offered the French Company £1.4 million ($6.8 million) for its interests in "Barney's" mine. Barney made a higher offer, but withdrew it when Rhodes came to him with a proposition: If Barney would not bid against him, once Rhodes had acquired the French Company's interests, he would trade them to Barney for one-fifth interest in Kimberley Central. Barney would still be in control of his company, and a more powerful company at that, once the French Company's interests had been incorporated into it. Barney agreed, and it came to pass. Then Rhodes began buying more shares of stock in Kimberley Central and control of it dropped into his hands. At length Barnato agreed to the amalgamation of Kimberley Central and De Beers Mining Company to form De Beers Consolidated Mines Ltd. in 1888, the company that has controlled the world diamond industry to the present. Barney emerged as the new company's largest single stockholder, but Rhodes was in the driver's seat.

With time Rhodes and Barnato became political allies and then close friends. Both went on to make fortunes in the South African gold rushes that followed, fortunes that dwarfed their diamond profits. Barney, however, became unduly worried that his financial empire was toppling. He became seriously alcoholic and then began to suffer periods of derangement. In one of them, in 1897, he threw himself off the stern of a London to Capetown ship. He was forty-four.

The telegram to Rhodes announcing his friend's end arrived on a train carrying Rhodes to Rhodesia. It was intercepted by his secretary, who decided to hold it until the morning. When the secretary told Rhodes the next day, Rhodes was overcome by a confusion of emotions and lashed out at his secretary. "I suppose you thought this would affect me and I should not sleep. Why? Do you imagine that I should be in the least affected if you were to fall under the wheels of this train?"

The colossus had little time left himself. After making his fortunes in diamonds and then gold, he served as prime minister and virtual dictator of Cape Colony from 1890 to 1896, during which time the franchise was limited to the literate, thereby effectually disenfranchising nonwhites. After leaving office he devoted himself and his wealth to the colonization and development of the territories northerly of South Africa which were known by his name. Always in poor health, he suffered his first heart attack at the age of nineteen and several others before he died at the age of forty-eight in 1902.

Rhodes was proud to think that "the immense riches which have been taken out of the soil have not been devoted merely to the decoration of the female sex," that the wealth had been given over to "other things besides the expansion of luxury." Much of what he built with his diamond-born wealth in Northern Rhodesia, now Zambia, and in Southern Rhodesia, now Zimbabwe, lasted until yesterday. His legacy in South Africa itself may lead to further fearsome confrontations. His first great accomplishment, the creation of De Beers Consolidated Mines, Ltd., seems likely to be one of his more lasting monuments.

2

SIR ERNEST OPPENHEIMER
AND HIS COMPANIES

◆

De Beers Consolidated Mines was formed in 1888, with virtual control of the De Beers and Kimberley Mines, the two most important producers. Within a year it had taken over the other two Kimberley-area mines, Dutoitspan and Bultfontein, and in 1896 the newly discovered Wesselton Mine too became a part of De Beers. De Beers stockholders owned sufficient interests in the only other then-known mines, Jagersfontein and Koffiefontein, both in Orange Free State, to keep them operating as part of the De Beers network. For the fourteen years from its birth until 1902, De Beers' only "outside" competition came from the small output of the remaining diggers on the original river sites and their impoverished brothers in Brazil. As a practical matter De Beers had no competition—it constituted the diamond world.

De Beers' production monopoly began to fall apart in 1902 with the discovery of the Premier Mine far away from Kimberley in the Transvaal, some twenty miles northeast of Pretoria, a mine so vast that it could rival the giant. It is said that the mere sight of Premier's operations gave Alfred Beit, once partner of Rhodes, and De Beers' most influential director, the stroke that led to his death. In 1905 Premier unearthed the largest diamond ever found, the Cullinan, weighing 3,106 carats—a pound and a third of stone—and in 1908 (an aberrational year) Premier's production surpassed the combined output of all of De Beers' mines.

More diamonds were discovered in 1908 in the German colony of South West Africa, and two years later diamonds were found in the Belgian Congo. In 1925 large alluvial finds were made at Lichtenburg, South Africa, territory best suited for exploitation by the small-scale diggers, but their production in 1926 grievously upset the world diamond market. That year rich diamond finds were also made in Namaqualand, on the Atlantic coast of South Africa.

De Beers coped as best it could: It bought out and absorbed Premier in 1921, and it profited greatly in the heyday years of the 1920s, when buoyant economic conditions meant buoyant diamond prices that enabled the company to suffer and survive most anything. But the death of Rhodes in 1902 had left it without strong leadership until the chairmanship of the company was assumed in 1929 by Sir Ernest Oppenheimer, who was to transform the company into the De Beers that dominates today's diamond world.

Ernest Oppenheimer was born into a large Jewish family in Friedberg, a small town near Frankfurt, Germany, where his father was modestly prosperous as a cigar merchant. By the time of Ernest's birth in 1880, his cousin Fredrich Hirschhorn had already grown rich in the diamond fields. Ernest's older brothers, Bernhard and Louis, joined the diamond firm of a distant relative, Anton Dunkelsbuhler, and when Ernest was sixteen, he was withdrawn from school and sent to Dunkelsbuhler's London office to begin his lifetime career in diamonds as a sorter. In England the young Ernest saw and savored the stature and status of the English gentleman, and the life that so many other German Jews had attained in England through diamonds and gold, a life much different from that in the Jewish ghettos of central Europe. He became a naturalized British subject. After six years, at the age of twenty-two, Ernest was sent to Kimberley to oversee Dunkelsbuhler's office there.

In Kimberley, Ernest became a boarder in cousin "Fritz" Hirschhorn's mansion. After his own successes in diamonds, Hirschhorn had become the representative of Wernher, Beit & Co., the leading diamond-buying firm that had been established by Alfred Beit. He also served as the principal Kimberley representative of "the syndicate," the group of major diamond buyers, including Wernher, Beit & Co., Barnato Brothers, Dunkelsbuhler, and a few others, who bought the entire De Beers output and then sold it off in smaller lots to the diamond cutters of Amsterdam and Antwerp.

Hirschhorn was Beit's alternate on the De Beers board of directors, and would soon have a seat on the board himself. When Ernest accompanied Hirschhorn to the board meetings of De Beers, he could visit with the likes of Beit and Solly Joel, nephew of the departed Barnato and spokesman for the powerful and diverse interests of Barnato Brothers. Much of the talk revolved around the doings and threat of the recently discovered Premier Mine. Premier had set up its own selling organization, and Ernest's brother Bernhard was the brains of the rival selling operation.

Family connections and contacts provided Ernest the opportunity to create his own future. He prospered at work and began doing some investing of his own. In 1906 he married "well," to May Pollak, daughter of a wealthy Jewish London stockbroker, a past president of the London stock exchange.

Oppenheimer dabbled in politics as well. Rhodes, Barnato, and J. B. Robinson, the third great diamond man of the founding generation, had all served in the Cape Parliament, Barnato and Robinson on the Kimberley City Council, Robinson as mayor. Oppenheimer followed their steps, became a South African citizen, and in 1908 was first elected to the Kimberley City Council. In 1912 he was chosen by the other city councilors as mayor, a matter that could only have impressed De Beers' powerful board with the strong personality and abilities of Dunkelsbuhler's young agent.

The outbreak of the First World War sparked considerable anti-German feelings—much of it tinged with anti-Semitism—which devolved upon Ernest. Notwithstanding ugly rumors about his loyalties, he was reelected mayor in 1914, after the war's outbreak, but the sinking of the Lusitania in May of 1915 so aroused sentiment against anything "German" that Ernest resigned. Anti-German mobs roamed Kimberley, burning and destroying "German" property; they moved on the Oppenheimer house, but local police held them back. The next morning Oppenheimer secreted his family onto a Cape Town–bound train, and was preparing his own flight when a mob recognized him. They stoned his car, wounding him on the face, and pursued him on foot to the door of a nunnery where Oppenheimer—so recently Kimberley's first citizen—took refuge. He made his way with his family to England, intending never to return to South Africa.

This traumatic experience may have been responsible for Oppenheimer's decision to raise his two sons as Christians rather than as Jews. He almost certainly was aware that Alfred Beit's parents had converted to Lutheranism simply to avoid the anti-Semitism that threatened to block their children's paths in nineteenth-century Germany. The boys were entered in Anglican schools and were taught to identify themselves as such.*

The lure of business in Africa proved too strong, and after only a brief stay in London, Oppenheimer was back in South Africa again, this time investigating gold-mining possibilities for one of Dunkelsbuhler's corporate affiliates. Then he began buying gold-mining rights for a new company. An American, an influential mining engineer and future president, Herbert C. Hoover, brought entrée for Oppenheimer to the J. P. Morgan banking interests, which financed the new company; in recognition of the American role, the company was named Anglo American Corporation of South Africa. Before long Anglo American had an important role in the gold fields of the "east rand," east of Johannesburg.

The defeat of Germany in the war led to the establishment of its

* Innumerable South African and diamond Jews told me that Harry Oppenheimer, today's strongman of De Beers and the other Oppenheimer interests, had been bar mitzvaed (inducted into the religious duties of the adult Jewish male) at the Kimberley synagogue. Not so. By the time that Harry reached bar mitzva age, thirteen, the family was no longer Kimberley based, and by then he was a Christian. Subsequent to Harry's brith (ritual circumcision) there is no record of him at the Kimberley synagogue.

former colony of South West Africa as a "protectorate" of the Union of South Africa. When Oppenheimer learned that a restructuring of the nine German companies mining diamonds in South West Africa was imminent, he took advantage of the opportunity. He brought about the amalgamation of the southwest African producers as Consolidated Diamond Mines, Ltd., and his Anglo American emerged with the controlling interest in CDM. It was much as Rhodes had done in Kimberley years before. For the first time, Oppenheimer had his own card in the diamond game, a strategic position that he would use ultimately to take control of the diamond world.

He also reentered public life. In 1921 Great Britain knighted him for his contributions during the war and after (the most significant of which had been his role as secretary of a group that promoted the erection of memorials to the war dead) and no doubt for his contributions to the party of British Prime Minister Lloyd George, who prepared the list of honorees. Sir Ernest was now one of the "rand lords," the large and (except for Ernest) noisy gaggle of South African mining magnates who had been similarly honored for similar services in the past.

In 1924, at the request of South Africa's great leader Jan Christian Smuts, Oppenheimer stood for the South African Parliament as a candidate from Kimberley. The Oppenheimers had long before severed their ties with the community but, in the manner of the British party system, where a candidate lived did not much matter. He ran and, the days of the mob apparently forgotten, Kimberley elected him and then repeatedly reelected him. He served until 1938.

Oppenheimer's hagiographic biographer, Theodore Gregory, wrote that in Parliament "the protection of the diamond industry from ill-considered policies imposed a task upon him that must at times have been almost intolerable." His maiden speech was on a diamond control bill, and thereafter he addressed himself to Parliament's concerns principally when he had a personal financial interest at stake—not so bad as it might sound inasmuch as the interests of his Kimberley constituency were roughly the same as those of the mining crowd. There was nothing cynical about it; Oppenheimer was always able to convince himself that what was best for the mining industry really was best for South Africa.

Sir Ernest was widely known for his diplomacy and his humility—the latter a gentle and considerate way of dealing with others, whether his peers or domestic servants. This was more a matter of grace than of humility. Sir Ernest was not a humble man. He repeatedly commissioned portraits of himself, was inclined to use the papal "we," and idolized Napoleon, who, according to myth, was a man of diminutive height. Sir Ernest was scarcely five feet tall.

Like all South African mining executives, Oppenheimer always favored expanded job opportunities for black workers. The mines were starved for skilled employees and "job reservation," the rule embodied

in law that certain jobs were reserved for whites only, barred the way
to fuller development of mine potential and profits. His concern for
blacks, however, was also at least partially a moral concern. In correspon-
dence with son Harry he sometimes mentioned the need for the country
to do something to improve black living conditions. During World War
II he wrote: "We spend such large sums on the war and our revenue
is so buoyant that we can well afford when the war is over to continue
the big expenditure for a while longer in order to bring happiness to
our native population." In the mid-1950s, he organized a group of mining magnates to finance the construction of new and improved housing
in a new black township to house blacks living in slum conditions or
left homeless by redevelopment projects. His efforts represented the
first major infusion of private capital to improve black living conditions
in South Africa. There was some agitation to give the new township
the name by which Sir Ernest was known in the black community, Op-
ahama, but instead it was named Soweto. The Ernest Oppenheimer
Tower and Gardens there are a monument to his interest.

Oppenheimer's son Harry has written that his father would never
have favored transferring political power to the black majority; "on the
contrary, it was because he was convinced that they could not be allowed
to exercise power that he felt a special moral duty lay on the whites
to govern them wisely, justly, humanely and unselfishly. And in this
duty he thought white South Africa was failing."

By today's standards, the kind and degree of Oppenheimer's concern for the blacks are unimpressive, but in the South Africa of his
day he consistently took the most progressive "responsible" positions
on racial issues.

Oppenheimer's great interests were De Beers and diamonds. He
collected "fancy colors," the rare diamonds colored blue, pink, amber,
or intense yellow. He also collected De Beers stock, buying shares whenever possible. Throughout the 1920s he ached to break into the inner
sanctum of its board, but the insiders didn't seem to like him. With
the creation of CDM, however, Oppenheimer could no longer be treated
lightly. His role increased when Anglo American, together with Joel's
Barnato Brothers, reached an agreement giving them control over the
sale of the diamonds produced by new fields in Angola and the Belgian
Congo that were then being developed by Forminière, a Belgian mining
house.

The CDM/Forminière productions could be sold through the same
syndicate that bought and merchandised the De Beers output, thereby
keeping the market "tight," or it could be sold "outside," thereby threatening everybody's game. Oppenheimer demanded his own interest in
the prior syndicate in exchange for his cooperation. The syndicate was
then led by Ludwig Breitmeyer, whose firm had succeeded Wernher,

Beit & Co. Breitmeyer may have viewed Oppenheimer as unfriendly, but the syndicate's other leading members were well disposed toward him: Barnato Brothers, which had already learned to work with Oppenheimer, and Dunkelsbuhler, where Ernest's brother Louis had become the guiding light. Anglo American became a member of the syndicate, and Oppenheimer contributed to it the production under his control. But not for long. At the end of 1924, Oppenheimer withdrew from the syndicate. Anglo would sell its products independently, thereby threatening diamond world stability.

The following year a new syndicate, an Oppenheimer-led group composed of Anglo, Barnato Brothers, Dunkelsbuhler, and another Barnato-related company, bid for the exclusive right to buy and merchandise the De Beers output. With Barnato Brothers as the principal stockholder in all of the major South African producers, the new group won the contract. Breitmeyer had been shuffled out. Oppenheimer's group took over the assets and the debts of the previous syndicate, and also its impressive stock of rough, which was to prove a highly profitable asset in the remaining years of the roaring twenties.

With his new role as leader of the syndicate, Oppenheimer's allies within the De Beers board (principally Solly Joel of Barnato Brothers, De Beers' leading stockholder) were able to prevail and Oppenheimer finally won his seat on De Beers' board. As a board member he pushed for consolidation of all diamond interests under the De Beers umbrella, to the unquestionable advantage of the corporation and, not incidentally, of himself.

Meanwhile he kept an open eye for further opportunities to enhance his own role in the diamond world. In 1927 he and Joel acquired the most promising of the alluvial tracts recently discovered at Lichtenburg. Oppenheimer wrote his brother, "Solly was not inclined, nor was I, simply to hand them over to De Beers. We both felt that it was a very useful thing, for bargaining in the future, to have properties of that kind under our control." They acquired mining interests in Namaqualand as well. Questions would be raised later by other De Beers directors as to whether interests like these acquired by directors of their corporation should not instead have been acquired by the corporation that Oppenheimer and Joel were honor-bound to serve. Then in 1929, just prior to the stock market crash and the onset of the Great Depression, Oppenheimer acquired the vast hoard of rough that had been prospected, mined, and collected by Dr. Hans Merensky, one of the pioneer Namaqualand prospectors.

Meanwhile, Oppenheimer angled aggressively for the chairmanship of De Beers, over the opposition of those directors, including his cousin Hirschhorn, who argued that it would be an impossible conflict for the head of the diamond-buying syndicate to serve as well as the head of the principal producer of diamonds. But Joel's holdings, together with

Oppenheimer's impressive stock interests in De Beers, proved too powerful for the opposition, and Ernest Oppenheimer acceded to the chairmanship of De Beers in December 1929, just as the world entered the
gloomy economic period of the 1930s.

De Beers immediately embarked upon Oppenheimer's plan for consolidation of interests. It purchased from its new chairman Anglo's interests in CDM, and the controlling stock in the Jagersfontein mine owned
by the chairman's ally, Barnato Brothers, and their other diamond-producing interests. A new corporation was formed, the Diamond Corporation, owned half by the southern African diamond producers (De Beers
and its corporate subsidiaries) and half by the members of the prior
syndicate (Anglo, Dunkelsbuhler, and the Barnato companies), to take
over the merchandising operations of the previous syndicate.

The chairman of the Diamond Corporation was none other than
Ernest Oppenheimer. The Diamond Corporation bought up the contracts and business of the syndicate previously controlled by Oppenheimer, including stocks of unsold rough, and the chairman's recently
acquired Merensky diamonds as well. This impressive acquisition came
as the world entered a depression that had already made diamonds
almost unsalable. It would be fifteen years before the depression and
World War II were past, when a healthy demand for diamonds would
at last reemerge, making De Beers a rich entity in the mid-1940s.

Within a couple of years after Ernest's accession, all of the old-
timers died out, leaving Oppenheimer as the last surviving link with
the diamond's corporate past. Increasingly De Beers became an Oppenheimer fiefdom, the family firm that it is today. When Anglo American's
Chairman Oppenheimer needed vast sums of capital to develop new
Anglo American gold mines in the late 1940s, the wise investor who
took the plunge was Chairman Oppenheimer's cash-rich De Beers, which
also acquired interests in other of its chairman's enterprises. Minority
stockholders grumbled about abuse of office, but there was precedent:
Rhodes had done the same.

Oppenheimer's life was not all success and happiness. In the mid-
1930s, he suffered a series of personal losses in close succession: the
death of his nephew Michael, Bernhard's son, in an airplane crash in
September of 1933; Mrs. Oppenheimer's death in February 1934; that
of his brother-in-law, friend, and deputy, Leslie Pollak, in June of that
year; and finally the death of his younger son, Frank, in a swimming
accident in April 1935.

Oppenheimer turned to religion for solace. He had never been
"religious," and had always kept himself distant from the large Jewish
community in Kimberley. Opportunism had probably had something
to do with that. The general atmosphere of the day in South Africa
was unfriendly to Jews, so neither Anglo nor De Beers employed many.

Oppenheimer became a devout Bible reader, especially of the Book of Job, the story of the truly good man who was "tested" by God by being deprived of his family, health, and property. He studied Christianity, was confirmed as an Anglican, and became a regular churchgoer. He married again, to the widow of his deceased nephew Michael, a Christian by birth. Still later in life, close to his death in 1957, he became attracted to the tenets of Roman Catholicism, though he never formally became a Catholic.

The Jewish diamond men accepted his peregrinations good-naturedly. Many of them still believe he died a Catholic. One Yiddish-intoned diamond dealer said to me, "Vy did Sir Ernest become a Catholic? So ven people asked him, 'Catholic? Vut did you used to be?' he could answer, 'Church of England!' " Oppenheimer himself supposedly told the Jewish diamantaires, "To my friends I am a Jew and to my enemies I am a Jew." As to the last he was surely correct: Long after his conversion important Nationalist Party political leaders would continue to denounce the domination of the country by "Anglo-Jewish capitalists." Everyone in South Africa has always understood that such references were to Oppenheimer or to his son and successor, Harry.

Today De Beers is very likely the most cash-rich business entity in the world. As of January 1, 1981, its cash assets on hand (converted from rands to dollars at the then-prevailing rate of $1.34 per rand) amounted to a little more than $1 billion—more than the net annual income of most of the most powerful American corporations. Its stocks of diamonds were listed in its accounts at $930 million, but these stocks, many on hand for years, were valued at "cost bases," and conservatively figured must be reckoned at having a current-day fair value of not less than $1.5 billion. The market value of the listed securities the company owned stood at $3.5 billion. These liquid and more-or-less liquid assets totaled $6 billion as of January 1, 1981; assuming that the value of all of its mines, equipment, and buildings was zero, and that it had no value at all as a going business, each of its 360 million issued shares still had a "hard" value of $16.66 a share—at a time when De Beers was trading at $9.75 in New York.

The company's running profits, according to its annual report for calendar year 1980, came to $1.1 billion after taxes, or $3 million a day; its per share earnings were $3.18 per share per year. David Fitzpatrick, the London-based Merrill Lynch analyst who follows precious commodities stocks, doubts it: he believes it to be *more*. The company suffers an embarrassment of riches, which it disguises as best it can by portraying its financial picture as conservatively as possible, so as not to make the South African, black African, and Soviet governments with which it must live and deal too suspicious or too greedy. De Beers is in the almost unheard-of position in the corporate world of understating the strength of its position. Fitzpatrick regards De Beers stock to be very much overdiscounted for the political clouds that overhang its environment.

De Beers' role in the diamond world is almost as strong today as it ever was, despite a sharp decline in its world role as a diamond producer. In 1902 De Beers lost its 99 percent control over diamond production, and never regained it. Its 1980 production of 14.7 million carats represented under 30 percent of the world's output by weight, but because of the unusually high proportion of gems among the De Beers stones, its output represents closer to half of the dollar value of world output. Its strength and power lie in its control of the merchandising of not only the products of its own mines, but also those of some of South Africa's most implacable foes: the Soviet Union, Angola, and other countries in black Africa.

De Beers today is still a very stuffy concern. Though women are its raison d'être, no woman has ever held a seat on its board, and none is likely to in the foreseeable future. Diamonds are something that men do for women. It is still largely closed to Jewish job applicants. When I asked a De Beers spokesman if I was counting right, he agreed that there did seem to be relatively few Jews in the De Beers ranks—particularly small when one considers that after the diamonds leave De Beers' selling agency, the network of diamond distribution is "strictly kosher." He pointed out that "when a Jew knows something about diamonds, he doesn't want to work for somebody else for a salary; he wants to be in business for himself." Whether it is the acknowledgment of realities or passive anti-Semitism, De Beers' unwritten policy disfavors the hiring of Jews.

Oppenheimer's great creation and monument, however, is not De Beers but Anglo American. The "American" interest became insignificant after 1922, when the Morgan group sold its holdings. Since then, under Oppenheimer and his son, Harry, Anglo has become the world's leading gold producer, with other interests that go far beyond gold: it is Africa's leading mining house, an octopus with extensive mining involvements in all of the base metals and coal, in Africa, North America, and Australia, and interests—often controlling interests—in every aspect of the South African economy. Its corporate subsidiaries and spin-offs (among them the powerful British mining house Charter Consolidated) and the subsidiaries of the subsidiaries number in the hundreds.

Anglo's relations with De Beers today are complex and confusing. Most of De Beers' prospecting is done by Anglo or by Anglo employees, and De Beers' technical backup and auxiliary services are all largely provided through contracts with Anglo. The two intertwine at so many junctures that at points of tangent it is difficult even for corporate officers to know exactly where the one begins and the other ends. Except for the independent stockholders of both, it really doesn't make much difference: Anglo and its subsidiary Anglo American Investment Trust (Anamint) own a combined 31 percent of De Beers while De Beers owns a 38.5 percent interest in Anglo. Anglo controls De Beers or De Beers controls Anglo, but in any case, the Oppenheimer family controls both.

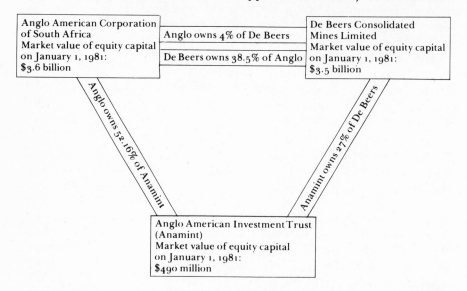

The two giants, De Beers and Anglo, dominating both of the world's most glittering markets, have produced incomprehensible wealth. Yet the companies are sometimes as inscrutable as the diamond itself.

3

A GRAIN OF SUGAR
IN A HUNDRED BAGS OF RICE

◆

Some spend a lifetime in diamond mines and never see a diamond. I was lucky.

At De Beers' Wesselton Mine, Peter van Blommestein, a technically oriented member of the company's public relations staff, guided me about the underground. As we inspected an unstable area from a safe distance, van Bloomestein's headlamp picked up a glitter—"Look there!" He pointed. A diamond!

I had been in a mine for only an hour and had seen a diamond embedded in its kimberlite matrix far underground—unless . . . I suggested to my guide, "You leave one there to show the tourists?" He reacted with some impatience to my suggestion that the company had planted a diamond: "Listen, this is a working area and we do not leave stones around in working areas in order to im—" His words were drowned out as several tons of stone crashed down and covered the specimen with rubble. I never did hear his response.

My diamond sighting was in a shaft mine, but most kimberlite pipes are worked "open cast." In open-cast mining the blue ground is simply blasted free from the floor of the pipe, creating a hole that grows deeper as the work progresses. As the pipe deepens, however, sections of the "reef," the nonkimberlitic country rock into which the pipe has intruded, begin to slough off into the hole, making open-cast mining risky while overburdening the blue ground with useless debris. If the pipe is rich enough, however, it may pay to continue mining exploitation by underground or shaft mining.

Shaft mining dates back to King Solomon, and Barnato introduced it to diamond mining at the Kimberley Mine in 1883, prior to the amalgamation that formed De Beers Consolidated. Mine shafts are not drilled, like oil wells, but are excavated by blasting. The surface area of the proposed shaft is loaded with explosives that are detonated; the rubble is then hauled out. More explosives are set at the bottom of the resulting hole; they are detonated, and more rubble is hauled out. And so on, until the shaft has reached the required depth.

Shaft mines have at least two shafts, a main shaft for the transportation of men and materials and one for ventilation. The main shaft is usually located amidst firm country rock some thousand feet away from the pipe to be mined, and is connected with the pipe by tunnels leading off the shaft into each of the working areas within the pipe. These tunnels are excavated by blasting or, when the tunnel enters the body of the pipe, by use of horizontally placed rock-eating drills.

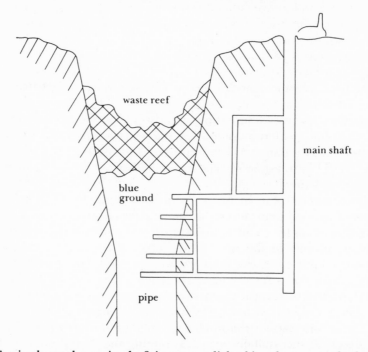

A trip down the main shaft is accomplished in a huge rough elevator, packed with perhaps a hundred miners, some white, mostly black, each in his yellow coverall, each wearing a hard hat with a miner's headlamp. Most of the headlamps are white lit, but some have red lights. Those identify the men who may be carrying explosives. The elevator travels down sometimes as much as a half mile beneath the earth's surface in a matter of minutes. The speed does not upset the equilibrium, but the first-timer will have butterflies anyway.

The visitor disembarks into a brightly lit area. The more permanent working areas are laced with cavernous hallways and tunnels, a subterranean railroad, and a network of highways over which a fleet of huge trucks rumble. Major intersections are governed by traffic lights. The kimberlite carrot that lies beneath the 79.5 surface acres of Premier Mine is beehived with almost two hundred miles of big and small tunnels.

The visitor's introduction to the underground is awe inspiring, but the atmosphere becomes more eerie closer to the mine face, the area where kimberlite is actually being removed from the pipe.

Farther away from the main shaft elevator, the ceilings become lower, the highways become paths. The string of "street lights" ends, and now only headlamps light the way, occasionally reflecting the glitter of a gold earring in a black man's ear. The winds that hurry through the main ventilation channels become faint, the temperature becomes warmer, almost uncomfortable. The air becomes thick. The farthest reaches of the mine are inhabited not by men but by metal insects: the great winch scraper, a man-made beetle that lumbers through the rock dust with a ton of kimberlite in its maw, and the huge bug-eyed drill-snouted creature that opens new paths in virgin rock. Occasionally there is a muffled explosion from far off in the night. It is here that mining, the mightiest of industries, is groaning, driving, striving, succeeding, performing a drama of terrifying reality.

The actual process is somewhat more prosaic. At most shaft diamond mines, the blue ground is mined by a process known as block caving, which is also commonly used in iron and copper mining. Block caving involves undermining—weakening—the floor of the pit, and then letting it collapse of its own weight, under controlled conditions, so that the collapsed kimberlite can be hauled out and hoisted up to ground level for processing. At a selected depth beneath the floor of the pit, a series of cone-shaped caves are blasted across the pipe, the wider end of each cone being closest to the floor of the pipe, the narrow end pointing downwards. This leaves the floor hanging with very little support. The force of gravity collapses it into the cones. The process can be speeded up with selected blasting if desired. The kimberlite debris falls through to the narrow end of the cones, which funnel the kimberlite into "scraper drifts," long concrete-lined tunnels located farther underground. Winch scrapers collect the kimberlite in the scraper drifts and dump it down a slot to the next level, into small railroadlike freight cars. These carry the stone to another dumping slot, where it falls into a crusher that crushes the kimberlite into six-inch chunks. The chunks drop from the crusher onto a conveyor belt, which carries the kimberlite back to the main shaft where it is hoisted to ground level for further processing and retrieval of the diamonds. When the floor has been completely block caved, the process is then repeated at a lower depth.

The economics of diamond-processing plants require that they run continually, and this means that it is necessary to remove kimberlite from the pipe continually to keep feeding the plant. Most diamond mines work on a twenty-four-hour basis.

Separating the diamonds from the mined kimberlite is something like searching for one grain of sugar hidden someplace in a hundred bags of rice. Even at De Beers' most diamondiferous mine, the Finsch Mine, diamonds represent only 1/6,000,000th of the total material processed.

The first step in liberating the diamonds from the kimberlite at most diamond mines is done with crushing machines that gently break up the kimberlite chunks. Unless the crusher should catch a diamond at a "cleavage plane"—at one of the points where its structure makes it prone to splitting—the diamond is not likely to be broken in the process, and losses are few.

When the kimberlite has been reduced in size, the next step in the process of separating out the diamonds is "heavy media separation." Diamond has a specific gravity of 3.52—that is, a given volume of diamond will weigh exactly 3.52 times as much as the same volume of water. Because diamond is heavier than water, if you drop a diamond in a glass of water it will sink. Kimberlite, though also heavier than water, is much lighter than diamond. If you increase the weight of the water by adding powdered particles of heavier material, and keep the particles in suspension in the water by swirling, you create a "puddle" in which diamonds and other heavy materials will still sink, but in which kimberlite and other lighter materials will float. The principle of separating heavy materials from light materials, "sinks" from "floats," was first applied in the diamond industry in Kimberley in the 1870s, using low, round, rotating pans. Rotation pans are still used almost everywhere; more sophisticated heavy-media separation devices that rely on the same principle are often used as well.

Larger kimberlite floats are further broken to release diamonds that may be hidden within, and then the process of separating sinks and floats is repeated. Floating kimberlite pieces are repeatedly broken and reprocessed until the kimberlite has been reduced to particles too small to hide anything of value.

Most plants use a series of heavy-media treatments, each of which contains a slightly different puddle, each of which produces a concentrate that is heavier in weight-per-volume than the one before, each one progressively richer in diamond. When the concentrate has been refined as much as is feasible by heavy-media techniques, something under one percent of it will be diamond, but the ratio of diamond to nondiamond will have been reduced to a manageable proportion. At relatively small mines, mechanical separation ends here, and the concentrate is then picked over for diamonds by human hand and eye. Well-financed operations use further mechanical techniques to separate the diamonds from the other materials, before the human hand enters the process. Earliest of these to be devised was the grease belt, which relies on the principle that diamonds are more likely to stick to grease than are other materials. Grease belts have been adopted into grease tables, grease vanners, and grease wheels.

More recently, X-ray separation of diamonds from kimberlite has replaced grease-based separation. Diamond and a few other materials will fluoresce in an X-ray beam. This discovery was developed into the X-ray based separation machine by the Russians and then by De Beers. In an X-ray–based separating machine, the concentrate is passed before an X-ray beam on a conveyor belt. When any matter on the conveyor luminesces, an air jet targets the bright matter and knocks it aside, out of the stream of materials and into a catch box (which has a secure lock). A properly tuned X-ray separator will catch virtually 100 percent of the diamonds passed before it, together with almost five times as much other material; but to be certain that no diamonds have been missed, concentrates are usually given three trips under the lights.

Whether heavy media separation is followed by grease or X-ray refinements, ultimately human beings do the final extraction, the winnowing out of the diamonds from the chaff. The belief in the industry is that women are better suited for this work than men—"sharper eyes and faster hands," said the supervisor at the CDM sorting room in Namibia. There, and many other places, sorting is women's work. At CDM, a hatful of concentrate—by this point it is upward of 20 percent diamond—is plunked onto a table with low sides to stop anything from rolling off. The woman beside the table quickly shuffles through the concentrate using her hands and a small metal triangle, pushing the diamonds to one side and the worthless particles to the other. The sorters work with such speed that one would think they worked inefficiently, but they pick out 98–99 percent of the diamonds in their piles of concentrate, and to be on the safe side everything is then picked through a second time.

In a typical day almost six thousand carats of diamond—better than two pounds of it—will pass through the hands of the CDM sorters, almost all of it very high quality, good-sized gems. The sorters are monitored by a string of closed-circuit TVs.

The security at different sorting rooms varies. In the CDM sorting room, the watch is closer because the sorters at CDM actually touch the diamonds with their hands. At the De Beers mine at Orapa, Botswana, and in many other diamond-processing plants the sorters work through "glove boxes": the diamond concentrate is deposited into a glass case with gloves fitted into the case. It is impossible for the worker to get a diamond out of the glove box except through the hole in its bottom through which the diamonds drop into a locked safe.

What the sorters reject is ultimately pulverized (to minimize any temptation on the part of sorters knowingly to reject diamonds) and is then added to the tailings dump, the huge pile of materials—everything other than diamond—that is regurgitated by the processing plant. Tailings dumps dominate the landscape at all diamond mines.

Kimberlite wastes may be the world's most useless substance. Kimberlite is prone to expand, contract, and disintegrate, so that it cannot be used as a substitute for either sand or gravel in the construction industry. It is useless even for fill. About all that kimberlite is good for is yielding diamonds, haunting landscapes—and being reprocessed at some later time when improved recovery techniques may make it profitable to sift through it all again.

De Beers operates a number of pipe mines in South Africa, most of them old mines with significant places in the history of the diamond industry: Premier, the greatest of diamond pipes, still one of the biggest contributors to De Beers' total caratage; Koffiefontein in the Orange Free State; and four pipes in Kimberley that date from the days of the great South African diamond rush of the late 1800s. These have been joined by newer mines, Finsch and Letseng-la-Terai.

Finsch, discovered only in 1960 and still mined open cast, is now the company's most productive South African mine. Letseng-la-Terai (or, translated into English, "the diamond mine at the turn by the swamp on the roof of Africa") is located in Lesotho, a small tribal country entirely surrounded by South Africa. It was opened by De Beers after other international mining houses became satisfied that the Letseng pipe could not be made payable, reportedly in response to a plea from the king of Lesotho to Harry Oppenheimer. De Beers went in to develop the pipe in partnership with the government of Lesotho partly as a matter of philanthropy and partly as a matter of politics: many of Anglo American's black gold-mine workers are the king's subjects. Letseng was probably expected to run at a loss and it probably does, though De Beers never reveals that kind of information.

Diamond pipes probably do not have bottoms, but they do have economic bottoms. As mining proceeds farther down the pipe, diamonds tend to become fewer in number and smaller in size, while mining costs increase with depth. A point comes when it no longer pays to work a pipe. That was the fate of the greatest of the Kimberley-area mines, the Kimberley Mine, now known as the Big Hole of Kimberley, over which Rhodes and Barnato had their great fight for control. It closed forever in 1914.

The Big Hole has taken on a personality and a mystique of its own in diamond lore and fills an important place in the cultural as well as the economic history of South Africa. It was the source for the most significant portions of the wealth that enabled Rhodes, Beit, Barnato, and J. B. Robinson to develop the gold fields of the Transvaal Province, and their development led to the further industrialization of the country. In that sense, the Big Hole was the womb that gave birth to modern South Africa.

4

ORANJEMUND: SYMBOL OF EMPIRE

◆

The German government proclaimed most of the southern reaches of its colony in what is now Namibia to be *sperrgebiet*, forbidden territory, closed by the government in 1908 to protect the region's diamond wealth. It remains forbidden and forbidding. Most of it is naked desert. Incessant winds pick up the sands and swirl them into blinding dust storms. Along the South Atlantic coast, where the diamonds are, the *sperrgebiet* is cold, chilly even during the Namibian summer and bitterly cold for most of the rest of the year. Workings in this inhospitable terrain have for many years produced more revenue for De Beers than any of the company's other mining ventures.

In the terrible desolation of the *sperrgebiet*, De Beers' wholly owned subsidiary CDM (now its official corporate name) has created an oasis, Oranjemund, with wide boulevards and tended grass for the community's ten thousand-plus residents. Built, owned, and operated by CDM, Oranjemund is self-contained and almost entirely self-sufficient, as pure a company town as any in the world.

Oranjemund refines its water needs from the nearby Orange River and maintains farms that provide much of its food. There are doctors, dentists, a hospital. "Downtown" Oranjemund features a big and well-stocked supermarket, a "fashion shop," a branch of Barclay's Bank, a cinema, a florist, a cleaner's, and trash receptacles exhorting the citizen to "Keep Oranjemund Clean & Tidy," or, alternately, to "Hou Oranjemund Skoon & Netjiesch." (Half of its white residents and most of its blacks are Afrikaans-speaking.)

As an antidote to the isolation, De Beers has created at Oranjemund what one contented employee calls a fool's paradise. The company has attended to every possible need and service. There is free housing, free domestic help, free utilities, no tax bills, a subsidy for meat. Living expenses come to substantially nothing at all. Every manner of athletic facility is available. CDM has the only fully grassed eighteen-hole golf course in Namibia, and membership in the golf club costs $9 a year, with no greens fees. The tennis club costs $3 yearly. There are hockey and rugby teams, squash, horseback riding, volleyball, judo/karate, a fishing club, three shooting ranges, and a yacht club whose unostentatious vessels (one would think of them as "boats" rather than as "yachts") ply a company-created inland "sea." There is a bridge club, a chess club, a photography club, amateur theater, and three churches, each with its own round of social activities. CDM has all the amenities of suburbia, and all free or almost free.

For those who can become involved in one of the organized activities, life at Oranjemund can be pleasurable. For those who cannot, especially company wives, the isolation can become unendurable. There are few employment opportunities for women in a mining community, and those wives without children to occupy them are likely to suffer loneliness. The women, more than the men, are likely to drink a bit more than they do on the "outside." Many wives, however, have made nice adjustments. "Home is where you make it," one told me.

The insulation of the community has its own side effects. Said one employee: "The company does everything for us, perhaps too much for some. It doesn't make for self-reliance." Once adjusted to life at Oranjemund, residents find it increasingly difficult to leave, and anyone there too long is likely to become unable to cope with the problems of everyday life in the real world. Whether to give more employees a chance to enjoy the easy life at CDM or to limit the adverse effects thereof, De Beers generally moves company personnel after about three years.

Diamonds were first found in Namibia in 1908 by Zacharias Lewala, a black railroad worker who had worked at the diamond mines in Kimberley. He was shoveling sand near Kolmanskop, close to Lüderitz, when he discovered crystals that he recognized as diamond. His find started a diamond rush to the area, some 150 miles north of today's production center at Oranjemund. Diamonds were so rich that at first mining technique consisted of sending armies of blacks to crawl along the desert to collect the diamonds that studded the surface sands. To protect the diamond wealth, the German government proclaimed a belt running 60 miles inland from the coast and 220 miles north from the Orange River *sperrgebiet,* and limited mining rights within it.

The easy diamond finds were exhausted rather quickly, and in the 1910s capital-intensive diamond mining was begun by the predecessors of CDM. Gradually they (and after its founding in 1920, CDM) moved south to continue mining at Elizabeth Bay, Pomona, and Bogenfels. By the mid-1940s, Oranjemund had become the center of CDM activity.

Oranjemund's diamonds are seemingly born of the oceans and are mined from the beaches. Geologists speculate that the stones CDM retrieves from the seashore of Namibia originated in pipes hundreds of miles inland—probably in the region of current-day Kimberley—which were eroded, their diamonds washed down the Orange River and into the Atlantic. The ocean then disbursed them up and down the coast, finally depositing them like seashells on prehistoric beaches.

Mining of beach diamonds involves stripping away the overlay of "modern" sand with heavy earth-moving equipment to reach the ancient beach, which is then dug out and removed for processing. The visitor can observe the operations from "ground level," far above the excavation, and see gigantic and bizarre machines at work. Bowl scrapers, great ant-shaped vehicles made by the Caterpillar Tractor Company and costing over a quarter of a million dollars each, roll across the dug-out flats with Ovambo tribesmen at the controls. The scraper part of it digs into the earth and then the machine requires a push from a couple of bulldozers to move it farther forward. The scraper churns up the floor and pushes the earth into the bowl of the machine. When its belly is full, with thirty to thirty-six tons of sand and gravel and perhaps half a gram of diamond, the bowl scraper lumbers away while another approaches to continue excavating.

The richest finds are made in the crevices and potholes in the bedrock itself, and when the machines have done as best they can, human "miners" carefully sweep the bedrock with small hand brooms. Here is the chance for an illiterate black man, the least skilled man on the De Beers payroll, to become rich by secreting away just one large diamond. The bedrock sweepers are watched by a security man, but only so well as one man can ever watch a group of men, and only for so long as the watchman himself remains true. As an honesty incentive, the sweeper is given a small reward for each "pickup" he turns in, and teams are given a periodic bonus for the total number of pickups that their group has handed over, thereby bringing team spirit and peer-group pressure to bear to reinforce the tenets of the Eighth Commandment. Still, theft and collusion are not unknown.

At selected spots CDM is also mining the foreshore area, the section of "land" (if that be what it is) that is beach at low tide and ocean bottom at high tide. Foreshore mining involves diking back the sea with sand, boulders, and very little nonnatural reinforcement, and holding the ocean at bay just long enough to remove the gravels of the foreshore and sweep its bedrock. CDM is mining as far as two hundred meters beyond high water level, and as much as twenty meters below mean sea level. Costs of establishing the temporary dikes and then fighting constant ocean seepage through them make foreshore operations considerably more expensive than digging out deposits under marine terraces on dry land, but the larger-sized diamonds in the richer of the foreshore areas make it economically feasible for the moment.

The diamondiferous materials, whether from beach or foreshore, are trucked to the closest of CDM's four plants for processing. The diamonds are separated out from the silt, sands, and common gravels by the same processes as are used to extract diamonds from crushed kimberlite at the pipe mines.

A glance at the pile of the day's production at CDM plainly shows the superior quality of alluvial stones over the diamonds being dug out of the pipes in Kimberley, the source from which CDM's stones probably originated. The alluvial stones are of much finer overall quality than pipe-mined stones. Even the poorest quality diamonds can get by in the insulated environment of an underground shelter but alluvial diamonds have to be better to survive a million years in the rough and tumble world of running water. The lesser quality stones were destroyed in the process of transporting them from the Kimberley region to the beaches of Namibia. Something like 98 percent of CDM's 1980 yield of 1,560,000 carats was gemstone. For years Oranjemund was undoubtedly the world's largest source of gem diamonds, until the Russian mines in Siberia reached full production in the 1960s.

Most of CDM's 6,500 employees are Africans, virtually all of them Ovambo tribesmen from Ovamboland in the far north of Namibia. In the early days of diamond mining in Namibia, the Ovambo were willing to travel the great distances to the mines, and began working them in the German period. They have held the jobs ever since. By now, most of CDM's Ovambo employees are second or third generation CDM people and when there are job openings, preference is given to the sons of present or past employees. This is an incentive to fathers to make a good record at the mine, thereby increasing the possibility that there will be jobs there for their sons. Family tradition promotes loyalty to the company, and to an extent helps to reduce the problems of theft.

CDM employs about 5,200 Ovambo, and they are very likely the best-paid black workers in all of Africa. When I was there in November 1979 their average wage was 350 rand ($420) a month take-home, plus or minus a modest charge for room and board—this in a country where the average per capita black income is about 125 rand annually, one of the world's lowest. They get free medical care, transportation, participation in De Beers' generous pension scheme, and other fringe benefits. Most employers in Namibia pay significantly less and offer less attractive facilities for workers, with the result that CDM gets the most desirable employees.

The usual term of service for Ovambo employees at CDM is six or nine months at a stretch, followed by a three-month leave. They are flown back and forth to their homeland. The company moves about five hundred men a month by a company plane that does only the Oranjemund-Ovamboland run. Virtually everyone returns to the company at the end of a leave; the high rate of return accounts for the fact that the average age of the company's Ovambo employees is well into the forties. It also accounts in part for the poor possibilities of job advancement for younger Ovambo: the more responsible positions are held by senior men who never leave.

The full force of apartheid never struck South Africa's "protectorate" of South West Africa (now Namibia). Until the mid-1970s, however, CDM "respected local customs" and in Oranjemund a purely white section coexisted with an entirely black section of similar housing reserved for the higher-ranking Ovambo employees. In an effort to encourage the latter to relocate their families to Oranjemund, the company built more housing in the black section, but despite generous subsidies, it was unable to attract sufficient Ovambo families to fill the units. Most of the Ovambo own a plot of land in Ovamboland, have left their wives there to tend the cattle, and look to the far north as "home." Ultimately the company moved whites into the empty flats, with the result that the "Ovambo" section of Oranjemund is now racially integrated. The town's school of five hundred pupils is integrated with about fifty children of those Ovambo who have moved their families to Oranjemund.

Racial segregation has formally ceased to exist at CDM, but continues on a de facto basis, the product of practicalities, distinctions based on job rank and status with the company, and natural social selection. At both of the packed pubs in downtown Oranjemund I noticed only one "colored" (mulatto in the South African scheme) patron, and no Ovambo. Ovambo faces are scarce in the center of town. The recreational facilities in the "white" section of town are open to all, but used almost only by whites. It is more convenient for the blacks to patronize the shops, recreation club, and facilities in "their" part of town, and probably everyone feels more comfortable that way. In the American North it has taken a long time for de facto segregation to begin to blend into an integrated society, and it will be a long time in Oranjemund as well.

The vast majority of the Ovambo employees live in one of five compounds, each a large dormitory complex, entirely black, with its own kitchen/dining facilities, library, chapel, recreational amenities (some including swimming pool or tennis courts) and company-subsidized shop and beer garden. I visited the "worst" one of those in the De Beers network, that at Affenrucken some fifty miles north of Oranjemund, and thought it not too bad, while many of the company's compounds both in Namibia and in South Africa are surprisingly attractive.

The company has established the Valombola Technical Center at Ongwediva, Ovamboland, at a cost of 1.5 million rand, to train more Ovambo for artisan roles—at CDM or elsewhere—but in some areas CDM may not be doing the most possible to train Ovambo for more responsible positions. In the heavy equipment repair shop, I asked a white mechanic whether, in due time, his black assistants would become more skilled and be given higher-ranked tasks. No, he said; at the end of their contracts they would go home on leave to Ovamboland, and when they returned they would likely be assigned elsewhere, with the result that they would never have sufficient exposure to his trade to become very skilled in it themselves.

The bigger stumbling block to Ovambo advancement, however, is their low literacy level. Those who might be suitable for more responsible positions are generally younger men, and it is difficult to assign younger men to positions of authority over older men. Many that have been promoted have been unable to exercise authority over their seniors and also over their former peers. The highest-ranking black man at CDM, a plant superintendent with many whites under him, is a Xhosa from South Africa, not an Ovambo. Difficult problems do not avail themselves of easy solutions.

Namibia is now approaching independence, its future political course uncertain. The two principal political arms competing for control are Southwest Africa People's Organization (SWAPO), a fragmented group favored by black nationalists, which operates both legitimately within Namibia and also from guerrilla bases in Angola, and the Democratic Turnhalle Alliance (DTA), a group of democratically committed parties favored and led by the white minority. As of this writing, DTA people are the "properly constituted authority," elected in SWAPO-boycotted elections, while SWAPO is recognized by the United Nations as the more nearly legitimate voice of Namibia. To most white settlers there, prospects seem grim.

In this environment, many believe that CDM is mining its tracts furiously with an eye to getting as much of the diamond wealth as possible out of Namibia before the deluge. De Beers denies it. Yes, they are mining three shifts a day at CDM, just as they are at all of their other mines, in order to meet current demand and not by way of flight preparation. The company has embarked on a $6 million general geological survey of 100,000 square kilometers of potentially mineral-rich lands, and it points to that and to its expenditures on the Valombola Technical Institute as evidence of its intentions to remain in Namibia. It has moved CDM's administrative headquarters from Kimberley to Windhoek, the Namibian capital. Harry Oppenheimer says that he wants to sustain CDM's contribution to Namibia's economy.

When the political situation settles down in Namibia, De Beers will be facing a very different situation. It approaches the future there with greater confidence than other white enterprises, however, because it and its sister company, Anglo American, have lived through and survived revolutionary change in other black African countries.

Over the years 1974–77, CDM—which uses virtually no governmental services—paid from 62.3 to 67 percent of its pretax profits in various forms of tax. The company has ended up with a third of its earnings and the government has ended up with two-thirds, and that two-thirds has come to slightly more than half of the government's total revenues. CDM is as important to Namibia as it is to De Beers.

SWAPO knows what happened in Zaire: Zairian President Mobutu Sese Seko stripped ownership of the diamond mines from Sibeka, the Belgian company that controlled them, and then found that he couldn't run the mines. He had to call Sibeka back to resume management. De Beers is an essential partner for the black countries in which it operates. Without De Beers the diamond mines—and the economies, to the extent to which the economies are dependent on the mines—would close down.

SWAPO's hints for the future are only that greater "social control" will be exercised over Namibia's mineral resources—which does not necessarily mean total nationalization. Harry Oppenheimer himself has met with Daniel Tjongarero, leader of one of SWAPO's two major factions, and the company is in touch with both factions, both in Namibia and in London. De Beers, a remarkably flexible political/diplomatic animal, lives with the Soviets, the Boers of South Africa (also politically difficult to deal with), the Angolans, and it can live with SWAPO if it must—and it is not yet clear that it will ever have to do so.

For how long is yet another question. The yield at Oranjemund has been falling off annually for many years as the richer locations are worked out, and CDM's role in De Beers' total profits has declined along with it. Projecting diamond-mine life spans, whether at pipe mines or in alluvial locations, is a very iffy matter. De Beers predicts that CDM has another fifteen years. Projections aside, they will just keep mining until it no longer pays.

The earlier diamond-mining towns of Namibia were abandoned as recently as the 1950s, and the sands immediately began to reclaim their natural territory. Dunes have made streets impassable, and drift in and then back out again from the abandoned houses of Kolmanskop, Elizabeth Bay, and Bogenfels. When the diamonds no longer pay, the same fate probably awaits Oranjemund.

5

BOTSWANA:
KUWAIT OF THE DIAMOND
WORLD

◆

The diamond mine at Orapa, Botswana, produces more diamonds for De Beers than any other mine in its empire—over four million carats a year, almost five pounds of diamonds a day, 365 days a year. Its diamonds, as a whole, are inferior to those harvested in Namibia, most of them usable only for industrial applications and worth relatively little, but while CDM's stones are being worked out, Botswana's diamond industry is just entering full flower. Oranjemund represents the company's fast-receding past; Botswana, its future.

Orapa, built from scratch by De Beers, sits in the midsts of endless plains of scrub brush. As a practical matter there is only one way for the visitor to get there: by Anglo American plane. Anglo aircraft make the four-hundred-mile run north from Johannesburg to Orapa six times a week. As the airplane approaches, you can see Orapa from a considerable distance—and especially the most prominent topographical feature of the community, a gigantic anthill just on the edge of town. As the plane begins its descent for landing, you can see that vehicles are moving on the top of the anthill. It is the tailings dump.

Orapa's processing plant is by far the biggest diamond-processing unit outside of Russia, and very likely the biggest and hungriest diamond plant in the world. It turns out something like two million pounds of tailings every hour of every day. The tailings dump is as high as it can safely be piled, and is moving out over the Botswanan countryside on two fronts at the rate of forty meters a month.

Botswana is a Texas-sized country with a population of perhaps 700,000 people, a density of about one person per square kilometer. The lonely Kalahari Desert blankets half of it, and swamps cover much of the rest. It has no industries other than diamonds, and no other prospects. Its diamond industry consists entirely of the mines operated by De Beers Botswana Mining Company, known as Debswana, which is owned exactly half and half by De Beers Consolidated and by the government of Botswana.

Botswana has enjoyed an excellent press and its longtime president, Sir Seretse Khama, who served as president from independence in 1966 until his death in July of 1980, received near-uniform accolades in the western newpapers. Khama established Botswana as close to a western-style democracy as there is in Africa. There is an opposition party with representation in the Botswanan Parliament; there are no political prisoners; corruption is less pervasive than in New Jersey. The country is truly an interracial nation, in which the majority blacks are politically dominant but in which white citizens fill important roles as equals. Botswana supports the efforts of black nationalists everywhere and maintains only informal relations with South Africa, but it is economically tied to and entirely dependent on South Africa.

Botswana's first diamond mine was discovered in 1967 and brought to production in 1971. Though most of Botswana's output is of "industrials," still it brings something over $32 a carat for the entire production (the 1978 average)—not bad for a diamond mine. All of the country's diamonds come from the mine at Orapa, in central Botswana, or from a much lesser two-pipe mine close to Orapa at Letlhakane. Another mine at Jwaneng in southern Botswana, outside the Orapa group of pipes, probably will enter production in 1982 and promises to be even more economically significant than the Orapa/Letlhakane mines. It should double the Botswana diamond production.

De Beers began prospecting for diamonds in then Bechuanaland in 1956. Its first efforts were concentrated in the Kalahari Desert. Over the centuries, billions of ants have tunneled down from the surface of the Kalahari to the water table as far as three hundred feet below, and in the process have pushed particles up to the surface that hint at the composition of the underground. De Beers systematically sampled the surface sands for pieces of garnet or ilmenite, minerals generally associated with kimberlite pipes, that the ants might have turned up. Though this prospecting technique has been successful in searches for other minerals in other areas, the company's efforts in the Kalahari were unfruitful. Meanwhile, the diamond-mining subsidiary of Selection Trust, a major British mining house, was prospecting for diamonds along the Macloutsie River, and discovered three small diamonds that must have originated in a kimberlite pipe someplace. When Selection Trust abandoned its efforts, De Beers sampled all along the Macloutsie and found occasional scattered diamonds and garnets, but no arrow of "tracer minerals" that might point to the location of the pipe. Then De Beers geologist Gavin Lamont theorized that the ancient course of the river might have been very different from its current course, and tentatively plotted an alternate course. The sampling teams following it came upon the world's second largest diamond pipe at what is today's Orapa. Kimberlite pipes invariably come in groups, and De Beers discovered many more kimberlites in the area of Orapa, but only the Orapa pipe and the smaller pipes at Letlhakane have proven to be economically diamondiferous. The prospecting effort alone cost $6 million.

Establishing a mine in the desert was an even more expensive proposition. Water was the most pressing need. Diamond-processing plants require vast quantities of water; the Orapa plant recycles much of its "used" water, but still requires an additional 5.3 million gallons of water daily. The nearest reliable water supply was 240 kilometers (150 miles) northwest of Orapa, in the unending Okavango swamps fed by rain from the Angolan highlands. The company reopened old natural channels from the region flowing in the direction of Orapa, and established a vast reservoir in a natural pan (depression) at Mopipi, 60 kilometers (37.5 miles) from Orapa, to meet the community's needs. The operation had a positive environmental impact. The channels had historically been kept open by the hippopotamus population until poachers killed off the hippos. Then the channels had grown in, closed up, and dried up. Now that man has done the work formerly done by nature and irrigated a broad swath of Botswana, all kinds of wildlife that had abandoned the region long ago have returned to it. The irrigation network established to supply Orapa will also enable development of other lands along the waterway. Meanwhile, in nine years of operation, Orapa has yet to suffer any significant water shortage.

A road had to be constructed to link Orapa with the railroad line at Francistown, and it was necessary to construct a separate rail depot there for Orapa-bound goods, to prevent the existing station from being ever clogged with Orapa supplies. Since then, provisions have been brought by rail to Francistown and then by truck to Orapa. A township had to be created at Orapa, complete with schools, stores, recreational and medical facilities, and a diesel-generated power plant. Before the mine was opened, De Beers had invested over $30 million in the Orapa project, the most sizable investment in the country, and a sum well in excess of the national budget of Botswana and many other countries.

Orapa township now has a population of between 4,500 and 5,000, half the size of Oranjemund. Its facilities are less complete and less impressive; emotional survival depends more on one's inner resources. The plight of the white "company wives" is harder than at Oranjemund. The government requires that any job that might be performed by a local citizen must be given to a local, so there are virtually no employment opportunities for white women at Orapa, and there are far fewer companions than at Oranjemund. Most "expats" get out once or twice a year on the Anglo plane.

The white industrial workers are a more motley crew than at Oranjemund or the De Beers mines in South Africa, with little or no company identification: rootless Europeans of miscellaneous origin, a rugged American mining engineer with one earring, a lot of South African roustabouts. You see them at the Orapa Recreational Club, intertwined with "local" girls, ready, willing, and able to break taboos. The senior white management staff are all "company people," presided over by Andrew Brittz, a stiff but honorable man with a lifetime of service to De Beers behind him. Together they form an Old India enclave at the edge of the Kalahari.

As of the fall of 1979, Orapa and its satellite mine at Letlhakane employed 2,100 people, most of them blacks from central Botswana. These are the least-paid people in the De Beers network. De Beers would like to pay more—as a matter of enlightened self-interest: to attract the best workers from elsewhere in Botswana to Orapa. The government, however, an equal partner in Debswana, keeps a lid on wages, to prevent the emergence in Botswana of an economic elite of very well-paid industrial workers.

The company has embarked on a Five Year Plan to "localize" the entire work force, and a good number of Botswanans are already employed in management spots.

Orapa is "integrated" in the manner of Oranjemund: there are jobs held exclusively by blacks and jobs held exclusively by whites and very few if any jobs that are truly integrated. Housing is allocated on a job-rank basis, making sections of Orapa integrated, and there are cordial relations but little social contact between the races. More segregation by practicalities and self-segregation.

The huge area of the Orapa pipe, 273 acres at the surface, is mined open-cast. As is common in such operations, layers ("benches") of kimberlite are blasted off from the matrix, moving backward from the center of the pit toward the rim, as many feet a day as the plant will consume in the next twenty-four hours. The rubble is trucked out over a rim road that connects the bottom of the pit to the surface levels, and is then brought to the plant. After nine years of operations, the pit has been excavated only to the depth of twenty to twenty-five meters and is deepening at the rate of only about three meters annually, or ten feet a year. The company estimates that it will be thirty years before it must convert to a shaft operation, and that the mine has a total life expectancy of seventy years. Operations in both the mine and the plant go on twenty-four hours, six days a week.

Letlhakane is a much smaller operation, removing only a third as much kimberlite, to yield only an eighth as much caratage. Because the gem proportion of the Letlhakane diamonds approaches 40 percent, as compared to a 15 percent gem content from the Orapa stones, the Letlhakane operation is profitable despite the relatively low overall yield. Preliminary processing of kimberlite is done at Letlhakane, and then four or five tons of concentrate are trucked daily the fifty-seven kilometers to Orapa for final processing and retrieval of the diamonds at the Orapa plant.

The government of Botswana has financed its interest in Debswana by loans from De Beers and from the international money markets. Its yield from the mines in taxes and its share of dividends come to 75 to 80 percent of the total pretax profit, in addition to which it collects income taxes from the otherwise lesser-employed work force. Diamonds are already Botswana's number one export, and produce close to half the government's total income.

Botswana has harnessed its diamond wealth better than most of the new countries in Africa. Sir Seretse discouraged premature urbanization; the country has substantial foreign currency reserves and a balanced budget; the *pula* (Botswana's unit of currency) is stable and respected, and national planners are looking for ways to utilize the diamond windfall that will have long-term benefits with only minimal adverse social effects.

Development of the Jwaneng mine will likely cost something in the range of a quarter of a billion dollars. It is remarkable to contemplate that this staggering investment is made as the first step in the production of articles of personal adornment, and that these articles are keeping Botswana afloat. When Jwaneng reaches full production in the mid-1980s, De Beers anticipates that Jwaneng's production will total upward of 6 million carats annually, which, together with Orapa/Letlhakane, will make Botswana the third biggest caratage producer after Zaire and the USSR, bringing a total cash price that may be second to none. With its small population, Botswana will be the diamond world's Kuwait.

6

ROBBERS AND COPS

◆

Considering the small size and high value of diamonds—their optimum stealability—it is not possible to imagine a diamond world in which theft and illegal diamond trade does not exist. The problem is greater in alluvial mines, where stones are loose and discernible, than in pipe mines, where they are usually hidden within the kimberlite; it is equally common in the processing plants; it is centralized in the separating rooms and in the sorting rooms at Kimberley and London; it is everywhere.

Some of De Beers' black workers on the mining level come from tribal groups whose cultures do not include strong belief in the myth of private property, and to whom distinctions about "legal title" and words like "theft" do not have much significance. Many whites, especially those of a conservative caste, believe that some black theft is politically motivated: that left-wing movements finance their activities by having the faithful steal diamonds. I much discount the proportion of diamond theft that is "political." I spent ten days at the Tourist Hotel in Antwerp, which caters to black Africans carrying illicit diamonds. There was not a "politician" in the hotel. The Africans with whom I spoke said yes, from time to time a radical shows up at the Tourist, but not often. When my wife asked one black smuggler if he was dedicated to Uhuru, the cause of black African freedom, he gave her a fatherly smile and replied, "I am a businessman." Most black theft, just like most white theft, is probably the product of simple greed. The grandest schemes are invariably perpetrated by whites.

How much De Beers loses through theft can only be conjectured. *Jewelers' Circular–Keystone*, the respected jewelry trade magazine, has ascribed confirmation of a $200-million-a-year estimate to an unidentified De Beers public relations person, but the company usually doesn't discuss this kind of thing, on the theory that the less one talks about security, the more secure things will be. Publication of a loss figure, whether the losses be high or low, would only be an incentive to further theft (and if the figure were high, would also shake confidence in De Beers' control of the world market).

Today security at the mines revolves around careful monitoring of everyone who enters a security area and random selection searches of those leaving. At many places, locked banks of doors are opened in such a manner that only one person at a time can enter a secured area. At the exit, everyone leaving a security area is subject to being searched, and a mechanical device selects on a random basis those who are actually subjected to the searching procedure. The percentage of people selected for search is constantly changing; one day the machine will select almost no one, the next day an inordinately large number will be chosen. The average is probably about 10 percent.

Random searches, of course, come in two kinds: random searches that are random and "random" searches that are not random at all. The machine that makes the selection can be programmed any way its operator wants. My guide at CDM, Estrellita Forbes, had been through the selector perhaps fifty times and never been selected, but a processing-plant supervisor with whom I spoke told me that he is selected perhaps 20 percent of the time that he goes through the gate.

I was randomly selected for search at CDM. I pressed my plastic identification card—every employee has one and every visitor is given one—into a slot and after a moment the indicator device showed that I was to go through the "search" door. Through it is a corridor lined with one-way mirrors, through which you are observed for signs of nervousness and to be certain that you do not drop anything. The corridor ends abuptly in a small antechamber. There is only one door out of that. As I approached it, a red-lit sign over the door commanded STOP. After two minutes the red light went out and a green light went on saying ENTER.

I entered a small room where one of two security men directed me to empty my pockets into a basket, and then to step up a few steps into a small alcove, and to turn my head to the right. I tried to engage the security men in conversation. "I'd rather not answer any questions," one of them responded for both.

After a respectable pause in the alcove, I heard a series of whirrs which were consistent with the operation of an X-ray machine. At CDM and Kleinzee, the search is performed by an X-ray scan, which will pick up stones hidden in body cavities or swallowed quicker and more easily than a human examiner could find one hidden in a smuggler's pocket. When the whirring stopped, I was directed to the exit. I was "clean."

Had I been "randomly" selected? Indeed, had I really been X-rayed, or was the whole thing a charade? The principal purpose of security is deterrence, and a soundmaker that emits X-ray-like sounds is as effective a deterrent as an X-ray machine, less expensive to operate, and involves no potential health hazard. Every time a worker is selected and "X-rayed" he is not necessarily X-rayed. But only the security man knows whether he has been working the X-ray or the soundmaker.

Premier and the Kimberley area mines have removed the X-ray machine; the selection is mechanical, but the search is human. In the days when their workers were confined to the security area for the six- or nine-month term of the employment contract, it was feasible to X-ray every man (or rather, every black man) when he left the gates on expiration of his term, but when the compounds were opened in the mid-1970s, and the black workers were permitted to come and go as they liked, regular X-ray examination became unfeasible.

If you are randomly selected for search at Premier, Kimberley, or Orapa, you may not actually be searched at all, or you may be subjected to a pat down search scarcely more probing than no search, or you may be asked to take off your boots or to partially disrobe, or you may be asked to totally disrobe. The extent of the search is largely in the discretion of the security officer who performs it, and he is likely to proceed diplomatically. Except for the X-ray machine—and they don't even have one in storage anymore at Premier or Kimberley—none of the standard search procedures will disclose a swallowed stone or a stone hidden in a body cavity.

Stone swallowing is relatively rare. A piece of rough that could be safely swallowed would not be worth swallowing or chasing; a stone big enough to promise its thief a lifetime of easy living would be difficult and dangerous to swallow. Rectums are another matter. A homemade candle-wax suppository with a diamond or diamonds bound into it makes a comfortable and perfectly safe "torpedo," as such devices are sometimes known. While the company has authority to insist on a rectal examination at the security gate, the odds on being asked to submit to one—unless the company has powerful suspicions about a particular suspect—are zero. The company relies on the same cross-cultural taboos that make it reluctant to request or perform an intimate body search, to inhibit would-be thieves from using off-limits hiding places. One divisional security chief with whom I spoke was uncharacteristically open about it: "My fingers aren't that long; if you want to put a diamond up there, you can have it!" Women involve further security problems; as a matter of delicacy, they are totally banned in the Orapa security areas (at the government's insistence).

Random searches result in the discovery of "very, very few" diamonds (the company doesn't like to be precise about such matters) but quite a few screwdrivers, wrenches, and the like. At Premier perhaps a thousand such items are turned in at the search rooms annually, just before the search is about to begin. Most of them probably do not spell an intended theft. Some men will take their favorite tools back to the compound at the end of the shift so as to be certain that they have their working equipment the next morning. "Hoarding" of tools is against company rules, but obviously a different matter than stealing, and the company views it lightly.

Random selection search is only the most apparent aspect of the De Beers security system. There are also closed-circuit TVs or human watchdogs at points where people handle stones. At CDM and Kleinzee, helicopters and security boats patrol the desolate stretches, watching for suspicious activity.

Security begins in the personnel office, where every job applicant is screened. Company officials do casual checks on every applicant, and deeper ones on anyone they have doubts about. The contract workers are drawn from a small number of tribes, and the company has its representatives in each of them, doing the same work. The high rate of return keeps new intake to a minimum, enabling careful scrutiny in the hiring process; low turnover makes for higher security. The company never advertises for workers in the sorting rooms, and anyone who asks for that kind of work is probably a bad risk. At the end, anyone questionable is eliminated.

To some extent—though the company would deny it—its hiring decisions are apparently influenced by the supposed "trustworthiness" of particular ethnic groups, most obviously in Sierra Leone where its extensive diamond-buying operations employ no Lebanese. The large Lebanese community of Sierra Leone pretty much controls the national economy, but the Lebanese there are not well regarded for rectitude. In South Africa, where Indians are commonly thought untrustworthy, the company has few Indians. At Oranjemund, the final recovery—not done through glove boxes—is done by white women rather than by the Ovambo, who do pretty much everything else at Oranjemund. South Africans commonly believe, as one told me, that "Ovambos are even less honest than Indians!" The company could give very acceptable (and possibly complete) explanations for the scarcity of Indians and the plethora of white women, and in their cases it may be that circumstances only incidentally coincide with common biases. As for the Lebanese, I asked one of the company's highest-ranking employees in Sierra Leone, why no Lebanese?, and he stuttered out this answer: "I'm not at liberty to disclose that."

In any case, there are very few professional thieves among the company's twenty-thousand-plus employees, only amateurs, human beings who will react to temptation as human beings will.

Much of the company security effort is devoted to removing temptations. Rare as it is for someone to see a diamond underground, the block caving method of underground mining introduced in the 1950s very much reduced the human handling of blue ground, correspondingly reducing the possibility of loss by theft. The use of glove boxes in the final separation process accomplishes the same, and the processing procedure has also been largely mechanized, insulating stones from human hands. The company's more humane approach to handling problems of security and people in recent years has largely coincided with the degree to which the company has been able to reduce opportunities for theft.

Compared with operations of twenty years ago, opportunities to steal are open to relatively few De Beers employees. Those who have them know that they are watched more closely than others. It would be safer for them to have somebody else carry out the goods, but it is difficult to know with whom to conspire because the De Beers operation is permeated (or so most employees believe) with undercover agents—spies.

In the past the company has also sent its own agents into the illicit diamond buying world outside company gates, both for intelligence and to participate in the entrapment of illicit dealers, and may still do so.

Vehicles make much better hiding places than humans, so De Beers maintains a fleet of vehicles within each security area to serve its needs. Each fleet remains within its security area permanently; at the end of their useful lives, the vehicles are relegated to junkyards within the same confines. Other vehicles stay outside the security gate, and when exceptions must be made and vehicles temporarily admitted, they are escorted in and out by security men who watch them at all times. The company is reluctant to sell anything at all from the security area as scrap, and when it does, it sells only to distant outsiders.

The security force itself is largely made up of Afrikaners, but is racially mixed, both as an aid to intelligence gathering and also as a dis-incentive to collusion within the security department. Collusion is less likely if it must cut across racial lines. For the most part, though, the security men seem uncorruptible. They are straitlaced, formal, and unapproachable; they keep their distance from the other employees as a matter of policy. Collusion between them and those that they are supposed to police is rare—though not unknown.

The whole system is bolstered by the rewards given workers who turn in pickup stones. The reward schedule varies from mine to mine. At the alluvial sites, CDM and the mines of the Kleinzee district, where pickups are a significant portion of total mine output, the usual bonus for turning in a one-carat piece of rough is about 4 rand ($4.80), and it is equally unimpressive at Premier—far less than the stones would be worth on the illicit market in South Africa, let alone in Antwerp. In Kimberley rewards are somewhat more generous, but only in Botswana are the rewards substantial enough to make it more rewarding for the worker to turn in a stone than to pocket it. At Orapa and all of the other pipe mines, however, the nature of the operation is such as to make pickups unlikely, and very few stones are turned in at them.

Stones that are stolen enter the "IDB" market, the market of the illicit diamond buyers. The going price there, according to Brigadier Hannes Erasmus, head of the diamond and gold division of the South African police, is about one-third of fair market value. Insofar as the statutes are concerned, illicit possession or buying or selling of an uncut diamond is a serious offense in South Africa, punishable by maximum penalties of a 10,000 rand ($12,000) fine or up to fifteen years imprisonment or both—nothing to be lightly contemplated. (In Namibia, however, the maximum penalty is a mere four years in jail—well worth risking for anyone in a position to bring out a batch of big stones.)

Illicit diamond buying is battled principally by the brigadier's four hundred-odd operatives, tough black, white, and colored men—and a few very attractive females. He is proud that in twenty-three years on the job, only two of his agents have been corrupted (to the best of his knowledge). His agents are everywhere that there are diamonds. They are in De Beers' underground mines, working alongside rank-and-file miners (and also alongside De Beers' own undercover security agents; neither batch of cops knows the other batch), but more of his "miners" are in the otherwise unsecured mines worked by the little guys who produce the "other" few percent of South Africa's diamonds. In the smaller enterprises, Erasmus' agents provide what security the entrepreneur has. The possibility of their presence in any particular operation—unknown for certain even to the entrepreneurs—also discourages management from trying to cheat the government out of income taxes and export duties. At the moment, a lot of small businesses are dredging for diamonds on the ocean bottoms off the coast of Namaqualand. Erasmus is there; he has had some of his men trained to be deep-sea divers.

The focus of crime prevention in the South African diamond world has always been on catching illicit buyers, on the theory—possibly correct—that the illicit buyers encourage theft, often instigate it, and that without them, the incentive to steal rough diamonds would dry up. Very few sellers, or people simply in possession of uncut diamonds, are ever caught or arrested. It is easier to curtail the illicit traffic by catching buyers, and they are caught in droves through the simple and familiar police practice of entrapment. Erasmus, a personable, outspoken, and colorful man, acknowledges that his branch works principally by trap "—well, we don't call it 'trap' anymore, we call it 'police action.' " Whatever it is called, it involves zeroing in on a suspect by undercover agents who to varying degrees entice the suspect into commission of the crime. The police operative, usually black, sometimes female, ingratiates himself or herself with the suspect; sooner or later the topic of conversation turns to rough diamonds—at the impetus of the one or of the other (and who brought up the subject is often disputed). A transaction is consummated, and at just the right moment the cops burst through the door, yelling the Afrikaans equivalent of "Hold everything!"

Erasmus denies that anyone is ever arbitrarily "tested." His division will consider assigning an agent to an individual only when in possession of a sworn statement from an informant indicating that the suspect has a past history of illicit diamond dealing.

Those arrested make a varied lot. In the first six months of 1979, the Rand *Daily Mail* reported the arrests on diamond charges of, among others, a well-known South African actor, a woman prosecutor, and a prominent millionaire. Virtually all of those arrested are white.

There isn't much to talk about in an illicit buying case, as most of the evidence has been tape recorded. Despite the harsh sound of the statute, imprisonment for first offenders is rare. The most common disposition is a hefty fine, a suspended jail term, and, perhaps most fierce, a forfeiture of any moneys that the buyer has paid to the undercover agent. A third of that goes to the informant. The forfeiture is often the most serious aspect of the disposition, as it can wipe out an offender. Erasmus notes that when there is a series of firm dispositions in the Kimberley court, diamond offenses seem to decline in the area; when sentences are easier, they thrive.

Finicky people may disapprove of the entrapment approach, but Brigadier Erasmus views illicit diamond buying as an evil that must be fought with hard methods. He sees it as involving much more than simple theft of private property. When one considers that something over half of De Beers' South African pretax profits goes to the state, a theft from De Beers is more nearly a theft from the public. Erasmus views illicit buying as "economic sabotage because our country is so dependent on diamonds and gold." From his twenty-five years on the job he concludes that illicit diamond dealing is usually an organized crime operation dominated by professional criminals, who are not entitled to any sympathy. He notes many shortcomings in the security system of IDB's number one victim: He regards the random selection system as it operates in Kimberley and at Premier as "not worth the metal in the turnstiles," and says that at a De Beers security area, "a mouse couldn't sneak in from the outside, but an elephant can get out unnoticed." He would like to see De Beers make greater use of X-ray searching; pay bigger rewards for pickup stones in order to dry up the illegal market; and step up internal detective work.

Erasmus himself sometimes works as an undercover agent in the field—risky business because often the victim becomes violent when the trap is sprung. In a lifetime on the job Erasmus says that every bone in his hand has been broken, and he has suffered more fractured noses than he would care to count. He is a personally dynamic man, with a style reminiscent of the crime-busting FBI men of the 1920s and the orientation, outlook, and character of the late J. Edgar Hoover—an accolade or an insult depending on the reader's own orientation. Though he is frank with interviewers, he imposes one rule: no photographs. A secret agent's "cover" must be protected or his utility ends, and the brigadier is still very much a secret agent.

7

HARRY OPPENHEIMER: SOUTH AFRICAN "RADICAL"

◆

Harry Oppenheimer is as he describes himself—"an extremely conservative old body"—and that is what one might expect, considering that Oppenheimer is without doubt the richest man in Africa. In South Africa, however, one's place on the political spectrum is pegged by reference to one issue alone: race. By local standards, the strongman of De Beers and Anglo American must be rated a political radical. Oppenheimer's is about the most aggressively pro-integration position held by any non-clergy, non-Marxist, nonstudent white.

Oppenheimer was serving in the South African Parliament when apartheid was first instituted in 1948. He opposed the premises and tenets of apartheid then and ever since. He has consistently favored the elimination of the pass laws under which blacks cannot enter white areas without official permission and a "pass"; an end to mass arrests and the denial of basic civil liberties; the elimination of "job reservation" (the law-enforced policy of limiting more highly skilled work to whites); the opening of all public facilities to blacks; an end to segregated educational facilities and equal rights in education; and the right of blacks to form labor unions.

He has gone so far as to defend "sedition" in South Africa during the Soweto riots of the summer of 1976: "In an atmosphere of smoldering social resentment it is perhaps not surprising that gangs of school-leavers who are unable to find jobs should roam the streets throwing stones and setting buildings on fire."

Though he opposes the immediate grant of universal suffrage, Oppenheimer favors the extension of the franchise to all people who meet certain educational standards.

He believes that the apartheid policies are not "designed cruelty," but represent only "an inability to see yourself in another man's shoes, particularly if the other feet just happen to be of another color."

Oppenheimer was born in 1908 in Kimberley, educated at Charter-house, and won a scholarship to Oxford's Christ's Church College, where he took the demanding course of study known as Philosophy, Politics and Economics. After graduating in 1931, he began work in the De Beers sorting rooms in Kimberley, then moved over to Anglo American, with four years out for battlefront service during World War II. Toward the end of the war he married Bridget McCall. The Oppenheimers have a daughter, Mary, born in 1943, whose romantic intrigues over the years have long been the favorite conversation topic for Johannesburg hausfraus, and a son, Nicholas, born in 1945.

On his return from the war Oppenheimer resumed work at Anglo. In 1948 he entered the Union of South Africa Parliament as a Kimberley representative for the minority United Party. His principal role in Parliament was as spokesman for the United Party on matters of business and economics. Like his father, Oppenheimer made his maiden speech in Parliament on the subject of diamonds and gold; like his father, he was never embarrassed to take positions that plainly favored his own financial interests. As he viewed things, the benefits to himself were purely incidental. To Nationalist Party spokesmen on the other side of the aisle, notably Hendrik F. Verwoerd, later prime minister, Oppenheimer was "pretending to work in the public interest while in reality serving only the interests of capitalism." There was much merit to the claim of Nationalists that Oppenheimer and the United Party stood for the combined and related interests of integration and the monied powers. For the South African businessman, economic and moral considerations coincide: the terrible shortage of skilled labor in the country makes it imperative for the growth of private profits that blacks be trained for more highly skilled positions and moved ahead.

When his father died in 1957, Oppenheimer resigned from Parliament to take full control of the Anglo–De Beers interests. He describes his years of attempting to pursue business and political careers simultaneously as "a rather unsuccessful attempt to combine the two."

In 1959 the United Party grew "soft" on apartheid and the Progressive Party, a splinter offshoot of the United, was formed with Oppenheimer's personal and financial backing. The Progressives have now replaced the United Party as the opposition party in South Africa, and Oppenheimer is still with them and still outspoken on racial issues. Generally he frames his argument in nonhumanitarian terms that are more likely to be effective in the atmosphere of his country, as when he cites "the urgent economic need of having an educated, stable, and prosperous African work force," or when he argues the unreasonability of expecting blacks "to defend free enterprise and individual freedom against communism while they are excluded by official policy from most of the benefits which free enterprise brings."

Positions such as Oppenheimer's may strike the American reader as representing no more than common decency, but in South Africa of the period 1948 to 1975 (and even today, though to a lesser extent) common decency on racial matters has been an unpopular position.

During his period in Parliament, the political climate of South Africa was that of mid-1930s Germany, and its ruling Nationalist Party had a decidedly Nazi bent. SS-like rowdies occasionally menaced United Party gatherings where Oppenheimer appeared. Dr. Albert Hertzog, leading "intellectual" of the *verkrampt* (constricted) wing of the Nationalists, spoke about the "British-Jewish internationalist capitalists who are controlling our economy," much as did Hitler's "intellectuals," while even less civilized elements sniggered about "Hoggenheimer the Jew." Many argued that Anglo American should be nationalized, and one Nationalist bellowed at Oppenheimer across the floor of Parliament, "Perhaps we'd better raise taxation on the mines. How would you like that?" As recently as 1977, Prime Minister John Vorster challenged Oppenheimer to state "where he stands" in the fight against communism. That year the South African government determined not to sell a state-owned magnesium producer when the high bidder turned out to be Anglo American.*

Some blacks and left-oriented whites dismiss Oppenheimer as a "mere reformer," looking out for his pocketbook, attempting to preserve ill-gotten gains from the justice of social revolution, or at best assuaging a properly guilty conscience. They point to old statements in Parliament (never repudiated) in which Oppenheimer, while favoring an end to economic apartheid, favored continued social and residential segregation, and to the fact that when it comes to extending real equality— political equality—to the blacks, Harry Oppenheimer is opposed ("for the time being"). They point out that, notwithstanding his anti-apartheid statements, no one has benefited financially to a greater extent from apartheid or from exploitation of the blacks than Harry F. Oppenheimer.

Oppenheimer's wife, Bridget, has been a moving force behind Women for Peace, a multiracial group of South African women formed in the wake of the Soweto riots of 1976, working to lower racial barriers. "We have all lived in our various ghettos for so long I think people want to get together," she told the *New York Times.* Her chauffeur's cottage has been turned into a classroom, where illiterate blacks are now learning to read and being taught handicrafts. She herself teaches embroidery to black women. Her efforts, like her husband's, are regarded as offensive by white reactionaries and are rejected by black militants as small and ultimately unhelpful palliatives.

Oppenheimer seems to be making efforts in his own companies— De Beers especially (and less impressively so at Anglo American)—to practice what he preaches. De Beers is as racially integrated as it can be consistent with the dictates of South African laws requiring racial segregation and the bottom-line insistence of the white unions with which it must deal. Everyone expects that De Beers' black workers will be

* The government, however, has long sold its own output of diamonds, mined from the small-scale State Alluvial Diggings in Namaqualand, through De Beers' sales organization.

unionized in the foreseeable future, introducing a countervailing pressure to that exerted by the white union. The company will then be in a position to move more rapidly.

There is still an eye-popping gap in black/white earnings at De Beers; whites are probably earning, on average, three times as much as blacks. (All are paid on the basis of the same wage scale, regardless of color, but blacks perform the least-paid functions.) Still, the company's blacks are probably the best paid in South Africa. As of January 1, 1981, the average monthly wage enjoyed by its black workers in South Africa and Namibia was 393 rand (almost $500) monthly, plus significant fringe benefits. On average, the De Beers diamond miner is earning close to double what the average black gold miner earns, and very much more than the typical black African industrial worker.

De Beers' black "contract" workers, who come to work at the mines from their tribal homelands for six- or nine-month terms, are housed in compounds. The compound at the Premier Mine is De Beers' largest, housing most of Premier's 3,400 black workers. The Premier compound looks like the dormitory complex at a well-financed black college, with grounds maintained to English landscaping standards. The housing itself is more nearly comparable to that found in a good army barracks. Most men there are living in very large, sixteen-bed "rooms," which consist of a sitting area with a series of bedroom alcoves separated from the sitting area, bright and well ventilated. Most of the sitting areas are carpeted—not with fancy carpets, but with carpeting nonetheless. The cleanliness of each room is the responsibility of its occupants, and the rooms are impressively clean. The compound has pretty much every recreational facility that anyone might want.

Until the mid-1970s, De Beers' compounds were jails within the maximum-security gates, the black workers required to remain within the gates for the terms of their contracts. Now all of the compounds are open, the workers free to come and go to nearby towns on their off hours. Many of them own cars and return to their homeland once or twice a month to see family and friends.

In Kimberley, where most of the company's black employees are local people, the company makes company housing available for local black employees and encourages them to buy their own small, new three-bedroom houses at De Beers' Ipopeng community, on company-subsidized terms. The net monthly shelter expense for an Ipopeng homeowner comes to only two or three days' earnings.

The front-line De Beers personnel officer is a youngish man, decidedly progressive on racial issues, his views on race shaped as much by moral/patriotic considerations as by business considerations. De Beers' attitudes are plainly paternalistic, which is to say understanding and affectionate.

The miners have repaid the company with a remarkable degree of loyalty. In the South African scheme, the black contract workers are only temporary residents of the white mine area in which they are employed. But the rate at which they reenlist, as high as 98 percent at Kleinzee, belies their temporary status. Most stay with the company their entire working lives and then retire as well-set De Beers retirees. A thirty-year man will be pensioned at 60 percent of his recent average earnings, leaving him with a greater income than most working South African blacks enjoy.

The company's policy toward its black workers has stood it in good stead. During the general civil disorder in South Africa born of the Soweto riots in the summer of 1976, De Beers was largely left alone—a good omen for De Beers in the event of revolution in South Africa.

De Beers' white employees are equally long-tenured. Most of its executives have been with the company for years at one or another position at one or another mine, usually at several of them. Executives and black and white laborers all tend to think of and identify themselves as "De Beers people." The company is very much a family firm—with its 21,500 employees, probably the biggest family firm in the world.

Oppenheimer, the head of the family, is basically a shy man, but his intellectual bent and his elegant speech always win him the favor of journalists. He mingles comfortably with leaders of many worlds. He has inherited his father's soft charm and mild manner, his unfailing courtesy, and the affection that company employees gave to his father. Rank-and-file employees usually speak of him as "Mr. Harry." A lab technician at De Beers' Diamond Research Laboratory describes him as "an exceptionally nice guy, open, obliging, and extraordinarily approachable." A remarkable accolade for a man of Oppenheimer's power and wealth.

Oppenheimer, his son Nicholas, and his former son-in-law Gordon Waddell, who despite a divorce from Oppenheimer's daughter remains very much a part of Oppenheimer's family, each own 18,743,943 shares of Anglo American, a combined 25 percent of the company's outstanding shares. With Anglo trading at 14¼ as of June 1, 1981 in New York, the Oppenheimer family's interests in Anglo would compute out to $800 million. The Anglo holdings provide the nub of Oppenheimer's economic power. Anglo controls 52 percent of Anglo American Investment Trust (Anamint), which controls 27 percent of De Beers; Anglo controls 36 percent of the many-armed Charter Consolidated, and bigger and lesser percentages of dozens of other corporations. Though Oppenheimer owns only insignificant interests directly in De Beers, Anamint, Charter, or most of the others, he controls them all—and all of their literally hundreds of subsidiaries and allied companies—through his Anglo interest. Pyramiding is more common and more respectable in South Africa than in the United States, and Oppenheimer and Anglo are the champs of it.

Oppenheimer permits himself to enjoy his wealth and the usual diversions of the super rich. He is also a thoroughly cultured man, perhaps the world's only working tycoon who really appreciates Dylan Thomas. He is old-fashioned in his tastes, occasionally "dresses" for dinner, and has never worn a diamond. "I belong to a generation," he told the New York Times in 1977, "in which men did not wear jewelry. Things have changed—I'm not against that change," he said with a grin.

Oppenheimer has been a noteworthy philanthropist, a rarer breed in his country than in the United States because the South African tax laws do not allow tax deductions for most charitable contributions. His Oppenheimer Fund gives most of its money to "areas beyond conventional charity"—which means to black-oriented causes, mostly to provide educational and medical facilities for blacks. His major and most significant philanthropic effort has been his cornerstone support for the Urban Foundation, the most important institution in South Africa today dedicated to elimination of racial discrimination in employment, and the impetus and financing agency for the construction of new and improved housing for blacks. It aims, as Oppenheimer says, to demonstrate that the private enterprise system "is not something which bears the label 'for whites only.' " The motives of the Urban Foundation are not only humanitarian; it hopes to divert the deluge by giving blacks a stake in the capitalist system and instilling in them bourgeois wants that can best be fulfilled through capitalism. Its effects, however, are both humanitarian and impressive. Most of the country's biggest corporations have made substantial contributions to the Urban Foundation, but the contributions of Anglo, De Beers, and the Oppenheimer family have amounted to about a quarter of its total income. Oppenheimer is chairman of the foundation.

Though he is thoroughly "Christian" by now, Oppenheimer has been generous to a number of Jewish charities, quietly channeling his contributions through other people—not so quietly that they are unknown in the Johannesburg Jewish community or in the Jewish diamond world, but quietly enough so as not to strengthen the general identification of him in South Africa as a Jew.

Every day Oppenheimer journeys from Brenthurst, the English-styled estate built by his father in the suburbs of Johannesburg, to Anglo American's conventionally majestic building at 44 Main Street, a vast structure but not vast enough to contain the Oppenheimer empire. Anglo, De Beers, and the other Oppenheimer companies spill over to most of the buildings around 44 Main. Just inside the main door of the Anglo building is the wing devoted to the offices of "E. Oppenheimer & Son," the family holding company and nerve center of the Oppenheimer interests. Here are the offices of Oppenheimer, "Mr. Nicky" (as son Nicholas is known), and former son-in-law Waddell.

Oppenheimer is a hard worker. Until recently he worked extra long days and then took work home with him at night. He has always found it hard to relax, though now, at seventy-plus, he is beginning to take things a bit easier. He regards himself as a planner, the man with the overview, rather than as an administrator. He appreciates the fuller responsibilities that accompany his role as the economic king of South Africa, and he considers the social effects of his decisions along with profit and loss figures. He will open a marginal mine or keep operating a losing one when more "prudent" men would make the contrary decision.

Ernest Oppenheimer concentrated power in his own hands; Harry Oppenheimer is a delegator. His highest-level lieutenants are generally regarded to be Waddell, Gordon Relly, and Julien Ogilvie Thompson. Because of their roles in Anglo/De Beers, each is a very powerful man himself, but they generally keep low profiles and leave the speechmaking to Oppenheimer. Oppenheimer likes it that way. Ogilvie Thompson is the Oppenheimer man who most closely follows De Beers, the man who would be its president if De Beers had a president (it has only a board chairman—Oppenheimer). A Rhodes scholar and the son of a distinguished South African judge, Ogilvie Thompson is a businessman, plump and plain, who has not yet demonstrated any of his boss's humanitarian concerns—"a very tough individual, but he seems to know what he is about, in my opinion," Oppenheimer says of him.

Most De Beers employees anticipate that when Harry goes, Mr. Nicky, rather than Ogilvie Thompson, will become the active head of the De Beers family. Nicky, educated like his father at Oxford, has kept a very low profile (despite his full beard), with the result that many regard him as shy. Only recently has he begun making public statements—which echo his father's positions. One De Beers higher-up told me, "If Nicky isn't ready to take over De Beers when Harry steps out, the company will be ruled by a regent until he is ready."

Until Harry steps out, however, Harry is the boss, and a protective one insofar as De Beers is concerned. Though his Anglo empire dominates the gold world as well as the diamond world, and is involved in every aspect of human endeavor, the diamond business is Oppenheimer's favorite. He explains, "People buy diamonds out of vanity, and they buy gold because they're too stupid to think of any other monetary system which will work—and I think vanity is probably a more attractive motive than stupidity." Oppenheimer is nothing if not detached.

8

DIAMOND DIGGERS

◆

Barkly West is a long way from the Oppenheimer mansion. It is one of the centers for South Africa's independent diamond diggers, the smallest-scale diamond-mining entrepreneurs who are still working alluvial sites along the Orange and Vaal rivers, much as did their forefathers in the early 1870s. Many of them are lineal descendants of the men of "Klipdrift," as Barkly West was known during South Africa's first diamond rush. These men, their employees, their black counterparts in Central and West Africa, and their spiritual brothers in South America, are the most wretched inhabitants of the diamond world.

Every so often one of the South African diggers makes a great find, and this keeps everyone else's hopes alive. In 1934 it was Jacobus Jonker, finder of the Jonker Diamond, a spectacular 726-carat chunk of rough which brought him £70,000 (then $352,000) from De Beers' Diamond Corporation, its diamond-buying arm, at the depths of the Great Depression. De Beers' selling arm sold it to Harry Winston, reportedly for twice as much. Winston had it cut by the great cleaver Lazare Kaplan and then sold the principal diamond cut from it to King Farouk for something like $1 million. Still, £70,000 was enough for Jonker. The papers at the time quoted him as saying, "I have been a poor man all my life and was down on my luck." He said that he would use the proceeds to buy a big farm, and of course he would take Johannes with him—Johannes, the faithful African "boy" who had remained loyal to Jonker through unceasing unsuccessful digs across the decades. It was Johannes who had actually found the Jonker.

Then there was Petrus Ramoboa, a black digger in Lesotho, who came up with the 601.3-carat brownish stone known as the Lesotho Brown in 1967, which brought him £108,180 (then $302,000). Ramoboa, the newspapers said, would invest his winnings in, among other things, another wife, which was going some, inasmuch as it was *Mrs.* Ramoboa who had unearthed the Lesotho Brown. But why not? After all, Ramoboa told the press, "I'm a big man now."

Diamond digging is part of South Africa's cultural heritage, thanks to a series of diamond rushes. A lot of the little men still at it participated in the greatest of the twentieth-century diamond rushes, that to Lichtenburg in 1925. Sim Schneiderman, a new immigrant to South Africa at the time, remembers the Lichtenburg fields well: the terrible life, survival on the grain porridge known as "mealie meal"; the bitter cold in the winter and the scorching heat in the summer, and at the end—"You were lucky to get a shilling a stone." He got out, but most hung in in hopes of finding "the big one."

The practical exhaustion of the Lichtenburg fields coincided with the onset of the Great Depression, and in the 1930s, the diamond diggers of South Africa constituted a social plight for South Africa parallel to that of the Okies in the United States, half of them suffering from advanced stages of malnutrition and all of them suffering from wretchedness. The American Okies picked up and fled their worthless lands, while South Africa's diggers remained, partly because they had no alternative, and partly from the hope against hope that the elusive big one would turn up in their sieves, as it had in the sieves of others. It rarely did.

Small-scale diamond digging trapped people into dead-end situations and marginal existences. Ultimately, the government concluded that this was socially undesirable and ceased issuing diggers' licenses to new applicants. Until quite recently it was impossible to get a license unless the applicant had been licensed as of 1948. Now those who have served a two-year apprenticeship with a licensed digger can get their own license, but there isn't much interest among younger people. The diggers who survive are mostly remnants of the class of '48, colorful codgers in costumes that smell of World War I. They reminisce nicely about the great stones that littered the past, and speak and live almost entirely in the world of long gone by.

The diggers work along the rivers near Barkly West and at a number of other alluvial spots in South Africa. Most are Afrikaners who employ a dozen or so blacks to dig down through the more recent overburden to the levels of older riverbank gravels that promise to contain diamonds. Then they dig out the diamondiferous layer. Most will process out the diamonds with the aid of ancient but still serviceable rotary pans. The white man himself will usually sort through the final concentrate to retrieve whatever diamonds there may be.

One or two of the black employees are likely to have been with the white man for years, and there is a high degree of loyalty between these long-tenured blacks and the Afrikaner *baas*. Most of the employees, however, are short-term people, floaters. There is a common belief among diggers that Africans will spot a diamond sooner than a white man, and will pocket it for sale on the illicit market. It is a simple matter to do: The thief can sell a hot stone to a licensed digger downstream, who can claim to have recovered it himself. The short-term employees almost never turn a pickup stone over to the white boss.

There are also a number of black and colored licensed diggers, most of whom work solo or in pairs. All of the diggers, black or white, work in reliance on instinct and past experience. Fifty years of science and geology have passed them by.

The diggers' claims are now pretty much worked out. Hugh Austin, a Lichtenburg veteran, an old one-eyed man with an extra heavy brow over the vacant orb, told me that his crew of fifteen sometimes goes weeks without finding anything at all. It was easier in the old days— "There were a lot of diamonds then, but the prices were low. Now the price is high but there aren't many diamonds." Another old man in short khaki pants and a wide-brimmed hat, the "foreman" of the "Gong Gong Diamond Company" was of like mind: "Diamonds are scarce," he said with a despairing shake of the head.

Liberia, Sierra Leone, Guinea, the Ivory Coast, Zaire, and the Central African Republic all have their diamond diggers and all have experienced diamond rushes. Liberia's was perhaps the most spectacular in terms of numbers and raucousness.

Diamonds were first discovered on the Lofa River in Liberia around 1954, and sparked a rush that denuded the country's farms and plantations of their workers, attracting upward of eighty thousand people to the remote banks of the Lofa and neighboring creeks. Only the businessmen who provisioned them at astronomical prices did very well. Those few diggers who struck it rich squandered their wealth by washing their newly acquired autos in beer, lighting their cigarettes with dollar bills (the US dollar is the official unit of currency in Liberia), and similar acts of ostentation.

In 1956 the government determined to license and regularize diamond mining. As a start it decreed that all diamond mining activity cease, and sent in troops to close down the diggings. Many diggers resisted the soldiers. At the end, 62,000 *recorded* diggers were expelled from Liberia's diamondiferous region.

A licensing system for diggers was established, but the diamond areas were all superficial, and interest in diamond digging declined after 1962. There are still a number of diggers in the country, however, all "hinterland" people.

Most of the smallest West African operations are pit mines: the diggers dig a hole through the overburden along the stream bank, down to the level of diamondiferous gravel, and then dig out this layer, which is set aside for processing. They dig another hole a few feet away, dig out the gravel, and then tunnel out the gravel between the two holes, joining the pits. Many of the best West African pits are dug by members of the Maracca tribe, so the pits are sometimes known as Maracca pits.

A Maracca-dug pit may be no broader than a yard and may go twenty feet straight down. Because of the high water table, mechanical pumps are sometimes needed to pump out seepage water and keep the pits workable.

To prevent cave-ins and injuries, the Liberian Bureau of Mines insists that excavations, whatever their shape, be dug in steps, with a four-foot-wide plateau ("bench") for each six feet of depth. A properly dug excavation, viewed from above, should look something like a stadium. The bureau proscribes tunneling. To the typical operator, such rules involve senseless waste of the manpower that must be used to strip away vast quantities of valueless overburden. The rules are commonly ignored, with the result that a digger is killed every so often in a cave-in.

Only rarely do diamondiferous gravels look anything like what one would recognize as the "gravel" used by American road builders. More commonly the gravels are accumulations of coarse dirt and silt. Little pebbles will be mixed among the dirt and silt, but usually the pebbles are not visible in the mass. Washing removes all but the pebbles, which become concentrated and visible in the washing process. Among the pebbles are the diamonds. Though a few diggers have slightly advanced processing systems, most do not, and the technique commonly used by West African diggers is used with variations by most diggers worldwide:

The gravel is placed in a round-bottomed copper bowl that has holes punched in the bottom, very similar to a kitchen colander. The bowl of gravels is submerged in water and agitated by a hand thrust inside the bowl and by swirling. The sands and lighter materials either seep out the holes in the bottom or get splashed over the top. The heavier materials and the concentration of pebbles remain in the bottom of the bowl. The pebbles are then placed in a round, flat-bottomed sieve. The sieve is submerged in the water and agitated very gently, up and down, back and forth. The heavier materials, among which would be the diamonds, concentrate rather neatly in the middle of the sieve, and the diamonds, the heaviest of them, gravitate to the very center and bottom of the sieve. After a couple of minutes of agitation, the sieve is taken out of the water and is quickly upended and plunked on the ground, so that the pebbles fall upon the surface in the same arrangement as they had in the sieve, only the bottom layers are now uppermost. Because the heavier pebbles usually have a large amount of ferrous material along with them, the area of heavier material is clearly darker in color and crisply delineated from the lighter materials surrounding it. The diamonds will be within this darker inner circle of pebbles, which is rapidly picked through.

Virtually all the diggers of Guinea, the Ivory Coast, Zaire, and the

Central African Republic are working illicitly, often in the face of brutal sanctions if caught.

The independent buyer of rough diamond is every digger's "uncle," and most diggers are tied either by contractual obligation to a diamond buyer who finances their operations or by bonds of loyalty to a buyer who "helps them out" with money from time to time. When the digger gets a little bit ahead, he is likely to spend improvidently. In *Diamond Rivers* (1977), an educational film produced for television by Bill Benenson, one old-timer, one of the last one-man Brazilian diamond diggers, tells about himself and what impels him and small diggers everywhere:

> I think I was born looking for diamonds. My father was a prospector and he died without having anything. And I, as old as I am, I don't have anything either. But I have never stopped looking. Not for long, anyway. Why do I do it? Because I like it, and it is what I know best. If I was lucky, when I went to town and got money I would buy good clothes, a good hat, good boots, a good revolver to put in my belt, and then I would go party. Beer, wine, cognac, and sing and dance and party some more, and then, when the money was gone, I would come back to the river and look for more. Where is the prospector who invests his money, buys land or a house? They do not exist, I tell you. He is a man without a future, only living for the day. . . . There were some good days. . . .

9

ANATOMY OF A MONOPOLY

◆

The diggers' output worldwide is minuscule when compared with that of the major diamond-mining enterprises, all of whom sell their diamonds through De Beers' Central Selling Organisation (CSO), commonly known as the Syndicate. Through agreements with the key non-De Beers diamond-mining houses, the CSO limits the amount of rough that each will introduce to the market annually, and commits each to sell its allocated share to the Diamond Corporation, a CSO entity.

The CSO feeds out the stones to the market—the Diamond Corporation's acquisitions along with the De Beers-mined diamonds—or stockpiles them according to overall world economic conditions and trends, the number of stones it believes to have been accumulated by diamond-polishing works and wholesalers farther down the distribution pipeline, and the state of the diamond market. The CSO's constant concern is that the market never be oversaturated with diamonds. The tremendous cash position of parent company De Beers, with access to Anglo American's cash as well if it should ever need more, enables the CSO to buy and hold for stock whatever it believes should be stockpiled for however long it deems it desirable to keep goods off the market.

According to De Beer's 1980 annual report, the CSO "markets over 80 percent of the world's diamond production." The 80 percent figure which De Beers has cited for years (in 1977 and 1978 its reports claimed "approximately 80 percent") is both too high and too low. Something over 15 percent of total world diamond production consists of industrial diamonds mined and consumed entirely within the USSR, outside the CSO operation, and Russia merchandises another few percent of total world production as polished diamonds, outside the purview of its relations with the CSO. Russia alone, therefore, reduces the CSO's market role to about the 80 percent level, and disorganized productions surely push it beneath. On the other and much more significant hand, however, the 80 percent figure is low indeed. Russia's domestic consumption of its own industrial diamond production has no effect on free-world diamond-market conditions, and its sales of polished diamonds are made in semi-consonance with CSO policies. The stones that Russia sells as rough it sells through the CSO. The most significant flow of stones outside CSO control probably consists of those stones that are pilfered from CSO-cooperating producers and sold surreptitiously, together with Ghana's 3-or-so percent of total world output. Because Ghana's stones are exclusively of industrial quality, they have no effect on the gem market, which constitutes just about the whole diamond game. Much of the output of the diggers and of the lesser mining companies with whom the CSO does not have contracts is acquired by it anyway. It buys their diamonds in competition with other buyers on what is known as the outside market, the market that operates outside the CSO. These stones are therefore converted into "inside" rough. In terms of gem diamond rough that is made available to the diamond-polishing industry—practical terms—CSO control must be upward of 90 percent.

CSO spokesmen like to describe the CSO as an association of cooperating producers, but they are not going to quibble if people want to use words like "cartel" and "monopoly." De Beers public relations people can say calmly, without hesitation or trace of embarrassment, ". . . we are a marketing monopoly." Monopoly is a neutral word in the De Beers lexicon: There are good ones and bad ones. As they see it, theirs is a benevolent monopoly. Harry Oppenheimer says, "Whether [the CSO's] measure of control amounts to a monopoly I would not know, but if it does it is certainly a monopoly of a most unusual kind. There is no one concerned with diamonds, whether as producer, dealer, cutter, jeweler, or customer, who does not benefit from it."

Technically, "CSO" denotes the collection of diamond trade and trading entities controlled by De Beers and other Oppenheimer-group companies that together make for a central selling organization and constitute the CSO. Its principal arms are the Diamond Corporation, the Diamond Trading Company, and Industrial Distributors.

The Diamond Corporation is now a wholly-owned De Beers subsidiary. It contracts for the output of the major producers other than De Beers and buys such further stones as the CSO may acquire on the "outside" market.

The Diamond Trading Company (DTC) is the entity that sells the gemstones and near-gems within CSO control. Fifty percent of it is owned by Anglo American Investment Trust—Anamint—which is 52 percent owned by Anglo American. The ownership of the other half of the DTC is not traceable, but it belongs to other Oppenheimer-group companies, possibly E. Oppenheimer & Son, the family's private holding company. De Beers owns no share of the DTC. Most stones, however, are channeled en route to the DTC through "Purtra" (Diamond Purchasing and Trading Company), which funnels off some of the profits from the selling function, and De Beers owns a 53 percent interest in that.

Industrial Distributors is the CSO arm that sells the group's natural and synthetic industrial diamonds. Though most natural diamonds are still classed as "industrials," a larger share of them is classed as gems today than was the case ten years ago. In the meantime, the price of industrials has dropped significantly, due to the introduction of synthetic industrial diamonds, while the price of gems has increased even more, with the result that, in dollar terms, the economic significance of industrials, or of Industrial Distributors, to De Beers or to the diamond world, is now relatively small. De Beers owns 32 percent of Industrial Distributors.

Dealing with the CSO is not half so complicated as trying to understand its corporate makeup. Selling to it has important advantages for a producer.

Diamond Corporation contracts are usually for five-year periods and guarantee the producer that the Diamond Corporation will purchase the producer's entire output up to the agreed quota. The CSO's quota system is the diamond world's production-control mechanism; it operates at the mining level as a restraint on diamond production, and is the first step in De Beers' ongoing effort to ensure that diamond supply remains below diamond demand.

Each producer's quota represents his share of the market. It is adjustable upward in the event that DTC sales volume increases, but is not adjustable downward regardless of what weaknesses the market may develop during the term of the contract. The agreement therefore gives the producer the ability to formulate long-term plans without having to worry about the vagaries of market conditions, an important consideration in any industry but especially important in mining, where measured increases and decreases in output are difficult to arrange.

The price for all this varies from contract to contract. All are written in terms of discounts from DTC list prices: The Diamond Corporation will purchase the agreed-upon quantities at current and changing DTC list prices minus a percentage commission, which may be as low as 7.5 percent or as high, perhaps, as 12 percent. When one considers the CSO's substantial administrative and overhead expense, the interest expense of carrying its stocks and of remaining liquid (whether interest paid or interest lost by virtue of otherwise investible capital being tied up or reserved), the costs of the institutional advertising that De Beers and the CSO bear for the entire diamond world, and the very considerable value of the expertise of the De Beers selling organization, it is difficult to believe that the CSO can provide its services for such modest commissions. Nobody seriously believes that it does.

The CSO, like all diamond-world entities, "buys with this hand and sells with that hand," with some percentages lost in the switch of hands. The Diamond Corporation tends to view stones conservatively when it buys; after purchase, the stones are resorted, recategorized;

and when the time comes for the DTC to sell, it tends to view the same stones more optimistically. What may be called a 10 percent discount at time of purchase often turns out to have been a 20 percent discount—which is what the usual margin probably amounts to after the hocus-pocus.

Most of the producers, possibly all of them, have independent consultants who, with varying degrees of fidelity, audit their dealings with the CSO to ensure that this sort of thing does not happen. When requested, the CSO will provide these experts with samples of current DTC sales packets with prices for their review. The producers' representatives may conduct sporadic negotiations with the CSO over classifications. But the producers themselves are directed by mining engineers or by political administrators, totally unequipped to evaluate their output. As for the independent experts—well, in the diamond world virtually nobody is independent of De Beers.

Each producer's deal is a little different, depending on its overall bargaining position at the time that the contract is entered. In order to keep the Soviet Union cooperative, the CSO probably gives the USSR a better deal than other producers. The Soviets' participation is thus subsidized by everybody else, each of whom must bear a correspondingly greater proportion of the total overhead. At the other end, Zaire is almost certainly getting the worst deal on paper and even worse in practice. With its huge volume of decreasingly desirable industrial stones, its bargaining position is hopeless.

Other than De Beers, the great producers are now all controlled by governments: Sierra Leone, the Soviet Union, Zaire, Angola, and Tanzania. It is the cooperation of each that gives De Beers its monopoly power in the diamond world.

10

SIERRA LEONE AND THE CURSE OF RICHES

◆

Corruption may be a constant in all governments, but in Sierra Leone it can be attributed to a specific endeavor: Corruption in Sierra Leone revolves around the diamonds. Licenses to dig for diamonds, to buy diamonds, to export diamonds, permits to reside within the diamond areas—all are bought and sold. Government officials connive with illicit diggers, buyers, sellers, and smugglers. The army and police must be moved in and out of the country's Kono District, the principal diamond area, for two related reasons: one, if they are left there too long they become totally corrupted; and two, to give everyone a chance for a slice of the pie. Everyone, black and white alike, insists that the diamond corruption reaches "right to the top," without naming President Siaka P. Stevens, but that's whom they have in mind.

Diamonds probably account for 60 percent plus of Sierra Leone's exports, and probably meet a goodly part of the government's total operating budget, but statistics are hard to come by in Sierra Leone, and people tend to be secretive about them. The last public report of the Government Diamond Office was issued in 1972; the last public annual report of the National Diamond Mining Company (Diminco), 51 percent government-owned, was in 1974. I was referred to the Ministry of Mines by both Diminco and Diamond Corporation people for statistical detail. I went there for all the answers.

As I waited for my interview with Simeon Jonjo, permanent secretary of the Ministry of Mines, his secretary, a staggeringly beautiful young girl, extended her right arm across her desk, placed her left hand over her right bicep, placed her head upon the top of her left hand, and went to sleep.

The permanent secretary did not keep me waiting long. He asked me what were the kinds of things I wanted to know—all statistical things, nothing potentially embarrassing—and then explained that before he gave me that kind of information, he would want to be very certain that what he told me was correct. I should outline my questions to his deputy, Mr. A. B. M. Kamara, Jr.; Mr. Kamara would prepare a written response and then *he* would review it before passing it along. I went over the questions with Mr. Kamara, who mentioned that after preparing the material he might be able to speak "informally" with me himself, but that there would be some expense for maps and the like (Maps? Nothing I asked involved maps) and could I advance some expense money? I slipped him 25 leones (1 leone equals from 95¢ to $1.04 at legitimate exchange bureaus or 77¢ on the black market), and then later another 25 leones for "postage," but of course I never got any response. *Gems & Jewellery*, the official publication of the government of India's Gem & Jewellery Export Promotion Council, reports that in 1978–79, Sierra Leone's diamond exports totaled 835,100 carats valued at 117 million leones (140 leones per carat), and that's about the best statistic available. At that rate, Sierra Leone's production, though small in cara-tage, is still the world's fourth most valuable output, after South Africa, the USSR, and Namibia.

We will spend a lot of pages in Sierra Leone, not alone because of its importance as a diamond producer, but because the Sierra Leone experience nicely illustrates a number of aspects of the diamond world: production, distribution, commercial mechanics and machinations, trad-ing techniques, and corruption. Sierra Leone makes a neat case history of a diamond country.

The Sierra Leone diamond industry is a three-cornered power strug-gle: the giant, De Beers and its network of merchandising subsidiaries, striving for continued control of the world diamond industry; Selection Trust, once a significant power in the diamond world, whose diamond power has been waning on all fronts; and finally, the forces of seeming disorder, symbolized for our purposes by Jamil (Jamil Said Mohamed), leader of the world's Lebanese diamantaires, who both represents and dominates the "bad" tradition in the Sierra Leone diamond story. Chro-nologically, Selection Trust came first.

Rich alluvial diamond fields were first discovered in Sierra Leone in 1930. Sierra Leone Selection Trust (SLST), a wholly owned sub-sidiary of Consolidated African Selection Trust (CAST), which was in turn majority-owned by Selection Trust Limited, a British mining house, obtained exclusive rights to exploit the country's diamonds until the year 2033. SLST began work in the Yengema area of the Kono District in the eastern part of Sierra Leone, still the base of operations of Di-minco, SLST's successor. SLST marketed its entire output through the Diamond Corporation.

Everything went fairly well until around 1950, when illicit diamond mining, commonly known in West Africa as IDM, began in Sierra Leone. The earliest illicit miners were probably SLST employees, who observed that heavy machinery was not necessary to retrieve the precious stones, that simple equipment and groups as small as a single man could dig the gravels along the riverbanks and process out the diamonds. Selection Trust officials have since been heard to grumble that "we're just running a mining school here."

The ranks of the earliest illicit miners were joined by other Kono people and then swelled by Sierra Leoneans from distant parts of the country and by foreign Africans. Principal among the foreigners were the Maracca tribesmen from the great Muslim tribe of south Saharan well diggers, whose traditional occupation made them especially suited for diamond digging.

The first illicit miners appreciated that what they were doing was "illegal" (was contrary to the laws made by the white men), but surely their digging for diamonds was a very different matter from stealing stones from the SLST sorting tables; it did not offend morality for indigenous people to dig diamonds merely because rights to do so throughout their country had irrationally or corruptly been promised by white governors to a big white foreign company. By 1956, thirty thousand illicit miners were digging up the diamond regions and outproducing SLST.

The diggers found their earliest buyers in the Mandingo traders who crisscross Africa dealing in whatever can be bought cheap and sold dear, and then in the Lebanese merchants in their own neighborhoods. At first the Mandingo buyers took their stones wherever else they traveled on their routes; the Lebanese took them to Freetown, the nation's capital and transportation center, and then smuggled them out of the country, generally to Beirut and thence to the diamond trading centers. In 1953, however, internal security between Kono and Freetown became tight, so Lebanese buyers, and increasingly Mandingo as well, began smuggling their wares across the Mano River into Liberia. By 1954 a thriving community of Antwerp-based diamond buyers had sprung up in Monrovia, the Liberian capital. To keep as much of the trade as possible under its control, De Beers' Diamond Corporation also opened a buying office in Monrovia.

Illicit diamond mining quickly developed from a somewhat bucolic calling into a major enterprise. Large combines of diggers emerged, now with more elaborate equipment, with financing from buyers in Monrovia or from local Lebanese. The illegal industry was taken over by toughs. Itinerant buyers were occasionally murdered by hard-pressed diggers. According to one source, by 1954 forty-five murders had already occurred in the diamond areas, including one case of a digger who had been disemboweled in search of a stone that he had been seen to swallow.

The diggers' camps and the towns into which they crowded became epidemic breeding grounds, dominated by a swaggering elite who caused trouble, invited vice, squandered their winnings, and raised prices to levels beyond the reach of law-abiding citizens.

As police increased enforcement efforts, teams of diggers began employing their own "security forces," often subcontracted, who engaged the police in battle and occasionally attacked isolated police stations.

De Beers, interested in curtailing any traffic that threatened its control over sources of rough diamond, joined on the side of law and order. It retained the services of a Lebanese adventurer, Fred Kamil, to command a corp of mercenaries, patrol the Liberian border, capture diamond smugglers at gunpoint, and turn them and their diamonds over to the government of Sierra Leone.

As the situation deteriorated, the government was faced with two alternatives: It could protect SLST's interests and the security of the tax revenues from SLST by repressing the illicit trade with such methods as might be necessary, or it could come to terms with the diggers. If the diggers were allowed some turf on which to operate legitimately, they could be licensed, regulated, supervised, and they then would begin making some contribution to the national treasury through export duties. Political considerations dictated this latter course: the diggers were largely Sierra Leonean, whereas SLST was a white foreign concern that had always been a political whipping boy in the country. The adoption of a plan that might allow for little men's diamond mining would also open broad new horizons for local political leaders and chiefs (many of whom served in Parliament) to line their own pockets through a rich new source for bribes.

In 1956 the country purchased a release of SLST's rights over most of the country at a price of £ 1,570,000 (then $4,380,000). By agreement, SLST's preserves were limited to two large rich areas (by now further reduced to one of 158 square miles centered at Yengema, and another less significant area at Tongo), with all of the company's rights to lapse in 1985. Most of the rest of the most promising diamond areas, and the regions that were already popular with the illicit operators, were opened up to licensed diggers who might operate pursuant to the newly enacted Alluvial Diamond Mining Scheme. Many of the diggers became "legits"; others, and especially those who were operating within the areas that continued to be reserved for SLST, continued illicitly.

At the suggestion of SLST, the country invited the Diamond Corporation to establish buying offices in the field to purchase the output of the small diggers. Other buyers also were licensed, but the Diamond Corporation was the only buyer given an export license; in the end, the others would all have to sell to the Diamond Corporation.

The marriage between Sierra Leone and De Beers was an ideal one: The country needed a buyer/exporter that could be counted upon to keep honest books and to pay the export duty, while De Beers needed a handle to control the flow of Sierra Leone's diggers' output—which had previously been flowing out of its control. In 1961 Sierra Leone ceased to do business with that South African entity, the Diamond Corporation, and switched its patronage instead to a new British company, Diamond Corporation of West Africa (Dicorwaf)—operated by the same pack of gentlemen as the Diamond Corporation.

For a little while, not long, things worked all right, but by the end of the fifties, SLST's remaining preserves were again overrun by illicit diggers who appreciated that the company had kept the best tracts for itself. Meanwhile, SLST also had a falling out with the Diamond Corporation.

In the later 1950s, SLST noticed what it took to be an unfavorable disparity between the price that the Diamond Corporation paid to alluvial-scheme diggers and what it paid to SLST. The more that SLST studied the market, the surer it became that it wasn't getting a fair shake. SLST produced mostly "premium" stones, diamonds that sold on the open market for more than the Diamond Corporation's marketing twin, the Diamond Trading Company, charged its customers. To SLST this meant that the DTC was selling its stones too cheaply—and therefore, that the Diamond Corporation was buying from SLST too cheaply. SLST was convinced that this was especially true with regard to its "special stones," those very large stones for which the DTC does not maintain any "book price." A check with a major New York cutter, Lazare Kaplan & Sons, confirmed its suspicions: SLST wasn't getting enough for its goods.

De Beers' margin of profit also grated on Selection Trust people. SLST's contract with the CSO called for a 12 percent commission, a sum that was not unreasonable to charge producers of stones that might have to be bought and held in stock for long periods before being sold, but that wasn't the case with SLST's output, which was much in demand. For SLST's stones, 12 percent seemed exorbitant to those of SLST's directors who were independent of De Beers. Some were not independent. De Beers had a substantial stock interest in CAST, the sole owner of SLST, and representation on its board.

A bitter in-house battle took place at the SLST board room between the De Beers–nominated directors and the independent directors, before the independents outvoted the De Beers people and determined to fight—or to secede from—the diamond cartel. SLST demanded that the commission be reduced to 4 percent; De Beers held firm at 12 percent. When SLST's contract with the Diamond Corporation expired, it made a contract in August of 1961 instead with Harry Winston, the biggest New York cutting firm, to sell its production to Winston at a 4 percent reduction from DTC book. Winston had long been chafing to be independent of the DTC, and at last he was. Whether he quit or was fired from the rolls of DTC customers, their relationship terminated, while Lazare Kaplan was simply purged from the roster of those permitted to buy direct from the DTC.

The change from 12 to 4 percent made a difference in SLST's pretax profit of about £ 400,000 ($7,120,000) a year, of which 60 percent was newfound money for the tax collector of Sierra Leone. The government, however, was unfavorably impressed. The DTC argued with government officials that if SLST were permitted to break loose from the cartel, the whole system might be imperiled; the Diamond Corporation might be unable to continue paying the alluvial scheme diggers as well as it had. From a long-range point of view, the government and people of Sierra Leone would therefore be better off if SLST were required to sell to the Diamond Corporation, even though doing so would generate less tax money for the country.

The legislators of Sierra Leone were somehow convinced. In January of 1962 they made law that all diamonds, including SLST's, could be sold for export only to the Government Diamond Office. And the GDO—which was managed for the government by the Diamond Corporation—sold only to the Diamond Corporation. For SLST it was principally a loss of face, with some loss of money; it was worse for Winston, who was now out in the cold. Both lobbied for some "adjustment."

A compromise was reached in the summer of 1962: SLST production would be sold one half to the Diamond Corporation at a 10 percent discount from book, with the remaining half sold to Winston and others at a 4 percent discount. Both Winston and Kaplan were restored as customers in good grace at the DTC. Kaplan and another New York buyer, Leon Tempelsman & Son, a firm whose principals were (and are) close to the Oppenheimers, joined Winston to divvy up the "outside" half between them. Tempelsman—and with time and politics, Winston as well—began turning most or all of their share of the SLST production over to the CSO anyway, leaving only the Kaplan share, the smallest portion of the SLST output, outside CSO control. De Beers, as usual, had won.

Kwame Nkrumah, founding father of Ghana (home base of SLST's parent, CAST) and intellectual impetus to today's African pan-nationalism, suggests in *Neo-Colonialism: The Last Stage of Imperialism* that the fight between SLST and the CSO was a mere charade, "a facade aimed at maintaining the fiction that Selection Trust and the Diamond Corporation are unrelated entities, a fiction retailed even by a press one would assume knows better." If so, it was a charade that left bitterness that lingers to this day. When I asked a Selection Trust officer how De Beers had won, he responded with a gesture: He waved his wallet at me. De Beers people, on the other hand, attribute their success instead to the intense distrust in which the Sierra Leoneans held SLST, believing—"possibly incorrectly" (says the fellow at the Diamond Corporation)—that SLST had had "secret vaults" and had been channeling off stones behind the back of the tax collector.

Thereafter Selection Trust limped along, losing its continuing battle with the illicit diggers. As the areas properly allocated to the alluvial scheme were worked out, more and more diggers switched their attention to SLST's lease areas. As soon as company prospecting teams made promising finds, the diggers would move in, digging up and spoiling the locations before the company could exploit them. In 1970 SLST abandoned prospecting efforts as pointless: Anything they discovered would only be stolen. Its employees often conspired with the diggers. SLST trucks carrying newly dug gravels to the processing plant sometimes detoured via the criminals' lairs, where gravels that had already been "washed" were substituted for the company's virgin gravels. Outright highjackings of gravel trucks took place. Rapacious diggers dug up highways and airfields and undermined houses. There were more open battles between illicit miners and police or company security forces, and a band of illicit miners attacked a company washing plant in reprisal for company harassment of their efforts. SLST increased its security force to a high of 1,200, a quarter of its total personnel, but the more security men it had, the more security men it had to watch.

Diamond dealing is prohibited by law within the lease area in order to minimize temptations, but no one paid any attention. Koidu, within the lease and close by the center of SLST operations, became the center for the illegal operations, and a Wild-West town dominated by lawlessness and by its Lebanese diamond buyers. The buyers competed for trade principally on the basis of ostentation: He with the fanciest Mercedes Benz, the most prominently displayed guns, the largest pile of chips at the gambling casino, the fanciest office, and the loudest mouth was probably the man who was getting the most for the stones that he sold to the Diamond Corporation (as the Government Diamond Office was fuzzily but not inaccurately known) or in Monrovia or Antwerp, and he was therefore the man who could pay the most for the stones that he bought from the diggers and lesser dealers. That man attracted the most business.

The Lebanese would report each other to the authorities for any of the offenses that all engaged in, and their raucous and sometimes violent feuds and vicious badmouthing of one another contributed to giving the Lebanese community an unsavory cast. Many in Sierra Leone tell stories about Lebanese buyers who capitalized on the vulnerability of the illicit miner: A licensed buyer would have an accomplice policeman arrive at his premises when an illicit miner was expected with a really big stone; the cop would arrive on schedule, bust down the door for show, and demand to see the digger's license; then the Lebanese would plead for the black miner and ultimately persuade the policeman to leave without making trouble. Then the Lebanese would "steal" the stone from the intimidated native.

Though the tax collector was the big loser in raids on the Selection Trust lease, government efforts against illicit operations were always sporadic and unsatisfactory. Whenever SLST became particularly piqued over the situation, the government would clear the area of Mandingos and Maraccas and deport a clutch of Lebanese, many of whom would reappear in a few months, but when it ejected Koidu diamond buyers it invariably left the most powerful offenders alone. When it sent in troops to bust up illicit mining gangs, the soldiers sometimes traded their guns for shovels and joined the digging too.

In 1967 Siaka Stevens was elected president. Selection Trust had never much gotten along with Stevens, not since the early 1950s, when the company abruptly evicted him from the lease area for some long-forgotten reason.

Stevens was first elected as the People's Party candidate, and the people of Sierra Leone have always been "for" illicit diamond mining, the little man's only hope for wealth. A lot of the people who elected Stevens were inexorably bound up with the illegal activity. Stevens debilitated what anti-IDM efforts were then under way.

Soon after, the government began moves to nationalize a majority interest in SLST. In 1971, as a negotiated matter, a new corporation, National Diamond Mining Company (Diminco), owned 51 percent by the government and 49 percent by SLST, took over SLST's mining interests in Sierra Leone. The government paid SLST $6 million in bonds to cover a 51 percent interest in the fixed assets, plus $2.1 million in cash to cover a 51 percent interest in SLST's current assets.

Part of the rationale for the nationalization was that the government's battle against illicit mining (halfhearted though it was) looked as if it were siding with a white outsider against its own people; after nationalization that could not be said. And surely it could not. But the government's campaign against illicit mining since then has neither been stepped up nor become more effective now that the victim of the thefts is a 51 percent public-owned entity. Tens of thousands of Kono people have come to depend on the economic spin-offs of illicit diamond digging; the economic as well as political repercussions of smashing it would be too great, the benefits of suffering it are too inviting.

DIMINCO TODAY

Today, Diminco is run by a board of directors composed of eleven, six nominees of the government and five from Selection Trust. In theory, Selection Trust is in charge of management, with the right to name the top Diminco officials, but in practice Stevens names top management, and as representative of the majority owner (the government and people of Sierra Leone) makes many key Diminco decisions himself. Though different names hold different portfolios in the country's government, there is only one minister in Sierra Leone: the president.

Stevens was a miner, organizer of the country's mineworker's union, and the minister of mines himself during an important period of the country's diamond history, so he is not ill-suited to be making these decisions—except that he is a political person who invariably curries favor. In a wildcat strike not sanctioned by the union in 1978, the government determined to make concessions while many of Diminco's Stevens-appointed senior staff felt that the strike should be resisted. "The government always makes concessions," one high-ranking Stevens appointee said with disappointment.

A. A. Koroma is Diminco's general manager. Koroma was jailed for two years for "treason" during one of the coups of the late sixties, but his fortunes took a better turn with the accession to power of President Stevens. In 1976 Selection Trust appointed him general manager of the mine—according to Koroma, on the urgings of Stevens. Koroma is a Kono District person, a lawyer by training, educated in both England and the United States, an affable and charming man and no doubt an able administrator, but he seemed foggy about such matters as the number of company employees, the size of the company payroll, and the breakdown of company production between its alluvial operations and its small kimberlite-pipe workings. He knows, however, where his loyalties lie. When I asked him how much the company's gross profits were last year, he said that I could get that information from the Ministry of Mines: "I'm not certain how much I should reveal to you: my obligations are to the company stockholders—and principally to the majority stockholder."

Selection Trust's role is now very much second place. Of Diminco's gross profits, 70 percent goes to the government for taxes, and Selection Trust gets 49 percent of the rest, or a net 14.7 percent of gross profits—if the government-controlled Board of Directors votes to declare a dividend. Because it controls the board, the government is in a position to determine whether or not Selection Trust gets anything at all, but because the government always needs the dividend income, it does declare the dividends.

Still, it is not a happy position for Selection Trust to be in. The company finds itself in this position because it neglected its public relations front. Its people were always mining people, technologists rather than politicians, let alone diplomats. They hoped to run an efficient mine free from interference, but ignored the public relations work that was necessary if the company was to operate as it might hope. And, one of their officers told me, they refused under any circumstances to pay a direct or indirect bribe. Nearly everyone that deals in black Africa with whom I spoke insisted that he was operating from a competitive disadvantage because of his refusal to deviate from the strictest standards of western ethics. I disbelieved most of them. Selection Trust, however, has been so consistently and uniformly unsuccessful in Sierra Leone that honesty may be the most reasonable explanation.

Most of Diminco's mining involves diverting rivers. After it has diverted the river into a new channel, it fills in the old channel and compacts it in order to make a firm surface on which its heavy equipment can operate. Then it excavates the channel with its new filling and a good swatch of the bank on either side of the channel, and removes it all for processing. Diminco is also doing some "terrace" mining, mining the streambeds of antiquity that dried up long ago. Most of this is "high terrace" work that requires the removal of thirty or more feet of overburden to reach the gravel layer. Most of the more accessible "low terrace" sections, with little overburden, were spoiled by diggers long ago. Diminco is also doing preliminary mining of the small kimberlites within its lease.

Diminco's diamond output has declined considerably, from just under a million carats in 1970 to 220,000 in 1978–79. The stones have also been declining in size. Meanwhile, the company must process more and more material in order to retrieve the fewer and fewer carats. Still, some 60 percent of the winnings are gemstone, and diamond price rises combined with the very big stones occasionally found have kept the operation economically viable.

Diminco now employs just under three thousand people on its two lease areas. The Africanization of its management began long before nationalization. In the mid-1950s, Selection Trust, a progressive company, began sending Sierra Leoneans to school abroad to train for responsible management positions in the mine. More than half of its senior staff, including both the general manager and the assistant general manager, are Sierra Leonean.

Most Diminco employees are paid the minimum national wage for mineworkers: two leones a day. When one considers the value of the amenities offered by Diminco, the employees are well off by Kono standards. They can buy their food at subsidized prices, and more than half of them live in subsidized company housing. By the standards at the De Beers mines, the company housing that I saw in Yengema is relatively unappetizing, much of it not electrified, but Yengema is an older installation with rapidly fading prospects, and Diminco is majority-owned by a financially pressed government.

When SLST was nationalized in 1971, two new potential buyers of the Diminco output entered the picture: Jamil Said Mohamed (known most often as Jamil, more formally as Jamil Said, but almost never by his full name or as Mr. Mohamed) and Industrial Diamonds, Ltd., the leading non-DTC affiliated dealer in diamond rough. Jamil had come to have considerable sway with the president, while the Swiss miracle worker Adolph Pleuss, a man of powerful influence throughout black Africa, spoke for Industrial Diamonds. Two Pleuss two equals five. Stevens determined to cut Jamil and Industrial Diamonds into the allocation, and told Winston that his 20 percent share of the Diminco stones would have to be reduced to make room. Winston surrendered the whole of it and withdrew from the Sierra Leone market. The emergent allocation was: the Diamond Corporation, 50 percent; Tempelsman, 27 percent; Jamil, 12 percent; Industrial Diamonds, 8 percent; and Lazare Kaplan, 3 percent. Jamil, as the intimate of the president, was the architect of the reshuffling, and when he was awarded his Diminco share it was with an executive direction that he be given the goods at a price no higher than "anybody else," which meant that he was to get the same 10 percent discount that the DTC was getting, rather than the smaller discount that had traditionally been given to the non-DTC buyers.

In practice, De Beers is the actual buyer not only of its own half, but of all or virtually all of the Tempelsman allocation and, by now, probably much or all of Jamil's share as well. It wants stones channeled through it, plain and simply, and is willing to pay to have them channeled through it. Maybe Tempelsman and Jamil sell to it at a profit (in which case Diminco is not getting top dollar for its goods); if not, the DTC has other ways of sweetening things for them. Jamil's Antwerp-based operative, Said Sulaimen, became a DTC "sightholder," one of the select group that buys diamonds direct from the DTC, in 1977, and Tempelsman has been one for decades. De Beers can repay courtesies by giving them choicer allocations of DTC goods, or better prices on special stones.

Illicit miners no longer plague Diminco to the extent of olden times. There is no point to Diminco's appealing to the government for help in combating the remaining problem. The government has essentially washed its hands of the situation as a matter "beyond solution," and Diminco officials themselves are philosophical about it: "We live with it now," one told me.

Diminco also has the routine security problems that all diamond mines have. Thefts in the field occur whenever an employee spots a stone. The company offers a reward of one-half value for any pickup stones that anyone in the field turns over, but a company officer says, "In this environment we cannot expect people to turn in pickup stones." It is just too easy to sell a stone in Koidu, no questions asked. The company almost never actually searches anyone.

Diminco has only a few years left in its alluvial workings, and then perhaps it can reprocess and rework select areas for a while longer. The company expects to phase out its alluvial workings by 1984 and to continue on as a kimberlite mining operation. Administratively, that will be a relative delight. There is no such thing as illicit mining in a kimberlite mine, and security problems are otherwise minimal.

Diminco's small kimberlite pipes have been known for many years and have been worked on a limited open-cast basis since 1968, but until recent diamond price rises they have been too small, too difficult for major development on a paying basis. There are two kimberlite pipes in the Yengema lease, both minute when compared with Premier's seventy-nine acres of surface: one is six-tenths of an acre and the other 1.1 acres. They represent just the tails of pipes that have been eroded down to almost nothing, presumably the roots of the pipes that scattered diamonds all over southeastern Sierra Leone. By the time the alluvials close up, Diminco hopes to be able to move ahead without interruption into a full-scale kimberlite operation. By then, the company's current digging into the pipes will have progressed to such depth that one of the pipes will require an immediate changeover to shaft operations, and the other will require a shaft not long thereafter.

The development of the kimberlite mines will cost an estimated £ 25–40 million or more—not much when compared to the costs of opening diamond mines elsewhere, but still a staggering sum for Diminco. Selection Trust would probably have little difficulty putting in its 49 percent, if it determined to continue in Sierra Leone. The government of Sierra Leone may have trouble coming up with its 51 percent of the outlay, especially since it is confronted with more important financial needs, such as paying for the Organization of African Unity conference. Sierra Leone hosted the OAU in 1980 at a final cost to the nation of probably $200 million—several months' gross earnings for every employed Sierra Leonean, and several times what it would cost to develop a kimberlite mine.

If financing is secured for the development of the pipes, there will be a new set of problems: cost factors in kimberlite mining, and especially shaft mining, are so much greater than in alluvial mining that the shaft operation will leave no profit, not even a gross profit available for taxation, unless the labor force is greatly reduced. The kimberlite process requires a much smaller work force, so that Diminco could reduce the personnel enough to make it pay, but for a quasi-governmental agency to dismiss employees makes for political problems. If the kimberlite operation is to pay, unpopular moves will have to be taken. These are decisions that Stevens seems to be particularly ill-suited to make.

Then there is the question of who will run the kimberlite operations: the existing Diminco, guided by Selection Trust expertise, or a somewhat different entity that looks elsewhere for management and technical guidance. One Sierra Leone mining official told me crisply, "Selection Trust doesn't know anything at all about kimberlite mining; they have no experience whatsoever." Who does? De Beers. The giant might even finance the whole operation for the government. All that remains to be seen; but in any case, the days of lots of easy money for the government of Sierra Leone will end with the last shovelful of alluvial ground.

THE DIGGERS AND THEIR WORLD

Many of the independent diamond diggers in Sierra Leone could more accurately be characterized as miners, and all of them prefer to be called miners. They are known, nonetheless, as diggers. Some of them actually dig down to the diamond gravels by hand, and some have a small corps of employees who dig manually, but others use mechanical equipment, and are actually running small mining companies.

Diggers may work legitimately under the alluvial scheme within the areas allocated to alluvial-scheme operations, or illicitly within or outside the alluvial-scheme territory. There has never been any moral distinction drawn between licensed and illicit operators in Sierra Leone; whether a digger operates as the one or the other is purely a matter of practicalities. Not even Selection Trust officials view the individual illicit digger with any moral contempt.

Most of the small operators are now financed by members of the commercially dominant Lebanese community. As non-Africans, and therefore noncitizens (though most of them were born in Sierra Leone), the country's Lebanese are barred from diamond mining in the country on their own account, but they are not prohibited from taking a financial interest in legitimate mining enterprises conducted by—sometimes only in the name of—Sierra Leonean Africans.

When the digger finds his stones, the financier customarily has a share interest in the finds, and equally important, the digger is obligated, legally or morally or both, to offer them for purchase first (sometimes exclusively) to his Lebanese backer. Out of the proceeds, existing loans must be repaid, and more often than not, all that is left is what charity the Lebanese wishes to give. The illicit diggers are even more inexorably tied to their financiers.

At the somewhat extensive alluvial-scheme mine where I first witnessed the washing procedure, a fully and somewhat formally dressed black man was squatting near the seminaked laborers who were doing the washing, holding an umbrella over his head for protection from the sun. He was the "security force." Small operations usually do not have any security at all. Also present was a young Lebanese man, the project's financier. He just happens to show up at washing time pretty much every day. He told me that he had considerable experience in gravel processing, and came to render advice when needed. No, he agreed, his advice was not often needed.

Under the alluvial scheme, the licensed digger is permitted to employ up to twenty "tributors," men who work not for a wage or a salary but for rice and shelter and a share of the finds at reckoning-up time. Virtually all of the digging manpower comes from tributors, who work in the hot sun, their bodies glistening, wearing only shorts in varying stages of disrepair.

It is unusual for the tributors' share to be set and agreed in advance. When the finds get liquidated, expenses and the financier's share are paid off the top and then the tributors negotiate with the license holder as to how much of what is left will go to the workers. If the boss is reasonable, his tributors will stay with him for years and not steal very many stones from him. A lot of the tributors are transitory and untrustworthy, but then, a lot of the bosses invite as much, and are no more trustworthy themselves in their dealings with their Lebanese backers. At most every level, diamonds is a dog-eat-dog business.

The Diamond Corporation's Role

At the time of institution of the alluvial scheme, the Diamond Corporation established a number of field offices, with buyers who lived in grass huts and actually visited the diggers on the job sites. To compete with the illicit buyers stationed at Koidu, the Diamond Corporation established a buying office nearby and just outside the lease area where it purchased illicit stones almost exclusively. ("We don't *know* they were illicit," a company spokesman points out.) Now that things have quieted down, the Diamond Corporation's buyers and its only buying office are in the town of Kenema, the buying center for legitimate alluvial-scheme diamonds.

In 1974 exporter's licenses were opened to others, and there are now ten licensed exporters, all but one of whom have nominal offices in Kenema (the exception being Jamil, whose buyers operate out of Koidu) but of them, when I was in Kenema in December of 1979, the only fully operating offices were those of the Diamond Corporation and of Industrial Diamonds. A gaggle of licensed buyers (without export licenses), almost exclusively Lebanese, also were open for business. No one other than the Diamond Corporation, however, was doing much business. Price rises have forced American jewelery retailers to cease buying substantial quantities of diamonds for stock. The rough buyers other than the Diamond Corporation can no longer afford to buy everything and anything, and none of the buyers was eager for routine trade. They were interested only in real bargains (which come principally from illicit operators) or in large stones for which there was then significant demand. The Diamond Corporation, however, is always interested in doing business.

At the Diamond Corporation's offices, the sellers sit in a roofed and screened porch outside the walls of the building, and deal with the buyers through windows to the interior. The flavor of the operation is corporate rather than personal. The Diamond Corporation's buyers are guided by a constantly updated price book, and for the most part their hands are tied by it.

The Diamond Corporation will refuse to purchase from anyone who is not a licensed digger or dealer. Now, if an illicit operator wants to have a licensed party carry his goods into the Diamond Corporation, that's not the Diamond Corporation's concern. It does not want to lose trade by being overly finicky.

As a matter of policy, the Diamond Corporation has always declined to finance diggers.

At the government's behest, in the late 1950s De Beers began training numbers of Sierra Leoneans to become diamond appraisers and buyers, and one of them, Joe Sisay, has risen to the top of its Kenema operations. Sisay himself deals the more important stones, and passes the lesser ones for evaluation and negotiation to one of the pleasant young white lads from the CSO's London offices, who assist him.

Sisay's traffic is mostly with Mandingo, Maracca, or Lebanese traders. (The Lebanese pass their wares on to the Diamond Corporation or not depending on market conditions.) As I visited with him, a trio of Lebanese dealers brought stones to him, and I found them to be colorful and animated bargainers.

The first Lebanese tried both vinegar and charm with Sisay: "Give me just a little profit, Joe." "Jesus Christ, Joe! Cost me ten thousand!" Then, "Five fifty-five a carat?" Smiling, "Put yourself in my place, Joe. . . ." Finally the would-be seller made a firm and from *his* tone manifestly fair demand: "I'll give it to you for twelve-and-a-half !"

At this point the Lebanese's sidekick interjected urgently, *"Take it, Joe!"* But Joe didn't. Throughout Sisay said virtually nothing, but his reticence contained the Lebanese's answer: No interest.

When the seller left I asked Sisay if the Lebanese were the hardest bargainers, and he said that there were none harder, but that the Maraccas were just as difficult.

The second seller drew Sisay out a little more, principally because of his opener: "This one's 'first color' [best possible color]." Sisay barely glanced at the stone before responding, "I'll show you 'first color.' " He started to reach for his master stones, his set of stones that exemplify the various qualities of color, when the seller backed off: "Never mind!" But Sisay insisted on demonstrating that the stone was not, in fact, first color, maybe not even second color. It was psychologically advantageous for him to deflate the seller as much as possible as early as possible, and the seller did lose most of his spontaneity. Still, no deal was closed. When the seller left, Sisay explained to me that the stone had had one black spot, and that the body of a stone, compared to the black spot, always appears whiter than it is, whiter than it will be when the black spot has been polished away.

The last was a young man with one stone on consignment from a digger. Sisay asked the seller, "How much do you want?"—his usual opener. The young man replied, 'I offered the man [the digger] eight hundred, but he said he had to have a thousand." He claimed to have already received a thousand offer elsewhere. Implicitly he was looking for a profit for himself.

Sisay weighed the stone, consulted his book, did a little scribbling, and then said that he came only to 968, but that he would round it off at the thousand. No profit for the Lebanese. The young man did not for the moment accept the offer, but he left the stone in Sisay's care anyway, thereby eliminating the possibility that Sisay might withdraw the offer. He would return to his prior offerers and probably tell them that the Diamond Corporation had offered 1,050 and that he was soliciting final offers.

Sisay said that the fellow was probably being reasonably truthful with him; that most of the people with whom he deals regularly deal more or less on the level with him—without, of course, being so candid as to leave no room for a final haggle. Sisay does the same: privately he valued the stone at 1,060.

The Lebanese Role

The Lebanese community, and principally the Koidu Lebanese, represent the alternate market in which the diggers and small dealers can sell their stones.

The Lebanese are the dominant economic factor in Sierra Leone, and in much of the rest of West Africa. They first began to arrive in Sierra Leone in the mid-1890s. They arrived very poor, lacking skills or useful experience, ignorant of the country and of the native languages. They took to trading and shortly became established participants in the life of the country. Until the diamond rush of the 1950s, however, they remained a largely impoverished community, many of whom lived in the style of the black Africans, some of them marrying Sierra Leonean women.

At the time of the illicit diamond rush, the Lebanese were in a position to take a big chunk of the traffic, but the Mandingo were ahead of them. Until the late 1950s the Mandingo held their own against the Lebanese for control of the non-Diminco production, but gradually the Lebanese became the dominant factor. "They are firm and controlling people and they know the black," an Antwerp rough dealer explained to me. H. L. van der Laan, author of *The Lebanese Traders in Sierra Leone,* believes that it has more to do with historical and economic circumstances: The Lebanese had greater access to finance; they could make bigger deals and could finance mining operations that were beyond the Mandingo traders. They also had greater rapport with the officials of the British colony of Sierra Leone, and after 1961 with the officials of the independent nation of Sierra Leone. Mandingos found it increasingly difficult to get or to renew buyers' licenses.

Today virtually all of the Lebanese are wealthy by Sierra Leone standards, and many of them are wealthy by American or European standards, living as well as is possible in an "underdeveloped country," and refueling with regular vacations abroad. Though their wealth originates in the diamonds, they have used their diamond money to gather control of every other aspect of the country's economy, with the predictable result that most black Sierra Leoneans resent them. Where has the country's diamond wealth gone? Any black man in Sierra Leone can tell you in a word: "Beirut," a convenient oversimplification.

The diamond diggers and smaller African dealers are largely very tribal people, and though they may have ill will toward the Lebanese, still, they feel more comfortable dealing with a Lebanese whom they have known for years than with a European. They are more likely to trust a Lebanese—especially those diggers who either began or are now operating illicitly. Every digger knows that he can bring his stones directly to the Diamond Corporation in Kenema for sale or for an offer, but few do, even though they know that their Lebanese buyer may sell their stones to the Diamond Corporation at a profit. Many of them are financially tied to a particular Lebanese, and most of the rest are tied to one by a sense of trust.

In the days when the Diamond Corporation was the only exporter, a Lebanese could tell the buyer that if he didn't get his price, he would take the stone away. The buyer understood what that meant: that the stone would be smuggled across to Monrovia and sold on the "outside market" to a competing buyer—the stone would be traded outside De Beers' control. But that kind of talk did not make much sense coming from a native Kono digger. The result was that the Diamond Corporation did pay the Lebanese a better price than the African—and may still.

Koidu, the commercial center for the Kono district and the Yengema lease area, and center of the Lebanese diamond traffic, is a busy, out-of-repair backwater city of tin shacks and shanties and scattered masonry structures that house the Lebanese-owned stores. In Koidu everything turns on bribery, from electricity and telephone service to the more conventional corruptions of police. Diamond dealing has always been illegal in Koidu.

The Koidu trade is much less active today than it was in the raucous fifties and sixties, but is still very far from dead. Much of the trade is "licit" from Sierra Leone's point of view—except for the fact that its mere existence is illicit. It involves buying the diamonds illicitly mined in neighboring Guinea, which are smuggled from Guinea into Sierra

Leone. Koidu is on a convenient road link to the diamondiferous area of Guinea; it is closer to Guinea than Monrovia, where the Guineans would otherwise go; there are more buyers—and thus more competition—in Koidu than in Monrovia; and the Koidu Lebanese are officially unofficially (or unofficially officially) permitted to pay for Guinean stones in US dollars (also the official unit of currency in Liberia). Many of the Koidu dealers end up smuggling stones to Monrovia principally to get dollars with which to purchase more Guinean stones. The Guineans are fond of Liberian currency, more than of leones, let alone of sylis (the Guinean unit of currency).

Jamil, charming and colorful, shrewd and hardworking, has risen to the top of the heap. He is an Afro-Lebanese (his mother is from the politically important Temne tribe) and an ostensible Muslim, though not one that would pass any mullah's muster. He drinks liquor and works on Friday.

Jamil started, so it goes, as a lorry driver involved in small-scale diamond smuggling, then became bigger and with the aid of a "handyman" was able to rope lesser illicit dealers into his arena. Out of it came an empire that extends to most aspects of the Sierra Leone economy, and to all of the seamier aspects of it. President Stevens is generally believed to have interests in many of Jamil's ventures, and Jamil is reputed to enjoy a second-to-none influence with the head of state. This is the kind of legend that revolves around one or more people in every African country; in the case of Sierra Leone's Jamil, it may have some truth to it.

In 1959 Jamil was arrested, sentenced to six months in jail, and banished from the Kono diamond district for unlawful possession of diamonds—no disgrace in Sierra Leone, where diamond offenses have always been viewed as tut-tut matters. In 1965 he was rehabilitated, issued a diamond dealer's license, and permitted to return to Kono. There he quickly rose to the top as the partisan of the prime minister, Sir Albert Margai. When Margai used the threat of expulsion from Kono to raise campaign contributions from the Lebanese, Jamil was one of the bag men, assessing "contributions" on an "ability to pay" basis. Meanwhile, Henneh Shamel, Jamil's main rival, cast his lot with Stevens and the opposition party, and with Stevens' success, Jamil faded rapidly into obscurity, while Shamel rode high and ostentatiously to the front as the king of the diamond dealers.

In November of 1969 an SLST shipment of one month's diamond production was waylaid at the small Hastings Airport south of Freetown by armed thieves who made off with $3.4 million worth of stones. People high up in company security had to have been involved. Shamel was arrested and charged with having masterminded the theft, but at trial he was acquitted. The presiding judge criticized the prosecution for having presented its case badly. Two days later Shamel left the country.

Shamel was declared a prohibited immigrant and barred from re-turning to Sierra Leone. Thereafter, Jamil began working his way into Stevens' good graces, and has continually improved his position since. Insofar as the country's diamond policy is concerned, he probably has more input than anyone else in Sierra Leone. His allocation of the Di-minco production is likely to increase—at least so long as President Stevens remains in office—to the extent that it is advantageous for Jamil to have it increase. He was almost certainly responsible for the govern-ment decision in 1974 to make export licenses available to others than the Diamond Corporation. He became a licensed exporter, but so long as the export duty remained pegged at 7.5 percent he exported almost nothing through official channels. Within ten days after the duty was reduced to 2.5 percent in 1978, Jamil surged past the Diamond Corpora-tion to become the number one alluvial-scheme exporter.

Jamil's considerable experience has made him a thoroughly compe-tent rough evaluator, and he now has a network of trading and diamond-cutting contacts in Antwerp, but at this point he is more of a financier than a diamantaire himself. He is the godfather of the Lebanese diamond traders, most of whom conduct their diamond businesses to greater or lesser degrees as his agent. Any Lebanese who becomes big enough works for Jamil or gets out. One of his Koidu operatives explained why: "He's got the cash, the guts, and the power. He gets people to cooperate with him." Jamil doesn't have to use threats of violence to secure coopera-tion (though many claim that he will); he influences people through matters such as who gets a renewal of his diamond dealer's license or a permit to reside within Kono. Most of the Lebanese export under Jamil's license, sending their goods either to Jamil's Antwerp man, Sulaimen, or to other buyers. Sulaimen gets the biggest chunk. He too is an Afro-Lebanese and brother to one of Jamil's higher-ranking lieutenants.

The De Beers and Selection Trust crowd resent Jamil's advantages, and especially the government's unofficial but well-established policy of suffering the Koidu dealers to remain and, worse, permitting them to deal in dollars—for "Guinean" stones only (but who is to say what stones come from where?). This makes Koidu a Monrovia outpost plumb in the heart of the Diminco lease. It also facilitates the laundering of black market currency transactions of whatever origin. But, says a De Beers person, "We've learned to live with that kind of thing."

Notwithstanding Jamil's overriding interests, diamond dealing among Koidu's buyers is a highly competitive matter. Koidu dealers buy principally from Kono diggers, from the more sophisticated Maracca illicits, and from the Mandingo, many of whom are carrying in the Gui-nean stones. Something over 90 percent of the black sellers are Muslim and come to the offices wearing gowns and either fezzes or the black

Muslim equivalent of the yarmulke. There is also considerable trading between the Lebanese themselves, and many stones have been traded several times within Sierra Leone before they are actually exported.

The Koidu dealers are a refreshingly honest lot of rogues, tremendously likable. They are quite open about the fact that all of their Guinean customers are smugglers; that many of the Sierra Leone stones in which they deal are illicitly mined, and that some of those stones may even have been stolen from Diminco; that they themselves have been knowingly if indirectly involved in illicit dealings in the past—and quite possibly, even right now. Nobody seriously maintains that the success of their operations depends principally on legitimate trade, and many of them are involved exclusively in illicit operations. Some are second-generation diamantaires and have been in the business all their lives. "Said" (as I will call him) is one of these.

Said is a solid and personable young man. He studied for two years in London but says that he did not approve of the dissolute life of hash smoking and wenching that typified the English college crowd, so left without taking a degree. He prefers life in Koidu to the sleazy sophistication of student London.

Said is only about twenty-four years old, but he represents twenty-four centuries of Phoenician tradition. I asked him, "Is it better for a digger to sell his diamonds in Koidu or to the Diamond Corporation in Kenema?" and in response he gave me most of what understanding I have of Lebanese trading techniques:

> That depends on whether you want to deal with *me*. I make you laugh, I make you cry, and I help you out in times of need. You have a bad time? Paid too much for a stone? Your old lady's sick? You can tell me about it. I will listen, I will help. We never forget a person who is in need. The Diamond Corporation doesn't want to know.
>
> I give respect, dignity, I talk to them fine, and they appreciate that. In the bad times I couldn't give good prices, but people came anyway. They said, "He's a good boy, he gives good prices." Maybe they knew it wasn't so, but they came anyway because when I didn't give good prices I still gave respect and dignity. It's feelings you work with, not only money; you touch his feelings—he'll never forget that.

Said works out of an office where he greets the sellers in their tribal gowns in his own informal western clothes. He deals with them good-naturedly, joshes, and has an easy and friendly rapport with them. They have obviously come to like him and to trust him. The trust element is all-important in Koidu, as it is throughout the diamond world. Occasionally stones are left with him for safekeeping by potential sellers who must return to Guinea to discuss an offer with a partner; they may not return for their goods for over a month.

All of the Lebanese dealers have tremendous expenses for charity, handouts, and uncollectable "loans." I watched while Said dispensed

a stream of leones to needy people who came in for help. To a great
extent such kindness is a rather cynical casting of bread upon waters:
Small courtesies today may give the opportunity for big killings tomorrow.

Said works all the time. When things slow down at his office, around
six thirty at night, he closes up and goes home, but any seller can come
to his house and he will return to his office at any time to close any
transaction. "Work!" he said out of nowhere. And then he added,
". . . Money."

For Sierra Leone, diamonds have been a curse of riches. It was
once an exporter of its people's basic staple, rice, but the diamonds
and their lure drained off the agricultural workers to the diamond diggings. Now it must import rice and leave most of the potentially rich
paddies idle.

The illicit dealings to which diamonds so nicely lend themselves
have promoted a general spirit of lawlessness within the country and
have corrupted the nation's officials. At every turn, laws and practices
have been changed to accommodate the illegal conduct of the diamond
community, each time at a greater cost to the country and its citizens
at large, theoretically as an effort to entice the illicit element into more
nearly legitimate avenues, but at least partly as a bid by the politicians
to win the goodwill of the criminal element.

By opening the diamond lands to the diggers in 1956, the country
gave up the significant tax income that would otherwise have come to
it from the much more heavily taxed SLST and reduced the country's
total mineral wealth potential by giving lands over to less efficient producers. About all that was gained for the country was the "legitimizing"
of the diggers, and the dubious possibility that the diggers might henceforth pay some export duties. There was no point to asking them to
pay income taxes. If required to do so, the newly legitimate diggers
and dealers would retaliate by smuggling their stones across the border
to Liberia, and the country would lose the export duty as well. On De
Beers' advice, the diggers and dealers were exempted from the income
tax. Everyone else must pick up the share of taxes that the diamantaires,
some of the country's wealthiest men, might otherwise have evaded
anyway. The exemption lures laborers to socially unproductive pursuits,
and encourages the channeling of Lebanese capital into tax-exempt diamond investments, rather than into investments that would be both
taxable and otherwise more desirable from society's viewpoint.

All this was done ostensibly in the hopes that the diamond people
would at least pay the export duty. But they didn't. Smuggling went
right on. So on the Diamond Corporation's urgings the export duty
was reduced from 7.5 percent to 2.5 percent, about the same as Liberia,
where a 3 percent duty is computed somewhat more leniently. Would

the diamond men at least give the state that much? The answer has been yes and no. With the drop in duty early in 1978, smuggling declined to very little. Then, a 5 percent devaluation of the leone in the fall of 1978 badly affected confidence in the leone and was an impetus to increased smuggling to Monrovia, where the stones could be sold for dollars. The hosting of the OAU conference and other government improvidences is likely to lead to further devaluation of the leone, and increased smuggling.

The country received real tax moneys from SLST, and both taxes and dividends from Diminco, but these moneys have largely been squandered, rather than invested in capital improvements or job-creating enterprises of lasting benefit to Sierra Leone. The country has gotten nothing out of the Alluvial Diamond Mining Scheme other than the increased popularity of its "statesmen."

It can't last much longer. Diminco will almost certainly cease to be profitable in the next few years, and the alluvial-scheme patches are already being worked over for the second and third times. Grave economic adjustments are ahead for the country when Diminco ceases contributing, and for the diggers when they have to hang up their sieves. When it's all over, all that Sierra Leone will have to show for it will be an emotional and fiscal letdown, and the remembrances of good days gone by.

11

COMMUNISTS AS CAPITALISTS: THE USSR

◆

Aikhal is a town of several thousand people and of interconnected apartment buildings, stores, and processing plants that stand on steel piers some ten feet off the ground in the Yakut Autonomous Soviet Socialist Republic, inside the Arctic Circle in northern Siberia. If Aikhal were built right on top of the rock-hard tundra, or "permafrost," frozen to the depth of a thousand feet, the warmth necessary to sustain human life would melt the permafrost, and the whole town would settle irregularly into a bog and crumble apart.

Aikhal's buildings are interconnected so that it is not necessary to set foot outside during the eight months of the year that are winter. Winter temperatures usually hover between 60 and 80 degrees below zero Fahrenheit, giving Aikhal one of the most severe climates suffered by any developed settlement in the world. In the summer the heat and the mosquitoes require that the whole of Aikhal be climate controlled, much of it air-conditioned. According to Soviet technical literature, it is "difficult to attract technicians" to work in Aikhal. Aikhal is a diamond town. It exists, like the Big Hole of Kimberley, for the vanity of women and the depravity of men—and also for the health of the Soviet balance of trade.

Aikhal is a satellite community of Mirny, some 560 kilometers (350 miles) to the south, and a major city for the Yakut ASSR. Mirny is the Oranjemund of the Arctic. In the late 1960s, Mirny's population was estimated at forty to fifty thousand, and it was the center for a Soviet diamond-mining industry that then employed 54,000 people—three times as many as De Beers. In the Soviet manner, something more than half of those 54,000 were women. This information is now roughly twelve years old, but in reporting on Soviet industry, being twelve years out of date isn't too bad.

Mirny, Aikhal, Mirny's other satellite communities, and the Soviet diamond-mining industry itself did not exist twenty-five years ago. Today Yakut may be second to Zaire in terms of total caratage produced; it may be second in terms of dollar value of its annual output to the combined South African and Namibian production. For all anyone outside the Soviet government knows, it may be first in both.

The Soviet diamond industry is an outgrowth of the cold war of the post–World War II period, when the capitalist countries that controlled the world diamond market embargoed the sale of diamonds to the Communist world. Diamond, being the hardest and most wear-resistant substance, makes the best possible bearings and cutting and grinding tools, and is essential to close-tolerance technology. Insignificant alluvial diamond output from the streambeds of the Ural Mountains, generated from some unknown kimberlite source, supplied a small portion of the Soviets' barest industrial and military necessities, and the rest they had to purchase on the Antwerp market semisurreptitiously (the diamond trading community has always been apolitical; total surreptitiousness has never been required) and at grossly inflated prices. Rather than remain dependent on a hostile West, the Soviets began to search for their own sources of strategic diamond.

The eminent Soviet geologist Vladimir Sobolev first theorized that diamonds would likely be found on the Siberian plateau after noting geological similarities between the area around the Vilyui River basin and the Kimberley region. He advised his government of his beliefs in 1941, but it was not until 1947 that the Soviets began serious geological exploration in Yukat. In 1949 they found small diamonds, along with quantities of pyropes, a kind of garnet that is usually found with diamonds. These came to the attention of two women geologists, who theorized that tracing the garnets would lead to a diamond pipe. In 1954 one of them, Larissa Popugaieva, traced the garnets to the first-discovered Soviet kimberlite pipe—in the Vilyui River basin as Sobolev had expected. Since then, countless pipes have been discovered in Yakut (many of them given ideologically inspiring names, such as the "Pipe of the 23rd Congress of the CSPPU"), as well as rich alluvial areas born of the pipes eons ago.

By the time production from Yakut became significant, the strategic importance of the finds had greatly diminished and would soon become insignificant—synthesis of industrial-grade diamond was accomplished in the mid-1950s. Now one of the regular buyers of *boart* (low grade industrial diamonds) sold from US government stockpiles is Diamtov, a Soviet government trading firm. At the same time, the Russians export quantities of synthetic industrials to the United States. But when the Soviet mines were developed in the late 1950s and early 1960s, the Russians were already proceeding with an eye-and-a-half toward trading Red diamonds to adorn the decadent bourgeoisie of the capitalist lands for chemicals, heavy machinery, grain, and the like.

Diamond mining for Russia today is principally a matter of obtaining foreign currency. Viktor I. Tikhonov, then the Mirny diamond administrator, was quoted in a 1967 East German press interview as saying, "We call ourselves the country's foreign exchange department." He estimated that the country had already recouped its investment in the diamond industry. Besides bringing in foreign currency, the Soviet diamond industry also helped to develop barren and remote portions of Siberia.

Technological problems of developing mines, processing plants, and communities in the trackless wilderness and fierce climate of northern Siberia presented great engineering challenges. In subzero cold, metal snaps like matchsticks, ordinary machinery and lubricants are useless, rubber becomes as brittle as a thin sheet of ice. That the Soviet diamond industry and its communities were indeed created under the horrific conditions of Yakut is surely one of the technical marvels of the century; *International Diamond Annual* (1971), which contains the fullest description of the problems and of the process of meeting them, describes the Soviet experience as "an astonishing story of almost superhuman endurance, dogged perseverance and dedicated determination." It was not accomplished without domestic opposition. Many Soviet planners argued that synthetic diamond plants could be constructed in inhabited, hospitable environments for a fraction of the cost of establishing mines in Siberia, and would then produce synthetic industrials that for most purposes would be preferable to the naturals. Ideologues argued simply that it was inappropriate and distasteful for a Marxist state to be in the diamond business.

Today the Soviets are mining kimberlite pipes as open-cast mines at a number of locations in Yakut. *International Diamond Annual* speculated that the Russians were probably using the heat generated by jet engines to assist in drilling into the frozen matrix. There may also be shaft operations at one or more of the Red pipes. The Soviets are known to be mining alluvial patches in "river terraces," operations similar in process (though complicated, again, by the weather) to those in Africa. In the brief summer the Russians also dredge the bottoms of the Yakut rivers with gigantic dredges that suck up, separate, and then spew out the river bottoms, relieving them of their diamonds in the process.

The Russians have at least seven scattered processing plants, which are likely to be among the most advanced in the world. Their scientists devised the technique of separating diamond from other materials by use of X-rays, and the Yakut plants may utilize other methodological improvements that have not yet been disclosed. Somehow they must have devised a system for providing their plants with the vast quantities of running water necessary to process out diamonds, a major provisioning problem in a climate in which water quickly becomes solid.

For the last several years the US Bureau of Mines has estimated Soviet diamond production at twelve million carats annually, second to that of Zaire, which produces about seventeen million carats a year, and ahead of the combined South Africa/Namibia production of about ten million. Because most of Zaire's production (or at least most of its "official" production) is of low-grade industrials, the value of the Soviet output is well in excess of Zaire's, probably second to that of De Beers. But only probably. The Soviets are highly secretive about all aspects of their diamond operations, including the quantities, qualities, and dollar values of their production. Though De Beers, as the selling agent for Soviet rough sales, may be in a position to hazard a very good estimate as to the details of Soviet production, it is invariably as discreet as the Russians are secretive when it comes to telling the business of its clients.

The gem/industrial breakdown of the Russian output is probably similar to the breakdowns elsewhere, with pipes yielding mostly "industrials" and alluvial deposits giving a somewhat better return of gemstones. Most observers believe that Soviet stones tend to be smaller than those from the South African mines and that truly large diamonds are even rarer than usual (unless the Soviets are hoarding them).

An unusually large proportion of the Soviet stones are perfect octahedrons. They are marginally "harder" than other diamonds, more brittle, and more prone to breakage in the polishing process. They tend to have a slightly greenish hue as rough, and a slight gray tinge when polished. Experienced diamond cutters believe that they can pick out the Siberian rough when it comes, undistinguished from the rest, in the boxes they receive from the DTC, De Beers' selling arm.

From the first Soviet sales in 1960 De Beers has been the selling agent for Soviet rough, strange bedfellows from the start, in a period when the Soviets were otherwise being uncooperative with western businesses (and especially outspoken against "monopolies"), and stranger still after 1964, when the Soviets backed the earliest Afro-Asian efforts in the United Nations to bring economic sanctions to bear against South Africa. At that time the relationship had an apparent breakdown. In a man-bites-dog announcement, De Beers told the world that it was ceasing to deal with the Soviets in retaliation for Russia's anti–South Africa position. Now the company prefers to explain the apparent breakdown on the fact that the relationship had become embarrassing for the Soviets. In any case, the breakdown was apparent but artificial; it simply went underground, where it has remained. Since 1964 the buyer-seller of the Soviet rough is no apartheid-tainted enslaver, but some politically respectable firm; for years it was Hambros Bank of London. Dealings may have moved behind some other front, but whatever the front, the sale of Soviet rough—and the profits derived therefrom—are still within the control of De Beers' CSO, which is what both parties intend. The Siberian stones are mixed in with those from all other consignors in DTC boxes, and sold like all the rest of the materials handled by the

DTC. In recent times, something over 20 percent of the rough in DTC boxes has been Siberian.

The relationship between De Beers and the Russians is not memorialized by a contract directly between them, but in complex documents covering a wide range of commercial matters to which the De Beers subsidiaries are third-party beneficiaries, but not signators.

No one has much confidence in a contract with the Russians, whether direct or "third party." Though contractually prohibited from doing so, the Russians occasionally do sell rough elsewhere, usually through Antwerp, generally only enough to "test the market" to be certain that De Beers is treating them fairly. Infrequently the Soviets will take advantage of temporary demand for particular qualities of rough, "go around" their agent, and very discreetly sell larger quantities of demanded qualities. Otherwise the Soviets edge around their contractual obligations simply by polishing the rough and then selling polished diamonds instead of rough diamonds. "Polisheds" are outside the purview of the Diamond Corporation's usual contract with producers. The Soviets will to some extent stockpile rough or move it on through the CSO depending on their cash needs, and their evaluations of the state of and the anticipated future price structure within the world rough-diamond market.

The relationship between De Beers and the Russians has always been a tenuous one, held together by practicalities: De Beers and the Soviets need each other. The Soviets need De Beers to maintain a stable market for diamonds through its advertising and its overall support of the diamond market, and as an ever ready buyer for whatever stones the Soviets may want to sell, at "list" prices regardless of the state of demand. De Beers needs the Soviet stones in order to maintain its control of the world diamond market—control that renders its own operations profitable. The two need each other to prevent price-cutting competition between them that would devastate both.

12

ZAIRE AND
ITS INDUSTRIAL DIAMONDS

◆

The hostility of the black world toward South Africa makes the relationships of Zaire, Angola, and Tanzania with De Beers politically embarrassing for them. Yet they are all "inside" countries, selling their output through the CSO. Black African leaders, when asked about their connections with De Beers, must respond in hems and haws or rely on transparent legal fictions: "Us? Deal with a white South African corporation? Never! We sell our diamonds to a Bahamian concern!" Nobody is fooled. The short of it is that they do not have much alternative but to deal with De Beers.

Going it alone is no matter for a diamond-producing country to undertake lightly. For those with small outputs, such as Tanzania or possibly Angola, both of which produce generally high-quality goods, it might be administratively and economically feasible to sell diamonds directly on the open market in Antwerp. They would have a serious problem, however, in finding experienced, trustworthy experts to direct their selling efforts, and more, in placing trust in their experts once found. The CSO is less likely to rob them (or likely to rob them less) than anyone else. Even under the best of circumstances, there would be periods when Angola or Tanzania would do worse selling direct than they do selling to the Diamond Corporation.

Bigger producers such as Zaire would have the same problems, complicated by the heavy administrative burden of establishing two intensely complex sales organizations, one for gems and one for industrials, and establishing relations with a hundred small cutters—most of whom would shy away from dealing with an "independent" out of fear of retribution from the DTC.

All producers are held back from "going it alone" by the knowledge that if any one of them did, other producers might also begin selling outside the CSO. One major defection or a couple of minor ones would inevitably cause the CSO system to fall apart, and diamond prices would disintegrate along with it. So they stay in line. Zaire is the most important of them.

At the time of the discovery of the "Bakwanga Hill," a grouping of diamondiferous kimberlite pipes in the south-central section of Zaire, geologists were dumbfounded by its immense size and by the richness of its yield of diamonds: often ten carats per ton of kimberlite—more than a hundred times the richness of the South African pipes, as much as four hundred times the richness of some others. Geologically, Bakwanga was and remains a most impressive marvel. The trouble was—and is—that the Bakwanga stones that still make up the great bulk of Zaire's exports are almost entirely industrials (between 85 and 98 percent, depending on the source of the estimate) too flawed for use in jewelry.

In 1918, when the Bakwanga kimberlites were discovered, there was virtually no demand for industrial-grade diamonds. The perfection of the diamond-studded grinding wheel in the late 1920s might have created a real market for industrials, except that the depression of the 1930s dampened the emerging demand. Industrials remained unsalable.

World War II was just what the Congo producers needed. Throughout the period 1940–45, and in the postwar years, new uses and applications for industrial diamonds were devised daily. Demand soared and so did prices. The Belgians unloaded the vast hoards of previously unsalable goods that they had been accumulating in milk cans and increased production. Sir Ernest believed that the Belgian companies (in which Anglo and De Beers were sizable minority stockholders) would be the controlling factor in the postwar diamond world. By 1954 the Belgian Congo (as Zaire was then known) was producing close to three-quarters of total world diamond output, selling its goods at a then impressive $20 per carat. That year General Electric announced that it had successfully synthesized industrial diamonds, and would soon embark on sales of synthetic industrials.

Users of the synthetic industrials found that for most applications the man-made diamonds were better than those created by nature. At first high costs of production retarded the threat to the "naturals" market from the new diamonds, but as engineers devised more efficient production techniques, the price of synthetics dropped, bringing down the price of natural industrials with it. Since 1954 the price of industrial diamonds, whether synthetic or natural, has dropped almost annually. By the early 1960s both General Electric and De Beers were manufacturing large quantities of synthetic industrial diamond and it seemed certain that the Zaire industry would be price-cut out of business in a matter of ten or fifteen years. Since then some new uses for naturals (as opposed to synthetics) have bolstered the demand for Bakwanga's production, and the staggering price rises in gem diamonds have made the small gem production from Bakwanga more valuable, enough to keep diamond mining there more or less viable.

Today Zaire's output of about seventeen million carats represents more than a third of total world diamond production—Zaire is still probably the leading diamond-producing country in terms of caratage—but while prices of everything else have gone up in the last quarter-century, the synthetics knocked the bottom out of Zaire's market. In 1978, Société Minière de Bakwanga (MIBA), which produced 10.5 million of the country's 17 million carats, received $81.6 million for its output—or, for its entire production of industrials and gems, $7.77 per carat. And 1978 was MIBA's best year in many.

MIBA is the child of Société d'Enterprise et d'Investissements du Bécéka (Sibeka), a Belgian mining house principally concerned with diamond mining, about 20 percent of which is owned by the Oppenheimer companies. Both MIBA and Sibeka have fared sorry in Zaire in recent years. The Zairian civil war disrupted their operations and brought massive social dislocation to Bakwanga. Prior to the civil war, the area had some fifty thousand inhabitants, largely but not exclusively Baluba tribesmen. During and after the war, most of the non-Baluba fled the area, while a massive influx of Baluba swelled the population to 350,000. Many newcomers turned to illicit diamond digging, poaching within MIBA's concession.

In 1969 the government nationalized a one-half interest in MIBA, and in 1973, as part of his campaign for "Zairianization" of the national economy, Zaire's President Mobutu Sese Seko expropriated Sibeka's remaining half interest and threw it out in the cold without a zaire (the country's unit of currency).

Mobutu eventually admitted that he needed the Europeans, and in 1978 he graciously gave Sibeka a 20 percent interest in MIBA, free of charge, together with the principal burden of management. MIBA is currently directed by a board of directors of eight, five appointed by the government (all people without familiarity with diamond mining or the diamond business) and three appointed by Sibeka. MIBA's managing director and general manager are both whites designated by Sibeka, with an assistant general manager nominated by the government.

Running MIBA in modern Zaire is no easy matter. Notwithstanding the fact that MIBA is 80 percent government owned, a quasi-governmental agency, it is plagued by the same kind of red tape that would affect any other private company doing business in Zaire—which is suffocating. There are not enough experienced, technically qualified black mining people to go around and it is not easy to get a non-Baluba black to go to Bakwanga. Securing a working permit in Zaire for a foreigner is a bureaucratic nightmare. Of MIBA's five thousand-odd employees about eighty are now, again, "expatriates," as whites are known.

The company is still plagued by poachers, who not only steal, but also spoil promising sites with their unsystematic operations. Internal theft may be an even greater problem for MIBA. The $2-a-carat goods are still coming in strong, but there has been a greater than normal decline in the number of larger gem-quality stones, warranting an assumption that MIBA's better material is being stolen by its staff—its black staff or its white staff, depending on the race of the man that gets to the particular stone first.

Of MIBA's gross sales, 12.5 percent goes for the export duty applicable to MIBA (a lower rate applies to other diamond producers), and another 7 percent for the country's turnover tax, both off the top. Zaire's corporation tax eats up exactly half of what profits remain after the first two taxes, import duties on what MIBA must acquire from abroad (almost everything), employment taxes, and the ordinary costs of production. In 1977 nothing was left at all for stockholders, but with increased prices in 1978, some 9 million zaires were left as aftertax profit for the "investors." A little under 2 million zaires were earmarked for Sibeka as minority stockholder—subject, that is, to Sibeka's contractual agreement with the government of Zaire that all dividends must remain in the company for a period of four years. Nothing was immediately due and payable to Sibeka as a dividend for 1978.

When I asked a high-ranking Sibeka official, "What are you *doing* in Zaire?" he had an answer: "We are in the diamond business, and we must go where there are diamonds. There are diamonds in Zaire and the country has great potential for the diamond business. That's what we are doing in Zaire."

The scuttlebutt in the diamond world is that Sibeka is profiting not from the mining of Zaire's diamonds, but rather from the distribution of them; that Sibeka's public evaluation of the MIBA production (from 3 to 5 percent gems and virtually all the rest usable only for grinding wheels and other low-valued applications) is egregiously pessimistic; that the MIBA stones are undervalued at every step prior to sale, and end up in DTC lots sold at favorable prices to interests in which Sibeka has interests. Or the Oppenheimer group may keep friendly Sibeka in Zaire in order to keep others out, and to ensure that Zaire's diamonds continue to be channeled through the CSO. The last is probably not the explanation. As one Sibeka official told me, "No other organization but the CSO can buy such large production on a regular basis."

One of the bigger dealers who would be in a position to handle the dollar volume involved more or less agreed:

> If I were to make an offer for the MIBA stones, the CSO would put pressure on Mobutu through the international banks that it works with; they'd hint, or maybe even tell him, that unless he stayed in line, they would refuse to roll over Zaire's loans. If I got in anyway, and controlled and was responsible for moving all those industrials, I would be confronted with price cuts

in the price of the synthetic industrials that De Beers makes that would eliminate the market for Zaire's natural production altogether, and maybe throw me into bankruptcy too. Only De Beers can handle Zaire's production, because only De Beers is immune from price cuts by De Beers. Mobutu isn't getting a fair deal on his stuff and he knows it, but there isn't anything he can do about it. Everyone's hands are tied.

As it is, MIBA and Zaire are profiting from their relationship with the CSO, whether or not "enough". . . ?

In 1978 MIBA's stones represented almost 30 percent of the CSO's caratage volume, but only about 3.2 percent of its total dollar gross—and a very much higher percentage of its administrative expense. Processing MIBA's volume represents a colossal burden. Notwithstanding the grumbling of black African nationalists and of "outside" diamond men about how the CSO takes advantage of Zaire, the profits earned by it from selling MIBA's output probably do not come to much. The CSO is not so much interested in the profits from the MIBA stones as it is in keeping MIBA's near quarter of total world diamond production under its control. Preserving market control is always the first objective of the CSO, and MIBA's output is important to that.

Of the total Zairian caratage, Bakwanga produces well over half and MIBA most of that, but the more valuable stones come from alluvial sites on the Kasai River and its network of tributaries in the province of West Kasai, centered at Tshikapa, some 350 kilometers or 200 miles west of Bakwanga. In West Kasai, the happy ratio of gems to industrials comes close to one-half gemstones. The total value of the West Kasai production probably exceeds the value of the Bakwanga output, but it is impossible to tabulate because the disorganization of the West Kasai production and the large portion of its output that flows into the underground diamond market conspire to make tabulation of West Kasai's yields impossible.

West Kasai is worked by about a dozen large, licensed mining operations, which employ heavy earth-moving equipment and as many as four or five hundred men each. These dozen are involved in fairly major projects, such as mining out the bottom of riverbeds, usually at meanders. This requires that the river be temporarily diverted into a newly created channel. The bed is then dug out by drag lines (a steam shovel-like excavating apparatus) and the materials are then processed for their diamonds. Or they may dig high-terrace sites, stripping away heavy overburdens of waste material down to the diamondiferous level of gravels that represents the streambanks of prehistory, and then remove those for processing.

There are hundreds of smaller operations employing upward of two dozen men each, working less challenging sites with little or no mechanical equipment. Many of these are licensed enterprises, and many are entirely illicit. Illicit mining can be a risky business in Zaire. In August

1979 the *New York Times* reported that "several hundred" illicit miners had drowned in a southern Zaire river, fleeing police who had caught them at work.

The Kasai miners are prohibited from exporting rough and are required by law to sell their output to one of the licensed buyers. There are only two of them, both with main buying offices in Tshikapa: the Diamond Corporation, which does business in Zaire as British-Zaire Diamond Distributors and which captures something over two-thirds of what sales are made through legitimate channels; and Meltax, a Swiss-based firm of Antwerp principals that gets the rest of the official transactions. If handling MIBA's output does not particularly attract the CSO from a financial standpoint, the gemstones of Tshikapa do. It is the occasional big stone bought in Tshikapa that keeps the company's Zairian operations financially viable.

As in all African diamond-buying centers, competition between the would-be buyers is fierce, even though there are only two of them in Tshikapa. But because the Diamond Corporation and Meltax must pay their top dollar in zaires, purchased by them for dollars at the government bank, an accurate and honorable valuation of a stone by either may bring the seller a lesser sum than a dishonorable evaluation by an illicit dealer who pays in cheaper black market zaires. According to the government of Zaire, one zaire is worth fifty cents US; according to black market money dealers, it is worth only a third of that. The disparity between official and black market rates means that if it is to stay in business in Zaire, while buying its zaires at fifty cents each, the Diamond Corporation must pay three times as much (in "real" money) for goods as the illicit dealer who buys his zaires at fourteen to seventeen cents each.

In other economic spheres—and almost certainly in diamonds as well—the government quietly sells zaires to respectable businesses at three, four, or five zaires to the dollar, so long as the recipients are discreet about it. Zaire cannot let it be known that not even it believes a zaire to be worth fifty cents. It probably gives the DTC and/or Meltax a "bargain" rate on zaires—but not enough to eliminate completely the advantage enjoyed by illicit dealers who trade in thoroughly discounted zaires.

The bigger mining operations in West Kasai must have a respectable flow of legitimate sales to show the government in case of audit, so they give the licensed buyers enough stones to make things look kosher, and then channel off the balance of their output to the illicit market. Even the unabashedly illicit outfits will occasionally sell stones to one of the legitimate buyers when they need cash in a pinch. An unlicensed miner need not worry about being asked by a licensed buyer for his own license at time of sale. He won't be asked. Though diamond miners are required to have a license, the law does not require the licensed buyer to see proof of the seller's legitimacy, and in Zaire neither the Diamond Corporation nor Meltax will ask to see proof. If either did, it would lose business to the other, or to the illicit buyers.

The output that is sold on the illicit market may be sold either in Zaire or abroad. Smaller operators generally sell to a "collector," usually a native Zairian. The collector sells to a bigger regional collector, who sells them, usually in one of Zaire's major cities, to a foreign black, generally a West African and most commonly to a citizen of Senegal, who may or may not be a Mandingo. Though the Senegalese are legally required to remain in one of Zaire's major cities, occasionally Senegalese diamond buyers will wander out into the hinterlands of West Kasai to do business. They bribe their way around the backlands without serious inconvenience. Everything is a matter of bribes in Zaire. Illegal enterprises thrive by paying bribes, and legitimate businesses must pay them too—or forget about doing business in Zaire.

The Senegalese bring their stones to Brazzaville, capital of the People's Republic of the Congo, a Marxist state formerly known as the French Congo, immediately north of the "Belgian" Congo. Or they may go to Bujumbura, capital of Burundi, a country dominated by its minority tribe that lies east of Zaire, or even to Antwerp to sell. In both Brazzaville and Burundi, the dollar-zaire exchange rate is realistic, and in either the seller can get immediate conversion of his payment from zaires to hard currencies if he wants. Bigger mine operators may take their output directly to the same marketplaces in which the Senegalese sell. There is always the problem of smuggling the stones out of Zaire, but that is not all that difficult in a country in which airport customs officials routinely solicit a baksheesh from the tourist. Everything worth getting out of Zaire is smuggled out, not only hideable parcels of diamonds, but elephantine shipments of raw copper ore, the country's economic mainstay (such as it is). There is a certain justice in this, inasmuch as everything worth getting into Zaire is smuggled in.

The exploitation of Zaire's West Kasai diamonds does not mean much to the government or people of the country. To discourage illicit mining, Zaire has removed some of the more important economic incentives to "going it illegal." Licensed diamond miners (other than MIBA) are exempted from the country's income tax on their diamond profits; otherwise, everyone would operate illicitly, thereby costing the government the export duty on rough diamond. And the export duty itself has been shaved to the point that it gives the country virtually no return. At the urgings of the Diamond Corporation, Zaire reduced the duty to 3 percent of value in order to keep it competitive with the export duties of Brazzaville and Burundi. Many regard the Diamond Corporation and Meltax as having been the real beneficiaries of the duty reduction.

Zaire would be economically better off (and almost certainly better off socially as well) if West Kasai's diamond production were exploited by an enterprise like Sibeka or De Beers, which could more easily be audited and could be taxed at some respectable rate. But it is far too late for that now. The producing sites of West Kasai are too many, too widely dispersed, and most of the individual sites too limited, to make West Kasai suitable for capital-intensive single-company exploitation—and especially so now that the diggers have gotten Kasai's diamonds in their blood.

13

JOHN WILLIAMSON'S
DIAMOND MINE

◆

John T. Williamson set out into the bush in 1936 in search of diamonds, and after five years of hardship and many of the illnesses known to tropical Africa, he still refused to be discouraged. By then he had become a living legend in East Africa as the driven, determined white prospector and dreamer, simultaneously admired, pitied, and dismissed as a romantic, a lunatic, and a fortune hunter. By the time he finally found the great diamond pipe in the remoteness of north-central Tanzania, he was destitute and chronically ill. It had been worth it.

The Williamson pipe was not only the biggest pipe ever found in terms of surface area—360.5 acres, four and a half times the surface of Premier, South Africa's biggest—it also had (and has) the largest proportion of gemstones in its yield of any kimberlite pipe in the world. Over the years Williamson Mine has given up more than thirteen million carats, almost as much as the Big Hole of Kimberley, and of overall better quality. For a long time Williamson Mine was the principal source for rare pink-hued diamonds, which command prices in excess of the price of the finest quality "white" stones.

Williamson was a Canadian who studied and taught at McGill University until he received his Ph.D. in geology in 1933. Then he went to southern Africa, worked in copper mining in Rhodesia for a couple of years and briefly for a De Beers subsidiary, and then set out to seek treasure for himself. Occasional finds of alluvial diamonds in the British colony of Tanganyika (today's Tanzania) drew his attention there. Other geologists had searched there for diamonds and no great lode had been found, but Williamson believed that the earlier prospecting ventures had not been intensive enough. He determined to do a more conscientious search. When he finally made his great find, De Beers offered him fortunes for his discovery. He refused.

Throughout the war years Williamson worked to create a new town, Mwadui, to service his mine, with the amenities necessary to support several thousand blacks and hundreds of whites and Indians (a sizable ethnic group in Tanzania). It was his town and his mine, the biggest, richest-yielding diamond mine in the world. He sold his early, still-limited production independently, but a slump in world diamond demand in 1947 left his wares unsalable, and forced him to sign with the Diamond Corporation.

By late 1949 the market had again firmed, and Williamson became dissatisfied with his relationship with the CSO. He could do better on his own. His contract bound him to sell his rough only to the Diamond Corporation, but it did not commit him to sell at all, so instead he began to stockpile his stones. He continued mining, increased production and threatened to increase it still further, while selling no stones. His growing hoard and his increasingly bigger portion of total world production threatened to blow open De Beers' diamond cartel—if, that is, he could hold out long enough. With the termination of his sales and increases in his expenses, Williamson's economic picture became severely strained. If he went bust in the process of fighting the CSO, that might be just as bad for the giant; the consequent unloading of his stones on the market might collapse prices.

When at last Williamson's contract with the Diamond Corporation expired in 1951, he was free to begin selling. Then he couldn't find a buyer! Those in a position to consider buying any sizable chunk of Williamson's rough well knew that anyone who bought from the renegade would be cut off from access to the 80–85 percent of the world's stones still controlled by the CSO. Its economic control over the potential buyers brought Williamson back into line. Thereafter he stayed in the fold, but he never liked it. Working with others wasn't in Williamson's nature.

Williamson's adventuresome history, fabulous wealth, continued hard work, and rugged good looks marked by a Clark Gable mustache made him a favorite with the journalists of the popular press, very few of whom ever actually saw him. From their sketches, he appeared a shy, charming man. His staff saw many different, bizarrely cut facets to him. From the biography by his chief of security, P. H. E. Burgess, he emerges as an emotional cripple and an egoist incapable of functioning in civilization. He was subject to irrational rages, in which he might hurl the day's production of diamonds about his rooms, and which sometimes left him crumpled in tears. At other times he would remain mute for long periods, even in the presence of guests.

Notwithstanding his riches, he became a recluse at Mwadui, in one of the world's worst climatic and social/cultural environments. Important visitors to Mwadui were lavishly entertained by his underlings, but the host himself almost never appeared. Strangers made him nervous, and the arrival of important people usually prompted recurrences of his tropical sicknesses. When business dictates brought him to the outside world, he rarely ventured outside his hotel room.

Williamson was a lifelong bachelor and misogynist like Rhodes, but unlike Rhodes, he had no affection for any man either. His emotional development was retarded at presexual levels. The only fondness that he ever displayed was for animals, especially dogs. He refused to permit steps to be taken to control large numbers of savage and mean-tempered dogs that roamed the mine property. Human beings rated lower. His white staff commonly believed that he despised them. He showed more interest in his African workers, though he did not have a high opinion of them, and he came closest to feeling comfortable with his Indian staff. He felt most nearly comfortable when he was alone. There was always a lighted cigarette close by Williamson's hand, and it was perhaps this that took his life through throat cancer at the age of fifty in 1958.

Soon after Williamson's death, his brother and two sisters agreed to sell Williamson Diamonds Ltd. to De Beers at a price of £4,140,000 (then $11,600,000), in addition to which De Beers was to pay the family's inheritance tax of £1.5 million ($4,200,000), making a total purchase price that represented less than the value of two years' output from the mine—less than De Beers had offered Williamson when he was alive. Harry Oppenheimer personally negotiated the deal with the surviving brother, Percy Williamson. Percy knew only enough about the diamond business to know that he did not want to run a diamond mine. The acquisition gave De Beers control of the only major "independent" diamond mine in the world, and the only possible threat to its dominance of the world diamond trade (until, that is, the Russian production began to blossom).

Tanganyika was on the verge of independence at the time of acquisition of Williamson Diamonds, and Oppenheimer realized that it would not be easy for a South African concern with recently acquired interests to operate in the traditional manner in a newly independent black country. At his suggestion the Territory of Tanganyika, soon to be the independent nation of Tanganyika (and after incorporation with Zanzibar, Tanzania), became a one-half owner of Williamson Diamonds. In satisfaction of the claim for death taxes, Tanganyika took a 26 percent interest in the corporation, and De Beers loaned the territory enough to purchase an additional 24 percent interest, giving it an even one-half ownership of Williamson Diamonds. The government would repay the debt, plus 6 percent interest, out of the dividends that it received from the corporation. To insulate the whole operation from the smell of apartheid, the De Beers half interest was placed in the name of Willcroft Co., an Oppenheimer-group subsidiary with a Bahamas mailing address.

Tanganyika became independent in 1961. De Beers, or rather, Willcroft, maintained good relations with the new government headed by Julius Nyerere, and continued to do so after 1967, when Nyerere's political philosophy evolved into "egalitarianism," a sweet, fuzzy, Walden-Pond Marxism. Consistent with the government's emerging policy, Williamson Diamonds Ltd. stepped up efforts at "Africanization." During the decade of the 1960s, the number of white employees was reduced from 350 to 90, opening all but the highest positions of responsibility for Tanzanians. The country found Willcroft to be a sympathetic and honorable partner for a new black nation struggling to establish its identity. The mine remained profitable and De Beers continued in control of its stones.

Though the Williamson pipe is very broad at the surface, its below-ground funnel shape tapers more rapidly than usual to a thin stem, making for an even sharper drop-off in productivity with depth than is usually the case with diamond pipes. Throughout the 1960s it was necessary to remove and process more and more kimberlite to retrieve fewer and fewer diamonds per load. By the early 1970s the economic life of Williamson Mine was clearly limited. Meanwhile, Tanzanian politics and ideology had evolved to the point at which it was no longer theoretically acceptable to the country to maintain a subservient relationship to a white foreign enterprise devoted to profit making. In 1973 the government determined that it was in the country's best interest to stretch out the life of Williamson Mine to a maximum, and to do so, the national interest dictated that Williamson production be cut back to a lower rate, a rate at which the mine could not be expected to generate an after-tax profit. Because the mine's prognosis was already bleak as a profit-making enterprise, De Beers was able to accede to the wishes of its equal partner nicely. Within a year only a handful of expatriates were left.

Anglo has continued to sell technical assistance to Williamson, and the CSO has continued as selling agent for the company's stones. Relations between the country and De Beers remain cordial. Willcroft continues to have representation on Williamson's board, nominally including Harry Oppenheimer, but accepts that full responsibility for operating the mine in a manner consistent with the objectives of national policy is now in the hands of the corporation's Tanzanian directors. As a result of his graciousness, Oppenheimer, the "good" neo-imperialist, is one of the few white capitalists who is genuinely respected and admired in Tanzania.

The evolution of Williamson Diamonds Ltd. might be viewed as an example of how an enterprise can be transformed from a white-dominated, profit-motivated operation into a black-dominated operation motivated by other than profit—peacefully and with good will between the races preserved. There are only minor blemishes to the picture: Today the Williamson Mine is perhaps the most inefficient diamond mine in the world; its management is bureaucracy-bound and preoccupied with tribal frictions and loyalties.

Profitable mining and processing-plant operations require greater volumes than Williamson is generating. Even with substantial increases in the price of diamonds, the economies of the industry are against Williamson Mine. For years its useful life has been estimated at only a few more years, but diamond price rises have continually forestalled the inevitable. Now it seems certain that it really is only a few more years before one of the great mines in diamond history is closed. Diamond people are not sentimental; Williamson Mine will be quickly forgotten—except by those who knew John Williamson.

14

ANGOLA:
FIDELISTAS FOR DE BEERS!

◆

The relationship between Angola, a black African Marxist state, and De Beers is perhaps the most bizarre of the many anomalies in the diamond world. While Angola sells its stones through the CSO and relies on De Beers expertise for the development of new diamond fields in Angola, to the mutual benefit of the country and the company, Angola and South Africa are engaged in a low-level shooting war. All of which goes to show only that economics is more powerful than ideology and that economic pressures make for seemingly unlikely alliances in the diamond world.

Diamonds were first discovered in Angola in 1917 in the northeastern quarter of the country, adjacent to the diamond fields of West Kasai in Zaire, and apparently part of the same geological phenomenon. Low-grade kimberlite pipes have been found in Angola, and these are probably the source for the rich lodes of alluvial diamonds in and along five diamondiferous rivers in northeastern Angola, and possibly for the alluvial diamonds of West Kasai as well.

The great bulk of Angolan production has always been from the alluvial workings. Companhia de Diamantes de Angola (Diamang) has operated the Angolan fields from the start, and perfected a unique technique for mining the bottoms of the broad Angolan rivers. It builds a dike down the center of the waterway and then channels all of the riverflow to the left side of the dike while it cleans out the right side of the river bottom and removes it for processing. Then it diverts all of the water to the other side of the dike and cleans out the opposite side. A large percentage of Diamang's finds are discovered in rough potholes on the river floors. Diamang's output has always contained a very high proportion of good grade gemstones, better than the stones from nearby Kasai.

Diamang obtained exclusive diamond rights over almost all of Angola for an effective fifty years in 1921, but concentrated its operations at Dundo in the Lunda district in the northeast quarter of Angola. Lunda became a company fiefdom, a state within a state, where the company dominated the local government and controlled the lives of Lunda's inhabitants. That was not so bad. If the Portuguese colonials deserved their worst-in-the-world reputation, Diamang was an exception: It assumed obligations for the health and well-being of everyone within its district, and represented a favorable example of industrial paternalism. When its original rights expired in 1971, much of what it had not exploited was removed from its control, but a broad swath of the area removed from its concession was given for prospecting and exploitation to a combined Diamang–De Beers combine, Condiama. Condiama has yet to indicate its successes (if any).

Diamang hit its peak of production in the first half of the 1970s, at about 2.2 million carats a year, making Angola the world's fifth or sixth biggest producer. At that time it was working upward of forty different locations, each with its own limited preliminary processing facilities, with final stages of processing and recovery of the diamonds centralized at a smaller number of plants. It then employed close to thirty thousand people, almost all of them black laborers.

All of that came virtually to an end with Angolan independence and the ensuing Angolan civil war. The Portuguese employees began quitting and pulling out after the revolution in Portugal itself in 1974, and their exodus stepped up with Portugal's grant of independence to Angola at the start of 1975. They stole as many stones as they could on the way out the door. The Portuguese government essentially turned its back on the matter of thefts by its returning expatriates (though the government of Portugal itself had substantial stock interests in Diamang). The flood of illicit stones that they carried threatened to shake the confidence of the diamond-cutting centers in the monolithic role of the CSO until the Diamond Corporation began fencing the loot— in the greater interests of diamond-world stability. They had done the same during the period of instability and thefts in Zaire during the Congo civil war.

Diamang continued to operate, but at grossly reduced levels. Lack of the expatriate mining engineers necessary for operations forced it to cease working most of its locations, and its place at them was filled by illicit diggers, some operating under political guise and some not bothering with such cover. In 1975–76 its concession was overrun by illicit diggers. Amidst the general civil disorder in Angola in the mid-1970s, complicated by the exodus of the Portuguese, company security completely disintegrated.

While the whites fled, the blacks ceased working. In an interview with the *New York Times* in 1976, João Martins, a Portuguese director of Diamang, said that "the Africans feel that with independence coming they do not have to work quite so much. Only six thousand are still at the mines." Diamang's production fell to under 400,000 carats in 1976.

That year the company essentially invited nationalization, with hopes that some role and profit might be preserved for its stockholders and managers in continued Angolan diamond operations. By then the Movimento Popular de Libertação de Angola (MPLA)—with which Diamang had remarkably good relations—had attained supremacy in Angola. In August of 1977 it nationalized a 60.85 percent interest in Diamang, taking most of the holdings of the small stockholders, largely private citizens in Portugal, and mostly leaving intact the stock interests in Diamang owned by the Oppenheimer companies, by Sibeka, by the successor to Forminière (the original developer of the West Kasai fields), and by other major international corporations.

Though Angola has yet to announce its position with regard to payment for the interests seized, the MPLA revolutionaries are trying hard to establish a good reputation in capitalist money markets, which gives the government some incentive to deal fairly when it gets around to paying for the interests nationalized.

Diamang, now principally government owned but expatriate directed, has begun reconstruction of its devastated empire, but it will be some time before its production of the early seventies is restored. When the Angolan diamond industry does revive, its prognosis should be bright. Angola diamonds are of overall good quality; yields per ton of material processed are respectable, and much of Angola's uncharted diamond reserves are believed to be rich. Marxist Angola is in a better position to control illicit diamond operations and theft than "democratic" countries like Zaire or Sierra Leone (actually corrupt oligarchies). In Angola they shoot diamond rustlers. It has a certain deterrent effect.

Through all of the turmoil, the CSO has remained in control of the distribution of the Angolan diamonds. The MPLA considered its alternatives (and whether it had any alternatives) to selling to the Diamond Corporation. It sent a high-powered delegation to the CSO to find out "what's what"—no grubby Fidelista types to lecture the Oppenheimer people about advanced socialist theory, but "bottom-line" guys. I asked David Neil-Gallacher, then chief of De Beers' public relations, how, with its connections in the land of apartheid, the CSO was able to continue in control of the Angolan stones, and he explained it. It was really quite simple: "We were very open with the Angolan delegation; we explained the mechanics of the diamond business to them; they decided that they wanted us to continue to handle their sales, and we do." It was as simple as that. Neil-Gallacher usually sports a pleasant smile, but this time I read it as a cat-canary satisfaction.

15

STRAY DIAMONDS

◆

Ghana was perhaps my favorite diamond country. It is also the largest diamond producer selling outside the CSO. Ghanaians are easygoing, gracious people, their government (at least at the time of my visit in November 1979, shortly after the country's then-most-recent coup) decent and optimistic.

Ghana is cocoa country: The Ghanaian economy depends on the cocoa crop, not on its diamond output. Much of the cocoa is smuggled into neighboring countries, where it can be sold for dollars rather than for cedis, the Ghanaian unit of currency. Smuggling cocoa is pretty tough to do when compared with smuggling diamonds.

Diamonds were first discovered in the British Colony of the Gold Coast in 1919. Organized mining began in 1924, when an American, Chester Beatty, established Consolidated African Selection Trust (CAST) to work two major concessions there. One of those has since ceased to be productive; the other, the Akwatia Concession, remains the center for diamond mining in Ghana. Small alluvial diggers were also licensed, and for many years their annual production exceeded that of CAST. All of Ghana's production is alluvial; the kimberlite pipes that gave birth to its diamonds have never been located.

In 1957 the Gold Coast became the first of the African colonies to win its independence and became Ghana under the leadership of Kwame Nkrumah. Diamonds were very important to the new country's economy. In the early days of Ghana's independence, its total annual output of some 3.3 million carats made it the world's second biggest producer, after Zaire. Though upward of 85 percent of Ghana's diamonds are sand-sized industrial stones, in that period, before the burgeoning of the synthetic industrial diamond industry, they commanded excellent prices.

Nkrumah, a scholarly man infused with Marxist attitudes, wanted nothing to do with what he regarded as the neo-colonialist imperialism of De Beers. He established the Free Diamond Market at Pra, near Accra, which he hoped might become the center for trade in all black African rough, through which all of his brothers might circumvent the CSO and reach the cutters more directly. The Free Diamond Market was to be a congregating spot where licensed buyers could buy rough from the licensed diggers and export it, all under close government supervision. It was expected to maximize the prices paid to the diggers, thereby ensuring the greatest flow of foreign currency into the country and also generating the maximum government revenues from export duties. The market failed to live up to expectations and in 1963 was replaced by a government agency, the Diamond Marketing Corporation (DMC), to which all diggers—and CAST—were required to sell their output. The DMC, in turn, liquidated (and liquidates) its purchases at auction. It is still the sole legal mechanism for selling and exporting all of Ghana's diamond production, but Ghana's output is now reduced to perhaps 1.3 million carats, and the overall role of diamonds in Ghana's economy now approaches insignificance.

In 1972 Ghana nationalized a 55 percent interest in CAST's operations and the name of the mining entity became Ghana Consolidated Diamonds. The terms were negotiated, but CAST didn't have much of a bargaining position and in the end had to accept the government's proposition. CAST was to be paid for the nationalized interest in cedis which could be exchanged for foreign currency at official rates and exported from Ghana. Payment, however, has been irregular, and since the nationalization dividends have been irregular too.

Ghana Consolidated has a more difficult position than most diamond companies. It is plagued by shortages, by the tendency of military governments to operate in a blizzard of decrees, and by the results of overrapid Africanization. Because of the small size of Ghana's goods, GCD must sort through a larger volume of media to find smaller and less valuable stones than other diamond companies, making for lesser hopes for profit. However, Ghana's stones have a desirable crystalline structure that gives them a better cutting edge for industrial purposes than synthetic diamonds or most other natural diamonds. They are especially desirable for setting into drill bits, which means that they can still command a respectable price for industrials. What gemstones there are in Ghana are almost exclusively "makeables," the less desirable rough that is usually cut in India. It is rare that the company ever recovers a piece of rough big enough to yield a one-carat polished diamond of whatever quality. Still, GCD's 1978 output of 1.25 million carats earned it an average of $12 a carat, as compared with MIBA's overall sale price of $7.77 per carat for Zairian goods.

Falling production is a bigger problem for GCD than low overall quality. Its output is now only half of what it was in the 1960s, and rapidly declining to the point when mining will cease to pay. People at Akwatia figure that it has only a couple of years left. Then, a fresh area on the lower Birim River might profitably be worked, if the financing necessary to bring it to production can be found. It is only a matter of years, however, before General Electric develops a synthetic diamond that will make a first-class drill bit, or until GCD's expenses, and especially the price of oil, escalate to prohibitive levels.

Ghana's small diggers may already have effectively terminated operations. In 1961 foreign exchange controls were first introduced in Ghana. Thereafter, diggers' sales through legitimate channels declined in direct proportion to declines in the value of the cedi. At most the diggers now turn over perhaps a few hundred carats annually to the Diamond Marketing Corporation, very much less than one percent of its volume, a great drop from the days when the diggers outproduced CAST. For these the diggers are paid in cedis, and—well, not even a Ghanaian wants a cedi. Whatever their real winnings are, they are smuggled out.

The Diamond Marketing Corporation sells the entire legitimate Ghanaian diamond production. It generally divides its merchandise into eighths: one-eighth is sold on the open market in Antwerp, so that the government can keep a pulse on the market; one-eighth is bartered with the People's Republic of China for bicycles and the like ("I don't know who ever gets the bicycles," said one GCD employee; "I've never seen one."); three-eighths are sold directly to CAST. The remaining three-eighths are auctioned off. Various licensed bidders make sealed bids for it, but CAST usually winds up with this portion too, giving it 75 percent of Ghana's production. Savvy Ghanaians explain this coincidence—quite possibly incorrectly—in terms of collusion. To left-oriented Ghanaians, steeped in the theory of the great Nkrumah, CAST's role as buyer negates the nationalization.

CAST's diamond-trading department consists of a man with the unlikely name of John Dimond, who operates for his concern as a one-man CSO. Dimond likes to try to control as much of the Ghana market as he can—like the CSO in the diamond world at large. He resells what he buys from the Diamond Marketing Corporation "various places." He acknowledges that "sometimes" CAST will sell to the CSO, but in my discussion with him he resisted any suggestion that CAST was buying merely as the agent for the CSO. He runs an independent operation. He has "other buyers," presumably in Antwerp. Like everyone in the diamond trade, he preferred not to be pinned down as to who or where.

Brazil, Venezuela, and Guyana are dotted with diamond miners' communities. Their overcrowded, unsanitary camps are peopled with whores, profiteers, and mostly by hardened mestizo adventurers, all with their peculiar seamy glamour. With few exceptions they are not "nice" people, and without exception, they are lawless people—except for the law of the jungle. Murders in fits of temper are common; so are murders for greed. Enter at your own risk.

How many carats South America produces is a matter of guess. Any official statistics there might be would be valueless because so much of the South American production is lost to the records in black market transactions and smugglers' pouches. Virtually all of its production is disorganized, the output of small mining companies and diggers, impossible to police or to trace. De Beers' estimate of the South American yield is a million carats annually, about 2 percent of total world production. Their guess should be as good as anyone's.

All of the South American production is alluvial, the workings concentrated along the rivers of southeastern Venezuela and central Guyana, and scattered throughout Brazil. In Venezuela there are men who dig and others who operate from dredges, but only one venture of imposing size, a dredging operation conducted by Sibeka, the Belgian company that directs the MIBA operations in Zaire. Makeshift dredges have supplanted the digger in most of Guyana as well. In Brazil, Sibeka and a few other combines employ million-dollar dredges, and hundreds or thousands of lesser entrepreneurs work from "vessels"—often wood platforms mounted on oil drums—with 1920s diving gear and buckets with which to haul the river bottom to deck level. There are only a few remaining diggers in Brazil, mostly old men reworking the rich areas of their youth. All of the Brazilian diamond miners must cope with one of the world's most corrupt, venal, and omnipresent set of officials.

South America is largely a closed market, which consumes most of the diamonds that it produces. In Guyana, for example, there is a large local market for diamonds, polished there in rudimentary factories and bought and sold surreptitiously by Guyanese who are thinking of flight insurance, or for protection against devaluation of the Guyanese dollar. The local market can usually pay more than export buyers can, and when Guyanese production is low, scarcely anything can be bought for export. Even when production is big, prices for those dealing at official exchange rates are usually higher than Antwerp market prices. Only by taking advantage of black market currency opportunities can an export buyer ever buy profitably there.

In Brazil probably 90 percent of the diamond production is consumed domestically, after being polished by the well-developed domestic cutting industry. Only in Venezuela are many diamonds left over for export, but rough prices in Ciudad Bolívar, the gateway to Venezuela's diamond territory, are usually in excess of Antwerp levels. Still there are usually a number of Antwerp buyers, an Israeli or two, and maybe a New Yorker in Ciudad Bolívar surveying the goods and generally making mistakes.

The Diamond Corporation claims to have no buying representatives anywhere in South America, and possibly does not. Because most of the South American goods are consumed domestically, South America

The modern history of the diamond world begins in Kimberley, South Africa, with the discovery of the diamond pipes, volcanic plugholes filled with diamond-bearing kimberlite. The pipes were dug out by small entrepreneurs, who worked their tiny claims at varying paces and hauled out their diggings by cable. The chaotic situation made consolidation both necessary and inevitable—and everyone with any imagination connived to centralize the control in his own hands. Above, the Kimberley Mine in 1877.

De Beers Consolidated Mines, Ltd.

A bizarre, driven giant, Cecil Rhodes (above) ultimately triumphed over Barney Barnato (right) to form De Beers Consolidated Mines, Ltd., in 1888. The company has controlled the diamond world ever since.

Rhodes's creation was in time taken over by Ernest Oppenheimer, son of a Jewish cigar merchant from Friedberg, Germany. Like Rhodes, Oppenheimer was to control many aspects of South Africa's economy.

Anglo American Corporation of South Africa

Anglo American Corporation of South Africa

Oppenheimer's son, Harry, remains in control of De Beers and of the other far-flung Oppenheimer interests. His Anglo American Corporation of South Africa is the key entity in the world gold trade, making him "King of Gold" as well as "King of Diamonds."

De Beers Consolidated Mines, Lt

Six of the eleven diamond pipes currently being worked by De Beers are mined "open cast." The Kimberlite is simply dug out of the pipe, creating a hole that constantly grows deeper. The other five pipes are "shaft mines" in which the miners travel far underground to burrow out the diamondiferous rock. The principal arteries in the shaft mines are cavernous, well lit, and well ventilated (above), but quarters are somewhat less comfortable in the farther reaches of the underground (below).

De Beers Consolidated Mines, L

The first step in separating diamonds from quantities of other material is to place everything in pans along with the heavier-than-water fluid. The mass is then rotated. Diamonds and other heavy materials will sink, but most of the lighter minerals will be swirled away to the sides and out the pan's exit hole.

De Beers Consolidated Mines, Ltd.

De Beers Consolidated Mines, Ltd.

Often the diamonds and the other heavy material are then passed with a stream of water over belts smeared with grease. The diamonds will stick to the grease, but most of the other material will be washed away.

Final separation of diamonds from chaff must always be done by human hands, sometimes working through "glove boxes." The only exit for a diamond is through a hole in the bottom of the box—into a locked safe.

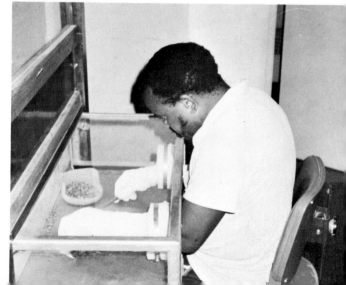

In the early days of the Namibian diamond industry, mining technique consisted of sending armies to crawl across the desert to collect the diamonds that studded the surface sands. It evolved into a capital-intensive operation directed from Oranjemund (below), a self-contained and self-sufficient symbol of the De Beers empire.

Much of the Namibian industry involves mining diamonds from the beaches. Millennia ago diamonds from the interior of South Africa were carried by rivers to the ocean, which disbursed them up and down the Namibian coast, depositing them like sea shells on the beaches of pre-history. The first step in recovering them is diking back the ocean. The men can work behind the dikes unconcerned about the angry seas beyond. Below, they are digging out the overlay of sands. The richest finds are usually made in the nooks and crannies of the bedrock itself. These are carefully swept by men using small hand brooms.

A series of diamond rushes have made small-scale diamond digging part of South Africa's cultural heritage, and private diggers still work alongside De Beers. Above, claims stakers scramble for the best locations at the sound of the starter's gun. Lichtenburg, South Africa, 1926.

Every few years some digger finds a great diamond, which keeps everyone's hopes alive. At left, Petrus Ramaboa displays his find, the "Lesotho Brown."

has no significant ripple effect on the world diamond market in general. So long as prices there are healthy, the CSO can let South America go its own way. De Beers' interests there are confined to prospecting: It is searching for that great kimberlite pipe someplace in Brazil. So are a thousand crazy guys. It may not even be there.

India, once the world's only diamond-producing country, is still at it, although its production is now relatively minuscule. There is no longer any regular diamond-seeking activity in the ancient diamond fields that made Golconda a synonym for "source of great wealth." The focus of Indian diamond mining has shifted and is now well confined to the area around misnamed Panna ("emerald" in Hindi) in the Indian state of Madhya Pradesh in north-central India.

The kimberlite pipe at Panna is worked as an open-cast mine by the government's National Mineral Development Corporation (NMDC), whose main business is to develop India's iron resources. In 1978–79 the NMDC did a gross iron business of $120 million—but ran it at a financial loss. Its small diamond business, $3.3 million gross, produced a profit of just under $1 million.

How long diamonds can remain profitable for the NMDC is another question. Panna was never a great diamond pipe or even a commercially significant one and its production is declining. Only its low labor costs—the typical Panna employee earns 400 rupees or $50 a month—have kept Panna open.

NMDC's problems are complicated by outmodedness and inadequate security. Its process for recovery of diamonds from concentrate is scarcely advanced from that of the most primitive Sierra Leone diggers. When the rotary pans have concentrated the kimberlite/diamond particles as much as is feasible, the concentrate is poured onto a concrete platform; sari-clad barefoot women then quickly sort through it to pick out the diamonds. As a security matter, the women who pick out the diamonds from the concentrate are supposed to work with one hand only, and to keep the other hand firmly planted in the crook of the hip. The "unemployed" hand is never supposed to touch the concrete platform. During my visit to Panna, however, one of the three sorters on duty occasionally dropped her "other" hand to the sorting area. By a curious quirk, the small independent diggers who ring the official mining area occasionally turn up large and valuable stones, while the NMDC produces almost only "smalls." Meanwhile, the security guards at NMDC stubbornly resist promotions or transfers.

Panna's output is sold every two or three months at auctions held in Bombay, Panna, or Madras, but both total volume and individual lots are too small—and prices too high—to attract foreign buyers.

Because output is small, NMDC can make more careful sortings than bigger producers. This enables it to encourage participation by particular buyers, and to cater to particular—sometimes exotic—markets. NMDC sells, for example, a large class of brown industrials that might bring $7.50 a carat on the world market. Indian cutters polish them as gems and they are then mounted into dog collars, hot sales items on the Saudi market. India has a stranglehold on the Arabian market for diamond-studded dog collars. NMDC sorts with an eye on this particular market (among others) and at auction the dog collar rough brings $40 a carat.

Not far from the NMDC's pipe, diggers work alluvial patches using the basic techniques used by labor-intensive diggers everywhere. In 1978 the government issued some eight thousand licenses to diggers—who found a total of 1,084 stones, most of slight value. That they will work the four- to six-month digging season and find nothing at all, and then return season after season to try again, is a crisp example of Hindu fatalism at work.

Diamonds have been discovered at scattered locations throughout the United States, including one diamondiferous kimberlite pipe that is currently being "worked" at Murfreesboro, Arkansas.

The Murfreesboro pipe isn't much of a diamond mine by world standards. It was discovered in 1906, prompted a diamond rush to the area (momentarily known as Kimberley, Arkansas), and was worked commercially off and on in the early part of the twentieth century. It was never successful as a commercial diamond mine. Local people are wont to ascribe its failure to intrigues, suits, arson, and to the machinations of "Baron Oppenheimer," the precise nature of whose hostile moves nobody still living can be quite certain about. They resist the possibility that its failure was due to inadequate yields and qualities, and dismiss a 1948 US Bureau of Mines conclusion to that effect as having been based on inadequate testing. It is not unlikely that a fresh look, with diamond prices vastly increased in the past thirty years, might prompt a different conclusion, just as the "unworkable" pipes in Sierra Leone are now deemed "workable."

Commercial exploitation now seems unlikely, however. The pipe was purchased by the State of Arkansas and since 1972 it has been operated as the Crater of Diamonds State Park, a tourist attraction. Pay two dollars and come in and mine diamonds. Thousands of tourists do so annually. In 1980, 581 diamonds were found, mostly of nominal value only, with a total weight of 192.35 carats.

Most of the Murfreesboro miners come as families out for a day of recreation, scratching around in the "yellow ground" with simple hand garden tools, or merely peering closely at the surface in the hopes that a glitter may catch the eye. In 1975 one tourist found a 16.37-carat stone, the Amarillo Yellow, valued at $100,000 (by an anonymous evaluator). Fully half the diamonds, however, are found by a small corps of regulars, veritable diamond diggers who work that section of the park where the pipe's alluvials would most likely have collected. They dig their "Maracca pits" to respectable depths and process their diggings in a one-step modification of the washing technique used by diamond diggers in "serious" digging areas. Only a couple of them earn enough at it to make a living.

Murfreesboro diamonds are prized more as local curiosities than as diamonds, and their value declines the farther one gets from Murfreesboro.

The domestic need for industrials prompted Chinese exploration for diamonds. Xsinhua, the Chinese news agency, reported in charming dialectic in 1976 that "before the great cultural revolution China was slow in locating diamond deposits owing to obstruction resulting from Liu Shao-ch'i's revisionist line, and imperialists, revisionists, and reactionaries tried to strangle her by withholding supplies of industrial diamonds. In the great cultural revolution, China has mobilized the masses to work on locating and reporting on diamond and other ore deposits." The masses, possibly with the help of some trained geologists, have now located at least two major diamond pipes, probably more, with output estimated by K. P. Wang, Far Eastern expert at the US Bureau of Mines, at between 1.8 and 2.8 million carats annually. As a result, Chinese purchases of industrials from both the CSO's Industrial Distributors and on the Antwerp market, once of impressive levels, have dwindled to almost nothing. Xsinhua calls China's accomplishments a victory in "the struggle to beat back the right deviationist wind." Probably none of China's pipes have yet entered full production.

In the West one hunts diamonds for gems and the industrials are the by-product. The reverse is true in China, where domestic demand for diamond engagement rings is still unimpressive. The gems, probably 20 percent of the total caratage, are being cut by the embryonic Chinese cutting industry.

Australia could develop into the great diamond-producing country of the 1990s. Diamond findings in the Kimberley section in the far north of Western Australia (named after the same Kimberley who gave his name to the center of the South African industry) have prompted a diamond rush to the region, which is desolate and uninviting even by Australian standards. The major prospectors are not the adventurers and sourdough types of previous diamond rushes, but great mining houses, including both De Beers and Selection Trust. Most successful in its prospecting efforts to date has been the "Ashton group," a syndicate of mining companies led by Conzinc Riotinto of Australia, the leading mining entity down under, which has discovered a large number of diamondiferous kimberlite pipes and retrieved several thousand carats in the process. The Australian stock market is periodically abuzz with reports of Ashton's doings, and stock in Conzinc and the other Ashton participants has soared. After several years of exploration and testing and the expenditure of upwards of $20 million, however, it is still not completely certain that any of Ashton's pipes can be made payable, and if they can be made payable, it will be several years before they can be brought to production.

Prospecting alongside the corporate giants with their sophisticated techniques and unlimited capital are a large number of much lesser mining companies whose stocks are known in the Australia stock market as "penny dreadfuls." Then there are also the spiritual descendants of the men of the Klondike, the undercapitalized fellows who are prospecting and staking claims with more hope than knowledge. Many of these little men are clustered in the immediate vicinity of a curiously named body of water, Lake Disappointment.

De Beers' attitude toward the mines of the future is not hostile. Sir Ernest said in 1927, "A new discovery of diamonds, whether mine or alluvial, is in itself no danger to the trade. On the contrary, a discovery from time to time will secure the continuity of the diamond trade. The real risk in a new discovery is irrational exploitation of such a discovery." Irrational exploitation means production on an excessive scale or distribution of the diamonds in a manner that might threaten market stability—i.e., production and distribution outside of the CSO scheme. But just as the De Beers can work with the Russians and the Angolans, it can work with the Chinese and the Australians. If production is on a truly significant scale, it must be worked within the CSO scheme or be worthless—along with the output of every other diamond producer. Important producers need "the Syndicate" just as much as the Syndicate needs the important producers.

PART II

INSIDE AND OUTSIDE THE DIAMOND MONOPOLY

◆

I'm just a bee, going around picking at flowers and bringing honey to De Beers.

—One of De Beers' customers

16

MONOPOLY IN MOTION

◆

The Diamond Trading Company decides what to supply and how much to supply, whom to supply, when to supply, and where to supply. Its measure of control and power reaching all around the globe is an economic echo of the great British East India Company. When David Neil-Gallacher told me, "The sun never sets on De Beers," his face assumed a nostalgic cast; he was thinking of the good old days when there were a lot of things British on which the sun never set.

Neil-Gallacher was my most constant contact with De Beers—the face of the empire. He is a youngish man, a solicitor by training, and said that his position with De Beers was his first commercial public relations position. It took some prodding before he would disclose his next prior employment: he had been press secretary for "Her Majesty" for four years. Neil-Gallacher is correct down to his pin stripe, his walking stick, and his hard bowler hat—the traditional English executive's costume that has now been abandoned by most British executives. In the impeccable-English-gentleman department, he makes Sir Anthony Eden look like a noisy tourist from the Bronx. He is also a man of tremendous charm and not a little humor. His is an attractive face for an empire.

The office of De Beers' chief of public relations is furnished with the same concern for tradition that typifies the rest of the De Beers operation, with only one modernist touch: an electric wastebasket that shreds anything that might be tossed into it. De Beers has traditionally wrapped as much of its doings as possible in a veil of secrecy. This has given the company a more sinister aura than it now deserves, for it is becoming somewhat more open. De Beers and the DTC no longer "classify" everything CIA-style. With writers, at least, the company now seems to operate on the assumption that the suppositions of journalists are likely to be even worse than the truth, and that fuller, franker discussions are likely to produce more favorable write-ups. I was surprised and impressed with Neil-Gallacher's candor.

Still, many areas are off limits, and Neil-Gallacher's answer to many questions was the simple, "I cannot say." Profits are an especially sensitive area. De Beers publishes total group profit figures, but remains highly secretive about what portion of its profits come from its production of diamonds and what portion from its merchandising efforts. Its annual reports for years prior to 1979, however, did give a clue as to the division: The report for calendar year 1978 says, "The geographical analysis of Group profit after tax is as follows: South Africa, 33 percent; South West Africa/Namibia, 20 percent; Elsewhere, 47 percent."

David Fitzpatrick, Merrill Lynch expert on De Beers, estimates that Botswana's contribution to the "Elsewhere" column is about 7 percent, and that just about all the rest of the "Elsewhere" represents profits from the merchandising effort: 40 percent or about $350 million profit a year for distributing its own and most of the rest of the world's rough diamonds.

If accurate, $350 million would represent De Beers' share of the CSO profits, not total CSO profits, some of which flow to other Oppenheimer-group entities. From the collection of annual reports of all of the publicly traded Oppenheimer companies (De Beers, Anglo American, Anamint, and Charter Consolidated) it is impossible to know with certainty the profits derived from diamond distribution by any one of them, or to put together the profits picture of any of the CSO entities—let alone to compute out the total CSO earnings. The figure can be pieced together only very imperfectly, by building speculation upon speculation. Figure, maybe, $500 million a year out of total DTC sales (which the company does report) of $2.7 billion in 1980.

The CSO's margin of profit on the productions of the major producers who contract with the Diamond Corporation averages 20 percent, which after expenses probably nets the CSO operation roughly 8 percent net profit on those transactions. The rest of the CSO profits are generated by the sale of De Beers-mined stones. If correct, it probably means that the "cost basis" of the stones that De Beers mines is about 20 percent of the sales price; and further, that De Beers is allocating a very hefty share of the profit to the selling entities.

Oppenheimer-group decision makers are in a position to channel profits back and forth between their entities pretty much as they want, and almost certainly do so with an eye to tax and possibly other considerations. By adjusting intergroup sales prices the total Oppenheimer-group profits from, say, CDM's output can be apportioned so as to lie in greater or lesser amounts in Namibia, South Africa, or Britain. Many analysts believe that CDM looms significantly larger in De Beers' total picture than the company admits; that it has allocated an inordinate proportion of CDM-generated profits to the merchandising account, either to minimize the bite of the hungry Namibian tax collector or to fuzzy the degree of company dependence on CDM.

Just as profits can be moved within or out of the grasp of this or that tax collector, they can be moved into or out of the pockets of this or that set of Oppenheimer-company stockholders. Were any of the various entities United States corporations, the machinations of profit allocation would be subject to the scrutiny of potentially dissident minority stockholders, but that is not the case with British and South African corporations, where minority stockholders must be content with what they get or get out.

The DTC is the selling arm of the empire. It controls the flow of diamonds onto the market and the price of them, two interrelated matters. Its decisions turn on fine balances of economics, politics, and personalities.

Let us begin our discussion of prices and DTC control of diamond prices with some basic economic theory: if supply is great and demand is slight, prices will be weak. If supply is tight and demand vigorous, prices will be high. For many years diamond demand has been relatively inelastic: It has been some largish percentage of newly engaged couples, a percentage that has been influenced upward by De Beers' institutional advertisements. At the moment, 77 percent of American affianced, close to 60 percent of Japanese engaged couples, and lesser numbers of everybody else, are going to buy a diamond engagement ring, as predictably as death and taxes. Price rises will force the young couple to settle for a smaller or poorer quality stone than Aunt Mary owns, but are not likely to drive them out of the market.

The substitutability of lesser for better stones to buyers who have a budgeted amount to spend and are going to spend it (and maybe a little more) on whatever they can get, makes the concept of "too expensive" largely inapplicable in the diamond world. The DTC is therefore in the happy position of being able to restrict supply and push up prices free from the constraints that limit most purveyors. Solly Joel, Barnato's nephew and Sir Ernest's ally, commented at a 1917 De Beers board meeting, "Why sell a million carats for one million pounds when you can sell five hundred thousand for two million? . . . The higher the price the fewer diamonds we have to give them. I can assure you we shall give them very few for a lot of money." The problem for De Beers has been, simply, to determine how few it must give them to get the most money.

The principal check on the company's price list is its own enlightened self-interest. Neil-Gallacher said calmly, "Diamonds are only valuable as long as people keep faith in their value." Keeping faith in the value of the diamond is the principal objective of CSO policy; it means preventing a decline in the retail price of diamonds, which would shake the faith of the public in the "forever" quality of the diamond's value. Harry Oppenheimer believes that "copper can plummet in price without affecting its long-range prospects. But a sharp drop in diamond prices would destroy confidence—no one would buy them."

The company's pricing policy is therefore largely concerned with preventing diamond prices on the consumer's market from spurting to temporary highs that might be unrealistic in view of ongoing demand and that would be followed by faith-shaking retreats to lower price levels. Only when it is satisfied that the balances are right to support a permanent DTC price increase will the DTC increase prices. It is not interested in maximizing today's profits, but in maximizing the century's profits. This concentration on the long-term interest results in the seemingly anomalous situation of the monopolist keeping its own prices low. It is only an example of enlightened self-interest at work.

As the DTC tells it, it does not take the impetus to price rises, but rather trails the market, increasing its prices only as increased demand justifies doing so. It can follow the trend of demand by following the price of rough in Antwerp, where rough—most of it rough that came from the DTC—is traded back and forth, making an active if informal market at premiums or discounts from DTC prices. When premiums become substantial in Antwerp and sustained over a period of time, the DTC believes that it can safely increase prices, and it does. Its buyers and their buyers tell the DTC—through their own pricing conduct on the Antwerp market—when the DTC should raise prices.

It is also true, however, that to some extent De Beers does what most Americans believe the oil companies do: that it holds back goods in demand, aggravating a supply/demand imbalance that leads to higher prices on the open market; then it raises its prices and begins releasing more goods onto the market at the new prices. It follows the market upward—after influencing the market to move upward by restricting supply. Diamond people see it happening all the time.

DTC price rises are generally announced in terms of an overall price increase of a stated percentage, with different grades increased more or less than overall, those qualities of stones for which demand has most increased being increased the most in price. Since September of 1949, the DTC's overall price increases, as tabulated by the Technical Committee of the Gem & Jewellery Export Promotion Council of the Government of India, have been as follows:

Month of price increase		Overall price increase percent	New price (adjusted from base price of 100)
September	1949	25	125.00
March	1951	15	143.75
September	1952	2 to 2.5	147.30
January	1954	2	150.25
January	1957	5.7	158.80
May	1960	2.5	162.78

Month of price increase		Overall price increase percent	New price (adjusted from base price of 100)
March	1963	5	170.92
February	1964	up to 10	188.00
August	1966	7.5	202.12
November	1967	16.6	235.67
September	1968	2.5	241.56
July	1969	4	251.22
November	1971	5	263.78
January	1972	5.4	278.03
September	1972	6.10	294.99
February	1973	11.00	327.45
March	1973	7.00	350.37
May	1973	10.00	385.40
August	1973	10.2	424.72
January	1975	10.0	467.19
January	1976	3.0	481.20
September	1976	5.75	508.88
March	1977	15	585.21
December	1977	17	684.60
August	1978	30	890.10
September	1979	13	1005.81
February	1980	12	1126.5

When the DTC does increase prices, not even the syndicate brokers—the agents between the DTC and its buyers—get more than a few moments notice of the increases. But it does not much matter. By then everyone in the diamond world has been reading the flow of stones and hoarding those that have been coming into shorter supply, in anticipation of the price increase.

To the extent that De Beers does think in terms of maximization of short-run profits, it does so only in terms of keeping the price spread between rough and polished diamonds small, garnering as much of the price of the finished product as it can as the cost of the rough. Indeed, since the USSR has entered the diamond world, the survival of the CSO system has come to depend on its keeping the spread small. The Russians sell both rough through the CSO and polished directly to wholesalers on the world market. If the spread between rough and polished becomes too large, the Russians will cease selling rough and will sell only polished; the CSO's percentage of control will fall below crucial levels and the system will fall apart.

To date the DTC has been remarkably successful in "spread management." The price differential between the wholesale price of rough and the wholesale price of polished has rarely been as high overall as 25 percent.

Maintaining the ongoing value of the diamond while keeping the spread within acceptable limits makes for a task at least as complex as that of managing the value of the Japanese yen on the world currency markets. The DTC has been more successful than most central bankers or finance ministers, none of whom can claim to have preserved the value of their currency for as long a period as the DTC can boast: Diamond prices have increased steadily since 1934, without suffering significant setbacks.

17

SIGHTS AND SIGHTHOLDERS

◆

Because the CSO controls (we will call it) 80 percent of the world's rough diamond production and the output of all of the major, well-organized producers, the DTC is the only rough supplier big enough to be able to meet the needs of a major diamond-cutting works on a regular, reliable basis. It sells to some three hundred of them, known as sightholders, through "sights" at which the buyers appear, inspect the goods that are being offered to them (hence the name "sight"), and accept them or refuse them. They will not often refuse.

Sights are held in London, with less commercially significant sights held in Kimberley (for sale to South African–based cutters of diamonds mined within South Africa) and in Lucerne. Lucerne sights were inaugurated only in recent years, for sale only of melee rough, rough that will produce medium-small diamonds. In all three locations the sights are organized on the same basis, and run in very much the same way they were in the days of the first syndicate in the 1880s.

Ten times a year the DTC advises sightholders of the dates of the upcoming sight, and solicits their orders. The sightholders reply that they want so many carats of this and so many of that. All totaled, the CSO sorts into some 2,500 different size/shape/color/quality categories, any of which might be requested. Everyone would *like* the same thing: whichever of the 2,500 categories of stones are currently in big demand, whichever have a ready market, whichever are then selling at a premium over DTC list price on the open market. But everyone knows that they are going to get pretty much what they've always received, or maybe a little worse. There is no point to the Bombay operators, who have traditionally received the very worst quality stones, requesting the material that will produce one carat D-flawlesses, or even requesting "Israeli-type" goods. They are not going to get them.

Each buyer channels his request through his Syndicate broker, the London agent who represents him in his dealings with the DTC. The broker may make special argument to the DTC as to why it should meet his client's specific requests, but as there are only four brokerage firms, each with a long list of clients, no one sightholder can expect particularly vigorous representation.

When all the requests are in, the DTC makes up parcels for each buyer, attempting to give each his reasonable wants—as the DTC might regard them to be reasonable. No one ever gets precisely what he has ordered; everyone gets fewer of the stones he has requested. On the other hand, the DTC considers just as carefully its own position: what it wants to "move." Its power as the dominant seller over the most significant buyers of rough diamond enables it to foist unordered goods on the buyers pretty much as it wants, and most sightholders' boxes will include some stones that the sightholder has not requested and can't use. When the DTC believes that speculative buying in the Antwerp market has reached levels that are unhealthy for the trade it will attempt to crimp speculation by giving its sightholders significantly more expensive parcels than they have ordered, so as to sop up some of the diamantaires' extra capital.

When completed, there may be a few boxes priced under $100,000 (the DTC sells in dollars) being sold to Indian cutters and some $250,000 boxes going to small shops in the *kempen* (countryside) region outside Antwerp; there will be a few priced upward of $5 million. In 1979 the average box went for about a million.

Sights last a full week ("sight week") and are held in London every five weeks. Most of the sightholders will come to London from Antwerp, Tel Aviv, Bombay, or New York to inspect and accept or reject the parcel that has been specifically prepared and earmarked for each. Some sightholders will spend as much as two or three hours studying their parcel and may get a good feel for its contents and its value, but no one ever makes more than a general survey of the parcel. Others don't come at all, but leave the inspecting and decision making to their syndicate broker, who will invariably accept the parcel on behalf of his client. Most look at their million-dollar boxes only cursorily for ten or so minutes—"as a matter of courtesy," one of the ten-minute boys told me. Most go not to inspect but to kibitz with each other, exchange news and gossip from the different cutting centers, and speculate on what "the Syndicate" is going to do next. They learn even from the exaggerations (not to say lies) that they hear from one another. Many will bring with them their "great" stone, the major stone that each has recently cut, in hopes that one of their peers will insist on buying it. None of these stones is ever for sale—but of course, if you want to make an offer . . .

At the end, each is almost certain to take his box. The price is not negotiable and the contents are not negotiable. The company cannot permit buyers to pick and choose, taking some items and leaving others, because then it would be left with all of the least desirable stones. It is an axiom in the diamond business that when the good stones and the "rubbish" are sold as a lot, you end up getting more for the rubbish. If you do not like your box, no, you cannot look at an alternate box. It's a take-it-or-leave-it proposition, and everyone knows that if he leaves it, without a very powerful explanation, he will probably not be invited back again.

Depending on market conditions, the DTC may or may not give its buyers itemized bills for their boxes. At the time of my visit there in the summer of 1979 they gave only a bottom-line bill which could not be reviewed and added up like a restaurant check. The DTC wants its buyers to look at their parcels as a whole, rather than to focus on the price of particular components within their boxes. When the DTC gives a fully itemized bill, sightholders can compare what the DTC charged this one for that and that one for this; charges of favoritism, always made softly, are then made more loudly, and the DTC office is sometimes rocked by a chorus of kvetches. This makes for what the DTC calls "an unhealthy climate." Things are easier when only a gross bill is given.

While giving a gross bill makes it hard for the diamantaire to audit his account with the DTC, it also makes it hard for internal revenue services to audit the diamantaire, who is free to substitute in and out of his parcel, and to misrepresent to his country's taxing authorities what he has received for all that money paid to the DTC.

One class of stones is always closely inspected: "special stones," those over 14.8 carats. The DTC does not have a book price for these; each is separately evaluated by a team of DTC valuators who put a price on it. The sightholder can negotiate the price of a special, according to the company, "within narrowly confined limits." Sightholders insist that the limits are somewhat more flexible; that at London sights, the prices of special stones are invariably pegged very much above what the DTC expects to get for them. It expects to be bargained on every one of them, and it is. One sightholder told me, "It's their chance to be Jewish." A sightholder can refuse a "special" with no hard feelings.

The DTC is represented in such sessions by one of several experts. Americans usually meet with George Burne, a reasonable sort. Burne is one of the DTC's impeccable English gentlemen, but he can bargain with the best of Jews, which is what in fact he is doing. It is a highly sophisticated form of bargaining, very different from the colorful *hondling* (haggling) of the diamond clubs, where buyers say it's bad and sellers say it's good. The buyer must show Burne what can be made from the piece, and convince him how much the polished will bring. Burne argues back, but almost always concedes to lower the price, sometimes by as much as 40–50 percent. He has his own "price list," which tells him how low he can go. Occasionally a buyer can convince Burne that even his bottom-line figure is too high. Burne cannot go below that, but he can and will send the stone "back upstairs" for reevaluation and then put it back in the sightholder's box at a later sight at a new and lower price. Some suspect that the DTC plays games with special stones in an effort to test the sightholder's skill and mettle.

Routine stones make for routine profits or losses; special stones make for big profits or small losses. Everyone wants them.

Payment is made by bank transfer direct to the DTC's account. The DTC does not give credit. After payment is confirmed, the parcels are mailed to the recipients. Diamonds are almost always sent by registered, insured mail, and diamond people generally regard this as the safest mode of delivery.

For the past several years the DTC has generally sold at lower prices than rough was trading for on the open market. Equally important, buying from the DTC ensures the sightholder of a regular flow of stones, a regular flow of work for one's employees (not a matter of sentiment but of keeping good workers), and a regular stock of supply for his customers. Most who become sightholders become dependent on the DTC for virtually all of their supply, and live from sight to sight for the work that keeps them going. In the diamond trade it is a mark of real distinction and of personal recognition for a manufacturer to become a sightholder. Together the sightholders function as an oligopoly of their own, operating under the umbrella of the DTC monopoly. *Diamant*, the international diamantaires' magazine published in three languages in Antwerp, calls the sightholders "the monopoly within the monopoly."

There are disadvantages, too, to being a sightholder. During most of the first half of the 1970s the sightholder paid more for his stones than open market price, and those who sold their DTC boxes usually had to sell at a discount. Sightholders who profit from the relationship in the good times are expected to continue placing orders and buying goods in uninviting times and at uninviting prices.

Some few who might have the choice prefer not to cast their lot and fate with the sightholders. M. Fabrikant & Sons, one of the world's largest wholesalers of polished diamonds, is one of the big operators that is not, and does not want to be, a sightholder. At times when DTC boxes command large premiums, Fabrikant has it harder than the DTC sightholders, but even then, there are always some classes of material, rough or polished, that can be picked up at a good price in the right market. With its worldwide chain of offices and correspondents, Fabrikant has a pulse reading on every market. In lean times it is able to buy rough more cheaply than the sightholders and to pick up DTC boxes at discounts from the syndicate's price. The nonsightholder has greater flexibility, but his operation requires more coordination and fancier footwork than the sightholder's. Dealing with the DTC is the easiest way, and for the past several years has been the most profitable way to acquire rough diamond.

In the lean times when DTC boxes sell at a discount, it is fairly easy to become a sightholder, but there haven't been lean enough times since 1974 or 1975. For the past several years it has been very difficult indeed. What the DTC looks for in considering prospective sightholders is a well-established, sound manufacturing business with broad-based sales outlets, not dependent on a single important customer who may switch patronage or fold, and—perhaps most important—financial strength and stability. A lot of goods in weak hands might turn a temporary recession into a major collapse of diamond prices and imperil everybody's ship. Financially potent sightholders, however, are not going to make desperation sales every time that the market softens, as it periodically does; they are in a position to be patient and to hold the price line. Maintaining stability of diamond prices all along the distribution pipeline goes hand in hand with the maintenance of the stability of Oppenheimer-group profits; the two are the co-raisons d'être for the CSO system.

People can enter the diamond business with little or no fixed investment, and can leave without serious economic loss. It is most important for the prospective sightholder to impress the DTC with his determination to remain in the trade. Under the right circumstances a newcomer can make the requisite impression. K. C. ("Casey") Liu, Hong Kong's only sightholder, got in without prior experience as a diamond manufacturer. All it took was the construction of a brand-new factory building, especially designed as a diamond-polishing works and built on Hong Kong Island with its staggering land costs, and the installation of eighty expensive (and at the time largely unsalable) Piermatic Automatic Diamond Polishing Machines, merchandised by a De Beers affiliate. Liu was given no encouragement by the DTC: none when he first discussed his intentions with them; none when he showed them the plans for his factory building; none at groundbreaking; none even when he placed the order for his Piermatics. When it was done the DTC inspected and then spoke: It was good. The investment involved let the DTC know that Liu was financially powerful and determined to become, and to remain, an important factor in the world diamond trade—precisely the kind of person with whom the DTC wants to deal. The Casey Diamond Company became a sightholder. It was simple.

As a rule of thumb, the DTC will more readily consider people in a position to accept million-dollar sights. Except for the Indian manufacturers, who accept and process otherwise unsalable stones, it doesn't pay the DTC to talk to modest buyers. When they say "wholesale," they mean wholesale. Anyway, a modestly priced sight would not be particularly attractive: It would necessarily exclude the bigger, more expensive stones which promise the greatest profit to the manufacturer.

The DTC considers most closely the compatibility of the proposed sightholder's enterprise with its own long-term objectives. At the moment they are unreceptive to "contractors." A contractor is a manufacturer who has no cutting shop or employees of his own, but sends the rough he buys around to others for finishing on a contract basis. A contractor is more likely to be or to become a commercial parasite than a manufacturer with a factory and employees. Because he has none of the social responsibilities of an employer, the contractor is also less of a social asset to the country in which he operates. What is best for De Beers or the DTC often tends—quite incidentally—to be best for the diamond-producing and -cutting countries.

Geography matters too. At the moment the DTC would like to see more countries with low labor costs establishing cutting businesses, to serve as foils to the Indian manufacturers who are now the DTC's only outlet for low-grade "gem" stones. The DTC does not like to be without alternative outlets. The Indians demonstrated the risk to the DTC by refusing, en masse, to accept any goods whatsoever at one sight in the spring of 1978. Anyone who wants to make a significant investment of his own to open a cutting shop in a cheap labor country is likely to be viewed more favorably by the DTC than someone who wants a sight for yet another factory in Tel Aviv or Antwerp.

The prospective sightholder begins by talking things over with one of the four syndicate brokers, I. Hennig & Co. Ltd., W. Nagel, Bonas & Company Ltd., or J. P. Morgan. The broker will interpret for him the unwritten constitution of the DTC, and discuss with him those aspects of his operation that are likely to be viewed as negatives by the DTC, and what he must do to put himself in a better light in the eyes of the syndicate. The broker will work with him to put his house in order, and will begin talking him up at the DTC, educating the syndicate about the prospect and his role in the diamond business. He needs a persuasive man, a can-do spokesman, to become a sightholder. Generally the syndicate broker charges no fee for this service; his fee comes by way of commission after the prospect has been accepted as a sightholder.

Being a syndicate broker is not simply a matter of collecting commissions. There are real moral problems involved in his work: He is expected to represent both the syndicate and the sightholder who pays his fee. While he argues the client's position with the syndicate he is expected to—and does—function as an informal DTC agent vis-à-vis his client, and periodically reports on his client's doings—good or bad—to the DTC. He serves two masters who regularly have conflicting interests. Actually more than two. When the syndicate broker attempts to get hard-to-get classes of goods for client X he must frame his argument

with the DTC in terms of the relative "entitlement" of competing potential purchasers, and the situations that he knows best for comparison
purposes are those of his other clients. In his presentation he necessarily
must favor—if only by implication—the one or the others. He is at every
turn confronted with the question which of his many masters will he
serve and which will he slight. He operates more in the tradition of
the Jewish marriage broker than in the manner of the professional agent
in the American sense. In the end he probably resolves the question
of whom to serve in the same manner as most agents: by serving himself.

For grappling with the ethical dilemmas, the syndicate broker is
well paid: the client pays him a commission of one percent of his purchases from the DTC, call it $100,000 per client per year. When the
polished market is slow, DTC boxes are selling at a discount, and sightholders are continuing operations at a loss, the syndicate broker gets
his one percent anyway. When the DTC raises its prices to the sightholders' dismay, the syndicate broker must put on his long face and shake
his head in commiseration with his client, knowing, meanwhile, that
his own income has just increased by whatever percentage the DTC
has raised its prices. One percent of more is more. Over the past few
years, as the price of rough has doubled, the syndicate broker's commissions have doubled along with it, though his workload has remained
precisely the same. "If you should ever be born again," one sightholder
counseled me, "it should be as a syndicate broker."

"How do I become a syndicate broker?" I asked Neil-Gallacher.
"I really don't know the details of it," he said; "there hasn't been a
new one accepted in many years, not since Willie Nagel." I had heard
that name before; a nondiamond acquaintance had told me that his
friend Nagel had something to do with the syndicate in London; I might
call Nagel if I had a chance. I did, and the strength of his friend's name
brought an invitation to Nagel's office on Ely Place, just around the
corner from the DTC office on Charterhouse Street. When I arrived,
Nagel was on the phone negotiating the purchase of a choice diamond.
Diamond men are always on the phone, and Nagel feels most comfortable
with a telephone to his ear. He copes with an average of one hundred
phone calls a day. He makes most of them himself, many of them placed
during the middle of the night in London or received during the middle
of the night at the recipient's end, or both. I was shown into his office
mid-conversation, as Nagel told the party on the other end, ". . . maybe
someday it will be such a price, but not at the moment. What price is
your real price? If it's a serious price let me know, but not in telephone
numbers. . . . If you're not serious, I cannot offer you; give me serious
prices, all right?" He looked up and whispered to his new and unknown
visitor, "I can't get an answer out of this man!" ". . . How much? How
much?" Whatever the response may have been, Nagel pulled himself
away from the phone, looked at the receiver quizzically, and then turned

to me and muttered, "Let him be clever another time!" In a moment he was free.

After an exchange of pleasantries, I asked my question: "How does one become a syndicate broker?" Nagel answered with a you-don't-want-to-be-bored-with-that tone: "It's a secret." But no, I was serious: "How does one become a syndicate broker?" He gave the same answer again, but this time with a firmer tone: "It's a secret." He meant just that: It was a secret.

Nagel is a stocky man of medium height, with a bulldog quality to his face and a great lion's mane of gray hair. He is a vibrant, outgoing, and effervescent fellow, a bundle of nervous energy which he transfers to everyone around him; sharp, fast-moving, flexible; a powerfully attractive personality and a powerful, domineering personality. A can-do man. He continually works under high pressure and he works best under heavy pressure. He sleeps almost not at all and never has a real vacation because his mind is always on business. He is abrupt with his staff, but affectionately so; they have all been with him a long time, handle him with considerable success, and are not much intimidated by him. Nagel likes to talk and is talkative, but not as talkative as he is secretive. In many hours together he gave me the genuine hospitality of his warm household; amused me, buffaloed me, thoroughly charmed me; and from my first question onward, evaded all close questions and gave me virtually no information at all about the diamond world—and particularly, not about how one becomes a syndicate broker.

Once a manufacturer has been accepted as a sightholder he is likely to remain one as long as he abides by certain basic unwritten rules, most of which revolve around profiteering. Insistence that a sightholder order and buy regularly—and particularly in those times when he would really rather not—is an aspect of the antiprofiteering policy. In good times DTC boxes are a bargain, no one cuts back his order, and everyone wants as big a box as he can wangle. In hard times the sightholder is at a competitive disdadvantage with the nonsightholder. The sightholder may have to operate at a loss in slow times. These are the times when a sightholder might be tempted to pass up a sight or to cut back his order. He does so at his peril; if he reduces his order he will not be permitted to increase it during the next busy period. Worse, he has given the DTC a signal: He is unreliable.

Many will tell you about this fellow or that fellow: "One sight he missed, one; and the syndicate cut him off cold, after twenty years of doing business, just like that!" Neil-Gallacher insisted to me that such stories are apocryphal, that sightholders who pass up a sight "for good reason" will not be punished; and I spoke to a number of sightholders who have passed up sights with impunity. Still, the DTC considers regularity a most important criterion in evaluation of its sightholders. They, and the degree to which the CSO can rely on them, play an important part in the CSO's market regulatory effort. It does not need any fair-weather friends, and it does not like to be used.

Though the myth of one-pass terminations is incorrect, most sight-holders—even those who have passed up sights—more or less believe in it, and all appreciate the risks. Most sightholders have never missed a sight.

Box selling is more likely to bring retribution. In periods of vigorous demand (known to diamantaires as "bren markets," from the Yiddish *bren*, or fire), such as the early part of 1978, rough diamonds have sold for considerably more than polished diamonds. At such times a sight-holder can make a bigger profit and a much easier one by selling his box than he can by polishing his stones and selling polished diamonds. Such seemingly irrational markets periodically arise and threaten the DTC's control of prices, stocks, and supplies of both rough and polished. The DTC always attempts to combat such situations and restore an orderly market. Box sellers, however, fan the flames.

When the DTC awards a sightholder a box, it does so on the implied representation of the buyer that he is going to manufacture (polish) the stones and sell them as polished diamonds. The DTC wants to control the distribution of rough and it wants the DTC—not its sightholders—to make what profits are to be made from distribution of rough. It becomes very upset about those who sell off their boxes, other than the limited number of dealers who are given "dealer's boxes" with the understanding that the dealer will be selling the components at a profit.

Sightholders know as much, but the temptation is great in bren times, and one can usually sell his box quietly and safely. There are no papers within the box to identify the seller, and the outside identification marks can be obliterated from the box easily and without breaking the DTC's ornate wax seal. Any reputable rough dealer, whether a sight-holding dealer or an "outside" dealer, will be happy to handle the trans-action in confidence and in a manner that will preserve the seller's anonymity even from the buyer. The price will be DTC invoice price (the buyer never sees the name on the invoice) plus a premium, which in early 1978 approached 100 percent. A DTC box may be sold and resold several times before the seal is broken and the stones scattered to the ultimate purchasers.

Because the profit for the sightholder is fat and easy during a bren, and because boys will be boys, box selling is common. Neil-Gallacher told me, "If we terminated every time a sightholder sold a box, we would not have too many sightholders left." Still, the DTC regards box selling as a felony and will invariably discipline a box seller with tempo-rary suspension if not a permanent termination if they catch him. Recidi-vists will receive capital punishment—termination. Sightholders are even circumspect when selling off stones from their boxes that are unsuitable for their operations, so that the DTC does not get the wrong impression.

The DTC has to rely on circumstantial evidence in tracking down box sellers. If a sightholder is receiving a respectable allotment and is simultaneously laying off employees, the DTC knows that he is either selling his allocation as a sealed box, or is at least selling off significant portions of it. One former Antwerp sightholder told me of his own fate: He was receiving a manufacturer's box until one day a DTC agent stopped at his "factory." Where were his diamond polishers? The sightholder made explanations, but the explanations were not believed, and indeed, they were not true. He had closed up manufacturing and was hanging on as a surreptitious rough dealer for as long as he might. That week he was expecting a cable from the DTC soliciting his order for the next sight, but the cable never arrived. He was all done.

Even those with dealer's boxes do not have free range in their selling activities. A dealer's box is given to dealers who are expected to service those diamond manufacturers in their own area who are too small to receive a sight themselves. During the bren of 1978, the DTC asked the sightholding dealers of Antwerp whom they were servicing. It was given lists of names of small cutters in the *kempen,* cottage-industry people. When DTC agents visited the family-styled cutting shops they were told, no, the *kempen* cutters had no goods to polish; the dealers who claimed to be supplying them had ceased to supply them. Where had all the diamonds gone? To Israel, where the Antwerp dealers could get much better prices than their local customers could pay. The DTC wants to decide what goods go where, so that it can control, curtail, or support the growth and development, or simply maintain the status quo, of the cutting industries of the various cutting regions of the world. Heads rolled.

People may be terminated for reasons other than misbehavior. The DTC is constantly shifting its apportionment of stones between manufacturing sightholders and dealing sightholders. At the moment the dealers constitute a relatively small portion of its clients. In lean times, however, the DTC must depend much more on its dealing sightholders. Shifts of apportionments between the dealers and the manufacturers and back again lead to the dropping of "innocent" sightholders.

Usually the company will not lightly terminate a buyer. It does not seriously expect its sightholders to "be good" when momma is not watching, and most of them will not be. Occasionally a sightholder is "caught" and will be suspended from a sight or two or three, but only infrequently is one terminated, and then usually with heavy heart. Only when the company becomes enraged, as happened during the bren of '78, will it lash out in fury and terminate scores of sightholders for profiteering. Then, when it cools down, it takes many of them back.

On other occasions, however, the DTC may throw a sightholder out like an old shoe, merely because he has ceased to fill a role in the changing DTC picture. The DTC cannot permit—or at least operates as if it cannot permit—sentiment to interfere with its management of global diamond policy.

The syndicate broker usually has the burden of breaking the news to a terminated sightholder. The task is akin to telling someone of a bereavement, and the news of termination is likely to affect the sightholder in the same way. The economic implications are great and far-reaching. In addition to the economic losses incidental to termination, there is a tremendous loss of prestige and status among one's peers in the business, with customers and prospective customers, and with the bankers who deal with the diamond community. Termination cannot be kept quiet. Within a day of the DTC's decision, everyone at the local diamond club (the gathering places and bourses for diamantaires) knows that the DTC has terminated so-and-so. Competitors casually drop the word with one's customers. Terminated sightholders are likely to suffer adverse psychological and emotional effects, self-doubts, anxiety, and temporary sexual impotence.

Often sightholders in disfavor will be told that they have been "temporarily suspended." The DTC takes the position that those temporarily suspended must approach the company for goods afresh, like any other new applicant for goods, or almost afresh, and may or may not get them. Those temporarily suspended never know whether the suspension is really intended to be temporary. "Temporary suspension" is frequently a euphemism for "all done."

A distasteful degree of sycophancy is demonstrated toward the DTC by most everyone in the diamond world, and prompts major cutters to an undignified slobbering over the beauties of an operation *they* think to be squeezing them harder and harder. No matter their private thought, most diamantaires at whatever level, whether or not DTC sightholders, will curry its favor, in the hope that sometime in the far distant future, perhaps, the DTC may return the favor. Those who offend it, however distant from the font, may suffer for it—as a result of an indiscretion, they may never *get* to the font. On the other hand, getting along well with the DTC never hurt anyone. The Israeli government's onetime Diamond Controller Jonas Hatsor is now a better-paid employee of the I. Hennig firm of syndicate brokers; Amos Mar-Haim, once the Israeli cabinet official under whom diamond controllers served, is now a better-paid employee of Bonas & Co., another syndicate broker; one-time Diamond Controller Joseph Perlmutter left government service to become a better-paid employee of the syndicate broker W. Nagel. There are only four syndicate brokers, the fourth of whom does not yet have an Israeli diamond official, but if and when he gets one, it will not be one that has offended the DTC.

The minding of Ps and Qs was responsible for the lack of candor on the part of many of the men who granted me interviews. With some it was no doubt dictated by a sense of responsibility to employees and customers who would suffer as greatly as the diamantaire himself from any indiscretion. Others with whom I spoke, however, were ward heeler types interested in currying the favor of the big boy, hoping to be quoted in print singing paeans to the DTC. The ward heelers are an important element in the DTC's intelligence system. One diamond dealer told me, "The syndicate knows when you sneeze or take a leak. They have a spy system that would put the CIA to shame. They know everything there is to know about anyone of significance in the diamond world."

The company has faced only one rebellion and that one was abortive. In the spring of 1978, all but one of the fifty-six Indian sightholders failed to apply for goods for the May sight, as a protest against the prices and qualities of "Indian goods." At the next meeting of the World Federation of Diamond Bourses, an Indian proudly told me, "Everyone was congratulating us!" By the June sight, however, all fifty-six Indians were back in the row, nothing accomplished. And now the DTC is encouraging the establishment of cutting industries in Malaysia and other cheap labor countries. *Diamant* asks rhetorically, "Does it remember—and the Syndicate, like the elephant, never forgets—that the Indians, as one man, refused a sight in 1978?"

"We couldn't do what the Indians did," an Antwerp sightholder told me. "If we tried that, someone would call them up, tell them what was going on—and who the ringleaders were—and say 'but I'll take anyone's share that doesn't apply.' You have to admire the Hindus. . . ."

It should not be surprising that sightholders, whose fate depends on the DTCs, resent the supplier and their own role. They claim that DTC price rises in all but the larger and choicer qualities have outstripped the price rises in the polished diamond market, so that they have been "squeezed," their margins of profit—except on the larger and choicer stones—narrowed to paper-thin proportions. An Israeli expressed the common view to me: "The syndicate thinks they should get all of the profits, and don't want anyone else to get a fair share. Whenever they think we're getting too big a piece of the pie, they raise their prices and cut us down." Most of them do not believe the DTC when it speaks of its responsibility to get as much as possible for the producers; do not believe that the price increases are being passed on to the producers—at least not for a long time.

As for the larger, choicer, stones on which the diamantaires could make a big enough profit to make the whole operation worthwhile, a sightholder asked me, "Where are they? They aren't coming in my box. The syndicate says 'They're in short supply,' and I say *bubkes* [nonsense]. Yeah, yeah, I know, better stones are rarer than less good stones, but not *that* much rarer. They accuse *us* of hoarding; *they're* the ones that are hoarding. They're hoarding those stones off the market, keeping them in their vaults, and then when they've raised the price on them to levels that they like, that take away most of our profit, then we'll see them in our boxes. Don't tell me, 'in short supply.' "

Even on a personal level the typical sightholder does not much like the DTC. Most of them, Jewish or Gentile, are rather earthy guys without much polish, and they generally feel that the stuffy fellows at the DTC talk down to them and treat them with disdain. Some have dealt with their DTC counterparts for a decade, but none "know" them. One told me, "I don't mind being stuffed, but I like to be kissed when I'm being stuffed."

Most of them know relatively little about the workings of the DTC. The DTC likes it that way; the less information, the more dependence.

The more successful the diamantaire, the greater his own self-esteem, the more he resents his position and his dependence. None ever had greater self-esteem than the late Harry Winston, and none had greater resentment for the DTC; he described the CSO operation as "a very vicious system" to investigators from the United States Justice Department's antitrust division. Throughout life he searched for some great lode of diamonds that would free him from his dependence. In the early 1950s he hoped it might be Angola, and he negotiated directly with Portuguese dictator Salazar, almost but not quite to the point of success. When it looked like he was about to be successful, he told *The New Yorker,* "De Beers might make me a preferred client if I'd pass up the Portuguese deal, but I'd rather have an independent diamond supply, and I'm going to try to get it." It fell through. Then he tried Sierra Leone; then the Ivory Coast and Venezuela. But he died dependent on the group that he always believed was looking down on him—on him!

Many attribute isolated DTC decisions to corruptions within: this one or that one has a secret interest in this or that cutting firm, and uses his influence to favor "his" firm in allocation of in-demand rough; or, so-and-so bought his way onto the sightholder's list; or, DTC insiders trade on their inside information. When I asked Neil-Gallacher what, if any, internal checks the DTC had to prevent influential insiders from abusing their positions, he looked hurt and replied disarmingly, "We are honorable men." You just had to believe him—and I do. My own belief—and it is just a belief, there is no way to establish it—is that preferences at the DTC go to people who are commercially significant, rather than those who are well connected in a political sense or who try to bribe their way around; that top DTC decision makers have a rather high awareness of their responsibilities in both macro and micro arenas; that DTC operations are remarkably uncapricious; that those mistakes, unfairnesses, or injustices for which the DTC may be responsible are not based on whim or on personal likes and dislikes, and that to the extent that politics plays a role in DTC decision making, it is politics on a rather high level: special consideration (favoritism) is shown for those who are operating, or promise to operate, in accordance with the visions and plans that the DTC has for the future diamond world. This is not so bad: Within the diamond world, the DTC represents the most nearly socially progressive factor. All of this is hypothesis; the data necessary to test it would never be forthcoming.

Friction between the sightholders and the DTC reached unprecedented heights during and subsequent to the bren of 1978. If any single cause can be given for the bren or "fire" market in rough diamonds that climaxed in the spring of 1978, it is probably economic conditions in Israel.

From 1973 onwards, the Israeli diamantaires enjoyed an officially sanctioned tax holiday. They paid substantially no income tax. By early 1977 they were awash with cash, and no place to invest it. They witnessed wealth-evaporating devaluations of the Israeli pound, and a decline in the purchasing power of the dollar, the currency of the diamond trade. Instead of leaving their money in money, they began to put their money in the item that they best understood: diamonds, and especially diamond rough.

As the price of rough began to rise noticeably, those without cash began entering the upswing market. The government of Israel, in an effort to promote its export industries, subsidizes bank loans to exporters, and in the period of the bren, diamantaires could borrow up to 80 percent of the "value" of their rough. The valuators at the Israeli banks that cater to the diamond trade have always been "generous" in their valuations—and been encouraged by bank managements to be generous—so that 80 percent of value has often meant something in excess of 100 percent of the real purchase price. The interest rate for such loans at the time of the bren was 6 percent, less than the decline in purchasing power of the dollar, and less than the DTC's predictable annual price rises. More Israelis began to buy more rough at higher and higher prices. Prices on the open rough market in Antwerp rose, and DTC prices were adjusted upward by 15 percent in March of 1977 and another 17 percent in December of 1977, but as much as the DTC raised its prices, open market prices spurted ahead all the more.

Before the end of 1977 rough was selling at economic maximums. Open market rough prices for most goods then soared past the wholesale price of the polished diamonds that might be made from them, and premiums on rough approached 100 percent over DTC prices. Antwerp manufacturers and dealers shared as much of their goods as they could— at exorbitant profits—with the Israelis. Even Indian goods, not economically cuttable in Israel, reached premiums of 65 percent. Meanwhile, the world's diamond community stockpiled more and more rough and polished diamonds—some \$4 to \$5 billion in goods, and well more than double their usual inventories. Something over half of Israel's foreign currency reserves were lent and committed to fueling the speculation of its diamantaires, who could use essentially free money to buy goods that just seemed to keep going up and up. The Antwerp cutting industry was drained of its raw materials, to the impressive short-run profit of its diamantaires, and to the loss of its work force.

This kind of situation has multiple dangers for the DTC. It irritates producers, who see the diamonds that they sell through the CSO at \$X per carat selling on the open market for \$2X; they see themselves as being victimized, and begin to think about the wisdom of dealing with the CSO. It threatens to bring the bust that follows booms, that the CSO is dedicated to avoiding. It jeopardizes the balances between the cutting centers that the DTC maintains and controls in the best interests of itself and, arguably, of the diamond world.

The DTC was late in moving, but when it did, it moved on several fronts. Its most potent weapon was the institution for the first time of a "surcharge," a temporary price increase *declared* to be temporary. This made clear to the diamond world, and to its bankers, that the DTC was going to force the price of diamond rough to *drop*. A 40 percent surcharge was applied at the March sight. The surcharge sopped up some of the sightholders' extra cash, making it more difficult for them to participate in speculations (and also making for greater DTC profits). Then the DTC progressively reduced the surcharge to 25, 15, and 10 percent.

The DTC used its influence with the banks in hopes of tightening up credit. At first the Israeli banks, tied to their clients and eager for the government-subsidized business, were uncooperative, but when the DTC did reduce its surcharges, the bankers had to react more responsibly. They began tightening up, evaluating rough more realistically, and refusing to roll over their diamantaires' notes, thereby forcing liquidation of diamond stocks. The company announced in the world press in March 1978 that rough prices in the cutting centers were too high, one day after Tiffany, the important New York jewelers, had placed an ad in the *New York Times* telling the consumer that diamond prices were too high at the retail end. Together, the two announcements dampened enthusiasm for speculation as a sign of the lengths to which the DTC would go to kill it off.

The DTC arranged with the Belgian government to have the DTC's seals broken by Belgian customs and not replaced by customs' own seals, so that prospective repurchasers could no longer know with confidence that the box had not been tampered with. It also inaugurated a policy of jumbling goods within the box: The sightholder would view his merchandise in London, all carefully sorted into several hundred papers, each a different class of merchandise, but just prior to shipping all the papers were emptied out and their contents jumbled into a common bag. The effect of this (in addition to making for duplication of the tedious sorting effort) was that when the sightholder received his merchandise he would have to take it to his office and resort it with the help of his staff. They would know that he had gotten a box, and it would then be very much more difficult for him to take those stones away from his workers and sell them to Israelis. Jumbling also made it impossible for the diamantaire to sell the components of the box in their original DTC papers, representing them to be "as received from the DTC."

The DTC's heavy-handed battle strategy cooled off the bren rapidly. Before the end of the year premiums had been restored to normal levels, and the hoards of stones that had been accumulated by merchants in Israel, and to a lesser extent India, began being flushed out, at discounts of 20 percent. There were bankruptcies. The diamond trade suffered a recession as a result of the DTC's war against the bren, a difficult but necessary antidote to a threatening collapse that would have haunted the diamond world for a decade. Order was restored and diamond price stability was preserved—along with DTC control.

When the last of the surcharge was finally phased out in July of 1978, it was replaced the following month by a colossal 30 percent permanent increase in DTC prices, the biggest price rise in its history. Happy ending. To the DTC, the bren was just another example of the diamantaires' permitting their short-term profit motive from defeating the long-term best interests both of the CSO and of the diamantaires themselves.

Not surprisingly, the diamantaires—and especially the Israelis—tell it very differently. They lay responsibility for the bren squarely on the DTC, particularly two officials, Anthony Oppenheimer (son of Harry's cousin Philip, the ostensible head of the DTC), and Michael Grantham, chief of the DTC's Israeli desk. They insist that Oppenheimer and Grantham warned key Israeli diamantaires in mid-1977 that a severe shortage of goods was developing. Meanwhile, the DTC began reducing sight allocations to its Israeli buyers (or so the Israelis claim). The DTC well knew that the Israeli reaction would be the only responsible one: to stockpile (not "hoard") enough rough to be certain that their employees would have enough work to keep them going during the anticipated slowdown. So they did. Arieh Ketsef, longtime president of the Israeli Diamond Manufacturers Association, says, "If you're eating bread and hear there's going to be a shortage of bread, you must buy bread now."

The Israelis date the peak of the bren precisely: March 9, 1978—"two days before, everyone wanted to buy; on March 9, everyone wanted to sell," one told me. The DTC's surcharges followed, were instituted on the downswing, and were therefore unnecessary, according to the Israelis, who believe that the principal effect of the surcharge was to take diamantaires' money and transfer it to DTC pockets. Further, it forced those sightholding dealers who also bought on the outside markets to use up more of their capital for their DTC allotments, leaving less change for them to spend outside, and leaving a larger share of the outside market for the Diamond Corporation buyers. The DTC's announcement to the world—which the diamantaires commonly if inaccurately characterize as having said, "Don't buy diamonds"—was taken as an irrational and irresponsible spiting of faces: "They sacrificed millions for themselves in order to prevent others from making money too; they want everybody to be slaves for De Beers."

When the recession hit, the DTC, through those of its affiliated companies that deal in polished diamonds, reentered to prop up the polished market by buying up stones. The DTC's objective is to shore up diamond prices whenever, wherever, declines might influence retail prices. That does not mean that the DTC will pay top dollar for polished goods, or even that it will pay reasonable dollar. It means only that the DTC wants any distress sales that might be made to be made only to strong hands within the trade which can hold the goods until they can be sold at respectable prices. Their own hands will do fine.

As early as the first surcharge, *Diamant* blamed the chaotic market situation on "the carefully planned policy conducted for over a year now by the DTC," and in a major analysis of the bren, *Jewelers' Circular–Keystone* agreed. The DTC had planned the bren—planned it to make money, to push overall market prices higher, and most, to reestablish its flagging control and dominance over both producers and diamantaires. De Beers was clearly the big winner from the bren. Israeli industry leaders insist (as one put it to me) that "the syndicate should thank us. They should be honest about it and say, 'Thanks to the Israelis we made money.' " Everyone made money out of the bren except for those Israelis who were caught overextended. A lot of them ended up broke. Another Israeli complained to me, "The Belgians made the money and we lost the money, but *we* get blamed for it!" Go figure it out.

No matter whose story is accepted, one thing is certain: In the ongoing friction and jockeying for position that goes on between the DTC and the diamantaires, it is the DTC that invariably wins.

As ruthless as they regard their adversary (as they view the DTC) to be, diamantaires, whether sightholders, nonsightholding manufacturers, diamond traders, or representatives of producers, mostly appreciate that their product, polished gem diamonds, has no intrinsic value—"only an artificial value," one said—and that what value it has depends on the CSO. They appreciate that CSO advertising maintains the demand for their product, and that CSO market control preserves them all from periodic market readjustments much more painful than the recession that followed the bren. They know that such a product needs a strong hand to guide it if the prosperity of the majority is to be preserved. To some extent the sightholders appreciate that DTC discipline is necessary to keep them all in line for their collective—and therefore individual—best interests.

The CSO has a lot of people to keep satisfied, all very difficult people or groups of people, and it keeps on top by the strength of its existing position, by its consummate ongoing diplomacy, and mostly by the common realization—despite all the groanings—that everyone in the trade needs it. A sightholder who attributed every manner of corruption including the assassination of Patrice Lumumba to the CSO acknowledged that "the DTC is saving all of us." Most speak of it (when they speak frankly) the way that a sampling of adolescents might tell a psychiatrist about their parents: with a little disguised affection, some respect, and considerable resentment. One actually used the parental image in his comments: "The CSO is the father of us all, and it supports us like a father does, and like all fathers, it is sometimes arbitrary, dictatorial, and autocratic. But we could not get along without our fathers, and we couldn't get along without the CSO. It is the only thing that separates the industry from disaster. They are greedy, ruthless people— and we cannot do without them. If the CSO didn't exist, we would have to invent it."

18

THE OUTSIDE MARKET

◆

Barkly West, near Kimberley, comes alive on Saturday, diggers' day, when the area diggers bring their finds to town to haggle with the licensed diamond buyers who show up once a week. Even so, things are much quieter in Barkly West than they were in earlier times. Gerald P. Bosman, a Barkly West buyer whose father was a buyer, whose grandfather was a digger, and whose brother is a buyer at another of South Africa's once-a-week diamond-buying markets, remembers the days when there would be long queues of diggers waiting for the buyers to open their offices on Saturday mornings. Now the queues are gone and the sellers are as scarce as the diamonds.

Most of the Barkly West buyers are accommodated in one long, low brick building on Diggers Row, which has a series of narrow storefronts, each of which is occupied only one day a week by the diamond buyer who rents it. Upstairs in the same building are more buyers, and around the corner from it, upstairs over Barclay's Bank, is the office of the De Beers buyer. De Beers has six licensed diamond buyers stationed in Kimberley to buy from the diggers and the agents of the small mining companies that might show up at the company's world headquarters. One or another of the six will make the twenty-mile drive to Barkly West each Saturday.

The buyers begin arriving around seven or eight on Saturday morning. By eight or nine, the last of those that will come that week have arrived. Generally five or six will show up, sometimes eight or more.

All of the buyers are whites, as are most of the sellers. Mr. Bosman is a rotund, good-natured man who looks like one of Frans Hals's revelers, only in a leisure suit. He has been in diamonds all his life. He makes the rounds of several of the once-a-week markets and then sells his acquisitions to the South African cutters, most of whom are based in Johannesburg. If he can't get his price in Johannesburg, he will send his stones to contacts in Antwerp.

The diggers also straggle in, some as early as eight, but again, most of the players are there by nine. There are plenty of picturesque types, wizened old prospectors and an ancient toothless black man with his single stone to sell. Many of the diggers come to socialize with peers and buyers on Saturday mornings, even when they have no stones to offer. There are also a fair number of well-groomed young white men in late-model cars. These run medium-size modern mining operations— not modern when compared with De Beers, but still equipped with expensive earth-moving equipment and payrolls made up of several dozen or even a hundred employees. Every Saturday the same wretched group of beggars assembles on the sidewalk of Diggers Row. The sellers who have had a good week will give them something.

You can feel competition in the Barkly West air, and you can see its beneficial effects for the miners. In the South African markets buyers make "open" offers: once a buyer has made an offer he will stick by it for the remainder of the day. The open-offer system enables a seller to get offers from all of the buyers before accepting one, and to play the buyers off against one another. As I sat with the De Beers buyer, one of his callers tastefully and delicately tantalized him: "Gee, Bosman had figured that one at twenty-two." For whatever reason, the De Beers buyer thereupon increased his offer by a hefty percentage, clinching the purchase for the CSO. As I moved back and forth between the buyers' offices, I repeatedly encountered the same sellers, first at this one's office, then at that one's office, doing their "shopping."

The open-offer system puts the buyer at a disadvantage in any situation, but especially in one such as rough diamond buying, in which valuation is an imprecise and largely subjective matter. The high bidder gets the stone, and—at least in the eyes of the other buyers—has paid too much. In a highly competitive market, buyers will make mistakes, and especially on those Saturdays when a lot of buyers show up at Barkly West, and their competition is especially fierce. One digger told me that on those rare occasions when only one or two buyers come to town, their offers are miserly.

The dominant factor in the Barkly West market is De Beers. By informal agreement with the Barkly West buyers, the giant stayed out of their market for a number of years. ("Well, not really," one of the smaller buyers told me; "they had an 'undercover' buyer working for them here.") In the fall of 1979—after the death of its undercover agent—De Beers reentered the Barkly West market directly, its buyer told me, because it felt that prices were lagging in Barkly West; the diggers and small mining companies weren't getting their fair share. In addition to its eleemosynary interests, De Beers may also have been motivated by a concern that if prices are low anywhere in the world, some of its sightholders may increase their outside dealings and bypass De Beers.

When De Beers reentered the Barkly West market, prices immediately shot up by 20 to 40 percent. Its buyer told me that De Beers aims to buy in Barkly West at a 4 percent discount from DTC selling price. Bosman and the others cannot work on a 4 percent margin. Neither can De Beers. Its Barkly West operations are running at a loss, perhaps not an accounting loss, but certainly a loss in the sense that Barkly West does not carry its proportionate share of the overhead. De Beers can afford to do things that lesser competitors cannot.

Since De Beers came to town, none of the other buyers is doing much trade. The sellers will generally bring their stones to De Beers for first offer, then will shop around a little and end up back at De Beers to jockey for a few more rand and close the deal. Some of the other buyers have already ceased attending the Barkly West sessions. The competition is already being driven out; the monopoly power is being extended to one of the few remaining outposts for the small buyer. Whether the giant's willingness to "work" Barkly West on a 4 percent margin will continue when all the other buyers have been eliminated remains to be seen. At that point, Vaal River diamond diggers will be in the same boat as DTC sightholders: Take it or leave it.

The buyers and sellers are all in place at Barkly West by nine in the morning. They go through their movements, do what business they are going to do, and by late morning all the transactions that are going to be consummated have been made. By noon, everyone is gone.

Barkly West is one of the trading centers of the outside market. "Outside" means simply that the goods are not precommitted to the CSO. "Market" may be misleading. There is no formal market for outside goods, no centralized trading location. The outside market is anywhere that there is commercial activity in outside goods. It is an ancillary market, ancillary to the CSO's market (and it is again misleading to apply the word "market" to what transpires at the DTC).

Some entirely respectable transactions are conducted on the outside market, but the name has a generally unsavory connotation. For whatever else it may be, it is also the illicit market, the market for illegitimate goods, diamonds stolen from the mines or smuggled out of their country of origin, the market most rife with illegalities in its modus operandi— not so much in the South African trading centers as elsewhere, but even in four hours at Barkly West I noticed deviations from the requirements of South African law, committed even by the De Beers buyer.

Most of the outside market trading centers rotate on black market money. One buyer in Kenema, Sierra Leone, complained to me, "They aren't trading diamonds in Koidu, they are trading dollars and leones: the differential between the official and black market rate for the leone is twenty-seven percent; that twenty-seven percent is their profit. They can break even or lose money on the diamonds because they are making twenty-seven percent on the currency."

The situation is much more aggravated in Zaire, where the difference between official and black market rates for the zaire is three-to-one. The important outside market trading centers of Brazzaville, capital of the People's Republic of the Congo, and Bujumbura, capital of Burundi, trade mostly in diamonds smuggled in from Zaire, and their volume of activity depends more on changing black market rates for the zaire than on the state of world diamond demand. Their dealers, like those in Koidu, use diamonds as a medium of exchange by which currencies are profitably bought and sold. Rough buyers operating in South America told me that for them as well black market currency dealings were essential to the economic viability of their operations.

The outside market is a parasitic market in the sense that prices on the outside market are maintained and supported by the CSO's expensive overall operation, though outside transactions make no financial contribution to CSO overhead or profits. CSO people regard it as the freeloader's market—and one outside buyer with a contented smile acknowledged to me, "I'm just riding the syndicate's back." All but the largest sightholders will be discreet about the outside goods that they may buy, for fear of incurring the DTC's disfavor.

The outside output of West and Central Africa is more significant to the world diamond picture than that of South Africa. This disorganized production ultimately makes its way to one of the black African rough trading centers, principal among them being Monrovia, Brazzaville, and Bujumbura. There, the goods mingle with those smuggled out of Zaire, and with wares stolen from the more substantial mines from anywhere in Central or West Africa. Other goods may be brought directly from their countries of origin to Antwerp for sale, where a few dozen rough dealers and several scores of cutters—as well as the Diamond Corporation's buyers—are receptive to trading with tribal-garbed black men, no questions asked.

The traders who carry these goods are invariably black Muslims from West Africa, many of them Mandingo tribesmen, many of them nationals of Senegal. At international borders, their alternatives are three: smuggle, bribe, or a little of both. The choice, and the degree to which the courier must be secretive, depends on the border. The road between Kinshasa (Zaire) and Brazzaville is tight—safer to cross at an unguarded spot. Smuggle. That between Zaire and Burundi is easy. Bribe. An occasional Senegalese will carry as many as 150,000 to 200,000 carats—forty kilos—of low-grade industrials over twelve hundred miles of very difficult highway from Bakwanga to Bujumbura, relying on charm (and they are very charming people) and bribes to get his quarter-million-dollar cargo past occasional road checks and the international border. At most African borders, discretion and a baksheesh are sufficient to get baggage cleared without an inspection.

When it is necessary to be secretive, diamonds can be smuggled in hollowed-out utensils and secret baggage compartments. A quarter of a million in good quality rough will fit neatly in a plastic sandwich bag—no need for elaborate measures. When the heat is on, a smuggler may carry his goods on his person—which is sometimes a euphemism for *in* his person. In 1966 Zaire's Police des Mines recovered 1,500 carats in sixty-six separate plastic capsules from the rectum and connecting chambers of one John Wina, surely a matter for the *Guinness Book of World Records.*

What if you are caught at the border, a reasonable baksheesh is refused, the border official demands your diamonds as his baksheesh? You argue, you plead, and at the end, if you must, you give them to him. It almost never happens.

Despite the economic losses that smuggling spells to producing countries, there is relatively little ill will between the nations over it. Smuggling is part of the African cultural heritage. With diamonds, in particular, governments begrudgingly accept the economic principle: Rough diamonds will flow from countries with soft currencies into those with hard currencies, as surely as rivers to the sea.

When the courier reaches the trading center, he brings his wares to the office of one of the buyer/exporters. Though there are occasional independent buyer/exporters in business for themselves, most of these offices are operated by a major Antwerp or New York rough dealer or diamond-cutting firm, or are openly CSO agencies. Of the few independents there are, some are buying as covert CSO agents.

Many of the actual buyers (especially the Diamond Corporation people) are pleasant, polished, and engaging British colonial types; another will be a Kipling protagonist, a grubby guy in need of a shave, a hard-living adventurer using words like "bloody"; there are numbers of Mideasterners—Armenians, Lebanese, and Arabs; and a very few Jews. Their common trait is that they are all youngish fellows. Everywhere they work out of their air-conditioned offices and wait for the trade to come to them, or for the "steerers" to whom they pay commissions to bring the trade to them. Even if he should be close to a producing area, it is not practical for a white buyer to attempt to deal "in the bush," buying directly from diggers. The digger is a tribal person, extremely mistrustful of the European; anyway, it is uneconomical for the European to deal with him: He rarely has more than one or two routine stones on hand, and the buyer cannot efficiently deal in one- and two-stone lots.

Competition between the buyers is almost literally cut-throat: They connive against one another to get each other in trouble and deported for real, imagined, or even manufactured violations of local law. Competition often impels them to mistakes with overgenerous offers.

Though any of them will buy single stones from whoever might bring one to them, they function principally as wholesale buyers, buying largish mixtures of goods. Just like the DTC, the itinerant African diamond trader does not want to be stuck with the least desirable merchandise, and the buyer will make an offer on the lot, rather than offers on each of the separate stones in it.

The practice of trading lots rather than particular stones works out best for both buyers and sellers because of the vagaries of rough evaluation. Valuing rough is a highly speculative matter. The rough buyer must visualize what the final stone will look like after polishing and how much the piece or pieces of polished will bring, considering the color, quality, weight, shape, and purity of each. From that figure he works backward: he subtracts the various costs that will be incurred in transforming the rough into polished and his own margin of profit. The resulting figure is the value of the rough. "The value of a potato depends on the value of the potato chips that can be made from it," a rough buyer told me.

Even for buyers with considerable experience as cutters (and almost no rough buyers in the outposts have any significant cutting experience) evaluation is difficult and imprecise. Rough buyer Gerald Bosman asked me, "When you look at a man, can you see inside and know his character and personality? It is the same with rough diamonds." The process is fraught with possible error on the valuation of any particular piece of rough. Experienced diamond traders believe, however, that the overvaluations and undervaluations of particular stones in a lot are likely to cancel each other out, leaving a realistic total figure for any largish lot.

When the parcel is handed to the buyer, he pours it out onto his white blotter pad (diamonds are customarily viewed against some shade of white background) and sorts them into piles. The buyer then calculates the value of each pile. He is guided by a price list provided by his home office, which is updated on a regular basis, but he has the price list in his head. He does not openly refer to it, and the seller never sees the price list. For each pile he jots down a figure on his pad, usually a figure somewhat lower than the price book would authorize. This all looks very authoritative—and open, inasmuch as it is common for the black seller to "audit" the white buyer's jottings. The buyer offers the total for openers, and jockeying begins from there.

Buyers (other than the CSO buyers, who are usually bound by their price books) must be afforded considerable discretion to pay more than book figures on particular transactions in order to win the trust of particular sellers. When a white buyer has convinced a black seller that he is giving him the very best possible price, then he has won the seller's trust and will have a long-term supplier. Trust is a valuable asset.

The objective of diamond buying in the outposts of Africa (or South

America) is simply to buy big stones at a small fraction of real value. The black traders can pretty well value the common stones themselves on the basis of past experience, and generosity on routine items builds the black's confidence in his white buyer. However, even successful and long-experienced black traders will have little or no previous experience with big stones. They generally undervalue them. When the time comes to sell the big, valuable stone, the black will turn to his white buyer. He cannot know whether he is really getting fair value and must rely on his trust. When that big stone comes along, his trust will suddenly become inappropriate.

Everyone in the diamond-buying outposts is looking for, dreaming of, that one in 100,000 stones that falls his way just right, and that makes a whole decade profitable and memorable. If he must, a white buyer can stand small losses on thousands of stones in order to make the big killing on that one big stone, and buyers will cultivate innumerable small black men with generosity as well as charm in order to have the big one routed to himself when it comes along. (This approach to business, of course, is true not only of diamond buyers but of pretty much anyone, anywhere, who buys a specialized item and has an expertise advantage over the person on the other side of the table.)

At the same time the white buyer is attempting to win the black man's trust, he pursues a different and conflicting goal: keeping the African trader as ignorant of diamonds and of the intricacies of the diamond world as possible, partly to keep the African dependent on himself, partly the better to take advantage of him. The most successful buyers exhibit tact, an understanding of psychology, patience, good nature, and even paternalistic affection for the sellers.

When the buyer first deals with a black trader new to him, he will often be confronted with a demand of ten or twenty times reasonable value. The buyer's response is to "low-ball" just as severely on his opening offer. Otherwise he will never be able to consummate a transaction at roughly fair market value. If the buyer becomes certain that the black's expectations are unrealistic, he switches to his alternate goal: to be certain that if he cannot buy himself, at least none of his competitors will be able to buy. This is accomplished by "burning":

In the markets of Central and Western Africa, buyers do not permit sellers to force them to bid against each other, as happens at Barkly West. The unwritten but recognized rule of the trade is: Any offer made must be honored so long as the seller is in the office. Once the seller leaves the office, the closing of the door behind the seller operates as a withdrawal of any offers that the buyer might have made. Sellers cannot visit competing buyers, hear their offers, and then return to an earlier stop and say, "I accept the offer."

Assume that a Mandingo comes to a buyer's office with a single stone for which he asks 10,000—a stone that the buyer thinks is worth

2,000. The buyer offers 400 and then moves up step by step to around 2,000, but when the buyer is satisfied that the Mandingo is not going to sell for anything within the range of reason—that even an offer of 3,000 will be rejected—he offers the 3,000! If he has judged right, the offer will be rejected. The Mandingo leaves, visits other buyers and gets offers of 1,700, maybe as much as 2,200, but he will not get as big an offer as 3,000 because the stone is not worth 3,000. The buyer has "burned" the stone.

The Mandingo realizes that the first offerer was not so bad after all. He will return to that man. At that point he will sell the stone for 1,900–2,000, because he knows that his only other high offer was 2,200, and that there is no point in going back to Mr. 2,200, because Mr. 2,200 will only drop his offer to 1,800.

There is a risk to burning: If the buyer has judged his man wrong—if, perhaps, some previous buyer has burned the stone at 2,800—and the Mandingo says he will accept the 3,000 offer, then the buyer must buy and call it a mistake. The ethic of the trade dictates that offers made in the buyer's office can be accepted prior to termination of the negotiating session. The buyer who weasels on an offer will be black-listed. An experienced stone burner told me that "some of the rules of the trade are dishonest, but they are honestly adhered to."

The man on the other side of the table is a black man. Generally he has purchased his wares either from the digger or from another black trader who has purchased from the digger. The digger himself is invariably preliterate, little removed from the tribal state. He cannot price his stone in terms of market value because he is hopelessly removed from the market, and he is not competent, technically, to evaluate his wares. The black man to whom he sells, a trading black, has somewhat more expertise. White buyers, perhaps rationalizing their own conduct, insist that the black traders take merciless advantage of the diggers.

The black trader has paid something for the goods and wants to make a profit over cost, but usually his conception of value is based only on personal experience: How much did the last somewhat similar stone bring? Though closer to the real market than the digger, he is still far removed from it. When Antwerp prices go up, the white buyers will try to pay "old" prices for as long as the competitive situation permits. On the other hand, when prices are on the decline, buyers will try to keep up the prices that they pay to their regular clients for as long as possible, in order to maintain hard-won rapport. When, however, the white man must reduce the prices that he pays, then the black trader must reduce the price that he pays to the diggers. It may take a year for price changes to filter from Antwerp to the diggers in the bush, and by then the trend may well have reversed.

The Mandingo are the kings of the black African traders—"the best traders in Africa," says an Armenian who spent a decade buying in Monrovia. They come from Senegal, Gambia, Guinea, or Mali. Almost everywhere that they live they are a minority group—like Jews and Armenians, the great Caucasian trading tribes—and they like to describe themselves as "the Jews of Africa." Those Mandingo who are traders usually wear Muslim robes, as much an occupational uniform as a sign of pride in their background.

The typical Mandingo trader is usually not much better educated than any other black African, but he will develop some expertise about diamonds. He understands how to use a loupe (the jeweler's ten-powered eyepiece) and what to look for: the significance of the size, type, and positioning of the flaws within the stone, and color grading. When a buyer negotiates with an experienced Mandingo, discussion is likely to revolve around the placement of a particular stone within the series of piles into which the buyer has sorted the black man's offerings. The Mandingo develops his own price list—like the white man's, kept in his head—to which he refers when he buys from diggers or from other black traders.

The white buyer is more sophisticated in his analyses and closer to the marketplace, putting the Mandingo at an expertise disadvantage, but this is partly balanced by an intuitional advantage whites believe— possibly only the white man's projections—the Mandingo enjoys over the European. According to Henri Brunner, who worked for ten years as a Diamond Corporation buyer throughout West Africa, a Mandingo has a psychic intuition when it comes to pegging a white man: He senses what the white man really thinks a stone is worth. Like any other diamantaire, however, Mandingos make mistakes too. Brunner has seen Mandingos pale visibly when offered, seriously, a third of what the African had paid for a stone.

Prior to reaching the market there is considerable dealing back and forth between the black traders. When they reach the market, however, they cease dealing between themselves. Then they will sell only to the white man.

Things have quieted down a lot in the African markets of the outside world since their great days, 1954–66. Since then, the disorganized production has declined and the CSO has tightened its control over buyers. Once-active markets have died. Of the principal remaining ones, Monrovia is the busiest, and its volume is only a third of what it was at its peak.

At the time of my visit to Monrovia, there were then thirteen licensed buyer/exporters, almost all of them connected with specific major rough dealers or cutters. Buyer/exporters come and go in Monrovia and the other outside market towns. Their numbers depend on the state of activity in the world diamond and currency markets, the flow of goods into the city, and the amount of cash that the biggest men in the diamond world have left over after paying for their DTC allotments.

An experienced rough dealer can guess the country of origin of a stone with a fair degree of accuracy, but as for what percentage of "Liberia's" diamonds come from where—well, that depends on whom you ask. The buyer for Hatton Diamonds (the Diamond Corporation's Monrovia operation) told me that he trades almost exclusively in domestic Liberian rough, with perhaps a very few Sierra Leone stones mixed in. Another licensed buyer/exporter smiled as he answered the same question: "Liberia?" He almost never sees a domestic stone. Possibly they travel in different circles.

Unlike in Liberia, there is no problem figuring out the percentage of domestic traffic in Brazzaville or in Bujumbura. It is zero. Neither the People's Republic of the Congo nor Burundi has any domestic diamond production at all. Fictions to the contrary maintained by both governments and by those who buy there are only halfheartedly maintained. What diamonds are dealt in those centers are illicit if only because they got there illicitly. Many are illicit for other reasons as well. While they are illegal or illicit stones, people in the trade are quick to take offense at fuzzy diction. One Brazzaville buyer jumped when I suggested that he was a fence, dealing in stolen goods:

A: Why do you call them stolen? A lot of people dig these stones just like MIBA's are dug stones!
Q: Are they legally dug?
A: Maybe not legally dug, I wouldn't know about that, but not stolen either. They are won by the sweat of the brow. A man who takes a stone from the sorting room, that's a stolen stone. Some of the stones I buy may actually be stolen, but those are the small minority.

The governments that host the trading centers get very little for their participation. Duties everywhere have been trimmed to keep them competitive. Liberia's duty is now 3 percent. The country has retained the CSO to value all diamond exports, and computes its export duty on the basis of the CSO appraisal. The valuator that the CSO has put on the job is Jerome Wotorson, who just happens to be the younger brother of the Liberian minister of mines. This happy coincidence probably doesn't hurt the CSO's standing in the country. Wotorson knows his stuff, but the practicalities of the situation make it impossible for him to appraise exports realistically.

When the exporters bring their stones to him for his appraisal and for the calculation of the export duty, most of them regularly underdeclare the value of their shipments. One buyer told me that he always lies to "Jerome" and that most people regularly lie to Jerome. "The key to doing business in Liberia is to take your cue from the first syllable—Lie." Wotorson either buys it or not, and will usually negotiate to push the value and the duty upward, but he is a reasonable man. "He has to be. Otherwise, I'll smuggle all my stones around him," one buyer told me. "Jerome" knows as much.

Many stones are smuggled around him anyway, not so much to avoid the duty but to avoid the eyes of tax officials back home, or of the CSO (for reasons set forth farther along). The official statistics show that in 1978 Liberia exported 300,000 carats, valued at $30 million. The total duty yielded in 1978 was $900,000, not much in the total picture, and the infusion of the foreign trade into Liberia has virtually no multiplier effect on the national economy. Liberia's cut of the game is $900,000.

The situation is much the same in Brazzaville and Burundi: The diamantaires deal less than honorably with the government; the governments tolerate it in order to get the "found money" that should be going elsewhere anyway. I asked one Brazzaville buyer whether he insured his parcels for the amount on which he paid duty and he said no, that he insured for more, but "the insurance company is in Belgium, not in Brazzaville, and if the government should ever ask me about such things, I will tell them whatever I feel like telling them."

The big boy on the outside market is a familiar one: the CSO. A large proportion of the outside goods are outside by virtue of illicit activities, so smuggling and illicit digging and dealing are as great an enemy of the CSO as they are to the governments of the producing nations. The two are natural allies. The company's first tactic whenever a new source for outside rough becomes active is to fight smuggling by reporting suspected smugglers and illicit traders to government and police. When, however, the CSO determines that smuggling from a particular area cannot be confined within acceptable limits, it changes tack and goes into the smugglers' den as friend, and happily buys whatever goods are brought to it. Its objective is simple and consistent: to control the flow of diamonds, licit or illicit, through cooperation with authorities to the extent possible, and by cooperating with the diamond underworld to the extent necessary. When it must get in bed with criminal elements, it does so politely.

When the CSO doesn't have an acknowledged buyer in a particular market, the local diamond buyers will all suspect—with some degree of accuracy—that one or another of their fellows is a covert CSO operative, and which one of them it is. Geopolitically it is desirable for the CSO to do regular, if limited, buying on all of the African markets on a continuing basis. What happens in Bujumbura today may affect Antwerp tomorrow.

The CSO is not much concerned about the fact that it makes no profit on those stones that flow in the outside market. Its concern is more profound: the more stones that flow outside CSO control, the harder it is for it to control its sightholders, the world's most important cutting firms, and the harder to control the total flow of diamonds in consonance with retail demand. Its principal effort in the outside markets is therefore to ensure that as much of the otherwise outside production as is reasonably possible becomes inside rough, bought by a Diamond Corporation buyer and sold by the Diamond Trading Company. It buys for strategic reasons, not for profit on individual stones, and it is prepared to work on zero margins or losses.

Most of the biggest of the other rough buyers in the outposts, including Arslanian Frères and Diamond Distributors, Inc., probably the two biggest, are themselves DTC sightholders. Any rough dealer who becomes a power in the outside world will probably be "invited in" and given a DTC box. Once "in," the DTC has considerable power over him. By increasing or decreasing his DTC allotment, it can control the amount of surplus capital at his disposal with which he can compete against the Diamond Corporation buyers in the outposts. The outside-dealing sightholder will put up with it because he makes more profits, and steadier and more reliable profits on the goods that he gets in his DTC box than he does on the stones that he scrounges in Monrovia or Bujumbura. It always pays to play ball with the DTC. When I asked one nonsightholding outside buyer to compare his operation for me with those of the Arslanians or of the Jolis family (Diamond Distributors), he said, "My dear fellow, Mr. Arslanian and Mr. Jolis are entirely caught in the DTC net." In 1977, at a time when the DTC was cutting back on the number of dealer's boxes and was closed to new dealing applicants, it made an exception to "catch" Said Sulaimen, the Antwerp operative for Sierra Leone's Jamil, in the same net by making him a sightholder. To the extent that the sightholding outside rough buyer represents a threat to the CSO it is only a threat to one-time profits on specific stones, not to control. He is in line, part of the network.

The outside rough dealers who do not receive DTC sights are not in line. The smaller operators among them commonly believe that the CSO will ignore little guys, but that "if you get too big, or make too much money, the CSO will move against you, and then it will stop at nothing." They keep low profiles to avoid the giant's glance and possibly its ire. Many of them will smuggle large portions of their purchases out of the countries in which they deal in part so that significant volume is not attached to their names on the official records, which might attract the CSO's attention. They appreciate that the CSO could crush any one of them at any time that it wanted, either by focusing its competitive efforts or through still more nefarious tactics. One dealer insisted, "They will use means in Africa that they would not use in Europe." People cited examples, but no, don't use my name; they believe that the CSO will lash out against someone simply out of spite.

That is how the smaller outside operator views his chief competitor.

For the view of the bigger ones, I checked with Jack Lunzer of Industrial Diamonds, Ltd., probably the world's biggest nonsightholding dealer in rough diamonds, gem as well as industrial. Lunzer is a distinguished-looking man in one of the few truly elegant offices in the diamond world, situated in London's diamond district just around the corner from the CSO headquarters. After the tea was poured, I mentioned that I understood that the CSO could be a ruthless competitor. He gave me a confused look, blinked his eyes a few times, and then said that he knew most of the people at the CSO; that they were "terribly good fellows, terribly charming . . . terribly."

Except when the CSO is making war in one or another marketplace, either zeroing in on a particular dealer or just flexing its muscles (as it has done increasingly since the bren of '78 rattled its control), competition between its buyer and the outside buyers is tamer than that between the outsiders themselves. At most times the CSO buyer will be offering something very close to DTC selling price. The outside dealers peg their offers to Antwerp open market prices. Which is higher, DTC or Antwerp price, has traditionally determined whether stones were sold to the Diamond Corporation's buyer or to an independent. Brunner, recalling ten years with the CSO in Africa, says that "we were almost never in anybody's way. Either the market price was above DTC selling price, in which case we couldn't buy, or it was below us—our buying was supporting the market and nobody else wanted to buy."

While every independent buyer wants to make advantageous purchases himself, if he cannot, he would rather that the CSO got the goods than that they went to one of his independent competitors. Rough bought by another independent will come to Antwerp to compete with his stones, whereas goods that go to the CSO buyer will probably end up in some cutter's box, not on the open rough market where he deals. Most of the outside rough buyers headquartered in Antwerp will occasionally sell portions of their "overstock" to the Diamond Corporation's Antwerp buyer, and be treated not too badly by the man with the upper hand. In the diamond world, not even the independents are really independent.

PART III

CUTTERS AND
THE DIAMOND TRADERS

◆

The only good diamond is the one that is sold and paid for.

—*Romi Goldmuntz,*
legendary Antwerp diamantaire

19

DIAMOND CUT DIAMOND

◆

Around the time of Charlemagne, Europeans began to lose interest in the diamond, and continued to lose interest in it to the same extent as they lost confidence in its supposed supernatural qualities. The Renaissance man Benvenuto Cellini, a lapidary as well as most everything else, ranked it far behind rubies and emeralds in terms of both aesthetic and financial value. If one did not believe in the diamond's magical qualities, a rough diamond just couldn't be valued for much. The light-reflecting qualities of diamond that might make a diamond attractive were locked up in the stone and required cutting and faceting of the rough stone in order to be released.*

The invention of diamond cutting and the development and refinement of cutting techniques would give the diamond its brilliance and an aesthetic appeal to replace the waning appeal of its supposed supernatural qualities. Cutting (and the CSO) restored the diamond to its place of preeminence among gems. Diamond is uncuttable by any other substance, but it is not evenly hard in all of its planes and directions; one plane may be over a hundred times as hard and abrasive as another. When hundreds of small particles of diamond are placed on a flat surface, some of them will fall so that their most abrasive plane is facing upward. If they are somehow affixed to a revolving wheel and another diamond is pressed against the wheel, the most abrasive of the particles on the wheel will slowly cut away the diamond being worked.

We do not know by whom, when, or where this basic discovery that gave birth to the diamond-cutting industry was made. Diamond cutting probably developed more or less simultaneously in both India and Europe, possibly in Venice, but it is clear that the art was already fairly advanced by the time of Lodewyk van Berken, traditionally accepted

---

* I use the terms cutting and polishing interchangeably, as is sometimes done in the trade, to refer to the process of converting diamonds from rough to polished, though technically they are not identical.

as having "invented" the process of diamond cutting in 1476. By that time diamond cutting was already flourishing in India, Venice, Nuremberg, and Bruges in Flanders (now Belgium). Van Berken became the leader of a nascent diamond-cutting industry at Antwerp.

Some conservative types resisted the processing of diamonds: "In the same way as a virgin is preferable to a harlot, so we prefer a diamond in its natural state to one which has been worked," wrote Garcia ab Horto in 1565. But the unattractiveness of the rough, when compared with that of the polished—even those stones polished by early techniques—made the increased acceptance of polishing inevitable.

The first cutters made the "table facet"—the flat uppermost surface of the finished gem—merely by grinding away the top of the stone, reducing it to powder. Sometime in the 1600s, cutters discovered how to "cleave" the diamond, to split it delicately into two parts, one larger, one smaller, each of which might become a finished gem. The division plane left a flat surface on each portion that with minimal grinding might serve as the table for the finished stone. This enabled cutters to make more efficient use of the piece of rough. Cleaving, together with the earlier-developed ability to abrade away unwanted parts on a diamond-charged grinding wheel, completed the basic technology necessary for the development of the modern cutting industry.

The earliest cutters developed a number of styles for polished diamonds. Each style in succession made fuller use of the light-reflecting qualities of diamond, but each advancement in the science of cutting, each fuller exploitation of the material's light-reflecting qualities, led to increasingly greater loss in the bulk of the rough, and so to smaller (ergo, less obviously impressive) end products.

The advances were evolved through trial and error by men with no sophisticated understanding of optics. Progress in theory and practice was hampered by the basic character trait of diamond cutters through the ages: They are highly conservative people, not much interested in experimentation, always principally concerned with the eternally high cost of their raw material, and with ways to preserve as much of it as possible.

It took more than five hundred years for the blockish product of the early 1400s to mature into the most popular cut today, the round "brilliant" used in engagement rings. This cut gives greater brilliance, greater light reflection, than any of its predecessors—and involves a

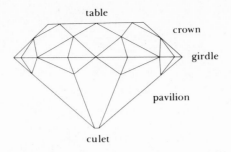

greater loss in the volume of the rough than any of them. The modern brilliant has a table, a culet (the tip at the bottom, usually flattened off to prevent inadvertent chipping or fracturing of the stone), and, usually, fifty-six other facets between the table top and the culet bottom, all surrounded by the circular outer rim or girdle. The facets act as a series of tiny, aligned mirrors, reflecting the light that strikes and enters the stone back out the table.

The basic form of the brilliant usually is attributed to a Venetian, Vincenzio Perruzzi, who is believed to have created it around the year 1700. Working on an unscientific, haphazard basis, cutters improved Perruzzi's design, developing an instinct as to how many facets—and how placed—would maximize a stone's brilliance. They learned that two of the diamond's attractive optical qualities competed: brilliance (the stone's ability to reflect light) and dispersion (the stone's ability to separate the colors that go to make up light, giving the rainbow effect described in the trade as "fire"). By increasing or decreasing the crown angles (the angles between the girdle and the table when the stone is viewed in profile), the cutter might increase visible dispersion at the expense of brilliance or vice versa. On the underside of the stone, the "pavilion" side, cutters discovered that greater or smaller pavilion angles (the angles between the girdle and the culet) and proportionate depth of the pavilion, led to greater or lesser "leakage" of light from the underside, thereby affecting the stone's brilliance.

Cutters also learned that every consideration of angles, depths, and percentages must be balanced by a consideration for the greater or lesser loss in the original weight and volume of the rough. Weight and bulk are objective matters that any prospective diamond buyer can appreciate; fine distinctions in the optics of a stone will be wasted on most customers.

In 1919 Marcel Tolkowsky, a mathematician from a diamond family, worked out and published what he regarded to be the ideal proportions for the polished diamond, those that would maximize its brilliance consistent with a high degree of fire. An ideal diamond, according to Tolkowsky, would be cut in the following proportions relative to the diameter of the girdle, and with the following angles:

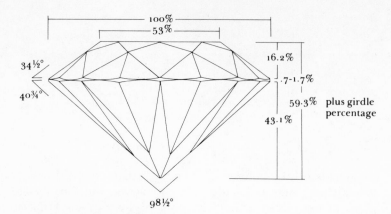

Tolkowsky theoretical brilliant cut
Courtesy Gemological Institute of America

Today Tolkowsky's proportions are honored mainly in the breach. Only rarely does one find a table as small as his "ideal" table—just 53 percent of the girdle diameter. For technical reasons, cutters never liked the 53 percent table, and current aesthetic tastes are in tune with the cutter's bias. Still, Tolkowsky remains a basic standard for evaluating the cut of a round brilliant. The publication of his book *Diamond Design* led to rapid advances in diamond-cutting theory and application. The result is that the modern American or Japanese affianced has a more attractive brilliant (albeit a smaller stone) than any diamond owned by Marie Antoinette.

Other popular shapes for diamonds (e.g., the marquise, emerald cut, pear-shaped, oval, and heart-shaped, all of them collectively known as fancy shapes) have been created and adapted over time in order to make more efficient use of the weight and volume of particular pieces of rough, though at the expense of maximization of the optical properties of the basic substance. The round brilliant remains the most popular form, and carat per carat, the most expensive of the finished products.

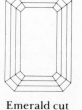

Marquise   Oval   Emerald cut   Heart   Pear shape

Courtesy Gemological Institute of America

It is common in the trade to characterize brilliants as being for the "meat and potatoes" crowd, fancy cuts being for fancier types.

THE DIAMOND MANUFACTURER

The diamond manufacturer is the entrepreneur who buys rough and causes it to be transformed into polished diamonds, Most manufacturers have diamond-polishing experience themselves. Theirs is a business with a small margin of profit, a margin that turns on the competence of the rank-and-file cutters, so personal experience in cutting is almost indispensable for the success of a manufacturer's enterprise. Harry Winston was the exception; he had no cutting experience himself and entered manufacturing only after he was already well known as a successful retailer. But Winston was an exception in everything.

Diamond manufacturing is a business in which a shop with eighty employees is a giant of the trade. There is no GM or Pan-Am equivalent. Only one firm exclusively engaged in cutting and wholesaling, Lazare Kaplan & Sons, Inc., is a publicly traded corporation, and only Kaplan and Baumgold Brothers, another major American wholesaler, attempt to stimulate demand on the retail level for their own "brand" of diamond through advertisements in popular journals. Kaplan employs about 225. Such economies as there are in large-scale diamond processing are not impressive. On the other hand, successful manufacturing requires close supervision of every step along the way by principals, and this keeps the industry "small." In the mining end of the diamond world, big capitalism is probably more efficient than little capitalism, but the reverse is surely true in diamond manufacturing.

The biggest and best-established manufacturers are DTC sightholders. For the past several years the nonsightholding manufacturers have had to pay premiums, often substantial premiums, for their rough. It is possible for one who must pay a premium for the raw material to survive in the diamond world, however, because every manufacturer's overall costs picture, sales contacts, financing arrangements, expertise, and expectations differ. Thousands of nonsightholding manufacturers do make livings, some of them good ones. The nonsightholding manufacturers buy their rough on the open market, from sightholding rough dealers, outside rough dealers, or in the diamond bourses or clubs they may frequent. A big enough nonsightholder may buy an occasional secondhand DTC box, and work it over a few months. Every sightholder's box will include some "sorting goods," items ill-suited for the particular sightholder's operation, and these may be sold directly to a nonsightholding manufacturer who regularly buys the same sightholder's castoffs.

A manufacturer may own his own cutting works or factory, in which case he is also called a cutter, or he may contract to have his rough processed by various outside cutters, truly independent contractors, in which case he is called a contractor. Most big factory-owning cutters also contract out some stones for processing.

Contracting can be done on a shoestring. Hundreds of people in New York's 47th Street diamond district are sporadic "manufacturers," buying an occasional piece of rough and contracting out the various steps in the processing. The expense to become a contracting manufacturer is the price of the piece of rough plus cutting expenses, which rarely come to as much as $60 a carat. You can begin with a $100 piece of rough and call yourself a diamond manufacturer.

To own one's own factory on a modest scale costs only a little more. Diamond-cutting equipment is relatively inexpensive and space requirements are minimal. Diamond cutting can easily be done in a residential apartment (or cottage; diamond cutting is a prototypical cottage industry). A factory-owning manufacturer often employs cutters as "independent contractors," and they are usually paid for piecework so that the entrepreneur is plagued neither by unproductive workers, fringe expenses, nor government forms. In short, diamond manufacturing, either as a contractor or as a small factory owner, is an easy-entrance business.

It is not, however, an easy business. The manufacturer is caught between two very different beasts, the rough market and the polished market, both of which threaten to consume him. The two are about as similar as the iron ore market is to the girder market: There are different risks and problems in both, and developments, supplies, and prices in the raw material market may be very different from those in the finished product market.

The rough market in which the manufacturer must buy is a seller's market. Production controls and stockpiling by the CSO, together with the inefficiencies of the disorganized producers, keep supply of rough beneath demand. The DTC makes no concessions to buyers, and rarely are concessions made by those who control what remains of the rough. Employer-manufacturers, however, must keep buying rough, whatever the price, in good times and bad, to keep their employees working, even when they will have to sell their polished at a loss. The employer who runs out of work for a good worker is going to lose that man permanently. Diamond manufacturing is a cyclical business, and the manufacturer always knows that next year he will recoup the losses he has suffered this year—if he can hold out until next year. When times are bad, he will put his people to work on less expensive rough to limit his losses, but he will proceed knowing that he is proceeding at a loss. At the time of my visit to Tel Aviv in the summer of 1979, most manufacturers had been operating at a loss for almost a year and fully expected to continue operating at a loss for several more months. They were still buying rough, and the DTC and the rough dealers were still dictating the terms to them.

The polished market, on the other hand, is more nearly a buyers' market in which manufacturers compete fiercely, and in which somewhere there is usually some seller in distress, willing to sell for less. Buyers shop around. Thus, the manufacturer is at a disadvantage in both of the markets in which he must operate. This keeps his margin low. Generally a manufacturer feels he has done very well indeed if the sale price of his polished, after rough and labor costs, leaves him a 5 percent margin of profit. Rarely will it be that high.

Not surprisingly, diamond manufacturers *kvetch* more than other people. One dealer who keeps out of manufacturing told me, "Manufacturers always talk about the times when they lose money, and they talk about it for years after they have recouped. But they forget about the times when they made money, and that . . . that they forget immediately!"

THE PROCESS

Planning. The cutting process begins by planning the stone, determining the cuts that will be made. Each piece of rough is peculiar to itself and should be individually planned to maximize the sale value of the polished diamond or diamonds that will emerge from it.

Usually the planning will be done by the manufacturer himself, because a minor judgmental error in the planning of one stone can wipe out his profit on a dozen successfully planned ones. The planner must have an innate sense of spatial relations, and must be able to balance science, economics, and art.

The planner peers into the piece of rough through his loupe and thinks through how best to process it—where to make the cuts so as to maximize the sale value of what is left after processing. Will it be maximized by producing the one or two biggest polished diamonds that the rough stone might conceivably yield? Or by drawing several polished diamonds out of the single piece of rough? By converting the rough into brilliants or fancies or one or more of each? By cutting away the flaws within the rough, thereby producing a "cleaner" finished product but one of less impressive size, or by leaving the flaws in the polished, perhaps planned so that they will end up in an unimportant portion, thereby preserving bulk and weight, though detracting from the internal quality of the end product? Which course will produce a higher total sales price on the polished market?

The planner approaches "make"—the quality of the proportions that the finished product will have—from the same vantage. It is not too hard to chart an ideal cut, but relatively few pieces of rough are well suited for the ideal from an economic point of view. The planner is concerned with economics—which will bring more money, a smaller finished diamond with very good proportions or a larger polished diamond with inferior proportions?

Manufacturers know they will make more money if they are flexible enough to deviate from high standards. P. Nathan Ferstenberg, leader of Antwerp manufacturers for over twenty years, advises that relatively flawless stones of good color should be given high quality make, but with poorer quality stones, weight preservation is more important: lightly flawed stones should be given a lesser make, and with poor-colored, spotted pieces of rough, "You try for a third make."

If planners are preoccupied with any single consideration, it is with preservation of the bulk and weight of the rough. (Diamond people speak of "weight," but they use it as a shorthand for size or volume or bulk, which are most easily quantified in terms of weight.) They are concerned to preserve as high a percentage of rough weight as possible, to maintain as high a "yield" as possible. Manufacturers' and cutters' minds are bedeviled by small differences in yield. By outsiders' standards, yields are never impressive. The typical Israeli manufacturer's yield will be between 42 and 45 percent: just over half of the weight and volume of the rough will be lost in the polishing process. With very large pieces of rough, the yield is even lower, and on the tiny "makeables" that the Indian industry processes, the yield is rarely as high as 30 percent—over two-thirds of the precious raw material is ground into dust.

Diamond planners shed tears over the losses because rough, most of which is ground up into dust, represents the greatest component of the final price of the polished. On large stones, more than 90 percent of the sale value of the polished diamond is likely to represent the cost of the rough—less than 10 percent represents the costs of processing and the profit. The smallish stones processed in Israel involve somewhat more labor input (carat for carat), but rough costs still represent some 75 percent of the wholesale price of the polished. On very small stones, in which labor costs are still more significant, the rough value is still slightly more than half the price of the finished diamonds. Obviously, just a little improvement in yield will make for a very big improvement in profits. A. P. Palshetkar, a leading Indian manufacturer, writes in *Gems & Jewellery* that for every one percent improvement in yield, the manufacturer will achieve at least an 8 percent improvement in the price of the finished diamonds—all of that extra being profit.

The trait that makes for a highly successful diamond planner is an ability to see ways to exclude the rough's more serious flaws (there are occasional flawless polished diamonds, but there are virtually no flawless pieces of rough) without wasting as much weight as the next fellow, and to preserve weight whenever possible without deviating as much as someone else from optically desirable proportions. New York's greatest living cutter, Lazare Kaplan, and Antwerp's Ferstenberg both attribute their success to this ability. Diamond planning is a mechanical matter, but as in all fields of endeavor, the addition of imagination and flexibility to well-grounded mechanical skills makes for greatness.

As is the case in most professions, however, most diamond planners are only marginally competent at their work. Legions of people in both Antwerp and New York make respectable incomes buying the poorly planned products of others and having them recut to refined plans, losing some weight but transforming bigger, duller stones into smaller more sparkling gems of greater resale value. The products of the larger and busier manufacturers, who are less able because of time and volume constraints to do careful planning, can often be reworked profitably by a more patient or scientific planner farther down the line.

Important stones are always planned as a group effort. The manufacturer and his top-ranking foreman may study a stone for months before the actual cutting operations begin. Kaplan together with his eldest son, Leo, spent over a year studying the Jonker rough, its structures and its possibilities, making multiple models of it and computing out the innumerable possibilities within the five ounces of rock.

When the planner has completed his study, he commonly marks the stone with India ink, showing where the important cuts and divisions are to be made. His markings represent the fate and future of any piece of rough.

Division of the Rough: Cleaving and Sawing. The actual processing of most gem diamonds probably will begin with the division of the rough into two parts, creating the uppermost plane, the table facet, for two polished diamonds. The planner usually plans to make one larger and one smaller. This minimizes wastage and is also harmonious with the economic law that larger diamonds are worth proportionately more, grain per grain (other factors being equal) than smaller ones. The planner therefore plans to make one as large as possible consistent with a full-sized table, the smaller being fashioned from whatever scrap is left over from the larger. The division may be accomplished by cleaving or sawing.

A diamond, whatever its apparent outward shape as a piece of rough, has a tightly formed crystalline structure with a distinct grain. Struck just right along its grain—along one of its "cleavage planes"—a diamond will split in two. The first step in cleaving involves locating the appropriate plane. When it has been determined, a small groove or kerf is worked into the diamond at the right place by rubbing it with another diamond, and a chisel is placed into the groove. The chisel is then tapped with a counterweighted mallet with precisely the right degree of force. If all of the studies of the stone and the calculations have been properly done, the diamond will cleave in two. If they have not, perhaps nothing will happen; or perhaps the diamond will shatter into many pieces; or perhaps it will remain in one piece but will fracture internally in a shell-shaped pattern of cracks. Every apprentice cleaver is likely to render several pieces of rough worthless in the course of his training, which is why an education in cleaving is open only to the sons or nephews of cleavers or to those who can pay very well indeed.

Exciting stories, most of them apocryphal, are told about the cleaving of the great diamonds. Best known of them pertains to the cleaving of the best-known diamond, the Cullinan, by the legendary cleaver Joseph Asscher of Amsterdam in 1908. Asscher's competence would determine whether the Cullinan would be successfully opened for further processing or destroyed.

Asscher had a history of heart attack, and during the suspenseful cleaving of the Cullinan, the biggest and most valuable stone in diamond history, he had two physicians on hand. He poised the heavy steel rod that he had devised as a mallet for the assignment and came down upon the steel cleaver's wedge resting on the Cullinan. Everyone gasped: the wedge had shattered, but the Cullinan remained intact. Asscher placed another wedge and raised his mallet again. This time when he tapped it the Cullinan cleaved neatly in two, and Asscher, though he did not have the feared heart attack, fainted dead away.

Asscher's nephew Louis has insisted with no little irritation that the story is "absolutely untrue"—a matter of puffery that someone cooked up. The key to Louis Asscher's irritation: "No Asscher would ever faint over any operation on any diamond." Perhaps the nephew takes it too personally. It was, after all, the tale of Joseph Asscher's faint—symbolizing the drama of the moment—that made his uncle the legendary Joseph Asscher, rather than the late Joseph Asscher.

Similar stories surround the cleaving of most of the great diamonds of recent times. According to the *New York Times*, during the processing of the 726-carat Presidente Vargas diamond in 1941, Harry Winston's cleaver Adrian Grasselly, a nervous sort, lost six pounds; he begged off having a public cleaving of the gem, tried to stop operations when the first two blows failed to cleave, and was trembling after the successful third clomp of his mallet divided El Presidente in two. Most of this kind of stuff is part of the fabricated mystique of the diamond—and more particularly, the fabricated mystique of the Winston Diamond—which Harry Winston, the purveyor of most of the biggest stones and the diamond world's all-time greatest showman/salesman, fostered.

Sawing, the other common method for making the initial division, lacks the romance of cleaving but is now very much the more usual beginning of the process. Like cleaving, the technique dates to the seventeenth century, but sawing never quite caught on until technical advances of the early twentieth century made it increasingly attractive for initial division of the rough. The modern diamond saw looks, and seems to work, like the circular saw employed to cut wood in lumberyards, only the diamond saw is a small, high-tolerance piece of equipment. The saw blade is a disc of phosphor-bronze, rarely as thick as 1/200 of an inch, kept rigid between sturdy supports applied to either side of the blade. An electric motor spins the saw blade rapidly. The diamond to be cut is glued into its dop (holder) with specially designed diamond worker's cement, and is then pressed against the rapidly spinning saw blade by a weighted arm. No matter how rapidly the wheel spins and how great the pressure applied, bronze will not cut diamond. Only diamond cuts diamond. The wheel is therefore charged with a mixture of diamond dust (small particles of powdered diamond) and oil—castor oil, olive oil, corn oil, any will do almost equally well. The revolutions of the disc rub this abrasive mulch repeatedly over the India ink line indicating where the diamond is to be divided, in time abrading it. Once the sawing is actually under way, the diamond being sawed generates its own dust to recharge the wheel, so that the diamond is cut by its own offal. It is the diamond dust that actually does the cutting, and what looks to be the saw is merely the vehicle that distributes and agitates the dust against the diamond being sawn.

The length of time required to saw through a diamond depends on its size, shape, and internal consistency, the degree of pressure with which it is held against the saw, and the thickness and speed of the saw blade. An "easy" one-carat rough may be sawn through in as little as a couple of hours; a more difficult one-carat stone may require a day. Large stones take days or weeks of continuous abrading. The impatient can now have their rough divided by laser beam, which essentially cuts through a diamond by focusing intense heat upon the division line, actually burning through it. Laser is often used on stones that might otherwise be sawn but for internal knots that might make sawing perilous. Otherwise it is not popular because it is a very much more expensive procedure.

Cleaving is done with the grain and sawing across the grain, so that the method of division chosen is dictated by the alignment of the rough as planned; one will be appropriate and the other inappropriate. Some stones will require both sawing and cleaving in their processing.

Whichever initial division is used, the manufacturer, even those who run their own small factories, will usually contract it out. Few shops have sufficiently regular need for a cleaver to maintain one on a full-time basis, while sawing is more efficiently centralized because one sawyer can tend a whole bank of diamond saws. Only large factory-owning manufacturers maintain their own sawing facilities. A sawing factory may contain hundreds of saws operated by several sawyers. The cleaver, however, is almost always a one-man operation, serving several manufacturers as an independent contractor.

Brutting: Applying the Girdle. When the stone has been divided, the rough is then given to the brutter, also known as the girdler,* who cuts the stone's girdle, giving it its circular equator. He is not concerned with topographical irregularities in the crown above the girdle or the pavilion below it; those will be handled by whoever grinds the facets.

The stone to be girdled is cemented to a lathe and caused to revolve rapidly. The brutter brings another diamond against the revolving stone. This second diamond, known as the tool stone, is cemented to a short pole, and the brutter moves it into play or out by leaning his torso forward or back. As the revolving stone repeatedly knocks against the tool stone, the out-of-circular portions of the stone being worked are knocked off and the girdle is rounded. Occasionally the brutter will tap the lathe head with a hammer, knocking the stone being worked slightly out of alignment and thereby making stubborn sections of the stone more directly accessible to the tool stone. The little pieces chipped off in the process, actually minuscule particles of diamond dust, are collected in a box that sits immediately beneath the theater of operations and are used in other aspects of the diamond-polishing operation.

Delicately done, a girdle will be smooth not only to the naked eye and thumb but also when viewed through the loupe. A stone that has been hurriedly girdled will show numerous minute hairline fractures extending a short distance into the stone, known as bearding. The patient brutter avoids bearding and also preserves more of the stone's original weight than the hasty worker. A fine-tolerance brutter will have left an occasional "natural"—a section where the natural skin of the rough has remained untouched because it did not need to be cut away—in a perfectly round girdle. A careful brutter can girdle a one-carat stone in an hour. The brutter's most valuable instrument is an experienced eye; otherwise, he works only with the simplest of tools.

Faceting. When the stone has been brutted it is ready for faceting. In all, a finished brilliant will have a table, a culet, and fifty-six other facets, making a total of fifty-eight. In modern cutting operations, the work is commonly done by four different men. The top blocker finishes off the table and applies the eight basic facets on the crown; the bottom blocker flattens off the culet and applies the eight basic pavilion facets. Together the two blockers do the "blocking," and produce a recognizable brilliant known as the eight-cut (or single-cut), which has a total of eighteen facets (or seventeen if the culet is left pointed). Processing of small stones is often terminated at this point, and they are then wholesaled as *achtkants* (eight-cuts). Most stones, however, will be passed on

* I have called anyone engaged in the diamond-cutting process a cutter, but in the trade "cutter" is customarily reserved for the brutter, while those who place the facets are known as polishers, not cutters. From a technical standpoint, only the sawyer is a cutter— only his work involves cutting.

to the top brillianteerer, who takes the eight-cut and applies another twenty-four facets to the crown before turning it over to the bottom brillianteerer, who puts sixteen more on the pavilion, thereby finishing off the diamond. A one-carat diamond can be totally faceted in something less than one man-day.

Whichever role a faceter fills, he proceeds in the same manner, with the same tools. The diamond is faceted by grinding down the stone into flat planes or facets on a grinding wheel, known as the scaife (plural: scaives) or lap. The scaife is a flat, cast-iron disc, which is incised with a gridwork of grooves. The surface of the disc is rubbed with a mixture of diamond dust and oil, which fills and temporarily remains in place within the grooves. An electric motor spins the disc just like a phonograph record turntable, but much faster.

The diamond to be faceted is secured into a dop or holder, either with cement or solder; the dop is then attached to a tang, a short wooden arm, but long enough so that one end of it will rest outside the scaife, the dop end being dropped onto the revolving scaife like the arm placed on a record turntable. The cutter holds onto the tang and can apply some manual pressure to it and press the stone harder against the scaife if he wishes. Or he can rest lead weights on the tang, thereby applying steadier pressure. As the scaife revolves, the diamond dust resting in its grooves cuts away and flattens out the portion of the diamond set against the scaife. Periodically the cutter checks how things are going—more often as he approaches the completion of the facet—by lifting the tang, with its attached dop and diamond within, to eye level and peering at the product through his loupe. Each facet, each angle, must be placed precisely, but most old-line cutters scorn any but the most rudimentary of handheld protractors, and then only for the "basic eight." The work is done by eye, and with impressive accuracy.

When one considers that a one-carat stone is only 1/142 of an ounce, it is astonishing to think that craftsmen can place fifty-eight facets, each at about the right angle one to the other, on such a small item. And one carat is really big in the diamond world. I have seen one-point diamonds, each 1/100 of a carat, each scarcely bigger than a speck of beach sand, 14,200 of them to the ounce, each "full cut" with fifty-eight facets ground onto them, almost a million facets to the ounce. The process is a bit like inscribing the Lord's Prayer onto the head of a pin. It takes a man, or more often a group of Indian adolescents, perhaps an hour or two to do. The work isn't very carefully executed—maybe some of the fifty-eight facets aren't really there, especially on the pavilion side—but their "quality" doesn't much matter. The ones that I saw in the New York offices of JDR Diamonds, Inc., were being offered to the wholesale trade at $4 apiece. As Mr. Krakowski of JDR unwrapped the paper in which he stores the one-pointers, he told me, "Every time I open this paper I lose one or two of them."

Modern equipment is now available to the faceter, particularly semi-automatic and automatic dops that will set angles precisely and switch to the next when "told" to do so by the operator. These are resisted by most workers. Even the factory hands in the diamond world are profoundly conservative and resist change.

THE WORKERS

The entrance door to Suite 428 in one of the narrow tall buildings in New York's 47th Street diamond district is a cacophony of plaques that announce some but not all of the various businesses that operate from within. The visitor rings and when identity has been established, a buzzer buzzes the caller inside a cluttered two-room atelier, cramped and not very clean (which by diamond district standards means very clean). It is a communal diamond factory, one of hundreds on 47th Street or in Antwerp or Tel Aviv. Most are filthy, but all are well lit. Light is vital to quality diamond working.

The "landlord" of 428, the man who actually rents the two rooms from the building's owner, works in the smaller of the rooms with his son. They do a little contracting, a little dealing, and the son does the blocking on many of the stones that they manufacture.

The larger room houses eight scaives, each worked by a man who rents both scaife and space. Each person in Suite 428 is a separate business entity, in business for himself, doing work for contracting manufacturers. They may use old-fashioned, semiautomatic, or fully automatic dops depending on the type of work involved, the character of the stone, and their own temperament. Some will do the entire faceting process, both blocking and brillianteering, crown and pavilion, but more will do only one aspect of the faceting. "I could do the whole thing well myself," one told me, "but it would take me longer. My output and my earnings are much better if I just stick to bottom brillianteering."

There is also a brutter in 428. The brutter owns his own equipment and rents only space. The brutter told me that it takes him about fifteen minutes to girdle a small stone—he had been getting mainly small ones of late—and that his rate on them works out to about $5 a girdle, or $20 an hour. Most brutters in New York earn less, closer to $10 an hour, but some may earn as much as $30 an hour. Diamond work is almost always piecework (actually paid so much per carat worked, rather than so much per stone worked). Because per carat rates differ on the basis of the individual's abilities as a worker and as a bargainer, and because everyone's rate of output is different, average hourly earnings of diamond workers may vary tremendously. In any case, as an independent contractor, the diamond worker in New York gets no benefits.

The landlord does not give work to any of his tenants; it would be difficult for him to give work to some and not to the others. All the workers have different customers (some work only for one contractor) and very few contractors will use more than one of the workers at 428. Diamond polishers are not interchangeable: Some will preserve greater weight than others, some will produce stones with more nearly perfect symmetry, or a better quality finish, and contractors are not interested in the convenience of using subcontractors from the same atelier. Every contractor likes to work with the subs that he is used to working with, and they are superstitious about changing subs.

The men at 428 are not taken up with the mystique of the diamond. I asked one worker there whether diamonds meant anything to him, and he said, "Yes, this: dirty hands and dirty face." The gray solder-like cement with which most diamond workers affix the stone to the dop gets polished into dust along with the diamonds, and leaves a thin gray film on the worker and his work area. ("White" lung disease, however, is quite rare among them.) One man told me that his wife owned a diamond, but "Nothing special. If I had bought a couple of one-carat D-flawlesses a few years ago, I'd be worth a lot today, but what did I know? 'Me? Invest in diamonds?' I said. 'Come on, I work with diamonds!' . . . Go figure it out."

The workers at 428 take pride in what they do. Each can recognize his own work long after the stone has left his hands. They are proud of the aesthetic quality of the work that they turn out, but they are perhaps proudest of their "yield," the weight that they retain. To most, the hallmark of work well done is "returning good weight." Labor costs are low when compared with the high cost of rough, so that the cutter who saves weight is worth very much more than the hastier cutter who "overcuts." The cutter who cuts least is paid best.

The men in 428 are all Jews of varying degrees of Orthodoxy, from just plain Orthodox on up. They range in age from the late twenties up to eighty. They speak Yiddish. When I arrived they were taking a break, clustered in a card game together with a couple of bearded, yarmulked men from down the hall. Only one of them had remained at his work: a strikingly handsome black-bearded young man with a face as full of timeless character as any painted by Chagall. He was bent over his scaife. His clothes were visibly tattered. His black yarmulke was held tight against his skull by the headband of the stereo earphones through which he was listening to a rock and roll station. There have been some changes in the business, though not many. At 4:00 PM every day the men break for an organized session of communal prayer; then, some may work far into the night.

Farther up the street from 428 I visited the small shop of a factory-owning manufacturer. His men too are all "independent contractors." This arrangement has historical antecedents in the early period of diamond polishing, when all diamond workers were in fact independent contractors, taking their assignments home with them. In today's world, calling them independent contractors—when they work almost exclusively for the same employer, in his factory and on his terms—is sham, designed to avoid a myriad of governmental forms, employment taxes, union problems, and the withholding of an employee's federal income taxes. It is given a color of legitimacy by the fact that each worker pays "rent" to his employer for space and scaife (a bookkeeping entry only) and each is nominally free to accept or reject work as he sees fit. Virtually every diamond cutter in New York is an "independent contractor."

There is considerable loyalty, an almost familial loyalty, between manufacturers, whether contractors or factory owners, and their workers. This is the manufacturer's best protection against "stone growing" by his workers: If a cutter owns a 23-point stone (23/100 of a carat) himself and polishes a stone for a manufacturer that turns out to be 25 points after polishing, he may simply substitute his own stone for the manufacturer's stone. Then he has a 25-point stone, which by the same growth process becomes a 28-pointer; or perhaps his 28-point "H" colored stone improves by substitution for a more desirable "G" colored stone. In this manner, given sufficient time, volume, and discretion, a 10-point "K" colored stone worth perhaps $15 can mature into a stone of impressive size, quality, and value.

Some diamond workers will occasionally act as manufacturers themselves. One of the men at 428 told me, "There are always guys coming in here with an odd piece of rough hoping to sell it to one or another of us. I know if I buy a piece of rough from one of them, it's fifth hand; no one else wanted it. But sometimes I'll buy. You can never tell with a diamond. Maybe from the rough you'll think it's a "J" [an undesirable color] and it polishes up as an "F" and you've made a killing. It's happened to me a couple of times. Then maybe a stone will break on you and you'll have to do five or six just to make up the loss. That's happened to me too."

Good diamond workers must be patient and painstaking. Because they are paid for piecework, there is a natural tendency for them to rush through their work to increase their output and make more money. By increasing the speed of his scaife or applying greater pressure, the polisher can turn out more stones and receive more pay, in the process leaving "burn" marks on the polished which must either be suffered by the manufacturer or eliminated by more polishing and greater loss of weight. The brutter can girdle more stones if he consistently "overcuts," or if he works at a rate of speed that leaves his girdles bearded. The eager worker may be tempted.

The patience that is essential to top-quality diamond work is sometimes equated with lack of conventional ambition, and while patience and lack of ambition are not the same, there does seem to be a correlation between them in the world of the diamond worker. In New York, where much of the world's finest diamond cutting is done, the work force is composed mostly of Hasidic Jews and Puerto Ricans, two groups noted for top quality cutting with minimal wastage of weight. The Hasidim actually pride themselves on their lack of worldly ambition (their freedom from materialistic goals); they want to work only so much as is necessary to keep bread on the table for their large families, and to devote the rest of their hours to their religious duties.

For decades, more American cutting has been done in Puerto Rico than in New York, and thousands of Puerto Ricans have become highly skilled cutters. One manufacturer who spoke in pejoratives of blacks described Puerto Ricans as "very able mechanics with a fine touch and a fine eye." Yet there is no Puerto Rican manufacturer or wholesale diamond dealer of significance in either San Juan or New York. Why not? I asked a pioneer in the Puerto Rican industry. "*Kup*" was the answer—literally "head," but more commonly used to mean mentality: Puerto Ricans are not interested in empire building. Another major manufacturer said that "they are slow and patient; the *mañana* mentality makes for a good work product."

The lack of worldly ambition that is frequently found among quality diamond cutters tends to make them less steady workers than others. Manufacturers sometimes complain that the worker with an extra dollar in his pocket lacks any compulsion to work. He may go on long drunken benders, or take off days without apparent good reason, or he will do a couple of stones and then either take off the rest of the day or devote it to distracting other workers. Hasids don't go on drunken benders, but they are partial to *schmoozing* (long heart-to-heart chats over inconsequential matters), interminable telephone conversations, and impromptu breaks for religious study or devotions. As pieceworkers or independent contractors, diamond workers have a flexibility that—from the manufacturer's point of view—is abused by many. It is suffered because the requisite patience of diamond work so often goes hand in hand with the "irresponsibility" of the "unambitious" spirit.

Diamond workers in Belgium and Israel have unions, but they are weak unions when compared with those operating in other industries in their countries. Effectually they negotiate neither rates of pay nor job security. There are no diamond workers' unions at all in India or in Puerto Rico. Most cutters in New York City are quietly affiliated with the Association of Diamond Cutters, a union-like organization that posts bigger-slice-of-the-pie posters in many of the ateliers. No one pays much attention.

Most diamond workers who work in organized factories work in small ones, with a familial atmosphere that discourages union militancy. More important, the great differences in the quality of work produced by different diamond workers give them less uniformity of interest than is the case in other unionized industries. The workers are slow to identify their own self-interest with the interests of a larger group.

ASSEMBLY LINES AND AUTOMATION

In *Diamonds,* the standard in-trade text, the English gemologist Eric Bruton describes diamond cutters as temperamental people who still regard their craft as a highly personal art. Many will still carry their own tangs and dops, just as a French chef will carry his own knives, and some few will even decline to use the scaife provided by the factory but will insist on bringing their own familiar scaives as well.

Much of that is now fading, and fading very rapidly. Prior to World War II, the diamond cutter was a generalist, with the full range of skills required to polish a diamond, and often brutting and cleaving experience as well. He worked alone or in small groups, usually as a truly independent contractor. Increased diamond production since the end of World War II, together with increased retail demand, has led to a tremendous growth in the size of the world diamond industry. In the process, diamond factories have become bigger and the organization of the bigger ones has evolved into a rigid assembly-line system not very different from that in automobile factories.

The maturation of industrial organization in the diamond world was hastened by the birth and rapid growth of the "Palestinian" diamond-cutting industry during World War II. A cutting industry was created in Palestine overnight to replace those of Antwerp and Amsterdam, and there was not time to train generalists. Workers could be trained to do any one of the specific aspects of the work passably, however, in a very short time. The result was the fragmentation of the process into the steps set forth above, and the introduction of "chain-of-six" processing: sawyer, brutter, top blocker, bottom blocker, top brillianteerer, bottom brillianteerer. The efficiencies of narrow specialization led to rapid acceptance by manufacturers of chain-of-six operations in the postwar world. Today in the bigger factories in Israel, now the world's dollar-volume leader in cutting, and in Puerto Rico, a man may work his whole life in a diamond factory without learning more than his own task.

Diamond cutting as one of a chain of six is repetitive work, and no one pretends that it is an art. One Simon Legree manufacturer in New York told me, "Cutting isn't the spectacular work outsiders think it is. I could train a monkey to do it in six months." And an Antwerp manufacturer said, "They're even polishing now in Tunisia, and that proves that anyone can polish diamonds."

Chain-of-six workers in a large factory are generally regular employees (not independent contractors) but are paid as pieceworkers. To counter the incentive that piecework gives to shoddy workmanship, every stone must be checked at every step along the way as a constant quality control over the work of each separate workman.

Most manufacturers now operate chain-of-six on routine stones. Big stones, important stones, however, are still entrusted to a generalist and are likely to be worked by the same polisher throughout the process. Such stones are too valuable to be entrusted to other than the most highly skilled workers, artisans in the traditional mold.

Further impersonalization of the process is inevitable with increased industry acceptance of automatic polishing equipment. The industry has traditionally been highly resistant to change in basic tools. Prototypical automatic polishing machines were resisted by the trade and failed, until the Piermatic Automatic Diamond Polishing Machine was sponsored, developed, and "pushed" by the DTC in the late 1960s and early 1970s. (When the DTC suggests that manufacturers try something, they try it.) The Piermatic, merchandised by Bonas & Co. (not related to the syndicate brokers of the same name), a DTC affiliate, will do almost all the faceting that a diamond requires.

The Piermatic is used only after a stone has been brutted. The girdled diamond is set into a holder and its profile projected onto a graphed screen. The profile can be moved about the fixed graph and when it has been properly positioned the supervisor can quickly read from the graph the angles that the Piermatic should be programmed to cut in order to maximize the qualities of the particular stone. The machine does the rest, polishing in accordance with the settings. Four Piermatics will sit over each scaife, each polishing a different stone, each head switching periodically to the next facet. A red light goes on when any one stone has been finished. Then the operator removes it from the assembly and places the next stone.

In addition to saving labor, Piermatics require less costly labor because of the low skill required to operate them. A beginner can successfully operate a Piermatic in two or three days, and after two or three weeks he will be thoroughly proficient and able to handle a bank of Piermatics simultaneously. The Piermatic also allows significant savings in supervisory expense.

The burgeoning of chain-of-six manufacturing transformed the diamond worker from a craftsman to a skilled industrial worker. To the extent that it has been accepted, the Piermatic has reduced the cutter from a skilled industrial worker to a low-level factory hand. Most (possibly all) factories with Piermatics also have chain-of-six operations, and you can see the difference in the faces of the workers: the faces of the chain-of-six workers reflect their involvement in their work. The Piermatic operators have blank faces. In most places Piermatic operators are paid an hourly or daily rate, rather than on a piecework basis, and their earnings are meager. "They're minimum wage people, not too intelligent," a New York manufacturer says of his Piermatic operators.

By the time of publication of this book, there will probably be 5,000 Piermatics in operation worldwide, about 40 percent of them in Israel and another 20 percent in South Africa. Their use allows more than five thousand highly paid chain-of-six operators to be replaced by something less than one thousand lowly paid Piermatic operators. In countries with virtually no unemployment such as Israel and (for whites) South Africa, the loss of jobs does not mean much, but the change in the kind of work from skilled to unskilled may matter.

The Piermatic has not yet proved suitable for the processing of larger, more expensive rough, in which the cost of the labor has never been particularly significant to the manufacturer's total cost basis for the finished stone. It does not have the discretion that a human worker has. So far the Piermatic has proven most suitable for melee of appropriate form and quality, which is why it is most commonly used in Israel, where most melee is processed.

The machine, however, is constantly and continually being improved, giving it greater flexibility. It is becoming more sophisticated in every way. Its acceptance in the trade will increase with its improvements, partly because it makes economic sense and partly because the DTC, which markets the Piermatic, considers such matters as up-to-dateness of a manufacturer's operations when it makes revisions of its list of sightholders and allocates goods. Or at least sightholders *think* that it does.

Prototype brutting machines to replace human girdlers have been made on an experimental basis, and within the decade will be taking their place beside the Piermatic.

The diamond workers' unions in Belgium and Israel have been slow to appreciate the threat that automation holds for their members, and only now are union officials becoming increasingly uneasy about it. It is probably not feasible for them to take an effective stand against "progress."

20

THE DIAMOND TRADE

◆

"Jews are diamonds," Sir Ernest is reputed to have said. Whether or not he really made the statement, it is true that the diamond trade has been predominantly Jewish for over two centuries.

Jews probably began entering the trade in the sixteenth century when they flocked to the Netherlands because of its climate of religious toleration. In Holland, then the leader in the diamond trade, they began cutting and trading diamonds. By the late 1700s the higher levels of the diamond trade were entirely confined to Jews.

Possibly the first European to prospect for diamonds in Africa was a Jew, T. B. Kisch, who worked unsuccessfully in South Africa in the 1860s, and many Jews took part in the great diamond rush to the Kimberley area that began in 1869. In 1871, still in the diamond rush period of Kimberley's history, the Griqualand West Hebrew Association established its synagogue, which still serves the city's Jewish population. Somewhere around half of Kimberley's diamond buyers of the 1870s were Jews, as well as hundreds of diggers. Jews figured in all of the great early firms: Rhodes relied on Beit and on Rothschild money; the Barnatos were Jews, and many regarded J. B. Robinson's Jewish lieutenant, Maurice Marcus, to be his strongest asset.

As a group, however, Jews did no better than anyone else. In December 1873, one Marcus Heyman wrote an ethnocentric review of the situation on the Kimberley diamond fields:

> On the 8th ultimo, I left the above fields. Prior to my departure I ascertained that there were no less than fifty of our co-religionists in the various camps in a state of semi-destitution. Money was being collected every day to send some of these poor deluded victims back to England. . . .
>
> Diamond buying and selling on the fields is a thing of the past . . . you can hardly clear your expenses at it. Cape Town swarms with respectable Jewish young fellows who are unable to get employment, and who have not the means wherewithal to return to their parents.

Later, one of the important early diamond discoveries in Namaqualand was made by a Solomon Rabinowitz, presumably Jewish, and one of the few known women diamond diggers of the Lichtenburg rush was a Yetta Abrams, whose religious persuasion, again, can only be presumed, but which again must be presumed to have been Jewish.

Meanwhile, throughout the latter part of the nineteenth century and the early twentieth, eastern European Jews were fleeing the pogroms and abandoning the *shtetlach,* the Jewish communities of eastern Europe, and joining close or distant relatives in Amsterdam and Antwerp. Many got work as apprentice diamond polishers in Jewish-owned firms. By the outbreak of World War II, some newcomers had graduated to entrepreneurial roles, and the actual cutters were by then largely if not predominantly Christians. Changes in the trade brought about by wartime relocations established the diamond-cutting industry of Israel, in which the cutters, as well as the traders, are exclusively Jewish, and the cutting industry of New York, in which many of the cutters are Jews.

The trade today is highly ethnocentric. Everywhere I heard racial stereotypes, both from Jews and non-Jews: Chinese people have better eyes for judging diamond qualities, a Chinese dealer told me. Puerto Ricans make the best diamond cutters because they are lazy. "It is almost impossible to outsmart an Armenian," a Jewish diamantaire told me with a shake of the head bespeaking admiration. (There are many Armenians in the trade, and their role in it is far greater than their numbers.)

Sooner or later, almost everyone asked my background, no one with greater charm than Charles Ingber, secretary-general of the World Federation of Diamond Bourses, a distinguished-looking old man with a thick French accent:

> . . . aah, are you Jewish? [The reader must imagine the question being asked by Maurice Chevalier.]
> ME (*with affected Menasha Skulnik intonation*): What else?
> "CHEVALIER": I didn't think you looked *Mayflower.*

The Jewish diamantaire who does not "keep kosher" (observe traditional Jewish dietary laws) will keep it quiet, and there are plenty of insincere yarmulkes parading around the world's diamond districts.

The trade is not only highly ethnocentric but also clannish and cliquish. There is a seeming democracy about the human melange at the New York Diamond Dealers Club, or the Diamond Trade Association across the street from it, where Jews mix with Christians from Belgium and Italy, Chinese dealers from Hong Kong, and "Baghdadi" (as Iraqi, Iranians, and other middle Easterners are likely to be known), but the eastern European Jews clearly control Antwerp, New York, and Tel Aviv—the important centers of the diamond trade—and Christians insist that they treat each other differently than they treat "outsiders." A Christian dealer with a Jewish-sounding name and possibly Semitic features told me that he generally "passes" and that virtually no one knows the bitter truth about him: He is Episcopal. He tries to keep it that way. One such as Hong Kong's K. C. Liu (who does not try to pass for Jewish) will nonetheless pepper his conversation with occasional Yiddish expressions. It doesn't hurt any.

Outsiders include not only Christians but also Sephardic Jews, for it is the Ashkenazim who dominate the trade. In Europe and the United States (but not Israel), the Sephardim have been the urbane, "sophisticated" Jews. Their roots trace back to the golden days of Iberia, before they were driven out of Spain and Portugal by the Inquisition of the late 1400s and 1500s. Many of the Sephardim removed to the Lowlands and entered the diamond trade.

The Ashkenazim, the much more numerous branch of Jews, are the earthy eastern European Jews of Sholem Aleichem and Marc Chagall, from whom almost all American Jews are descended. In the seventeenth and eighteenth centuries, both groups vied for dominance of the diamond trade, and suspicions and jealousies made for considerable hostility and acknowledged distrust between them. Each group claimed that the other would give preferential treatment not only to their own, but even to *goyim* (Christians) rather than do a decent turn for a Jew of the other group. The Ashkenazim came to clear dominance of the trade by the end of the eighteenth century, and have preserved their role ever since. As for whether they still "discriminate" against Sephardim, I asked one Sephardic dealer and he answered, "I don't know."

I was surprised that not one Jewish diamantaire complained to me about the DTC's quiet policy of not hiring Jews, though they were full of complaints about every other aspect of the syndicate's operation. The diamond trade is not politicized. Anyway, one yarmulked young diamond man told me, "Jews couldn't hold together the DTC." Without the DTC's guidance "we would undercut each other and cut the whole market to hell."

Regardless of ethnic group—Jew, Lebanese, Armenian, Indian Jain—the diamantaire is almost invariably male. The diamond trade has always been a man's business, principally due to Orthodox Jewish attitudes toward the woman's role and men's relations with women. The Orthodox Jewish conception of the woman's place is among the most traditional in the world: Woman belongs in the home. Further, an Orthodox Jewish male is reluctant to have any significant contact (such as business contact) with a woman other than a member of his family. This attitude almost certainly has something to do with the evils of Eve: Women are likely to excite base appetites, distracting the God-fearing from the duties of piety.

Women have been exluded from the trade not only by the attitude of the men within it, but by their own culturally imposed limitations. Until very recent times, virtually all of the women potentially eligible to participate in the diamond trade, those from diamond families, came from very Conservative or Orthodox Jewish households. They were raised for marriage and children, and imbued with the "female" temperament and disposition, liking diamonds but not the tough, unsentimental world of diamond dealing. Diamond dealing was one of those things that nice Jewish girls didn't do. Ethel Blitz, a fifth-generation diamantaire, says that women [particularly those from diamond families] "don't have the same projection as men. We don't speak up." In 1978, after an assertiveness training course she became the first woman to become a full-fledged member of the New York Diamond Dealers Club.

There were earlier females in the cutting end of the business. Greta Neiman entered the industry during World War II, worked for many years as a cutter in the Harry Winston workshop, and for several years has been a self-employed brutter working from a 47th Street factory loft along with several Orthodox Jewish men. She does not work with them in the communal factory area, where she might distract the God-fearing, but in a small walled-off alcove.

Ms. Neiman is now a decidedly plump grandmother, attractive and powerfully likable, but not a clear and present danger to anyone's piety. Still, when she gets into the elevator to take her to her fifth-floor atelier, one of the Hasidim may disembark so as not to be left alone with the temptress. This is a matter of moral rank-pulling, a holier-than-thou routine. Religiosity is nonsectarian.

Ms. Neiman is herself an Orthodox Jew and appreciates the cultural background for the Orthodox man's attitude toward "strange" women. Her own background and religious training, and thirty-plus years in the New York diamond district, permit her to accept good-naturedly her role as a second-class citizen of the diamond world. But the men who disembark from the elevator get to her: "I wanna slug those guys!"

The most important diamond clubs, in which much of the trade takes place, have traditionally been closed to women, some but not all of them admitting the widows of deceased members as "affiliates," a less than equal status. Just outside the trading hall of the Antwerp Diamantclub are a number of small conference booths which are often occupied by women dealers and brokers excluded from the floor. One told me, "I suppose I could get in if I made a big enough ruckus, but why would I want to? I do a good business in the offices and I can meet people right here and not have to pay their dues."

There have been signs of progress. In 1977 the South African Diamond Club admitted Sharon Goldblatt as its first woman member in her own right; the following year Antwerp's Diamantkring, which trades mostly rough and industrials, accepted Nicole Polak. These are less tradition-bound arenas. Even the biggest and most influential clubs—the strongholds of the super-Orthodox—started to crack. The Israel Diamond Exchange *began* to allow the widows of deceased members affiliate status (but then reversed itself and resumed excluding the widows—thereby making it practically impossible for them to carry on their husbands' businesses). After a bitter internal fight between traditionalists and modernists, with a lot of abstentions by people caught in the middle, the New York Diamond Dealers Club accepted Ethel Blitz. (Her letter of acceptance began: "Dear Sir.") The DTC—which feels no more comfortable dealing with women as equals than do Hasidic Jewish males—accepted Blitz as a sightholder.

It seems likely that the number of female tokens in the trade will increase, but that on balance, the woman's role in the diamond world for the indefinite future is likely to be that of the past: consumer.

Diamonds are a truly international business. While New York dealers flock to Antwerp to buy, the New York Diamond Dealers Club is often crowded with Belgians come to buy in New York—to buy rough as well as polished. Who buys or sells where is more a matter of whom and what you know than it is of regional availability.

A particularly uncommon stone may make several peregrinations across the Atlantic, and maybe the Pacific, before reaching the ultimate consumer in Dallas or Kuwait. Alfred Montezinos, probably New York's leading dealer in "fancy colors" (naturally colored diamonds), bought a stone in Amsterdam and brought it back to the United States. A dealer from Antwerp heard that he had it and called and bought it from him. The stone was mailed to the buyer in Antwerp who resold it to a Hong Kong dealer who had a customer for it—in New York. Each oceanic crossing represents another handler's markup. This can happen, of course, only with the more nearly unique stones, unusually large fine whites or "fancies," for which there are no comparables, no "market value," and no check on price other than the profundity of the buyer's desire and pocket.

Certain types of stones have larger markets in certain areas: North of 45° latitude, a "Cape" stone, one with a distinctly yellowish hue to it, will be discounted on the retail level, but south of 45°, in Italy, Spain, South Africa, South America, or Southeast Asia, you can sell it easily. D-flawlesses, the best quality stones, are unsalable in London. If it is big you can sell it in the Philippines regardless of how bad it may otherwise be. The portability of diamonds, however, operates to minimize regional price differences on the wholesale level. Stones are likely to end up in those sections of the world that demand them.

Every diamantaire of significance on the global diamond scene has access to a telex machine, and the speed and availability of the telex quickly evens out significant price differentials caused by temporary demand in any particular market. If something is momentarily in great demand and therefore commanding a premium price in Tokyo, in a matter of hours every major manufacturer and dealer in the world knows it. The Tokyo demand will inch prices upward everywhere else on the demanded type, closer to the Tokyo price. In a matter of days, the Tokyo demand will have been satisfied and prices will settle at around the same level worldwide.

The trade is characterized by an impressive degree of trust. The contractor must trust his cutters not to grow stones with his merchandise. Because diamonds are more stealable than most wares, all employees must obviously be trustworthy. The regularity with which diamantaires use phony invoices makes for greater than usual embezzlement opportunities in the diamond trade; the boss must be certain that the only one robbing the enterprise is himself. Having a trustworthy staff is the only way to be certain. A buyer will view stones in the wholesaler's office, buy, and then leave them behind for the seller to mail to him. (For security reasons he would prefer not to carry them on his person.) In the interim, the seller could easily switch a few stones on the buyer. No one does. A broker reaches across a desk, grabs a million-dollar parcel of stones, and runs out the door to show them to the hot prospect leaving on the plane in an hour, without even knowing the seller's price demand. No one asks for a receipt, and it never dawns on the consignor to think that maybe the broker will run away with the merchandise. He won't. A Hong Kong diamantaire will sell to a diamond dealer from Jakarta, Bangkok, or another city from within the "smuggling zone" with no written evidence of the transaction whatsoever on sixty or ninety days' credit. As a practical matter, such debts are uncollectable, except to the extent that the buyer is honorable. He is.

There is nothing mysterious about this. The nature of the commodity requires that people deal only with people that they can trust, so diamantaires select those with whom they do business on the basis of established reputation for trustworthiness. Commonly a diamantaire will not deal with anyone unknown to him unless the party comes very well introduced. Character screening of prospective members by the membership committees of the seventeen diamond clubs scattered worldwide makes it likely that any member of one of the clubs will be trustworthy. Carefully selected with an eye to trustworthiness, the diamantaire's business associates are almost certain to *be* trustworthy.

Within their group diamantaires are quite possibly the world's most honest businessmen. Their standards are high and honorable: a man's word is his bond, a bargain is a bargain, and so on.

To some extent the level of commercial integrity that traditionally characterized the trade's internal dealings is beginning to decline. Years ago if a dealer forgot a stone on a table at the bourse, in all likelihood someone would turn it in at the desk; he would get it back. The diamantaire no longer has such confidence in the integrity of his fellows as a group. An Antwerp rough dealer says with a shake of the head, "If I send a parcel to Tel Aviv and by the time that it gets there prices have dropped, the Israeli will decline to accept the goods." The robberies that plague the diamond districts of New York and Tel Aviv are almost always perpetrated by people from within the diamond community. The change in the trade is reflected in a notice posted on the board at the New York Diamond Dealers Club advising of a new club rule: A member who may guarantee payments to be made by a visiting buyer can be held to his guarantee only if it is *in writing*. "Yes, this is a business of trust," a member told me, "but that doesn't mean that it doesn't get violated."

Most attribute the change to the growth of the trade. Before World War II it was a much smaller world, in which a diamantaire was brought into the trade by an uncle or grandfather. Everyone knew everyone else—and their children-successors. It was a highly personal world in which business honor and character meant a lot. Today many more people want—and can afford—diamonds, and there are more diamonds to be had, albeit smaller ones. Between 1969 and 1979, the DTC's gross increased by more than 1,000 percent, indicating a burgeoning of the business at every level and a manifold infusion of new people, expanding the diamond world to one of very different size and dizzying complexities. Most of these newer men are not "family" people, bred from birth with the ethic of the diamond trade. V. Barsamian, a leader of the Antwerp community, told *Newsweek* in 1978 that the diamond world was "usually one big family, but now it's becoming a Babylon. There are newcomers—wolves."

The importance of trust in the business is part of the explanation as to why diamond firms are usually family operations: Whom can you trust if not a relative? Virtually all of the world's major firms are family businesses conducted by brothers, grandsons, cousins, and in-laws, and almost everyone of significance in the trade is from a diamond family. Many diamantaires can trace the diamonds in their blood back to pre-Kimberley days, and many families have sprouted offshoots in different diamond centers. Joseph Schlussel of the Diamond Registry, New York, is only one of many with a brother in Tel Aviv and a brother-in-law in Antwerp, all in the diamond trade.

Commonly diamantaires will act on the assumption that one's family ties with the diamond business, or his lack of them, is an indication of his probable character. A family man is more likely to have been trained in the traditions of the trade, to appreciate and honor its ethics and code of conduct. Unless an "outsider" is brought in by a well-respected mentor who has "adopted" him, he may be shunned from important circles; dealers will be less eager to deal with him, and reluctant to give him goods on "memo" (consignment). The business lends itself nicely to family continuity; the father's goodwill and connections are visited upon the son because "I knew his father," but particularly because the son is presumed to have the father's character. What is not passed on, however, is the father's personality. Generally the founding fathers have come from humble origins and built their success on their "common touch," their ability to *schmooze*. Their sons were born into the upper middle class and to some extent lack their father's ability to deal on a personal basis. They are crisper, busier, more businesslike in the American sense, less willing and less able to haggle. When compared with their simpler, more personable fathers, diamond sons as a group may seem "arrogant," as government officials in two countries characterized them to me. The sons are not interested in *schmoozing*.

The family tradition is equally strong among non-Jewish diamantaires. Most of the most prominent diamond people in India are "family people," some fourth-generation diamantaires. One Indian sitting at a desk opposite his son told me, "I don't bring in outsiders to train; this is not a university." A black diamantaire that I met in Africa told me that he was bringing his teenaged son into the business. Why? He answered Jewish style: "Who else can I trust?"

The industry's honor code never had much relevance when the diamantaires have met the outside world. The average diamond man is no less willing to take advantage of another's ignorance than anyone else—quite possibly more so—and the typical consumer in New York's 47th Street diamond district has a slimmer chance than Little Red Ridinghood. The code of honor has even less relevance when the diamantaire meets an organized government, because, an Antwerp dealer told me, "cheating a government is not like cheating a person." Tax evasion has a respectable tradition in the diamond trade.

As the organization of the diamond trade has matured, the finaglings have matured along with it. One of New York's bigger manufacturer/dealers told me with pride, "We're big boys now; gray zone work doesn't pay anymore." Maintaining duplicate records, extra involvements with accountants and lawyers, and general worrying balance out to be more painful than the paying of taxes. To *some* extent I believe this to be true, though only among the larger American firms. Even the biggest, however, find it hard to reject the cultural traditions of an ancient industry. In the 1977 scandal over the tax returns of the Zale Corporation, the largest retail jewelry chain in the United States and one of the biggest factors in the world diamond trade, one of the allegations of impropriety was that Zale had maintained a gray-money fund in Antwerp for Zale's shadier transactions. For the most part, though, the allegations revolved around such matters as intentional misallocation of costs and profits— the same kind of impropriety in which any nondiamond firm might be involved. To the extent that yesterday's larcenies become outmoded, the diamond trade moves forward.

In world history, duties predate income taxes, and so smuggling predates income tax evasion in the diamond world. To smuggle or not to smuggle is a business decision. Leading members of some of the most respected diamond world entities have been caught and convicted of smuggling and related offenses. No disgrace. *Roselodge* v. *Castle,* an interesting 1966 British litigation, dealt with the question of whether a Lloyd's of London subsidiary could refuse to honor a diamantaire's theft policy on the grounds that the policyholder had failed to voluntarily disclose to it that one of his staff (not suspected of the theft) had once been convicted of smuggling diamonds. In the trial, the diamantaire, Harry Rosenberg, one of London's most colorful and candid dealers, testified that

> I have never had cause for one moment to doubt [the former smuggler's] honesty while he was with me; but there is a qualification I should like to make even though running a risk that my Lord may take a different or very serious view of it; but in the trade, in our trade we do not regard a man who has smuggled goods as having committed an act of dishonesty.

The diamantaire who deals with a professional smuggling operation can be confident that if his goods are intercepted, the smuggling concern will make good all losses, as surely as the Rock of Gibraltar. They too are men of integrity within the trade.

The diamond trade is only a little less secretive than the opium trade. A government official who deals regularly with diamond people described their reticence as "Like a prison system; if you 'talk' others won't deal with you, buy from you, or sell to you." The secrecy filters down to the lowest levels: The closest thing to a "union" among New York City's diamond workers, the Association of Diamond Cutters, is probably the only labor organization in the country that has an unlisted telephone number.

In my interviews I was able to elicit relatively little fearless discussion from the diamond people, and virtually nothing of significance was said in a formal interview setting. Even those who were themselves cooperative were tight with others' names. They do not want to expose someone else to the potential risks that go with speaking to a journalist—or of refusing to speak with a journalist. Writers mean trouble, and diamond people know it. With some few exceptions, they do have something to hide.

The diamantaires' legendary secretiveness is a symptom of one of the underlying tones of the diamond business, which is fear: fear that someone else will usurp "your" market or contact or clients, or fear of commercial reprisals both backward and forward on the distribution pipeline. All of them are afraid to see themselves quoted saying something that might jeopardize their position in the trade or might cast any ill reflection on any aspect of "the business." That might incur the ill will of their peers. Then there is the fear of the IRS, be it the American, Belgian, Israeli, Indian, or South African IRS. More recently, there is the fear of theft and of kidnappings. Fear is a constant in the diamond world.

21

THE DIAMANTAIRES

◆

The diamantaires might be studied anthropologically as a group, like some tribal culture or perhaps a subgroup of a culture. Just as Navahos are a subgroup of American Indians, diamond men form a subculture of "traders." The cultural traits of diamond men cut across apparent ethnic lines: the Indian diamantaires, almost entirely Jains, a Hindu off-shoot, are remarkably like their Jewish brothers in Antwerp and Tel Aviv. The reactions of the diamantaires toward me were parallel to those of the Samoans toward Margaret Mead; they viewed me with considerable suspicion and curiosity at first; only with time did they begin to relax with me, and they never accepted me as "one of their own."

To draw an anthropological stereotype of the diamantaire one might say diamantaires as a group are hearty, warm, and charming personalities. They are also very largely vain, egotistical, and prone to self-praise. They are mentally quick, clever or cunning, but only very rarely are they brilliant. The scoundrels among them that I met were nonetheless highly colorful and immensely likable.

Almost to a man, diamantaires are great raconteurs. "I said to the DTC man," one told me, " 'I'm gunna lose money on this stone—I'm gunna lose a quarter of a million dollars. Is that what you want? You want me to lose a quarter of a million dollars?' He told me, 'No, you aren't going to lose money; you are going to make fifteen percent.' I sez to him, 'I don't want to make fifteen percent, I only want to make five percent. Listen, why don't *you* keep the stone, just give me the five percent!' "

A diamantaire is generally of limited education but even those that are well educated in a formalistic sense usually have low cultural horizons and unsophisticated tastes. The diamantaire's judgment in art or decoration is undeveloped. At the theater he will avoid heavy message matters. He reads virtually not at all, not even diamond trade publications, preferring to get his information orally. Despite the zest that typifies the diamantaire, he lives in a confined and narrow world of diamonds, and his interests are never far removed from his business. Diamantaires are generally of very conservative political cast and in the United States they are usually right-of-center Republicans.

Virtually none of them would think of wearing a diamond. Notwithstanding De Beers' advertising effort to convince the world that "Diamonds Are for Him," most diamantaires personally believe that diamonds are not for him at all, but only for her. When I finally did see a diamantaire wearing a diamond, it was an earring: a man with a single diamond earring at Antwerp's important diamond club, the Beurs Voor Diamanthandel. My host told me that though the fellow with the earring was a rare eccentric in the trade, he was not what I might have thought. There are virtually no homosexuals in the diamond trade. Much to the contrary: From my conversations with diamantaires, I believe (and there are no statistical surveys on the subject) that a disproportionate number of diamantaires—for middle-aged, upper-middle-class Jewish men—have extracurricular sex lives of a thoroughly heterosexual nature.

An occasional diamantaire is caught up in the mystique of the diamond and has some real affection for his wares, but these are as rare as a big D-flawless. Diamonds are the diamantaire's stock-in-trade and he views them in the same light as the clothier views a bolt of cloth. In both trades the goods are called just that: goods. An ad by Baumgold Brothers in *Diamant* well expresses the diamantaires' view of their product:

**BEAUTY
FOR HER,
PROFITS
FOR YOU.
BEAUTIFUL.**

Most diamantaires, however, have private collections of diamonds, kept separate from their recorded business inventories, maintained either as flight insurance—the Nazi era has not been forgotten—or as a "private" trading stock which may be dipped into or upgraded. It would be interesting to know how many of these private collections ever get reported on death tax returns. Diamond people have an easier time evading taxes than others, living or dead.

Diamantaires are likely the most efficient businessmen in the whole world. Even a large diamond dealer will know every last stone in his inventory, and will conduct a major business with a staff of three. Ten employees makes a dealer a giant. Mostly the diamond firms are single-entrepreneur or father-and-son operations. The diamantaire must constantly make quick decisions which will involve occasional mistakes. It takes a self-confident man to stick with it, and self-confident men are loners. This personality trait of the diamantaire, together with the fact that no two diamonds are ever alike, explains why diamond dealing, like diamond manufacturing, is remarkably unconcentrated. Diamonds is a hoard of little businesses.

While diamantaires are efficient, they are not particularly farsighted. De Beers and its CSO are the only diamond world entities that follow the trend of world economy and economic developments on any sophisticated basis, or which attempt to do any long-term planning; the only ones that concentrate on long-term as opposed to short-term goals. The diamantaires rely on "the syndicate" to do their thinking for them, and they buy and sell for today and tomorrow only.

Most dealers have "specialties": melee, sizes or smalls, "Capes" or "whites"—there are dozens of specialties—but I repeatedly received the same answer to the question, What do you deal in? "I deal in anything that I can make a buck in." Partly it is a matter of making money and partly it is a matter of the game, the action. The typical diamantaire is commercially hyperactive and most are involved in more than one level of the business at the same time. A seller will act as a wholesaler selling to smaller wholesalers and simultaneously as a wholesaler selling to retailers. In the diamond world sellers regularly compete in the same arena as those who buy from them. Everyone understands.

Diamond people live a hectic existence, eating on the run, working all the time. Dr. Ami Sha'Ked, Tel Aviv's leading sex therapist, told me that to the extent that a diamantaire is sexually dysfunctioning, he is likely to be a premature ejaculator, because he is always in a hurry. They travel a lot, attending sights in London, visiting their factories in other countries, calling on important customers in the Orient, and when they are not abroad they are on the telephone. If ever a diamond man relaxes, it is on the telephone. When you eavesdrop on their phone conversations you can savor their real charm and flavor, and you must then "forgive" whatever shortcomings they might have. When I visited Sal Lipener, New York/Tel Aviv manufacturer and at the time chairman of the board of the New York Diamond Dealers Club, he had one phone to each ear, speaking Yiddish into one and "English" into the other: "Yes bubeleh, yes dahling, yes bubeleh," he was saying to the burly guy on the other end of the "English" phone.

Every last diamantaire is a hustler. Diamond men are hungry, figuratively and sometimes literally. When the World Federation of Diamond Bourses selected New York as the site for one of its biennial conventions, the New Yorkers determined to outdo predecessor host cities: They hired a sightseeing boat for a floating reception for their brothers from abroad. It was a grand success until the headwaiter announced that dinner was served. At that moment the ship lurched abruptly and alarmingly while the world's leading diamond dignitaries stampeded the buffet table. A reticent diamond man remains hungry, and the diamond world is no place for the reticent.

Diamonds is a tense business, one in which no one ever really knows what is better or worse, what is "worth" what today—or what will be worth what tomorrow, whether the trend is up or down, or how badly the fellow on the other side of the table wants to buy or to sell. Usually, it is a highly leveraged business, in which small general price movements can make fortunes or wipe out the diamantaire. It is a business of bluff and nerve.

There is a lot of smoking in the diamond world, probably a reflection of its nervous climate. More diamond people smoke than other people, and those that smoke, smoke more than other smokers. On the reception desk of Antwerp's Diamond High Council, the "Parliament" of the Antwerp diamond world, sits a basket overflowing with open packages of different brands of cigarettes for the convenience of callers. The Hasidic Jews of New York's diamond district smoke most of all. If there is a diamantaire's occupational illness, it is hypertension.

A diamond dealer is a man who buys and sells diamonds on his own account, either with his own capital, capital provided by a syndicate of backers, borrowed capital, or some of each. A dealer may also manufacture (and is likely to when polished are selling for significantly more than rough), but when he manufactures he generally does so as a contractor. (Manufacturers, possibly without exception, are also dealers, buying other people's output and stray polished diamonds to mingle with their own products and deal at a profit.) A dealer may deal principally in rough or principally in polished, but most deal in "anything I can make a buck in." Some serve a manufacturer as both the provisioner of the rough and as the buyer of the polished, with a little money changing hands for the manufacturer's expenses and margin of profit. This practice is quite ancient.

On a mechanical level, diamond dealing, whether in rough or polished, consists of sorting larger parcels into smaller, more narrowly classified parcels (and at the level of the retail consumer into one-stone parcels) to meet the needs of a continually narrowing class of potential buyers. Diamond dealers are really in the sorting business. Stones may be sorted and resorted ten times between the mine and the finger, with a very small profit turned at each refinement of the assortment. The total manpower, expertise, and expense put into the combined sorting operations often exceeds the manpower and expense that goes into the cutting operation.

On the most-wholesale level, dealers deal in melanges, large mixed lots that require refinements by the purchasers, whether the purchasers be other dealers or manufacturers. Farther down the distribution pipeline, people deal in "series," parcels made up of stones of substantially similar quality but differing sizes, and then, at the next level down, in smaller series, parcels of smaller weight and perhaps with a narrower spread of sizes and qualities. Most intertrade transactions involve purchase and sale of series, again a matter of the seller "moving" all of his merchandise, including the odd pieces that might not find a ready buyer on their own.

Virtually any dealer, no matter how big, will deal in refinements of his usual sales units in order to sell to the "picky" buyer, but the dealer must charge a premium for the stone or stones that are tailor selected for (or sometimes by) the customer. The removal of a stone or stones that are "just right" for a particular customer is likely to devalue the remaining stones in the parcel disproportionately. The dealer who "breaks the series" will insist on being compensated for it.

Those dealers who are principally rough dealers may be sightholders or not, dealing principally in inside goods from the DTC or in outside goods. Whichever he is, the rough dealer is likely to charge open market price without regard for costs, margins, or the DTC price list. Rough dealers are certain to divide their customers into two categories: those who buy rough regularly in order to keep operations going and employees working, and those who buy or don't buy depending on whether they are going to make money on the transaction. Their preferred customers are those in the first category, and a rough dealer can show considerable loyalty toward those.

The polished dealer may principally be a wholesaler's wholesaler, buying entire factory outputs and selling them off in melanges, or he may be a retailer's wholesaler, principally selling series to jewelry manufacturers or to retailers, or sending them small selections on "memo." The retailer's wholesaler buys melanges or large-lot series, sorts them into refined categories, and then stocks the stones to meet specific demands as the demands arise—just like any other wholesaler. If he can't meet the specific demand when the order is phoned in to him, he says, "Yes, I think I've got those in stock; look, I'm tied up right now, lemme call you back in an hour." In the meantime he runs over to the diamond club, or calls his buddies and brokers and rounds up the goods. ("You only need one source when you deal with me.")

It takes a lot of capital to maintain a wide-range stock of diamonds. In today's diamond world, it would be unreasonable to consider becoming a diamond dealer without capital of upward of one million dollars. To some extent bank financing helps, and a number of "diamond banks" in Antwerp and Tel Aviv specialize in financing the diamond trade, but the diamond dealer cannot expect to rely on borrowed money. When interest rates go above 10 percent per year (and they seem unlikely to drop below that ever again), slow-moving goods that must be stocked for a couple of years are going to be losers, and the dealer has to be able to absorb those losses.

The dealer with sufficient capital to be able to extend credit to his buyers is almost certain to be a success in business, especially in the tight-money times that promise to characterize the future as they have the recent past. Credit terms are at least as important as price and invoice recital, often more so.

In slow times the polished dealer has to sweat it out. There is no point to his cutting prices: If he has a stock of goods priced at $1,200 a carat and sells some of it at $1,000, he will not be able to get $1,000 for the next chunk of it that he sells, but only $900 and then $800. In the perverse economics of the diamond world, demand falls as prices fall. If he does cut, his competitors may be tempted to do so too, and if any one class of goods "breaks" it will have a ripple effect that will affect the grades above and below it and spread all across the diamond market. Each and every dealer must hold firm and maintain the price line, and there is surprising solidarity and very little chipping away at it. Peer-group pressure and fears of incurring DTC hostility help to keep waverers in line, and those who do cut prices in order to move overstocks will do so only "in confidence." The financial strength of the polished dealers—together with CSO buying intervention on the polished market—keep wholesale polished prices stable, much as the CSO shores up the rough market.

A diamond dealer operates on the principle, "Buy when people offer goods and sell when people ask for goods." Translation: Buy cheap and sell dear; buy when someone wants to sell badly enough to give you a very good price and sell when someone needs goods badly enough to pay well for them. The diamond dealer can drive as hard a bargain as anyone, and haggling can be an exhausting process. Generally the man with the strongest personality prevails. Many regard the late Joseph Goldfinger of Tel Aviv as the industry's strongest personality of recent times; the fellow on the opposite side of the table would always be a little awed by him, and when Goldfinger said a price, it was difficult to make the kind of counteroffer that one would make to a lesser being. (Ian Fleming was an expert on the diamond trade and almost certainly borrowed Goldfinger's name for his 007 mysteries.) The wise dealer, however, does not drive as hard a bargain as he might: He is interested in return business, not simply one-time profits. Moshe Schnitzer, strongman of the Israeli diamond trade and one of the industry's greatest salesmen, says, "The buyer has to have a chance to make a profit too. In any deal, I never take the last penny."

The broker in the diamond business, as in all others, is the man who finds buyers for sellers' merchandise, and receives a commission for his services. In the diamond trade the principals rarely meet and usually are unaware of each other's identity. The diamond broker is the intermediary for two anonymous people, more like the securities broker than like the real estate broker. It is not unknown for brothers to sell goods to each other through brokers without realizing it. In addition to people who are exclusively full-time brokers, every manufacturer or dealer occasionally brokers other people's goods.

The broker must convince the seller that he is getting top dollar for the goods while satisfying the buyer that he is buying at the very lowest possible price. An adept broker will leave both parties with the feeling that the broker has been "his" man in an adversary negotiation. By the custom of the trade, brokers are allowed considerable latitude in their oral representations. Thus it is not dishonorable (or not too dishonorable) for a broker to tell a seller "You won't get a better price" even when he feels certain that the prospective buyer will pay a little more, or to tell a buyer, casually, "This seller is firm so if you can't meet the price, that's all right," when he knows that the seller is on the verge of bankruptcy. Those who appear to be straight shooters, however, are likely to be more successful at brokering in the long run than those who are too manifestly scoundrels. All diamond brokers, whether relative straight shooters or relative scoundrels, are highly colorful and entertaining characters.

It does not take much expertise to be a diamond broker, and many of them are remarkably unknowledgeable about their wares. One told me that when he began brokering rough he knew nothing about diamonds, but, "You don't have to know anything about something to sell it. Does a real estate agent know how many bricks there are in a building? If you're the seller you say it's good goods; if you're the buyer, you say it isn't. It's all a matter of who can wear the other one down fastest." The job requires more *chutzpah* (gall) than expertise.

The broker is good for both parties. He saves the seller the expense of salary, fringe benefits, and expense accounts that a regularly employed salesman would require, and reduces the seller's merchandising expense to insignificant levels. Sightholders liquidating unusable DTC rough can safely sell it through a broker, knowing that anonymity will be preserved. Most buyers prefer to deal through brokers because they can deal harder with an anonymous seller than they can face to face. A buyer can offer a price through a broker that he would be afraid to offer directly for fear that it would be viewed as insulting, adversely affecting any further negotiations. He can drive as hard a bargain against a distressed manufacturer as the manufacturer's distress permits, without having to feel uncomfortable about doing so. A leading polished dealer told me that he always keeps a broker between himself and the other fellow because "I'm much too squeamish to deal directly."

The broker's commission in the diamond trade, unlike in most other trades, is paid by the buyer, and not directly by the seller, though the seller pays it indirectly to the extent that the buyer takes the commission into consideration in formulating his final offer. The commission is a modest one or two percent, but sometimes the broker is squeezed on his commission, and must shave it in order to close the deal. Commonly it ends up at one percent or less, making the diamond broker probably the lowest-commissioned salesman in the world. In addition, however, he gets "all he can steal," a New York broker-turned-dealer told me. The broker sometimes gets a little more from the buyer than he admits to the seller, and pays a little less to the seller than he tells the buyer. Except when the buyer is invoiced on the seller's billhead (as is required by the regularly ignored rule of many diamond clubs), the seller cannot really know what the buyer did pay, nor can the buyer know what the seller received. Or a broker may be given a parcel to sell at whatever the market will bear. In such cases he will unquestionably deal honorably with his consignor—honorably as dictated both by the ethic of the trade and by common western standards of conduct—on virtually all of the goods. When, however, he gets a request for a particular stone to fit a particular purpose, he will sell that stone at something more than market price, and pocket everything in excess of what the *normal* market would have borne. While this might be called embezzlement in any other line of work, in the diamond trade it is a legitimate form of stealing.

All in all a diamond broker can make an "honest" living. Some who bring buyers and sellers together who establish a permanent business relationship get a commission on their transactions for so long as the relationship lasts—sometimes a lifetime annuity, with commission checks mailed regularly to a retirement address on lower Collins Avenue in Miami Beach or to Elat, Israel. It is never an easy living, though.

A broker can be a rather pathetic sight. On the street floor of the 47th Street diamond district in New York, the outsider can see the broker at work on the lowest level, making the rounds of the more prominent stallholders. A young Hasidic man approaches the counter and takes a small black leather box, closed by a zipper, from inside his overcoat. The box is attached to a chain that leads somewhere within the Hasid's bulky garments. Inside the box are perhaps forty *briefkes* (diamond papers), each a small rectangular sheet of white paper folded into something like a blintz, with diamonds within. He hands a *briefke* to the stallholder. Inside are maybe ten small gems, some a little bigger than others, some smaller, apparently of the same color, presumably of about the same quality. It is a small series. They exchange a little conversation in Yiddish and then the Hasid moves on. In the course of an afternoon, a stream of brokers approach the stallholder, show him merchandise. He looks, displays little interest, they pass on to the next booth.

22

BARGAINING AND CLUBS

◆

As each broker approached Montezinos, he opened the offered *briefke*, looked at it for the shortest moment, folded it back up, and tossed it back at the broker with an expression of lack of interest. An experienced diamantaire can evaluate a packet of diamonds in the bat of an eye, and Alfred Montezinos, New York "fancy colors" dealer and former president of Cartier, is an experienced diamantaire. I was fortunate to witness his bargaining technique at Antwerp's Beurs Voor Diamanthandel.

Montezinos had positioned himself at one of the long tables, and brokers brought him goods that they thought might interest him. He is well known throughout the diamond world, and everyone knows what is likely to interest Montezinos: the world's best sizes and qualities of the rare intensely colored diamonds. His bargaining style with each differs depending on his previous experience with the individual. Some of the brokers with whom he deals are relatively straightforward (for diamond brokers) and with those, the ballet between buyer and broker is less complex. Montezinos prefers to deal in a more straightforward manner, but for those that insist on the full choreography, he knows how to dance. With some he can be quite polite: "No, but thank you for showing me the merchandise." With others he is abrupt, even rude. All of them handle in a surprisingly disrespectful manner the goods that are touted at the retail level in hushed tones of reverence.

The first *briefke* was opened and closed again in a flash. Too close a look in a *briefke* indicates a greater degree of interest than the prudent buyer will show. Montezinos rejected its contents with real scorn. The apparent degree of his lack of interest is inversely proportional to the degree of his interest. The broker showed him a different item, not the kind of stone in which Montezinos usually deals, but he admitted that it was at least "a lot nicer than the last one." After fencing on various items and some passage of time, he and the broker backed into negotiations on the first stone.

"How much?" Montezinos has made a science of interpreting the length of time that elapses between this question and its answer. The length of time it takes the broker to answer reflects the length of time it has taken him to figure out what he can get out of Montezinos. "How much?" he asked again, and the broker began to respond: "Twenty-sev—" Before he could finish his answer Montezinos interjected impatiently, "How much?!" and out tumbled the answer: "Twenty-two." Montezinos said simply, "No." He made no counteroffer, but he did mutter something softly to himself—a number. Fourteen hundred. The broker, "unfortunately," overheard. The comment, the number, pained the broker deeply. One must see a diamond broker's face overcome with a mixture of anger and hurt when presented with an eminently reasonable offer in order to appreciate why Jews have been so successful as traders and actors. Pained expressions are a diamond broker's stock in trade.

Meanwhile, another broker approached Montezinos with merchandise and Montezinos drifted away from the first and became intensely involved with the other—praising his wares—for the benefit of the first broker, still seated at his table. The first broker understood what was happening and excused himself abruptly, parting from Montezinos with a reciprocated intimation that Montezinos was an unreasonable person. Later that afternoon, broker number one just happened to pass Montezinos' spot at the table, and they renewed old acquaintances, ultimately to trade a *mazel* over the parcel at 1,700 per carat. Recitation of the word *"mazel"*—actually a short form for *mazel und brachah,* "luck and blessing"—seals a bargain for diamantaires.

Another broker approached with goods. Montezinos made his one-second evaluation, and returned the *briefke* with a "How much?" The price was stated. Montezinos put on his no-interest-whatsoever expression. "No interest?" asked the seemingly puzzled broker—who goes through this same routine twenty times daily. "Not at that price," was the answer—the same answer that I heard on my travels through the diamond world from different buyers in several different countries. At length the broker piqued his interest, and when Montezinos finally made his firm-and-final, the broker said, "Well, I'll have to ask the seller." The parcel was sealed, with Montezinos' offer noted on it. In a moment the broker returned; the offer was accepted. The moment was so brief that it was inconceivable that the broker had actually called the seller in the interim. Either the goods had been the broker's own merchandise or the seller had given him advance authority to sell at a lower price than Montezinos' bid. Lesson: He had bid too much.

All in all, Montezinos had a busy and successful day, in which he made a large number of purchases. It was his last day for that particular trip to Antwerp, and much as he tries to restrain himself, he is likely to "loosen up" a bit on his last day. The brokers understand as much, and sometimes hold back goods they think might interest him until his last day. He knows that they know. So he is always fuzzy about his timetable; most every day is likely to be his "last" day. This one was.

Most diamond transactions require bargaining, not only deals between two strangers but also deals between the world's biggest and most prestigious manufacturers and their best-established clients. Everyone I spoke with said that he would prefer to eliminate the bargaining, and some dealers, especially younger people in the trade, are now managing to dispense with it. A sizable number of sellers now operate from a firm "postbargaining" price list, particularly on smallish lots of routine goods. But most still feel that they "have to play the game."

The extent to which sellers inflate their realistic valuations to arrive at initial price demands, and buyers discount them to arrive at opening offers, varies as greatly as do personalities and temperaments. Bargaining techniques are as different as are diamonds. There is no typical "spread" between opening offers and demands, but if one were to create one, it would likely be: A seller will probably ask 20 percent more than he thinks the goods are worth, and a buyer will likely offer 15 to 20 percent less than fair market value to start, making a total spread of perhaps 40 percent. Thus, the seller will ask $1,200 a carat for goods he values at $1,000 and the buyer, if his valuation of the goods is about the same, will ofer $800.

Many buyers will decline to bid against a demand that the buyer thinks to be inflated by more than 20 percent: If the seller asks $1,400 per carat for a "$1,000" parcel, the buyer will refuse to make any offer until the seller drops to $1,200; then, the buyer will offer $800. On unusual goods—large, speculative pieces of rough; "fancy colors"; and other tough-to-value items—the spread is likely to be greater because neither party can have much of a feel for what the other party thinks the lot to be worth. The seller's objective, bear in mind, is to sell at the *buyer's* highest valuation; the buyer's objective, to buy at the seller's lowest valuation. Whatever the seller may quote for a price on a tough-to-value item, the buyer will respond, "We're so far apart that we won't be able to get together on this lot"; to which the seller must and will reply, "Make me an offer anyway—insult me."

Getting an initial price demand or an initial offer is not always easy. Sellers—usually acting through their brokers—play coy. They are not much interested in selling, and certainly not eager to part with their goods—or at least that is the pose. Anyone who wants (or needs) to sell will sell for less. Buyers, on the other hand, invariably affect simple boredom over the merchandise. When they begin to move into negotiations they spar a little before either makes a demand or an offer. The buyer asks, "How much?" The broker may respond, "Is it worth twenty-five hundred a carat?" That does not constitute an initial demand of $2,500; the demand may be more than $2,500—or less. The broker is merely asking a simple question. The savvy buyer will ignore the question, and may respond with one of his own: "Would you take seventeen hundred?" That response does *not* constitute an offer of $1,700. "Well," says the broker, "how much do you want to spend?" No one in the diamond world ever answers such a question. If a buyer says he wants to spend $1,800, then $1,600 goods *become* $1,800 goods—or $1,900 goods (but he'll let you have them for $1,850).

When finally the parties enter serious negotiations and reach a point where a buyer makes a seemingly firm and final offer, almost always lower than the price the seller has authorized the broker to accept, the broker needs time to consult the seller. The parcel is sealed in an envelope, and the offered figure noted upon it. It is most rare for an offerer to sign acknowledging his offer in writing, and even rarer for the prospective buyer to repudiate his offer. His reputation would be sullied if he did. The offer is understood to remain open for one business day (excluding weekends) for the seller to accept if he wishes. The life spans of offers may vary in accordance with differing customs in the various diamond centers, and may be altered by specific acknowledgement of the offerer.

"See this envelope?" a diamantaire asked as he showed me a small manila envelope stapled closed. "A man offered me twenty-one five for this stone today. I refused it. We left it that we'd sleep on it overnight. If I called him in the morning and said that I'd take the twenty-one five he'd never dream of denying that he made the offer, or of not honoring the offer, even if the value of the stone dropped overnight. And I'd never dream of opening the envelope to try to get a higher offer from someone else, and then putting the stone back in the envelope and stapling it back up—or of calling him next week and saying, 'You said that the offer would stay open a week—I accept it.' People don't do that in this business. In this business your word is sacred."

Nevertheless, breaches and subterfuges do occur: a broker may tell another prospect, "I offered it to Rabinowitz for a thousand; he offered nine hundred. I'll stick to the thousand with him if you'll pay nine sixty." That kind of conduct is clearly unethical in the trade, for which a broker may be censured and fined by the diamond club with which he is affiliated, but it does happen.

The most spirited and colorful bargaining takes place in the clubs. There are seventeen diamond clubs or bourses, four in Antwerp, two each in New York, Tel Aviv, and London, and clubs in Amsterdam, Johannesburg, Milan, Vienna, Paris, Singapore, and Idar-Oberstein (the small West German town southeast of Frankfurt that is the "Antwerp" of the ruby and emerald worlds). Each of these clubs is part of the World Federation of Diamond Bourses, which has a total membership of about eighteen thousand individuals.

Everyone who is anyone in the diamond world belongs to one or more of the clubs, and lots of people who are "nobody" in the diamond world belong too. Membership in any one of them opens doors at any other.

Prior to the war (which in the diamond trade is understood to mean World War II) the diamond club was every diamantaire's office. Membership in the great clubs of the day, the Beurs Voor Diamanthandel in Amsterdam or the Diamantclub van Antwerpen, was opened only to replace deceased members and then was highly selective; acceptance into either was a tribute to a man's character, as well as to his importance in the business. Charles Ingber, an Antwerp diamond dealer for all of his long life, remembers the day when his father was elected to the Diamantclub: The father was honored in the synagogue by being called to recite a blessing over the Torah, after which the family hosted a reception at their house.

Today, any manufacturer or dealer of substance has his own office as well as a club membership. In the interests of privacy all of the most important trade is conducted in the offices, and most dealers visit their clubs only occasionally. The bourse or club is still the office for those without, for the smaller dealers, and for the brokers. It is the arena for the small men. It was before the war too, but before the war there were, by today's standards, only small men in the diamond world.

What happens in the diamond club, however, comes as close to establishing a market barometer as there is in the diamond world. "How much would it bring in the club?" means, "What is its market price?" It is the small men dealing the small lots in the club that establish the market price and the market trends, to be followed by the big boys. Even the biggest may send their "slow movers" there in order to unload overstocks, and most diamantaires, big or small, will occasionally stop at the club for lunch, to get a feel on the pulse of the diamond market. And indigestion. Food at diamond club lunchrooms ranges downward from bad. Most of them claim to run kosher operations, but super-Orthodox people don't believe it.

The office trade has drained off some of the floor congestion at most of the clubs, and at all but the New York Diamond Dealers Club and the Israel Diamond Exchange membership is now open to those who can pass the rigorous screening and afford the membership fees. A prospective applicant for membership at most diamond clubs must have at least two years' experience in the wholesale diamond trade and must be sponsored by a member. He will be asked for trade and financial references, which will be checked. His picture will be posted on the club bulletin board, and objecting members will be given an opportunity to state their grievances. His picture may be removed if objections to him are brought forward and then reposted when the objections are obviated. The membership chairman of one club told me, "How well

I do my job depends on how many people hate me."

Once a new member is accepted, he must come up with the initiation fee, which ranges upward to a walloping $5,000 at the New York Diamond Dealers Club and $10,000 at the Israel Diamond Exchange. Thereafter, annual dues and assessments are generally modest by comparison, about $350 for each of the eighteen hundred members of the New York Diamond Dealers Club. For this, the member is buying into a communal office with excellent security and dependable, discreet telephone message service, and access not only to his own local trade but to that of out-of-town diamantaires who may visit the club to purchase or sell.

At Antwerp's Beurs Voor Diamanthandel, probably the world's busiest diamond bourse, or the Israel Diamond Exchange or the New York Diamond Dealers Club, a couple of hundred out-of-town buyers will stop each day. Each will be hosted by a club member, who may or may not sit by the visitor's side at the trading tables, but who will, in either case, guarantee the foreigner's financial stability, and receive one or two percent from him in exchange for this "hospitality." The brokers approach the visitor seriatim with their wares. Foreigners do some 7,300 transactions *daily* at the Antwerp Beurs.

Diamond clubs are almost always laid out in the same manner: There is a largely glassed north-facing wall, with long tables placed at right angles to it, so as to maximize the members' access to the northern light. A diamond is likely to show its least distorted color when viewed in a northern light (and particularly between 10:00 AM and noon on a moderately overcast morning during the spring or fall). Strong southern sunlight will make a diamond look better than it is. Some of the most agitated arguments at diamond clubs will involve who has proper claim to the seat closest to the northern window. (This is true in the northern hemisphere only, of course; in the southern hemisphere diamantaires seek out a southern light for inspection of stones.)

Club surroundings may be somewhat shabby, as at the New York Diamond Dealers Club; European-Victorian, as at the Beurs in Antwerp; or crisply modern, as at Antwerp's Diamantclub or the Israel Diamond Exchange. The atmosphere at all of them is likely to be discombobulating. At the Israel Diamond Exchange, probably the worst in this respect, the usual noise level is a maddening din punctuated by the incessant staccato paging system, through which a dizzying mix of bustling people move in a frenzy of activity. It is a pandemonium, an inferno for anyone with a contemplative bone in him—and I saw it on an "off" day.

The club represents the diamantaire's court as well as his bourse, and in Tel Aviv or New York, where one club is clearly dominant, that club will represent the diamond community's informal government. Members are bound to submit any disputes that they cannot settle between themselves to the club's arbitrators for determination. Anyone who goes to civil court without permission of the club will suffer expulsion and blacklisting, which is likely to put a diamantaire out of business throughout the diamond world.

It is common for people in ghetto communities, suspicious of the larger world beyond their neighborhoods, to shun the civil judiciary outside in favor of in-group adjudication by less formal arbitrators, but in the diamond trade a fuller body of precedents and a more formalized procedure has grown up than is usually the case. In the last century and before, the Talmud, the vast compilation of the Oral Law of the Jews as elucidated and elaborated upon by the great rabbis and commentators, provided a framework of law—Jewish international law—for diamond men to apply in their dealings between themselves, regardless of what national boundaries might separate them. The law of the diamond world today, as applied by club arbitration panels, is almost certainly an evolution of traditional Talmudic principles, adapted to meet the needs and customs of a specific trade.

Perhaps 150 disputes a year come to the board of the New York Diamond Dealers Club, of which fully half are settled by club conciliators, and never reach a hearing before the arbitrators. Those that must go to arbitration will be heard by three members chosen from among a large panel that is elected. On any given afternoon there is likely to be a hearing in progress at the club's boardroom. A lawyer usually is present to assist the panel with legal insights but only when asked.

Arbitrators at a diamond club will hear almost any matter concerning the diamond trade or business-related wrongs. Their most common form of work is presiding over bankruptcies, which the diamond clubs handle more or less in the same way as a United States bankruptcy referee: The defaulting diamantaire turns over his assets to the club, which distributes them among creditors on a pro-rata basis. At bankruptcy court, however, the debtor walks out clean. When the defaulting diamantaire leaves his club's boardroom, it is with an understanding as to what *further* payments must still be made to his creditors, as a condition of his remaining in the club and the trade. On one of my visits to the New York Diamond Dealers Club a defaulting member delivered $550,000 in goods to the club for the benefit of creditors.

Only infrequently do arbitrations become disputes over who said what, and rarely is a man's character an issue. Exceptions may occur, when one diamantaire impugns another's reputation, or equally important, his financial stability. An unsuccessful litigant in such a contest may be required to pay money damages to the wronged party, or to pay a fine, which is turned over to some recognized charity. When in the heat of argument one Jewish diamantaire made a viciously anti-Semitic comment to another, the arbitrators of the New York Diamond Dealers Club ordered the offender to contribute $25,000 to a Jewish charity.

Whatever its origins, arbitration rather than civil litigation is especially appropriate for the diamond world because the hearing officers, fellow diamantaires, already know the arcane customs of the diamond trade. A trial before a civil magistrate would require long testimony— possibly conflicting—as to the customs of the trade. Arbitration is also fast, and it avoids the sometimes staggering costs of litigation in the civil arena. And it keeps disputes inside the community.

The member who refuses to accept the arbitrators' decision is certain of expulsion from the club. An expelled member's photo, together with a description of his offense, will be circulated among all of the clubs belonging to the World Federation of Diamond Bourses, and will remain posted on the bulletin board of each for one year. An expelled member of any one of them will find himself barred from any of the others. He is out of business.

There are very few people blacklisted in this manner at any one time, and being blacklisted rarely carries imputation of moral wrongdoing. Most of those shunted out of the trade are purged for financial shortcomings, failure to satisfy in-trade creditors. A man's word is supposed to be his bond, even—especially—when it comes to paying for goods on a date certain.

23

THE DIAMOND CITIES: AMSTERDAM GIVES WAY TO ANTWERP

◆

Of the world's great diamond-cutting centers, Antwerp, Tel Aviv, New York, Bombay and Surat in India, and Johannesburg, the best workmanship is generally believed to come from Antwerp, Johannesburg, or New York; Israel's "make" is a lesser one; and India's work is generally regarded to be of the poorest quality. The ranking of goods has nothing to do with the basic abilities of Belgians versus Hindus: The difference in workmanship produced by the differing cutting centers is mainly a matter of economics and rough supplies. The quality of the make that a manufacturer gives to his wares turns mostly on the quality of the rough that he is working. Best rough, warranting top quality make, gets it; undesirable rough deserves and gets only "third make." The best rough goes to Antwerp, the worst to India.

"Indian goods!" a Bombay manufacturer repeated after me, affecting the tone of scorn that his wares are frequently accorded. "Why, our people can—could—equal the world's finest make. Have you seen our work in ivory? Our fine goldwork? Indian handicrafts are the very best in the world—and our diamonds could be too—if only we could get the rough. But the rough *they* give us is suitable only for poor quality make."

"They" means the DTC. The DTC determines what goods get sold for processing where. New York gets "sizes," largish rough, the only kind that it has been economical to process in New York, and slightly smaller goods for the New Yorkers' Puerto Rican factories; Antwerp gets good quality good-sized stones and "difficult" goods, stones that will require greater than usual expertise to process successfully; Israel gets melee, smallish pieces; India gets near-gems and smalls and other stones that a decade ago would have been sold as industrials. Pursuant to South African law, Johannesburg gets pretty much whatever it wants of what is mined in South Africa. Because different centers process different types of goods, the cutting centers tend to be complementary rather than competing.

There are historical reasons for the DTC's allocations to the various cutting centers. The Lowlands at one time processed all of the world's diamonds. During World War II the cutting industry scattered to Palestine and elsewhere, but Antwerp and briefly Amsterdam were restored to a near-monopoly position in the immediate postwar period. Then, as costs in the Benelux area increased, it became uneconomical to process smaller goods there, leading to the birth (or reemergence) of the cutting center in Israel, where lower labor costs enabled the economical processing of melee. Even in Israel, however, smalls and bottom-quality rough could not be handled profitably. These continued to be sold as industrials. As demand increased for bottom-quality "gems," a third major cutting center emerged in India. First come is still first served: Israel is still largely limited to what Antwerp cannot use, and India to what Israel doesn't want. The New York–Puerto Rican share, a holdover from World War II days, ranks least important in the total picture.

Of the diamond-trading centers, Israel is an important trading center for melee and New York for sizes; Hong Kong is the great trading center for diamonds and everything else in the Orient, while Singapore fills a similar role but for a more regional market in Southeast Asia. Antwerp remains the unrivaled leader, the capital of the world diamond trade.

Whenever any of these cutting or trading centers is threatened by hostile government action, their diamantaires rise as one man with the cry, "Remember Amsterdam!" It is helpful to pause for an autopsy on Amsterdam.

To generations of Americans past—and probably future too—Amsterdam has been and will continue to be known as the diamond city, principally because it has been so long touted as such. Many who live there believe that Amsterdam is the diamond capital, and no visitor passing through its busy airport can leave with any other impression: No fewer than four airport stalls offer diamonds to the tourist. Like most people, I too identified Amsterdam with diamonds when I began researching this book, and was disbelieving when a New York dealer told me, "There's no action in Amsterdam anymore; if you go to their bourse you'll only find maybe three or four people there, sitting in a corner playing cards." I hoped he was wrong, and indeed he was: When I went to the Amsterdam Diamantbeurs on July 3, 1979 at 3:40 P.M., it was open for business but there was nobody there at all. Even the card players had abandoned the Beurs, something akin to rats and ships.

It wasn't always that way. For the past five hundred years, the focus of activity has moved back and forth between Antwerp and Amsterdam. Charles Ingber remembers his grandfather and his father prior to World War I leaving their homes in Antwerp for several days at a time to trade in Amsterdam, then the world's diamond capital. The focus began to shift again to Antwerp with the great diamond discoveries in South

Africa in the early 1870s. Antwerp's diamantaires had better connections with the South African entrepreneurs than did Amsterdam's. The events of the Nazi era sealed Amsterdam's fate in the diamond trade. More of Amsterdam's Jewish population was lost in the holocaust than Antwerp's; Antwerp was liberated from the Germans much earlier than Amsterdam; and after the war, the Belgian government made efforts to encourage the revival of the Antwerp trade. Holland did not encourage it, but instead hampered it with what diamantaires describe as "rules and regulations"—that is, taxes.

Of Amsterdam's great houses, only one remains significant in the gem world: Asscher's (Asscher's Diamond Company). Asscher's labor force is now down to around fifty—probably more than a quarter of the entire Dutch cutting force—and Asscher's no longer takes apprentices or newcomers to the trade, an omen for the future of the Dutch cutting industry. They face staggering labor costs: management's per employee expense comes to perhaps $2,500 a month. Income and employment taxes take the difference between that and the employee's $1,000 take-home. In Antwerp the tax collector's share would compute out about the same, but it is largely evaded through under-the-table payments. How can fully taxed Asscher's compete with the largely tax-exempt Antwerp firms? Simple, according to Joop Asscher, twenty-eight, from the fourth and current generation at Asscher's: "The Asscher make is the best in the world. We won't turn out any naif, half-finished stones, or stones with false facets. Make will vary according to the stone, but every one will be exactly symmetrical, perfectly finished." I heard the same kind of talk from manufacturers elsewhere; in Asscher's case, however, it may well be true.

Of the other great houses of Amsterdam, D. Drukker & Zn now deals mostly in industrials (and is a significant factor in that market worldwide), while the once proud house of A. van Moppes & Zoon, founded in 1828, is now reduced to a largely retail trade, catering to tourists steered to it by concierges and taxi drivers who will receive a kickback. They give a nice tour at the van Moppes factory—which I recommend—and they are polite and "soft sell" in the showroom (where their prices compare favorably with those that will be charged by the typical American retailer). Amsterdam is a good place to buy diamonds, the van Moppes guide told us, because "there are no taxes at all, except for the duty and we don't declare anything; whether you declare it when you go through the American customs, well that's up to you." How much is the duty at American customs? The guide answered correctly: "Twelve and a half percent—if you declare it." Van Moppes is an especially good place to buy, the guide said, because "we sell only perfect blue-white diamonds."

What do they do with the ones that aren't perfect? "We send them back," the guide told us. Back where? "Back to De Beers. We have an understanding with them: any diamonds that are not perfect, we will not take them."

News of van Moppes' understanding with De Beers will probably come as a shock to every other diamond manufacturer in the world, all of whom have been operating on the assumption that the DTC does not accept returns.

Outside of Amsterdam, such industry as there is in Holland is also largely tourist oriented. Raoul Delveaux, director general at the time of my visit of Antwerp's Hoge Raad Voor Diamant (Diamond High Council), the parliament of the Antwerp diamond industry, told me:

> In every town in Holland there are two signs, one directing you to the town hall and one to the local diamond factory. If you go to the factory you will see a sawyer and a cleaver working side by side, as they never do in real life, and a girdler and a polisher and they're supposedly making the stones, and at the end of the line there's a coffee cup sitting in a saucer with a couple of diamonds in the saucer too, and the tourists see them and ask are they for sale and the manager says, "Well, I suppose well ... oh, I guess we could sell just one or two ... " And the tourist buys them and is happy because he has gotten diamonds that might still be warm—maybe because the saucer was warm—and maybe he's even saved a little money on what they would retail for at home; and the manufacturer is happy because he has made a big profit instead of the 4 or 5 per cent that he would otherwise have made; and we are happy too, because those diamonds come from Antwerp.

Antwerp is a drab and gray industrial city almost totally devoid of charm. The New Yorker who described it to me as "the European Newark" did it no injustice. It is paradoxical that this most unglamorous of cities is the heart of one of the world's most glamorous industries.

There is an odd quality to the light in Antwerp: It is very light, but the light is diffused, without glare or heat. It is surely one of the best places in the world for inspecting diamonds, but that probably has much less to do with its preeminence in the trade than the attitude of the Belgian tax collectors. One of the industry's leaders put it bluntly to me: "We pay what taxes we want to pay."

The diamond quarter faces the long gray exterior of the enclosed railroad tracks along Pelikaanstraat, and then strings out behind Pelikaanstraat onto Rijfstraat, Hovenierstraat, and Schupstraat. The row of drab buildings on Pelikaanstraat includes the most prestigious addresses in the diamond world. One would walk right by No. 62 without noticing it. Inside is the vast modern hall of the Diamantclub, with an internal communications system that would rival Cape Canaveral's. On the floors above the club are the offices of many of the most powerful people in the world diamond trade. Two doors away is the Beurs, with the only facade on the street that pretends any majesty, and it barely pretends. The only architecturally interesting building in the area is the Andimo Building at 21 Schupstraat, known locally as the Tower of London. It is here that the DTC and its various "affiliated companies" have their Antwerp headquarters, and keep watch on a trade that exists at its sufferance. Living in the shadow of Andimo, Antwerp's diamantaires are preoccupied and jittery about the DTC's steps toward vertical integration.

Security is good throughout the diamond district. The busiest "back street," Hovenierstraat, is closed to traffic by policemen at either end, who monitor comings and goings; entrance to most of the more important buildings is restricted; and many of the offices have highly sophisticated electronic security devices. It is preventive security: The Antwerp diamond district lacks the history of crime that has plagued the New York and Tel Aviv communities. Violence, incompatible with the Antwerp tradition, is almost unknown. Such crimes as have occurred have been quickly solved by the well-regarded constabulary. The Antwerp diamond community has excellent relations with the police, unlike their brothers in New York and Tel Aviv.

As elsewhere, the Antwerp diamond community is principally Jewish. Most of Antwerp's thirteen thousand Jews are involved in one way or another with the trade, and they support four synagogues and a Yiddish newspaper. Cognoscenti regard Antwerp's kosher food as among the best in the world. Moskowitz's, just down the Pelikaanstraat from the Beurs and the Club, is the favorite of the diamond crowd. It is a clean, ultramodern deli where your meal is warmed in a microwave oven and served in brass and copper pots, just as in many other places in Belgium, except that at Moskowitz's, the meal is kosher—kosher enough to satisfy the Hasids who pack the place. That's kosher.

One of the first Jews in Antwerp was Lodewyk van Berken. Trained in Bruges and Paris, van Berken moved to Antwerp sometime in the 1470s and established the city's first cutting works. Under the patronage of Charles the Bold, duke of Burgundy, his work became sought after by the rich and powerful, kings and popes, and was even acclaimed by Benvenuto Cellini. He attracted other European Jews as pupils, and they remained in Antwerp. With time the city replaced the trade leaders— Lisbon, Venice, Paris, and Bruges—to become the unrivaled center of the diamond world. Then, in the eighteenth century, Amsterdam took control of the Brazilian output of rough and eclipsed Antwerp as the diamond capital. The pendulum began to swing back in Antwerp's favor soon after the Kimberley discoveries. Hitler's conquest of both Holland and Belgium in May of 1940 put an end to the competition between the cities.

As the war drew to an end, Romi Goldmuntz, doyen of the Antwerp diamantaires, reentered the city just behind the British liberation forces. Scattered encounters with German soldiers were still taking place within Antwerp when he resumed work. At about the same time a Red Cross truck carried Nathan Ferstenberg, Goldmuntz's successor as leader of the Antwerp industry, home to Antwerp. He scouted out his prewar foreman, a Christian; the foreman rounded up ten of the old staff, and within a week the Ferstenberg enterprises too were working. Before the formal end of the war, Antwerp was again in the diamond business. The government of the newly freed country sent emissaries to the places of refuge that Antwerp's Jews had found, to entreat them to return to Belgium. Belgium wanted a diamond industry to give employment, to bring dollars into the country, and otherwise to aid in the restoration of Belgium. One by one the diamantaires filtered back. The government did indeed make them welcome: They were essentially left alone by officials on every level, and the country was left open to the importation of licit or illicit rough without serious inconvenience to anyone.

The DTC did most to help: It cut off supplies of rough to the new cutting centers that had grown up in Palestine, Cuba, and Brazil during the war in order to channel the rough back to Antwerp—a sign of loyalty to its oldest patrons, struggling to start over fresh after suffering the ravages of war. Or so it was explained. There was probably more to it than just noble sentiment: Belgium controlled the tremendous diamond output of the Congo, which Sir Ernest erroneously believed held the key to the future of the diamond world.

Since then Antwerp has had its ups and downs. Its role as the only significant cutting center was chipped away with the emergence of Israel (or reemergence of Palestine), now the world's principal cutting center in terms of dollar volume, and of India, now the world's leading cutting country in terms of total caratage handled. Even its role as a trading center seemed to be ebbing in the late 1960s and early 1970s. Israel's interests, coordinated by its Diamond Institute, seemed to be making aggressive inroads on all of Antwerp's provinces.

To combat what looked to be the adverse trend, in 1973 the Antwerp diamond community, with the encouragement of the DTC, established the Hoge Raad Voor Diamant, or Diamond High Council, commonly known as the HRD, to coordinate and represent their interests. The HRD engages in some scientific research and the testing of apparatus, operates a respected diamond-grading laboratory, and carries the public relations burden for the Antwerp diamond community. It speaks for the industry as a united front, but its practical effectiveness is hampered by the stubbornness and independence of the individual diamantaires, each of whom will predictably refuse to temper his own short-term interests in favor of the long-term interests of any community, even his own.

During the bren of '78, Antwerp's allotments of rough were channeled off by many of the Antwerp diamond people to Israel, leaving the local cutters without work. The HRD adopted a rule: All export of rough had to be submitted to the HRD, and exporters would be requested to withdraw from their shipments any rough that was deemed suitable for local processing. Compliance would be voluntary, although the names of the uncooperative would be made available to the DTC. According to *Diamant,* the diamantaires gave only minimal cooperation—"a few flowery compliances, hand on heart, and in a glow of self-conscious virtue"—while either hoarding their stock or exporting it surreptitiously. To the extent that net exports dwindled, *Diamant* attributed it to the saturation of Israel.

Antwerp survived the bren and still has the largest number of cleavers, the most highly skilled diamond workers, and remains the only place where difficult rough can be processed. It is the great generalist in cutting, capable of handling all classes of materials and all cuts. Its importance has declined a lot from the days when almost every stone passed through Antwerp, but still something over half of the diamonds that will be retailed next year will have been bought and sold as rough or polished in Antwerp.

Antwerp's five hundred-plus dealers and manufacturers handle every imaginable type, cut, and quality of diamond. For the buyer with differing needs, or the seller with varying offerings, it is the only place to go. In weak-market times, Antwerp is often the only place that stones can be sold at any price. The staggering financial reserves of Antwerp's dealers enable them to buy—at the right price—and to hold. Antwerp operates as a stocking mechanism that protects the polished market, much as the DTC stocks to protect the rough market—both for their own profit.

Availability of financing for buyers is another powerful attraction for Antwerp. Many Antwerp sellers can provide financing themselves, and others can arrange for it for their buyers at Antwerp's Banque Diamantaire Anversoise or one of the other Antwerp "diamond banks" that exist to serve the local diamond community and their customers. Many Indians prefer to buy rough from Antwerp rough dealers who specialize in "Indian goods" at a slightly higher rate than that for which they might buy directly from the DTC because they can get financing for their purchases through the Antwerp diamond banks, financing that would be unavailable in India (or from the DTC).

The freedom of the Antwerp market is also a powerful impetus to trading there. There are no import or export duties on either rough or polished, and no currency controls. And there are no questions. I asked an industry leader about illicit rough and he cut me short: "Once it gets to Antwerp, it is *legitimate* rough." Nobody asks the source of anyone's stones, and if the seller says that his name is "Smith," then his name *is* Smith. People are also discreet about the origins of moneys. A 1979 *National Geographic* article quoted Ferstenberg for the assertion that "submarine money" (as he called it) accounted for a third of Antwerp's sales. Those I spoke to thought his estimate very conservative.

There are actually two related but separately identifiable diamond-cutting industries in Belgium: the *grof* branch, which processes the larger and more valuable stones in Antwerp itself, and the *klein* branch, which handles smaller and less important goods in the *kempen* region, the country-side around and easterly of Antwerp. Together they employ perhaps twelve thousand workers, well under a tenth of the number of diamond workers polishing in India.

On a total weight basis, much more of "Antwerp's" cutting is done in the *kempen* than in the city, and the *kempen* industry is the more interesting, at least sociologically, because it is still largely a cottage industry. In Antwerp workers are employed as regular employees, for the most part in small but organized factories, generally on an hourly rate. Antwerp manufacturers appreciate that on large and important stones, where labor costs are dwarfed by rough costs, piecework is counterproductive. In the *kempen*, though many organized factories exist (paying piecework), many cutters still work the stones in their own homes. Their "cottage" is often a large, garishly furnished house in the garret of which the polisher has established his "shop." There he works together with his wife, often assisted by children of tender years, for upward of ten or twelve hours a day, every day. Outside is his Mercedes Benz, and perhaps his wife's Mercedes too.

Pay in the *kempen* comes to significantly below that of the Antwerp workers, but a *kempen* worker will ask himself, "So what if I earn only a pittance an hour; in what other line of work could I put in so many hours?" (Antwerp's workers are limited to eight-hour days by their union.) The *kempen* industry—and the mentality of its workers—enables Antwerp to compete with Israel in the melee and eight-cut markets, even though Belgium's costs of living are among the world's highest.

Kempen manufacturers and their workers are mostly Flemish Christians. They have traditionally been dependent on the Antwerp dealers for their rough, but since the bren of '78, when the Antwerp dealers (with few exceptions) "sold out" their *kempen* clients, the DTC has accepted about a dozen *kempen* manufacturers as sightholders in their own rights. Many others among them buy their rough from Diamdel, a sight-holding dealer which as a matter of policy limits its margin to a small markup over DTC prices even in wild bren periods. The controlling stockholders in Diamdel are Oppenheimer entities, which use it (and its sister, Diamdel of Israel) as an instrument of DTC policy. The DTC takes a protective attitude toward the *kempenfolk*, mostly to maintain an alternate market and foil to the Israeli industry, and perhaps partly because it wants the *kempen* industry to survive for nostalgic reasons.

Diamond dealing is a tough business everywhere, but, says one New Yorker, "in Antwerp everyone sees the immediate deal as the last.

Some guys I've dealt with in Antwerp for twenty years are still trying to give me a screwing." It represents the least sentimental market in which almost every deal is a difficult negotiation. Initial spreads between sellers' demands and buyers' offers are likely to be greater in Antwerp than in New York. Another New Yorker put it to me in terms of *chutzpah:* "They have greater *chutzpah* in Antwerp than elsewhere, no hesitation in asking wild prices and that means that the buyer has to answer with an insulting counteroffer. It isn't a pleasant way to have to do business, but it's what you have to do—or not do business in Antwerp."

When I reported all of this to an Antwerp dealer he dismissed the subject abruptly: "The trouble with Americans is that if they've had a hard season they expect price concessions when they come to Antwerp, which we are not in a position to give and are not going to give merely because the Americans have had a hard season." I told him the one about the *schnorrer* (beggar) who was disappointed when his regular benefactor gave him only half of his usual two shekel honorarium: "One shekel?" the schnorrer asked disbelievingly. "I had a tough day," was the response. "So you had a tough day—*I* should suffer?" The diamantaire didn't think it was funny.

Negotiations in Antwerp are usually in "guilders"—not the guilder that is the Dutch currency, but an esperanto money unit with no meaning in the monetary system of any nation. Buyer, seller, and broker will all convert the Antwerp diamantaire's guilder into the national currency of meaning to each. After you have concluded a hard negotiation in an office, a New Yorker told me, "If you're paying in dollars negotiations have to start all over, this time over the value of a dollar. Then while you're closing the deal, the guy's on the phone selling your dollars. In Antwerp they always have these angles!"

Everyone on 47th Street feels obliged to insist on the sanctity with which their community approaches Form 1040. Nobody in Antwerp thinks he must maintain such silly stances, and I found its diamantaires to be the most refreshingly forthright tax evaders in the diamond world. At my first Antwerp stop, an industry leader cut short my roundabout questions and responded instead to the underlying question: "Yes, we have a black market; everyone knows we have a black market; the tax people know that we have a black market. We pay what taxes we want to pay." Belgium's IRS will occasionally audit some diamond man just like anyone else; the diamond people have no blanket immunity. But the man's books will invariably be "in order."

On other than the most formalistic level, it is not possible to audit a diamond business—anywhere—but this is especially true in Antwerp. By law the Belgian diamantaires are permitted to do 25 percent of their business on "blind invoices," invoices that identify the other party either anonymously or not at all. That completely uncheckable 25 percent allows enough flexibility for a diamantaire to adjust his own taxes as he wishes. Further factors make it still easier for him: He does much of his business in cash, and much of what isn't in cash is by way of payment through Swiss banks. One of the keys to the Belgian income tax is valuation of business inventories, and a diamantaire can pretty well value his inventory as he wants, secure in the knowledge that no tax department accountant can second-guess him on it. Some of them (including most of the women brokers and dealers) operate entirely in the informal economy. Most Antwerp diamantaires do pay something, however, to the tax collector. All of the offices in the diamond district are high-rent spots, which practically requires that the diamantaire show some profit just to maintain credibility—and a greater profit than he showed in the old lower-overhead days. Diamantaires fail to claim dozens of legitimate tax deductions that they might honestly claim so that deductible expenses do not become disproportionate to their declared gross sales and net incomes. Antwerp diamantaires sometimes take unneeded bank loans to finance specific transactions solely for the purpose of hiding the impressive strength of their capital position from the possible scrutiny of income tax investigators.

There is sufficient unrecorded cash floating around for almost every diamond worker in Antwerp or the *kempen* to get a share. The unions negotiate minimum rates of pay, which are paid over the table and are subject to Belgium's voracious income tax. Then each worker will negotiate on an individual basis with the boss over how much above the minimum he is worth. This extra will almost always be paid—by agreement and as a matter of negotiation—in black money. The typical Antwerp diamond worker is likely to end up with 60 percent of his income above the table, subject to taxes, and 40 percent of it in black money.

Lens Diamond Industries—a creature of the DTC—tried unsuccessfully to buck the tradition. When LDI opened its vast sawing works in the *kempen* it introduced, or tried to introduce, a revolutionary policy: no black money. The DTC prefers to do things legit. Lens promised permanent job security, a rarity in the diamond world, in exchange for which it asked job applicants to sacrifice the tax advantages traditionally enjoyed by diamond workers. Everyone was going to be paid above the table. Completely. The result: LDI's personnel office was a morgue. Ultimately it had to throw in the towel. Even today it is the laggard in the trade, paying probably 70 percent of the payroll above the table and only 30 percent of it below, a source of constant irritation to its workers, who feel that they are being treated unfairly when compared with their brothers at other factories. LDI was opened with the financial backing of the DTC; works exclusively sawing stones for and on contract with the DTC; and its controlling stockholders (in all likelihood its only significant stockholders) are within the Oppenheimer group. It is probably the world's largest diamond-processing unit, the General Motors of the diamond world, and almost every one of its 585 production workers gets a portion of his pay in black money!

The government of Belgium has never made any concerted effort to bring the diamantaires into line. There is an unwritten but well-understood agreement between the government and the diamond industry: the diamantaires will cause dollars to flow into the country and will provide respectable employment for sizable numbers of citizens, in exchange for which the government will not insist on complete compliance with the Internal Revenue Code. The people of Belgium are satisfied that the diamond men are living up to their part of the bargain. One Antwerp dealer pointed out to me that Belgium has little to recommend it to prospective employers unless it be "flexibility" in taxes. It keeps people employed by looking the other way.

A medieval text reported in 1613 that "In Brussels, Mechelen and Lier were many expatriate cutters who had established their business there in order to avoid heavy taxes of Antwerp." Antwerp diamantaires today—or tomorrow—will have no hesitation in following their forebearers' example. If the friendly tax climate were to change, one told me, "We would all be gone in three weeks!" One of the traditional appeals of the diamond business is that the diamantaire's fate is not interwoven with that of his country of residence. Diamond men are portable people with portable assets, and very few of them have any powerful cultural, sentimental, or "patriotic" attachment to Belgium. Where would you go? "To Israel; perhaps South America; I don't know, but we can do a lot for a country; someone would take us."

The diamond community has its own man in Brussels to keep an eye on things for it: Jacques "Jaak" Nutkewicz, lawyer turned diamantaire, sightholder, board chairman of the Beurs, past president of the HRD, past president of the World Federation of Diamond Bourses—and senator from Antwerp to the Belgian Senate. Nutkewicz is an atypical politician, a dry man, important and well aware of his importance. He goes to the Senate in case the diamond interests should need protection. But they don't. All of Belgium's many political parties look kindly on the diamantaires and there is no criticism of the diamond industry. Within Antwerp the city fathers are grateful to have the diamond people there. The diamond community has always enjoyed excellent relations with the city's administration, controlled by the not-very-socialist Socialist Party. (Nutkewicz is a member of the not-very-liberal Liberal Party.)

Diamonds do bring dollars to Belgium, but those that flow in are largely offset by those that Antwerp diamantaires must pay abroad for goods, and most of the difference is channeled off as the diamantaires' share of the black money. In most years the official statistics show a minuscule differential in the dollar value of the exports and the imports, and in some years (1978 was one of them) the diamonds imported and exported through official channels represented a balance of payments deficit for Belgium. Oh, there were indeed profits, but the profits were wholly invisible, and Belgium did not benefit by receiving significant income through taxes on them. And yes, the industry does employ people, but in times of diamond recessions, those that have been freed of diamond employment have been quickly snapped up by other industries. In fact, the light reflected by the diamonds does not shine very far from the Pelikaanstraat.

24

WHAT PRICE DIAMONDS?:
ISRAEL

◆

Israel is supposed to represent a great struggle in which a united people are working together to hold a seemingly impossible position against overwhelming odds. The country's ability to do so depends on the we-are-in-this-together psychology. Most Israelis know, however, that "we" are not all in this together: The diamond men are not "in this."

Israel's diamond industry operates outside the Israeli economy, being dependent entirely on world economic trends rather than on domestic ones. Other Israelis see their shekels (until recently known as Israeli pounds) become worth less and less daily, sometimes hourly, devalued by Israel's dizzying inflation, while the country's diamond men are immune from this destruction of savings: they trade in the international currency of the diamond world, the dollar, and they keep their liquid wealth in dollars or in Swiss francs—or in diamonds. The diamond people cluster in their quarter in Ramat Gan, ten minutes from downtown Tel Aviv, almost all of them officed in the two connected Diamond Exchange buildings. The police never enter their buildings and even cases of outright fraud—which occur more frequently in Israel than elsewhere in the diamond world—are handled internally (and often with sympathetic understanding). Israel's diamond community constitutes a nation within a nation.

Diamond men have brought the same blessings to Israel as to Antwerp: an influx of foreign currency and employment opportunities. But they have not been unmitigated assets to their country.

Prior to 1977, when Israel effectually abolished currency controls, the diamantaires were the principal magicians who arranged for circumvention of the control laws, and diamonds were the most common vehicle for surreptitious export of capital out of the country. Much of the diamantaires' own trade was conducted outside official channels and profited by "the switch"—by black market currency transactions. Many of those in other export industries did as much. Then the government adopted a subsidy for exporters: For every export-generated dollar that the exporters channeled through official agencies, they were paid a small cash bonus in Israeli pounds. The more export dollars that the man turned over, the bigger bonus he received from the national treasury. The declared purpose of the subsidies was to encourage export industries; the real purpose of it was to encourage exporters to deal "white" by reducing (for export dealings) the spread between black and white rates on the Israeli pound, thereby making black market dealings less attractive to exporters.

For the diamond men, the subsidy was computed on the value of the imported rough, on the theory that that was a better gauge than exports. Imports rose at an encouraging rate, though exports did not. As it turned out, the diamantaires were importing rough, collecting the subsidy, smuggling the rough out, reimporting the same rough, collecting another subsidy, resmuggling it, and so on. It was theft plain and simple. The scam came to light in the fall of 1977, at about the time that Israel was getting ready to chuck the whole currency-control system, and the subsidies were abolished along with the controls. Not every member of the Israel Diamond Exchange participated in the thefts (though some of its leaders did) but pretty close to every one of its fifteen hundred members knew what was going on. No one peeped a word of it—one of those friendly secrets that you keep within the family.

Israel's greater effort to encourage exports has been by way of making government-subsidized loans to those in export industries, but again the diamond boys have shown that boys will be boys. For many years prior to 1978, the interest rate applicable on bank loans to the diamantaires was 6 percent per year, with the government (i.e., the taxpayers at large) picking up the difference between that and whatever the "going" rate might have been. Then it was changed to a sliding rate: at first 60 percent and now 70 percent of the interest rate on interbank Eurodollar loans. Every Israeli diamantaire, regardless of how wealthy he may be, avails himself of this cheap money, and in busy periods it is common for much of Israel's foreign currency reserves to be tied up by the diamantaires. It has not, however, been possible to police their use of the bank loans. Over the years most of Israel's diamond people—maybe every last one of them—have used "diamond" loans to finance non-diamond-related investments, principally in real estate. In that sense, diamonds is a "front" in Israel for all kinds of legitimate businesses that profit illegitimately by perversion of export inducement loans.

Crime has been a late bloomer in Israel, but it is now reaching adolescence there, and is finding the diamantaires comfortable company. Diamonds is the only business in Israel that is officially exempted from meaningful recordkeeping, so that the criminal element can easily hide its money in the diamond trade, and the gangsters feel at home with the diamond business's tradition of secrecy. Diamonds also make a good funnel for getting their money to safer terrain.

The Shimron Commission Report, a 1978 government study into crime in Israel, pointed to diamonds and the diamond industry as one of the most important links between the country's baldly criminal elements and the "respectable" world of Israeli business. Moshe Schnitzer, president of the Diamond Exchange and of the World Federation of Diamond Bourses and spokesman for the Israeli diamond industry, blasted the Shimron findings. Still, many "legitimates" in the trade are aware of the infiltration into it of the Bugsy Siegel and Meyer Lansky types, and are uneasy about it.

Meanwhile the diamond industry (or rather, the insurers for the diamond industry) was plagued in late 1978 and early 1979 with a rash of major diamond heists from mail shipments at Tel Aviv's Ben-Gurion Airport. The police claimed that the thieves had been tipped off by insiders about the shipments, and arrested five members of the Diamond Exchange for "fencing" the stolen goods. While the police may have laid it on a bit thick in discussing the degree of the diamantaires' involvement, no one could doubt that the robberies had been inside jobs. Schnitzer denounced the arrests and the imputation of wrongdoing on the part of any member of the Exchange, and he was joined by Israeli Minister of Commerce and Industry Gideon Patt, son-in-law of a sightholder, who said that the diamantaires' violations could and should have been "kept quiet" so as not to give an entire industry a bad name.

Diamantaires are about the most unpopular group in Israel. It is the special treatment generally given them—especially where taxes are concerned—that has led to their disfavor. One might expect the diamond men of Israel, as citizens of a Jewish state, to own up to their taxes more fully than do their brothers in Christian Belgium. It doesn't seem to work that way. While lots of Israelis are paying income tax in Israel's maximum 60 percent bracket, the wealthiest Israelis, the diamantaires, may end up paying 20 percent. Few pay that much. Minister Patt, a friend of the industry, was quoted in the *Jerusalem Post* as explaining, "Unless we give them a chance to declare their moneys at low tax rates, they will smuggle these moneys abroad"—a plain statement of fact, but not one that the average Israeli could be expected to appreciate.

There are other little things that irritate the man on the street: In Israel everyone has to spend three years in the military; they do it (and well, too) but very few really want to. There is an exemption from Israel's military draft for *yeshiva buchers* (students at schools for advanced study in Jewish theology). Countless of these highly devout are highly devout principally to evade the draft. Meanwhile they hold down jobs. In what industry? You guessed it.

The diamond community has been able to maintain its favored position essentially because of the posited importance of the industry to Israel—and because of the diamantaires' support for those farsighted political leaders, statesmen if you will, who appreciate their role. Diamond money is distributed to all of Israel's major parties.

The effect of the diamond men's political contributions is neither more nor less insidious than the effect of the money that the oil interests pass around to American politicians, and their contributions influence the process to the same extent and in exactly the same manner: often indirectly and subtly, almost never in an unabashedly corrupting manner. Whenever the diamond community has been threatened, however, there has always been a well-placed contact in a position to help.

Otherwise the diamond men have neglected their public relations on the home front. Every taxi driver in Tel Aviv has a cousin whom he dislikes, who he will insist is "one of the biggest men in the diamond business." When an inept diamantaire publicly comments on the portability of the business, "What happened to Amsterdam," and how they might all "be forced to relocate" if the climate in Israel became less friendly, newspapers respond with "We'll-pack-you-sandwiches" editorials. Closer thinkers have begun to analyze the real contributions of the industry to Israel and to tally the costs of it, direct (in terms of subsidies given it) and indirect. As in Belgium, most of the dollar influx is offset by a dollar exodus for rough, with much of the remainder channeled off to Switzerland, and responsible industry people acknowledge that the balance-of-trade value of the industry has been overtouted. (The official statistics are readily available, but impossible to adjust to correct for the diamantaires' assorted finaglings. As is the case with most diamond-world statistics, you are safer proceeding without them.) Diamonds do employ people, about nine or ten thousand production workers in Israel, but—as in Belgium—these could be absorbed with a few months of indigestion into other aspects of the burgeoning Israeli economy.

The principal adverse effect of hosting the industry is probably the extent to which the vast amounts of black money that it generates contribute to the general havoc of the Israeli economy.

People in Tel Aviv are beginning to strike balance sheets and to ask the tough question: What price diamonds? Whatever the net loss or gain to Israel, there can be no question that the alternative to continuing favored treatment is losing the diamond community. Talk about "what happened to Amsterdam" involves no idle threat: In fact, Israeli diamantaires are increasingly considering relocating to South Africa.

In the past ten years, Israeli diamantaires have made Israel the world's leading cutting country in terms of dollar value of goods processed. Its industry prospered not simply on government favoritism—Israel's diamantaires almost certainly pay more taxes than Belgium's—but on hard work. The typical Israeli diamantaire considers a twelve-hour day normal. It has also prospered due to hard personal salesmanship, and by carving out a big niche for itself: lesser-quality melee with lesser-quality make, goods ideal to satisfy the new demands of the increasingly more prosperous American middle class. The typical white-collar engagement ring will probably contain a diamond polished in Israel.

Zvi Rosenberg was probably the first Palestinian diamantaire. Rosenberg was a Hungarian, trained as a diamond worker in Antwerp, who migrated to Palestine in 1934 and went into the ice business (frozen water, that is). Three years later he went back to the other kind of ice, opening the first diamond-cutting works in Palestine in Petah Tikva, not far from Tel Aviv, where he did work on contract for Antwerp manufacturers.

The Jews of Palestine were principally socialist-oriented, and unsympathetic to encouraging such capitalist-tainted enterprises as diamond polishing. However, the mayor of Netanya, Oved Ben Ami, was a "revisionist" Zionist, a nonsocialist who saw diamond polishing as an ideal industry for the country that he hoped would be created. Diamond polishing required little capital investment for plants or equipment, no railroads or freight cars for transportation of materials, and little of the water supply that hampered development of Palestine and would later make the development of Israel more difficult. Ben Ami invited Rosenberg to transfer his operations to Netanya, and then lured other diamond polishers to the young community with its welcoming atmosphere and its magnificent beaches. When Hitler overran the Lowlands in May of 1940, Ben Ami journeyed to London to visit Sir Ernest Oppenheimer's brother, Otto, then the strongman of the DTC, to plead that allocations of rough be made directly to Ben Ami's citizens. Oppenheimer told the mayor that there would be no point to it: The war would be of short duration, and then the CSO would have to channel the goods back to its regular customers. Ben Ami persisted, established useful contact with the influential syndicate broker George Prins of the firm of I. Hennig, and when it became clear that the war would last much longer than Otto had imagined, Prins argued the Israeli case and prevailed. Netanya became one of the world's great cutting centers. Many of Israel's largest diamond factories and a third of the industry's work force is still located there.

With the end of World War II and the rebirth of Antwerp, the industry in Netanya was shut off by the DTC. Starved for supplies of rough, it shriveled to almost nonexistence, until after the creation of the state of Israel in 1948. Then the "Palestinian" industry began to reemerge and to grow very slowly, without encouragement from the DTC—until labor costs in Antwerp and its kempen increased to such levels that it began to become uneconomical to process melee there. Uneconomical, that is, for the DTC.

If the cost of melee rough plus finishing costs comes to more than polished melee can reasonably be sold for, the situation is uneconomical.

The provisioner of the rough must either reduce the price of the raw material (or at least stop increasing the price of it) or find customers who can process it more cheaply. Reenter the Israelis. Israelis worked (and still work) cheaper than Belgians, and their manufacturers were willing to operate on thinner margins. The "cheap" Israeli labor became essential to permit the DTC to maintain the price of melee rough and to continue making periodic increases in its price. As the price of melee rough grew over time, requests for it from Antwerp manufacturers dwindled, enabling the DTC to fulfill increasingly greater portions of the demands made upon it by the Israeli manufacturers. The process speeded up during the 1960s and early seventies, as the economic unimportance of the rough diamond sources in formerly Belgian Zaire became more apparent.

The Israelis, meanwhile, took to the airways to find and develop new markets for their wares. In a 1975 interview with the *Jerusalem Post,* Morris Zale, the aged founder of the Zale chain, recalled, "I used to see [the Israeli diamantaires] with their little envelopes containing perhaps two diamonds. . . . Then the next time they would have a few more. . . . Now I see them everywhere—in Japan, Hong Kong—there are the Israelis, selling and selling hard." According to Zale, "They're very hard bargainers, among the world's shrewdest and toughest, working at closer margins than anybody else."

The assistance of the Israeli government was essential to the success of its diamantaires. With time, Oved Ben Ami's attitude toward the diamond industry became the prevailing one, for his reasons and one other: Being exclusively export oriented, the diamond industry was capable of earning hard currency for Israel. In 1958 the government established Pituach, a government agency, to attempt to develop outside sources of rough for the Israeli industry to augment the niggardly supplies that the DTC was then providing. Pituach made its own contacts in Central and West Africa and initiated large-scale dealings with Diamond Distributors, Inc., the important American outside market dealers. Its increasing success in developing alternate rough sources (coinciding with the declining importance of the Congo region and with the economics of melee processing) was in part responsible for a more friendly attitude on the part of the DTC toward Israel. The DTC admires—or at least responds to—a good show of independence. The volume of DTC goods flowing to Israel increased, as did the number of Israeli sightholders. Pituach itself became an important sightholding dealer, and then, mission accomplished, eased itself out of the outside market. As the Israeli trade picked up, Pituach declined in importance, and was finally dismantled in 1978 amidsts charges of mismanagement and financial irregularities.

The more important aid given by the government has been its financial assistance by way of the subsidized interest rates on bank loans. Easy access to cheap money has eased the financial problems of Israeli diamantaires in buying rough or in stocking polished, and has enabled them to extend liberal credit terms to their overseas buyers, all to the direct profit of themselves and indirectly to Israel—and to the DTC, which is able to keep up melee rough prices in part due to the easy credit enjoyed by the Israeli melee men.

The Office of the Diamond Controller was created by Israel as a watchdog over the diamantaires, to ensure that Israel did in fact enjoy the anticipated benefits. Like so many of all governments' regulatory agencies, the Controller's Office became an advocate for the industry that it was supposed to police. It was stripped of its most important duties when currency controls were eliminated in 1977, and the office itself was slated to be abolished, but it was preserved on the urgings of itself and of Schnitzer and Arieh Ketsef, president at the time of the Diamond Manufacturers Association. Both saw it as a useful buffer between the diamond community and less friendly elements of government. Its officials still shuttle back and forth between Tel Aviv and Jerusalem—for a civil servant to remain stationary in Israel is to admit his insignificance—but they don't fool anybody.

Today there are some eight hundred factories cutting and polishing diamonds in Israel, employing some nine to ten thousand workers (down from thirteen thousand during the bren of 1978), or about as many as Antwerp, but because the Piermatic is widely accepted in Israel and little used in Antwerp, the Israeli output far exceeds Antwerp's. Some of the larger factories employ one to two hundred workers, and do all stages of the processing including sawing, but most are smallish units of ten to twenty-five workers. Large manufacturers maintain their own factories and also send work out to shops that process for them on a contract basis. For example, Paz Diamonds, Israel's biggest diamond exporter in 1980, employs some two hundred in its own factories, but generates work for another five or six hundred workers employed in contractors' shops. Though the industry is still principally involved in the processing of melee brilliants, Israel is also the world's biggest processor of smaller "fancy shapes," under one carat.

The degree of competition between Israeli diamond manufacturers is among the world's most vigorous, but when it comes to meeting the government, the union, or the DTC, they form a united front in the Diamond Manufacturers Association, long headed by the able, articulate, and flexible Ketsef.

Most Israeli diamond workers are employed as regular employees, with some few working as independent contractors, principally as a tax evasion device. Though Israel has a large Arab population, over 99 percent of the diamond workers are Jewish and most of the remaining handful are non-Muslim Arabs. Virtually all do piecework. Diamonds is the last industry in Israel that is still on piecework, the last stronghold of rugged economic individualism. The workers are also paid Antwerp-style, part over and part under the table.

Many of the smaller Israeli diamantaires failed during the bren and the recession that followed it. They were overfinanced, and when the banks began tightening up on credit and calling loans, those who had bought rough at inflated prices and had financed at inflated valuations were caught in the crunch. What little equity they had was quickly eaten up and they went under. As the recession lingered, the remainder of the small men and the newcomers were shuffled out. They had no experience in resisting hard times and no wherewithal to do so.

The big boys, who over the years have successfully ridden the trends and made millions in the process, give little sympathy to those who tried to emulate them but gauged the pendulum incorrectly. One tough Israeli told me, * "אם אינך יכול לסבול את החום אל תשהה במטבח". He can take it, and is still cooking, but the kitchen is getting hotter. The Israeli diamond industry is now seriously threatened by foreign competition.

The Soviet Union poses the greatest current threat to the Israeli industry: It polishes melee too, and does so very well indeed. Because its government-run polishing plants get rough "for free" from the mines in Siberia, Russian factory administrators are not bedeviled by the yield constraints that must preoccupy other cutters, and the Russians have been free to concentrate on a very high quality make. The Soviets give their melee the care and attention—and the scorn for mere yield considerations—that free-world cutters reserve for top-quality stones. DTC price increases on the melee rough supplied to Israel require that the lesser-quality Israeli goods sell for only a little less than the clearly superior Soviet product. At odd times Israeli goods become unsalable: When Moscow needs a quick hundred million dollars it sends orders to Almazjuvelirexport, its diamond selling office, to deliver the dollars; Almazjuvelirexport "dumps" whatever goods it must in order to come up with the cash, cutting its price below Israeli levels.

Ketsef has argued that DTC prices have made it practically impossible for the Israeli manufacturers to compete with Russia. But there isn't much that the DTC can do about it; its pricing policy for melee rough is not simply a matter of greed. It must keep the difference between the market price for polished melee and its own price for melee rough paper thin, or the Russians will cease sending any of Siberia's melee rough to the CSO, and will polish all of it themselves. If that should happen, CSO control of the overall world diamond market would be seriously, perhaps terminally threatened.

Assuming that Israel can weather the Soviet threat, South Africa's

* "If you can't take the heat, stay out of the kitchen."

manufacturers pose tomorrow's challenge to the Israelis. South Africans buy their domestically mined rough free from the country's export duty, so are buying for about 10 percent less than the Israelis. Traditionally, the high cost of white labor in South Africa more than offset this advantage, and prevented the South African manufacturer from competing in the melee market. In 1976, however, its manufacturers began employing cheap "colored" (mulatto) labor. This prompted a ten-week strike by the all-white union that was settled by acceptance of "carat-weight apartheid": Only "artisans" (all white) can work stones over 89 points, but "operators" (colored) can process the smaller stones. The South African labor force immediately swelled with the introduction of the coloreds, and Israeli mercenaries were imported to train them to work melee. (One Johannesburg manufacturer told me that the Israelis were a mixed blessing—that they insisted on acting out their opposition to apartheid in the bedroom, and that "this caused friction with the colored help.")

Government policy gives the South African manufacturers first dibs on the nation's 30-odd percent of the world supply of gem rough, and with their new source of cheap labor, and greater use of the Piermatic, they are increasingly likely to draw on the domestic melee rough. Israeli sight boxes are likely to be significantly lighter five years hence.

Israel will also suffer inroads on its territory from other fronts. The Israeli industry prospered on the differential between low labor costs in Israel and higher labor costs in other centers, but the Piermatic reduces that advantage to insignificance. With the Piermatic, melee can be processed in New York or Puerto Rico almost as cheaply as in Israel, and some American manufacturers are already working melee on Piermatics. For the Israeli industry, things are certain to go to worse.

Israel has become an important diamond-trading center, principally but not exclusively in melee. Melee would be enough: As the world's leading finisher of the diamonds with the most constant and predictable demand, Israel is visited by large buyers from everywhere.

Israel is also a major reexport country. It is one of the leading customer nations for Indian polished, which Israelis buy, mingle with their own wares, and then resell as part of a parcel of Israeli goods. Because of Israel's better reputation in the trade, Indian goods sold as Israeli merchandise will bring a better price than Indian goods that are sold as such. It imports Russian polished for reexport to the United States as Israeli goods. The United States duties Russian goods at 10 percent, but admits non-Communist melee free of duty. Israel is a forwarding stop for Japan-bound goods polished in Antwerp or in New York. During the stopover, the merchandise becomes "Israeli." Israeli diamonds are admitted free of duty in Japan as part of Japan's cooperation in the world effort to speed the industrial maturation of the "under-developed nations."

Israel effectively prohibits the import of most polished diamonds, so that most of the country's reexport trade has had to be conducted surreptitiously. This does not seem to have stood in anyone's way. The percentage of Israel's citizens who have professional smuggling experience is probably higher than that of any other country in the world. In the immediate postwar period, untold thousands of young men, newly released from concentration camps, sole survivors of their families, rootless and jobless, wandered about Central and Eastern Europe smuggling goods from Rumania to Hungary to Czechoslovakia and back again. One by one they filtered to Israel where they settled permanently and made new lives for themselves (some of them in the diamond business). They are now mostly in their sixties and are long retired from their illicit pasts, but they have left a heritage.

The greatest part of Israel's diamond trade is conducted from the Diamond Exchange buildings, two twenty-eight story towers connected by an enclosed bridge. Prior to the opening of the first of the towers in 1968, most of Israel's diamonds were sent to Antwerp for distribution, but its opening permanently shifted the focus of the international trade in melee to Ramat Gan. Many of the largest international buyers maintain permanent offices in the Exchange complex and several hundred—sometimes more than a thousand—foreign buyers enter it daily to visit one or another of its offices or the trading floor of the exchange.

Security precautions are among the tightest in the world, and 65 percent of the budget for the complex is spent on keeping it that way. Habitants, regardless of how well known, must show their pass every time they enter, and outsiders do not get inside until a security man calls "upstairs" to confirm that the caller has an appointment in one of the offices. The security man takes and retains the visitor's passport until the caller leaves. Then, just before the visitor enters, his hand luggage will be searched. This protects against political sabotage, a constant concern throughout Israel, and ensures that any crimes committed within will be "inside" jobs. After the thoroughness with which entrants are screened, everybody breathes more easily in the complex than on 47th Street in New York, where frequent crimes of violence keep everyone on edge.

Three banks, the post office, and the customs service are all located in the complex so that it is never necessary for anyone to carry anything of value in or out. The Office of the Diamond Controller, the Diamond Institute—a quasi-governmental diamond-promotion agency—and what remains of Pituach are there too. All manner of amenities are provided within, so that the diamantaire can spend his day there, conduct all of his business, and attend to some of his personal errands as well, without ever having to leave. This is a time saver ("Time is money"—diaman-taire's aphorism). Three restaurants in the complex vie for the distinction of serving the world's worst kosher food. It doesn't matter: They are so packed and hectic that only the strong-stomached can eat in them anyway.

Though most of the business is conducted in the offices, the heart of the Diamond Exchange complex is the Diamond Exchange itself, with some fifteen hundred members. Membership in it was closed and cliquish for years, with vacancies filled by the sons and nephews of members or by those with influential backing. Its closed membership list was largely responsible for the birth of Tel Aviv's second club, *Etgar* (Challenge)—the New Israel Club for Commerce in Diamonds, which was formed in 1974 as a challenge to Israel's diamond establishment.

The New Israel Club is what diamond clubs must have been like before World War II. The club is the office for almost all of its members, and though its trading floor is hectic too, there is still table space for checkers players, and everyone has a moment to *schmooze* with a stranger. Most of its members are small guys trading in small parcels which move from table to table, each time moving up in price by a percent or maybe even two percent, as the parcels join successively larger parcels, until sooner or later they find their way into parcels at the big boys' club, whence they get exported. Etgar's building is behind and literally in the shadow of the Diamond Exchange complex.

The Israeli diamond community is pyramid-shaped, and Moshe Schnitzer, president of the Diamond Exchange, sits on top of the pyramid. His power in the diamond trade and in Israeli political affairs, however, does not depend on his long tenure as Exchange president; he remains the dominant force in Israeli diamonds by virtue of his electric personality and dynamism. He suffers occasional lapses into self-impor-tance, but that is a common trait among diamantaires, and on a one-to-one basis he is a charming and winning man, a captivating person.

Schnitzer was born in Rumania, in the same village as Willie Nagel, the syndicate broker, and his family emigrated to Palestine before the outbreak of the war. He earned a master's degree in philosophy but today he lives and operates in a very different world, and such philosophy as he spoke during our interview was of the cracker-barrel school: "In life sometimes you have to let yourself be fooled, knowing you are being fooled. You'll come off much better." After school his father—"a very wise man"—pushed him into a blue-collar job at the scaife under the tutelage of a manufacturing friend, and a future in the diamond world. It worked out for the best. In most years since 1964 Schnitzer's firm has been Israel's leading exporter—of diamonds or of anything else. How come? Schnitzer lowers his voice and turns away modestly as he explains, "I'm supposed to be the best salesman in the business"—and

International Diamond Annual (1971) did headline its feature on him: "Diamonds' Greatest Salesman." Like all great salesmen, Schnitzer is a nonstop worker (he saw me at 8:00 AM). In the early 1950s, he says, "I started going round the world looking for customers and outlets and since those days I have been going round and round the world—looking every time for new connections and meeting new people." He is a natural publicist, with the same flair for publicity as Harry Winston, but unlike Winston (who shunned photographers), nothing brings a smile to Schnitzer's face like a camera, and he sneaks into more press photos than an Israeli starlet.

As a manufacturer, Schnitzer is a contractor who "works" fourteen different factories, each on a different basis. The DTC is attempting to weed out its contractor sightholders, but not Schnitzer; "Schnitzer is a special case," the DTC spokesman told me.

In the political world, Schnitzer is a tough operator who enjoys manipulating and maneuvering power blocs and he is usually very good at it. He is not, however, simply a backroom power broker; he likes to get into the fray and he never misses a fray to jump into. It is Schnitzer who captains the diamond team in its ongoing negotiations with the government over the thorny perennial: income taxes.

Dr. Jacob Arnon (Ph.D. in economics) was born into an Amsterdam diamond family. He was trained as a diamond cleaver and became a small sightholder himself before the war. After the war he emigrated to Israel, left the diamond business, he thought forever, and became a civil servant in his new homeland. Government work, though, brought him back into the diamond world as Israel's diamond controller. His understanding of diamonds was important in his new role, but even more important was his understanding of diamantaires.

From his experiences in the prewar diamond world, Arnon knew that if the government were to get from the diamond men tax money that bore some reasonable relationship to their actual incomes, the tax would have to be based on some empirical data, the compilation of which was not principally dependent on the probity of the diamantaires' books. He explained to me, "If the tax were based on books, the books would never, ever, show any profit to tax. . . . We could make them keep books, or we could make them pay taxes, but we could not make them do both!"

Arnon devised formulas by which a diamantaire's probable income might be hypothesized on the basis of empirical data: by juggling the amount of rough he imported, the amount of polished he exported, the number of his employees, and "typical" margins of profit within the industry, the government might arrive at a probable income for each diamantaire, and assess the tax against that sum. Books didn't matter.

The formulas were first instituted in the early 1950s, and were revised annually thereafter as the result of negotiations between the diamond community and the government. The diamond men grew to like the system—and to control the annual revisions of the formulas.

Arnon believes that until 1973 the system worked fairly well, producing hypothesized incomes for tax purposes that approached 70 to 80 percent of actual profits. If so, it was probably the most successful tax recovery program anywhere in the diamond world. In 1973, years after Arnon had moved to other branches of the civil service, the system started breaking down; formula-based income assessments began to bear less and less relationship to reality.

In 1973 Israel had a war and it needed money to fight its war. It turned to its citizens and asked them to loan the government the money. No sector responded more generously, more unselfishly, than did the diamond community; the diamantaires bought more than twice as many war bonds as they were asked to buy. And, by the way, the diamond community was troubled by one small little problem, that perhaps the government might be able to help with. As part of the annual income tax return, the diamond people, like everyone else, were required to file a declaration of net worth. Could, perhaps, the government waive this annual headache for perhaps a few years? It was a small favor for the country's most patriotic citizen-group to have asked, and of course it was granted. The diamantaires were exempted from filing the annually required declaration until March of 1979. Without the declarations— without honest declarations—the IRS could not know whether the formulas were cutting for or against the public, or just how severely they were cutting against the public. Thereafter everything went haywire.

In 1977 Deputy Finance Minister Yehezkel Flomin determined to restore some sanity to the system and inaugurated a two-year battle to force the diamond men to keep honest books and to pay their taxes on the basis of the books. His positions, however, were moderated by the diamantaires' considerable influence with Prime Minister Menachem Begin, who personally intervened with his underlings on behalf of the diamond community. Over the years Begin's Herut Party has probably been most dependent on the goodwill and generosity of the diamond community, and Schnitzer's personal relations with Begin date back to the late 1940s, when he supported a pro-Zionist terrorist movement then led by the young Begin. IRS failed to use all of the muscle that the Israeli Revenue Code put at its disposal. Begin's influence enabled the diamond men to outlive Flomin's influence. In the meantime, the diamantaires made public their objections to the keeping of books. It was a tactical error.

The publicly stated reason for the diamond community's not wanting to keep books proclaimed the dishonor of almost everyone with whom they dealt. They said, Much of the rough that we buy is sold to us by sightholding manufacturers who are selling off DTC rough in violation of their understandings with the DTC. When we sell, most of our buyers will demand phony invoices. Others of our buyers are dealing in hot money and want no record of any kind kept of their transactions.

In effect, the official position of the Israeli diamond industry was, We are honest and straightforward people who pay our taxes. But the people from whom we buy? The people to whom we sell? *Oy!* Are they *gonifs!* God, are they thieves.

Not surprisingly, the typical Israeli newspaper reader was unimpressed. The public temper was going against the diamond community, while Schnitzer's public exchanges with Flomin were becoming more heated, their private exchanges explosive. The situation in July of 1979, two years into the fray, was fast becoming an impossible political situation, which the diamantaires seemed destined to lose. And then Flomin fell from his position in an intraparty squabble. I saw Schnitzer three days later and he told me that he was optimistic that an accord would be reached momentarily. And so it was.

Compromise was reached in the summer of 1979, with a stunning political victory for the government: The diamond men fell into line. They would keep books (though they did not begin doing so until January 1981). And the government could tell the people as much: We whipped the diamond men into line. For the diamond men it was a mere economic victory. In keeping their books they are not required to reveal to the government the identities of the other parties to their transactions, and they are permitted to "correct" inaccuracies that might otherwise emerge from the invoices—so that it will never be possible for the government to confirm the accuracy of the books.

There is, however, one check on the situation: Plausibility. If IRS believes a man's books to be unreasonable, it will remain free to make an assessment the "old way" instead, on the basis of the formulas under which the diamantaires have thrived. The worst that can happen to a diamantaire is that he will get a 20 percent reduction in his taxes: henceforth he will save the 20 percent penalty that was previously added to his tax bill for his failure to keep books. As Israeli Commissioner of Internal Revenue Dov Neiger explained it to me, "Even if we should reject his books, he will have kept books, so he is entitled to be spared the penalty." It was an ideal settlement: credit for the politicians, savings for the diamantaires. Beautiful.

One aspect of the problem remains unresolved: the matter of the net worth declarations that were due in March of 1979. March came and went. The diamond men explained that they were running a little late; they needed until September to make their net worth declarations because some assets that might appear to be "theirs" were really the property of foreign principals. They needed the time to "clarify" the extent of ownership of these foreign interests, so that assets that were not in fact theirs were not erroneously reflected in their financial positions. And of course, they could not tell the government the names of these foreign owners. Of course. September came and went too, and as of January 1, 1981, the declarations of assets had still not been filed. The battle, therefore, is likely to go on a while longer, with perhaps temporary victories for this side or that side and continual rematches. At the end who will win? The diamantaires, by hook or by crook.

The highlight of my trip to Israel was certainly Bar Mitzvah day at Jerusalem's Wailing Wall. For two thousand years Jews have made pilgrimages to pray (or "wail," hence the name "Wailing Wall") before the western wall of the old city of Jerusalem. Nowadays, on Thursdays, bar mitzvahs, the official induction of the thirteen-year-old Jewish male into the spiritual duties of manhood, are held in the very shadow of this most sacred of Jewish sites. Bar mitzvah day at the Wailing Wall is not to be missed. I was fortunate to witness a Yemenite bar mitzvah there, with its traditions peculiar to the Yemeni and decidedly odd to the western Jew. Particularly curious is the role that the Yemeni women play in the bar mitzvah. As in all Orthodox Jewish religious proceedings, the official ceremony is limited to men, but the Yemeni women do participate. They stand outside a low barrier and literally yelp, like American Indians giving a war whoop, during the ceremony, and pellet the official participants with candies. They look and are dressed like any other Jerusalem women, and only their odd role in the ceremony—and their partiality for gold teeth—distinguish them from others in the crowd. Children and an occasional old man scramble to pick up the candies that they throw.

The official bar mitzvah party is small, not even a *minyan* (the ten Jewish men necessary to make the ceremony "official"), but at the crucial moment the rabbi, dressed more like a Greek Orthodox patriarch than like any "western" rabbi, cries out *"Minyan!"* which summons sufficient Jewish strangers (in Israel) to make up the ten. I was part of the *minyan* for this particular Yemeni bar mitzvah boy.

The olive-skinned "boychik," short and skinny, went through his paces in a faltering voice, stumbled at the rough parts of his text, but made it through and then carried the Torah, the sacred scrolls, which nearly outweighed him, back to the Ark (their repository) surrounded by elders who watched the Torah throughout the procession, in case the boy through nervousness should slip or drop the scrolls. When they were replaced in the Ark, the boy posed for photos together with his father and older brother. There was no "Today I am a man" speech-making.

As they left, I slipped the bar mitzvah boy a hundred pounds, about four dollars American, and uttered the diamantaires' *"Mazel und bra-*

chah"—luck and blessings. He took the present but did not respond. Dazed by the solemnity of the momentous occasion, he was really not aware of what was happening—just like many of his American cousins. This is no digression: the point is that bar mitzvah boys are like diamonds—international . . . beautiful . . . charming . . . forever. Fill in your own adjective.

25

INDIA:
DIAMANTAIRES' NIRVANA?

◆

India today processes 6o percent by weight of the diamonds processed worldwide and a still larger percentage of the total number of stones polished. By those tests it is unquestionably the world's leading diamond-processing country. It owes its success to the growth of the market for "democratic" jewelry, featuring lower quality and lower-priced diamonds. The labor component in these lower grade goods—the proportion of total costs that labor expense represents—is higher than it is in better goods, not because more labor is required, but because the raw material is worth very much less. It makes sense to process them where labor costs can be minimized, even if the quality of workmanship is lesser—in India.

I arrived in Bombay at the end of a long period of drought. Because much of India's electricity is generated by hydroelectric plants, there were severe power shortages which had interfered with every service that depends on electricity. Then, on the morning of my arrival, the first great monsoon storm of the season struck, bringing relief.

The rains lasted all day, but the next morning was bright and sunny, and promptly at 10:00 AM Dr. G. M. Pandya, executive secretary of the Indian Gem & Jewellery Export Promotion Council, arrived to escort me to an interview with the council's then chairman, Mr. M. G. Mehta. En route to Mr. Mehta's office, our taxi passed a flower-draped corpse, the first of many that I was to see in India. Dr. Pandya said that it was a good omen to pass a corpse going in the opposite direction.

M. G. Mehta is busy in a wide range of diamond and diamond-related enterprises, some of them sightholding ventures, some not. Still, he had plenty of energy left to throw himself into the work of promoting India's diamond exports through his work as chairman of the Promotion Council, a quasi-governmental agency to which every diamond exporter belongs by law. Mehta is brimming with optimism about the future of the Indian industry. He pointed out that the average age of the Antwerp diamond polisher was sixty-three, while that of the Indian polisher was seventeen years eight months. The average diamond manufacturer in India was in his early thirties. These young manufacturers, he said, can take the chances that must be taken to develop an industry. The Indian diamond-polishing industry has grown geometrically in its twenty-year life span; still, he described it as "an industry for tomorrow." Yes, there were some disadvantages to India's position, he acknowledged, but before going on he was interrupted by the telephone. Like diamond men everywhere, the Indian diamantaire is continually on the phone. Unlike diamantaires elsewhere, however, the Indian diamond man's telephone doesn't really work. "Hello, hello," Mehta said and then screeched into the toy at his ear. At first there was no response; then the machine croaked back at him, *"Woongk, woogtt!"* He looked at the receiver in disbelief and slammed it down. What is a diamond man without his telephone?

Mehta is a tall, well-built man with the imposing appearance that truly successful businessmen in any line anywhere have. Urbane and dynamic, he was wearing a crisp white "Nehru" suit and, as is common in India, was barefoot. A peculiarly Indian touch in a luxurious office.

I was to find that the Indian diamantaires are the most gracious people in the entire diamond world. Though most people in the trade tend to be narrowly focused on their commerce, some Indian diamantaires were catholic in their interests, and the few reflective diamantaires I encountered were in India. That is not to say, however, that the Indian diamantaire is any "softer" than his brothers in Tel Aviv or Antwerp. The only sentimentalists in the diamond world are the consumers.

The medieval Indian cutting industry became virtually extinct with the exhaustion of the ancient Indian mines and survived only in small, isolated pockets. One of these was in and around Surat in the western Indian state of Gujarat. During World War II a few refugees from Antwerp and Amsterdam relocated to Surat to continue their work, but all of the Lowlanders promptly abandoned India at the end of the war. In the postwar period the crushing Indian import duty of 20 percent on diamond rough made it economically impossible to process imported rough in India for the world market, and the rough from Panna was insufficient to support more than the minuscule cutting industry in Panna itself. Rebirth began only in 1959 when the government, in an effort to encourage diamond processing as an export industry, authorized the rebate of the import duty to those who subsequently exported polished diamonds. The Indian industry dates essentially from then.

The Indian diamond industry has throughout been controlled by Palanpur Jains (Jains: a religious group; Palanpur: a city in northwestern India), much as the diamond trade in the western world is dominated by Ashkenazim, and that in the African bush is the province of the Mandingo. Jainism is a small religious sect closely related to Hinduism, from which it evolved around the 6th century BC as a protest against the overdeveloped ritualism of Hinduism. It commands the allegiance of perhaps one in every three hundred Indians, but Jains are much more significant in the commercial life of India than their small proportion would indicate. Most share a small number of surnames, many of which refer to the occupation of one of their forebears. Mehta (meaning "accountant") and Jhaveri (meaning "jeweler") are the most common surnames in the Indian diamond world.

Jainism is an appealing religion. Jains are vegetarians, nonviolent, truthful, and are noted for charity, good works, and occasional monastic retreats. Traditionally they have been ascetic, rejecting all worldly pleasures, though that tradition is close to dead among the diamond Jains. In the first century AD their movement survived a serious schism over the duty of the religious to be nudists. The bashful prevailed.

Virtually all Jains and all of the Palanpur diamond Jains are members of the *bania* (or trading) caste, but in today's India all of that is at last beginning to go by the board. A civil servant who works closely with the diamantaires says that they are of the "five-star caste," the group of neo-rich who cluster in the five-star hotels and restaurants, send their sons to school in England, and are increasingly westernized.

Palanpur is a small city which in 1911 had perhaps fifty thousand inhabitants. That was the year when the first two Palanpur Jains ventured south to Bombay to open a trade there in jewelry, mostly in pearls. More and more Palanpur Jains moved to bigger Indian cities, Bombay and others, and the Palanpur Jains became the dominant factor in the Indian pearl trade. The development of the cultured pearl prompted them to diversify so as to remain essentially in truly precious jewels, and their trade increasingly gravitated to diamonds. Probably 60 percent of India's diamond manufacturers, almost all of them centered in Bombay, can trace their roots to Palanpur.

The Palanpur diamond Jains form a small in-group of sons, brothers, and nephews. Many of the great families, including those now headed by S. G. Jhaveri and by K. K. Doshi, trace their involvement in the jewelry trade back several generations, though the family's focus may have shifted to diamonds more recently. All of the dominant diamond firms are run by "pre-1959" dynasties, the progenitors of which were in the diamond end of the wholesale jewelry business before the Indian diamond industry really took off. One of the industry's leading men told me, "We are a close-knit community adverse to newcomers—unless we want them."

The newcomers have come, however—droves of them. A Palanpur Jain will not consider "stealing" another man's customer. If he has a foreign buyer whose needs he cannot fill himself, he will without hesitation introduce the buyer to another manufacturer who has the needed goods, confident that his competitor will not steal the customer; that the competitor will send a forwarding fee, and that the next time that the customer has needs, if he should visit the competitor directly, the competitor will refer the buyer back to the original contact. They will view the buyer who attempts to switch suppliers almost as dimly as they view the seller who attempts to take over another man's buyer. The newcomers to the Indian industry, however, do not understand any of this, and have brought about a weakening of commercial loyalties.

The Indian labor supply is both cheap and inexhaustible. S. N. Sharma, managing director of the Hindustan Diamond Company, says:

> In the United States you have a backup machine, so that if the first machine fails, the operator can keep working. In India you have a backup man, so that if the first man falls, the machine can keep working. That is how the Indian diamond industry operates, much like the Chinese army, where you have three men for each rifle. When the first man is killed the second picks up the rifle; when the second drops, the third picks it up.

The advantages to the Indian manufacturers of cheap labor, however, are largely chimerical. The DTC sops up most of the advantage by keeping the price of rough for "Indian goods" at a level that would be unsupportable except for the cheap labor. What advantages remain to the Indian manufacturers from the cheap labor are largely offset by the relative unproductivity of their labor force, when compared with productivity levels in Israel or Belgium. Their workers are hampered by inadequate training and by poor equipment. During the bren of 1978 probably 350,000, possibly as many as 400,000, people were employed polishing diamonds in India, or about thirty times the number employed in Israel, but the number of stones and the weight handled per Indian worker were both far short of the Israeli per-man turnover, and the quality of workmanship was uniformly lower. India is no Nirvana for the diamantaire—only for the DTC.

The leaders of the Indian industry, like those everywhere, are the sightholders. The DTC regularly awards sights to some sixty-odd Indian sightholders, who purchase an average of about $350,000 worth of rough at each sight. In addition to the sightholders, there are probably some two thousand other diamond manufacturers in India, who obtain their rough in Antwerp, India, or both. Hindustan Diamond Company, a joint venture of the government of India and the DTC, is the country's only "dealing" sightholder, but virtually all of the "manufacturing" sightholders do some rough dealing out of their DTC boxes, and a few of them are exclusively surreptitious rough dealers.

Most of the most important manufacturers in India own no factories at all, partly because it is easier not to own factories and partly because they are unsuited to own factories: Very few of them have any cutting experience. Cutting in India has traditionally been monopolized by the

Patel community, a caste of Hindus. The manufacturers send their stones to Patels for polishing in the cottages, mostly in or near the city of Surat, about 150 miles north of Bombay. A major manufacturer may keep several hundred cottages busy, which in turn will employ ten or twenty times as many workers.

The manufacturer sends his rough to his principal contact in Surat, who may be a nonequal partner. The contact divides the goods between ten or twelve foremen, each of whom distributes his share of the goods to eight or ten cottages. Each cottage will perform the complete polishing process upon the stones allotted to it. The cottage owner is paid for his cottage's output on a per-stone basis. The going rate for the complete processing of a fifty-eight-facet brilliant in Surat in August of 1979 was 10 rupees ($1.25) for any stone regardless of size up to 25 points, and 12½ rupees for those few stones between 25 and 50 points. The usual $1.25 must cover the cottage owner's labor expense, overhead, and profit. As of the summer of 1979, in the midst of the recession, most cottage owners were operating at a loss, and kept going on a much diminished basis in order to keep the most able of their work force together.

When the stones have been polished, they are returned to the foreman, who brings them back to the principal Surat contact for return to Bombay. Each of the foremen runs his own cottage and in addition to what income he derives from that he receives a commission of about 5 percent on the work of the cottages to which he distributes. Because of the way the system operates it is impossible for any manufacturer to have more than a vague idea as to how many people he is "employing," how much "his" rank-and-file workers are earning, or of the conditions under which "his" people are working and living. That is none of his business.

Surat is a Birmingham/Manchester equivalent, an industrial city, prosperous by Indian standards. At the depths of the diamond recession there were still probably 175,000 to 250,000 diamond polishers working in India, most of them in Surat's environs. If one were to add up all of the diamond miners and diamond cutters in the world, more than half of them at any moment will be in greater Surat.

Diamonds is the second industry in Surat. Textiles is first. Textiles was also originally a cottage industry in Surat, but has now largely moved into regular factories. Except during diamond brens, there are more textile workers in Surat than diamond workers. The textile industry has built the city's impressive public auditorium, the city's enclosed, court-yarded textile market, and its most prominent hotel, the Tex-Palazzo. Because of the way in which it is organized, the diamond industry could not be expected to have made such contributions to the city, and it has not. I was told that the diamond industry's principal contributions to Surat have been inflation, overcrowding, and sickness.

The cottages are the backbone and essence of the Surat diamond industry. A typical cottage has a workroom where the actual polishing is done, distinct from the building's living quarters. Since the Indian industry processes only *maakbar* ("makeables"), stones that are neither sawn nor cleaved prior to processing, brutting is the first step. Each cottage has one or more brutting lathes and two or more low, donut-shaped circular tables, each with a scaife in the center. The table-scaife unit, known as a *ghanti*, generally accommodates four workers, each of whom uses a quarter of the scaife. The unit polishes on an assembly-line basis, chain-of-four. A large cottage may have ten or more *ghantis*. Workrooms are often decorated with garishly colored lithographs of Ganesha, the four-armed elephant-headed god, and other Hindu deities, and photos of cricket players or of the two sainted figures of modern India, Gandhi and John F. Kennedy. Commonly a radio will be playing at the kind of volume that adolescents appreciate; the work force is predominantly adolescent.

Most of the workers are older than they look. Those who look twelve or thirteen are more likely sixteen, and the small boys that look nine are likely twelve. Their nutrition and every other aspect of their environ-ment conspires to retard their growth and maturation (and would even if they were not working in diamond cottages). During the bren children as young as eight or nine were brought into the trade, but when the recession came, the less adept of these children were shuffled out. The youngest workers that I saw were the youngest veterans of the bren, now eleven and twelve years old, sweet little boys who moved their stones from scaife to eye and back again with the same sureness and confidence as an old Hasidic Jew—and somewhat more grace. Except in the large modern Surat factory operated by M. G. Mehta and Tata Industries, I did not see any worker over the age of eighteen. I find it very hard to believe that the average age of the Indian diamond polisher is as high as the seventeen years that statistics show it to be, and suspect that some cottage owners "forgot" to tell the statistics compiler about some of their younger boys. Most of the boys have very little education, though many of them can read and write in Gujarati.

Pay varies widely from cottage to cottage. Everyone claimed that his payroll was typical but the average payrolls of different cottage own-ers ranged from 300 to 500 rupees per boy per month. The Surat dia-mond boy probably earns from a minimum of 250 to a maximum of 600 rupees per month, or $31.25 to $75. (Average earnings at the large Mehta/Tata factory are 600 to 700 rupees monthly, or close to $100 for the best paid.) Differences in their pay probably depend more on the vastly differing output of pieceworkers and on differing degrees of pressure to produce applied by cottage owners than on actual differences in pay rates. Whatever the pay is, it is take-home. Those earning indus-trial wages fall below the threshold of the Indian income tax, which is why Indian diamond boys are not paid in part under the table.

My first glimpse of a Surat cottage was chilling: a room full of boys, some quite small, sitting on the floor doing factory work, with a tall, unpleasant-looking man standing over them. I was witnessing a nineteenth-century Dickensian nightmare. In the course of my hour there, however, it became obvious that the boys were contented and happy and functioned well together in their chains. The boss was no Fagin, and on reflection, his looks were not really "unpleasant." He appeared to be a kind and considerate man who taught as he inspected each boy's work. The interaction between the boys themselves, ranging in age from twelve to eighteen, and between the boys and their boss, and the emotional atmosphere were all very positive. The younger boys smiled a lot. The surroundings were notably cleaner than the typical 47th Street atelier or Ramat Gan factory, the ventilation seemed adequate, and the lighting was only arguably less than adequate. Children acquire skills much more easily than adults, and inasmuch as most diamond boys come from deprived backgrounds—none of them destined to be shopkeepers, let alone neurosurgeons—learning a trade at an age when people learn trades most easily will probably serve them better in life than traditional schooling. I have seen the past, and it can work too.

It was different during the bren. Demand for diamond polishers prompted upward of a hundred thousand rural adolescents to leave school and the restraining influence of parents to make their own way in Surat or one of the diamond towns nearby. Boys with only a little experience could demand advances toward future earnings of sometimes staggering proportions as a condition of accepting employment. They were given pay packets beyond those of family men and they pushed the price of necessities out of the reach of those with family responsibilities. They squandered most of the remainder of their earnings on vices. Gujarat is a "dry" state and a moral state, and modern Hindus (unlike ancient Hindus) are illiberal about peccadilloes, but the diamond boys and their diamond money brought new industries to Surat: bootlegging and prostitution. VD became very common among the older diamond boys, and not uncommon among prepubescent diamond boys, who contracted it through being on the receiving end of the acts of their midteen compatriots. Tuberculosis became epidemic among the diamond boys, born of their long hours, poor nutrition, and close quarters. As the bren became frenzied, the boys were packed still more closely into their quarters; hours and pressures to boost output increased. Quality of work declined along with the health of the diamond boys.

Laws to protect children and child laborers in the cottage industries are probably unenforceable, but in any case, they are not enforced. In listing the advantages of cottage employment, one cottage owner told me, "In a regular factory they are limited to an eight-hour day but

here in the cottage they can work as much as they want! No one checks!"
(The Surat diamond boy will commonly work from 7:30 AM until 8:00
PM, with time out for lunch and a nap.)

Cottage owners take themselves outside the operation of India's
major industrial order legislation, the Factories Act, aspects of which
apply to any industrial enterprise employing ten or more people. By
way of evasion, the diamond shops register each group of lathe and
two *ghantis* as a separate industrial unit. Each employs a total of nine,
just below the magic number. The small workroom in a cottage may
contain five or six ostensibly separate industrial units, separate on paper
though in no other way. One is registered to the man and his wife;
the next to the man and his brother; the third to the brother and his
wife. It can go on and on, limited only by family size, which in India
is unlimited. Even the largest and most reputable of the "organized"
diamond factories evade the Factories Act in this manner. No one in
diamonds complies with it, though compliance in India otherwise is
almost universal.

As currently constituted, the Indian diamond business could not
survive if it had to comply with the Factories Act. Among other things,
application of the Factories Act would add 15 percent to labor costs
for deductions to the Indian Provident Fund. With rough costing what
it does, there is not 15 percent left over for the Provident Fund.

As a result of the evasions of the Factories Act, the Indian diamond
workers do not participate in the Provident Fund, and are the only
workers in India who do not enjoy any of the social benefits common
to Indian industrial workers. Kuber, the Bombay correspondent for *Diamant,* writes that when adult diamond workers are laid off in India, "They
and their families are facing virtual starvation."

Most Indian diamond manufacturers have been indifferent to the
conditions of the diamond polishers and to the social implications of
their operations. There are exceptions, however, notably Kantilal Chhotalal Mehta, who in business drops the "Mehta" from his family name.
Chhotalal is a Palanpur Jain, a sightholder since 1969, one of the country's leading manufacturers, India's most prolific contributor of articles
in diamond trade journals, and the most prominent social critic within
the industry. His social views rest as much on enlightened self-interest
as on moral bases.

Chhotalal says that cheap labor and freedom from social obligations
have been a bane rather than a blessing to the industry, because they
have encouraged the industry to overproduction: "If we had social obligations we would never have brought 400,000 workers into the industry
in the bren, when the most we could reasonably employ on a continuing
basis was half as many, and we would not have gotten ourselves into
the current situation [August 1979] when we have so many polished
diamonds in stock that we cannot get reasonable prices for them. Protec-

tion for the work force and protection against overproduction—which means protection for the manufacturer—go hand in hand."

Very little if any of the costs of better treatment for the work force would fall on the manufacturer, Chhotalal believes. Perhaps some of the costs would be passed on to ultimate consumers. More of the costs would be absorbed by the DTC by way of a halt in increases in the price of Indian rough.

Chhotalal prefers not to acknowledge the poor quality of Indian workmanship, but other social critics within the industry do, and tie it to the absence of positive working conditions. Sharma of the Hindustan Diamond Company is quick to admit that standard Indian cutting is under par. Until Indian pay and working conditions improve, he says, workers will not take pride in their work, and until they take pride in it, quality of make will not improve. Poor cottage quality, he says, is already costing the industry and the manufacturers money; everyone will be better off when the workers are better off. "Cheaper" is not cheaper.

The DTC appreciates as much. It has been one of the more socially positive factors in the Indian cutting world, principally by urging manufacturers to cease contracting and establish their own regular factories with tenured work forces. By the summer of 1979 it had already prodded six sightholders into opening major factories, and it is keeping on the pressure. Only 10 percent of the DTC's dollar volume goes directly to India and perhaps another 5 percent goes there indirectly via Antwerp, but the adverse effects on the image of "the diamond" caused by poor Indian quality loom larger to it than does its short-term profit on "Indian goods." It could live with smaller profits on them for a while if it had to in order to maintain the image of its product. The DTC is never interested in garnering quick dollars.

Indian diamantaires are perhaps more resentful of the DTC than any other nationality group in the diamond world, and air their complaints with astonishing frankness. "Yes," one acknowledged, "I am dependent on the DTC, but you have to think of your own dignity."

Most of their complaints revolve around the quality of the goods that are made available to the Indian industry. Those who admit to poor quality of workmanship usually consider it a necessary corollary to bad quality rough. A very few manufacturers believe that smalls and lesser qualities are and should be the Indian forte. Most do not. They want better-grade goods and think that the Indian industry—their workers down the line as well as themselves—would make more money with better-grade goods. Many take it as a personal affront to themselves and their workers that they are relegated to pickings in De Beers' garbage dump, and they are sensitive to references to "Indian goods," which

Guy Verwimp   Beurs Voor Diamanthandel

Antwerp, with its four diamond bourses, is now the unrivaled leader of the world diamond trade. Busiest of the bourses is probably the Beurs Voor Diamanthandel, above.

P. Nathan Ferstenberg, at left, has long been the doyen of Antwerp's diamantaires.

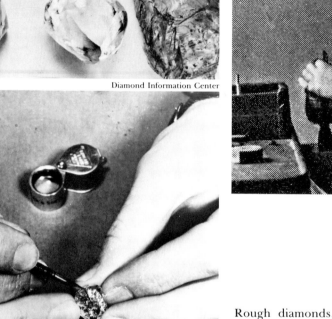

Rough diamonds, diamonds as they come from the mine, have a variety of shapes. They require cutting—processing—to release their light-reflecting beauty. The first step in the process is to mark the "rough" for division. Diamonds may be divided by "cleaving"—delicately chopping the diamond in two. In the historic photo above, Joseph Asscher is shown about to cleave the Cullinan diamond, the biggest diamond ever found. More commonly, though, diamonds are divided by sawing (left).

The stone's outer rim or "girdle" is shaped by the "brutter" (above, left). The polisher then "places" the stone's facets by grinding it down on a grinding wheel or "scaife," while continually checking his work.

Fuchs   Fuchs

Israel's diamond community constitutes a nation within a nation. Most
of it is garrisoned within the twin towers of the Diamond Exchange at Ramat
Gan.

The Israeli diamond industry is shaped
like a pyramid, and Moishe Schnitzer
sits on the top of that pyramid.

India's diamond boys working in cottage factories process more than half of the world's gem diamonds. The boy at the right is twelve years old—and has had four years' experience as a diamond cutter.

Lazare Kaplan & Sons

Because they are so numerous and so visible in the New York diamond district, outsiders assume that the Hasidim control the American diamond trade. But they are a small part of the business. More assimilated people like Lazare Kaplan, the most celebrated living diamond artisan, are the strong men of the New York trade.

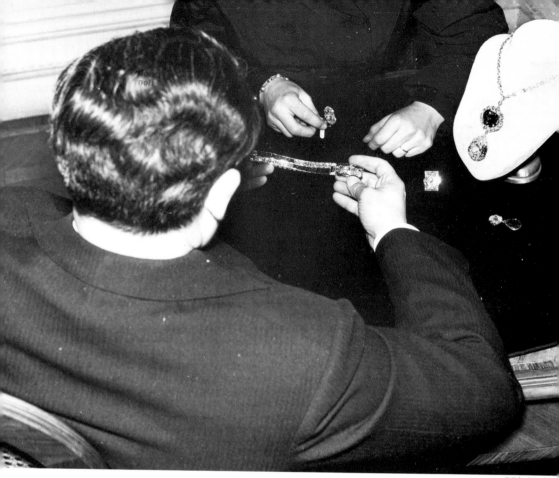

Harry Winston, the greatest showman/salesman in the history of the diamond, created the largest satrapy within the De Beers empire. As a matter of personal security he refused to allow full-face photos of himself to be published—explaining that his insurance company would immediately cancel his policies if he did. It added to the Winston mystique. Below are some of the famous diamonds that passed through his hands. Left to right: the Jonker, the Hope, and the Burton-Taylor.

When Randolph Churchill, father of Winston, peered down into the "Big Hole of Kimberley," the great worked-out diamond mine, and contemplated what it represented in human terms, he mused, "All for the vanity of woman." To which one of the women in the party added, "And the depravity of man."

they know to be a euphemism for "worst quality." "We can manufacture the best stones, better than the Russians, better than Antwerp," one told me. "From the cheapest goods we make fine stones. Small labor we can do like nobody else in the world. Our fingers are thin, supple. Your fingers, European fingers, Jewish fingers, are too fat for the best diamond work—it's a matter of the climate," he said, while he punctured the air above his head with the pudgiest set of digits east of 47th Street. ". . . If only we could get the rough!"

Things are getting worse, not better. Throughout the 1970s, as the polishing industry burgeoned in most of the diamond world, the DTC gradually but continually reduced the qualities it provided everywhere. Israeli boxes were downgraded by the inclusion of better-grade "Indian goods"—taken away from Indian boxes—and this has left the Indians with bigger and bigger percentages of purer and purer junk. Meanwhile the Indians are charged more and more for their rough, usually more on a per-carat basis than Israelis are paying for better-grade rough. There are historical and economic reasons for the DTC's position and policy, but one cannot expect the Indians to feel other than discriminated against. They commonly regard the DTC to be a "Jewish" business which favors Jewish businesses, and it would not be surprising if they were decidedly anti-Jewish. They are not.

The DTC's social influence in the Indian diamond business is almost certainly a positive one. Its provision of bottom-grade rough (rather than better material) is economically and socially desirable for the nation if not for its diamond manufacturers. The millions of tiny stones it sends to India make work for very many more people than the same value in melee would employ. And the Indian input involved in converting "garbage" into gemstones is a happy 43–47 percent: Processing in India adds 43–47 percent to the value of the rough, and much of that value added gets infused into the Indian economy in the form of hard currency. Processing adds only 22 percent to the rough value of the melee polished in Israel, and even less to the value of the larger and choicer stones worked in Antwerp or New York. Most Indian diamantaires, however, would reject this line of theory as rationalization for the maintenance of India's colonial status in the diamond world, and they resent the DTC much as colonial people have always resented their British overlord.

When the Indian industry complains to the DTC, the company spokesman replies, "We are working in the best interests of the Indian industry"—paternalistic talk that is maddening to the Indian diamantaire. One told me, "After enduring centuries of British paternalism we had thought in 1947 [when India became independent] 'at last we are free'— but not in the diamond business. We must still gulp it down and swallow." To a great extent the colonial comparison is appropriate: Like the best of traditional imperialists, the DTC attempts to be a positive

influence with and for the people with whom it deals, while preserving—
and profiting from—the power relationship between itself and the subjects of its empire.

If DTC control is "best" for everyone, it is least best for the Indians.
The status quo is always worst for the have-nots, and in the diamond
world the Indians are the have-nots. Many of them would prefer to
have a free market in the diamond world, and refuse to acknowledge
that the "stabilization" that the CSO brings has ever "stabilized" anything to their advantage.

Inevitably the Indians revolted when, with only one exception, they
failed to apply for any goods whatsoever at the May 1978 sight. They
were protesting, they said, the surcharges, a "punishment" that was
being visited upon them for Israeli sins, and also the continued decline
in the quality of goods provided to them. Both direct and indirect efforts
to find out who had organized the revolt of the slaves were unsuccessful.
No one will breach the confidence and jeopardize the fate of their secret
leader.

Over the years the Indians and their government have made some
effort to find and develop outside sources of rough. In the late 1960s
and early seventies, when the Indian industry was only a tenth of its
current size and was starved for rough, the government opened contact
with Zaire, hoping to make a direct rough connection with the world's
biggest producer of "Indian" rough. Zaire, counseled by DTC-linked
Belgians, wasn't interested.

Ghana, however, was eager for a foil to CAST (Consolidated African
Selection Trust) at its diamond auctions and encouraged the Indians.
India bought a large amount of goods in Ghana but then encountered
buyer resistance at home. The Ghana goods were of generally lesser
quality than the run-of-the-box material that was then coming from the
DTC, and the government found that most buyers preferred to deal
in Antwerp than to buy from their own government. Antwerp dealers
could often arrange advantageous financing for their Indian buyers, and
Antwerp dealers would finagle invoices for them. The government was
forced to drop out of the Ghana market and to abandon still more
ambitious plans to go into joint mining ventures in Africa and to enter
other African rough markets.

India's show of activity, however, was not without beneficial effects:
The DTC reduced the minimum stakes demanded of Indian sightholders,
admitted many new smaller Indians to its circle, and greatly increased
the total flow of rough to India. A government agency, the MMTC
(Minerals and Metals Trading Corporation), became a dealing sightholder. MMTC's allotment, together with much of the "Indian" rough
that was formerly sent to Antwerp dealers, has since been taken over
by Hindustan Diamond Company, which opened for business in the
fall of 1979.

HDC is a joint venture of the government of India (50 percent), the Bank of Bermuda (30 percent), and Industrial Investment Trust Limited, an Indian concern (20 percent), but everyone is quite open about the fact that the bank and the Indian corporation are only straw men for the DTC or some other avatar of the Oppenheimer group. India is rabidly anti-apartheid, and would never, ever get in bed with a South African–tainted entity like the DTC. No sooner than would the Soviet Union or the governments of Sierra Leone, Angola, or Tanzania. But the Bank of Bermuda is another story. Black people, as everyone well knows, are treated with genuine dignity and as equals in Bermuda! Under Indian law no foreign concern can own more than 40 percent interest in an Indian enterprise, so if the DTC was to own a full half of HDC, another "front" was needed in addition to the bank—thus the third stockholder, an Indian corporation with a shady reputation for its past involvements in gold smuggling. No one in India seems particularly embarrassed about the complex subterfuges that the government has gone through in order to cleanse its liaison with the DTC; and the syndicate, as always, is good-natured about dealing with those who officially scorn it. "Face" is the least of its concerns.

HDC, by far India's biggest sightholder and only dealing sightholder, was expected to operate something like the Diamdels, the dealing sightholders controlled by the DTC that operate on small margins and cater to "little guys" in Antwerp's *kempen* and in Tel Aviv. HDC operates on a no-profit 1.5 percent surcharge over DTC prices. Its originators had envisioned opening a branch in Surat and initiating cottage owners into diamond manufacturing on their own account, in hopes of enlarging the base of the Indian industry. Others had somehow had the idea that the government's HDC would also explore avenues for import of rough from sources other than the DTC, so as to free India from its dependency on the colonial overlord. It hasn't quite worked out either way.

Even the smallest manufacturers in Antwerp and Tel Aviv have access to financing, but Indian diamantaires generally do not, and HDC cannot offer financing, so that its clientele to date has been limited principally to the big manufacturers, people who do not need financing but who are eager to supplement their DTC allotments at a mere 1.5 percent premium. The smaller men are probably worse off than they were before HDC took the allotments that formerly went to India-oriented dealers in Antwerp. This has come as no surprise to S. G. Jhaveri, current chairman of the Gem and Jewellery Export Promotion Council, who predicted, prior to the official opening of HDC, that "two swords cannot stand in one sheath—a government monopoly cannot work together with a private monopoly without the impact on national policy being bad for the little man."

As for exploration for outside sources of rough, the DTC's involvement in HDC makes it most unlikely that HDC will ever make serious effort to pursue such avenues. If anything, HDC means that Indians will become even more dependent on the DTC, just as the DTC's accord with Israel's Pituach spelled the end of Israeli government efforts at "independence." If the DTC will deal with you, it is just too hard not to "play into its hand." Manufacturers who have attempted to make their own hookups with foreign diamond-producing governments told me that the Indian government had thrown too many roadblocks in their way. This was ascribed to a pernicious DTC influence in the Indian government. The word used was "corruption."

HDC, however, may prove to be a positive influence. Sharma, its managing director, is a mining engineer by training, a government official long associated with the Indian government's involvement in the diamond industry, and a man of impressive depth and breadth who speaks in an imaginative way about such things as "the man/machine factor" and "Maslow's law" (an American psychologist's theory pertaining to the hierarchy of human needs) as each might relate to the Indian diamond industry. He is societally oriented with respect to every aspect of the industry, and he is personally committed to the elimination of child labor and to improving the quality of life of the diamond worker. As head of HDC he controls sufficient economic power to have significant input into such matters.

India is not an important diamond-trading center, not even in Indian goods. Probably more Indian goods are traded in Antwerp than in Bombay. The Indians themselves hit the hustings, taking a page from their Israeli forefathers, visiting clients and contacts in Antwerp and seeking out direct buyers among the world's jewelry manufacturers. Most of their tiny stones ultimately become the "supporting" stones with which more important diamonds or rubies or emeralds are rimmed, or they are made up into pavé pieces, jewelry in which dozens of very small diamonds are set very close together, literally "paving" the surface with diamonds. The most important of their stones become engagement rings merchandised in American discount houses.

In the outside world the Indian diamantaire meets, buys from, and sells to Ashkenazim—"rigid men with rigid standards" is how one described them. Another said that the Jews with whom he customarily dealt were "amiable people but hard-bargaining and calculating." It is a puzzling world for them. When in Rome they do as the Romans and seal their bargains with the word *"mazel."*

The local diamond club (not affiliated with the World Federation) is the colorful Bombay Diamond Merchants Association. It maintains a long narrow trading room on Dhanji Street, close to the Zaveri (jeweler's) bazaar. Any passerby can look inside its open front wall and see its members packed inside, mostly barefoot young men sitting cross-legged on cushions and haggling animatedly. According to C. B. Jhaveri, Indian bargaining tactics are similar to those in western diamond clubs, except that the prospective buyer's stance is tempered. The Indian buyer will point out the defects in the merchandise offered, but without the exaggerated running down of the goods and the expressions of disgust typical of the Antwerp buyer.

Outside the hall overflow members and nonmembers do a brisk business dealing diamonds openly in the street, much as people once did on 47th Street, before the violence in New York's diamond district. Untouchables crawl on all fours at their feet, peering at the pavement in hopes of finding some lost speck. Occasionally one is found.

The men both inside and outside the association's trading room are dealing and brokering small stones in small quantities, entirely for the domestic Indian market.

Surat has its own local "bourse," Pipla Street. There is no formal club nor even a hall on Pipla Street. At noontime the street is crowded with dealers, small-time traders who stand on either side of the street with their scales and packets of stones. The local trade has some odd rules of its own: Always face the other person when the diamond paper is open; otherwise a flick of his tongue will steal a few stones from you. Much or most of the Pipla Street traffic is in "substitute goods," goods that Bombay manufacturers sent as rough to Surat for processing, where someone has substituted goods of slightly lesser quality for the original parcel. It is virtually impossible for the Bombay manufacturer dealing in vast quantities of low-grade diamonds to protect himself against stone switching in Surat.

There is a significant retail demand for diamonds within India, especially in Calcutta, where the rich are richer and the poor poorer than elsewhere in India. It is common to see an Indian woman wearing diamond earrings or a diamond-studded ear clip (a more elaborate piece of jewelry affixed to the ear) or most commonly, a diamond-ornamented nose stud, something like a shirt stud only affixed to the side of the nose that has been pierced to accommodate it. At weddings and other high occasions, a woman may wear a diamond ear clip and a diamond nose stud, the two connected by a veritable chain of diamonds. Diamonds are favored by Indians at time of marriage, something akin to De Beers' "engagement ring tradition."

Indians still associate diamonds with luck. Typically the consumer will take the diamond home on approval, without payment, for a few days to see whether that particular diamond brings good luck or bad luck. If nothing untoward happens in the interim, the retailer has almost certainly clinched the sale, but if the days are less successful, the diamond will be returned. The same diamond may bring good luck for one and bad luck for another, so the retailer will offer the rejected stone to the next prospect, until he finds the buyer whose stars are compatible with the diamond's.

Lesser-quality diamonds, however, are generally associated with bad luck and are shunned, so that relatively few of the diamonds bought by Indian consumers are products of their own cutting industry. Many of them are old stones purchased by well-to-do Indians prior to independence, currency controls, and import restrictions. Other diamonds are smuggled in and the best qualities cut in India may be quietly siphoned off and sold surreptitiously on the domestic market. While I believe the estimate to be grossly exaggerated, *Blitz*, a leading Bombay weekly, estimates that half of the rough imported ostensibly for processing and reexport under laws designed to facilitate the export business is in fact polished and then sold on the local market. According to *Blitz*, the black trade in diamonds plays an important role in India's "parallel economy." Occasionally the Indian press announces the arrest of a diamantaire for sales tax violations involving domestic diamond sales. It is easier for the government to establish a failure to collect and pay over the sales tax than to establish the other offenses involved in circumventing the law.

If any diamond man anywhere ever had an incentive to evade his country's taxes it is the Indian diamantaire. Indian economists believe that India may be the world's highest taxed country. Its income tax applies only to those earning in excess of 15,000 rupees a year (about $150 a month), which means that virtually everyone in India is exempt from it, but for those who "qualify" its rates rise rapidly to the maximum of 72 percent demanded of those with incomes in excess of 100,000 rupees, or about $12,500. In addition there is also a "wealth tax," which takes, annually, up to 5 percent of a man's net worth, or so much thereof as he may admit to. One industry leader told me that the two taxes together mean that about 94 percent of his [declared] income goes to the tax collector. Little wonder, then, that when I innocently asked him a purely technical question—"What do you show for a yield?"—he took it as a "pragmatic" question: "What do I *show* or what do I *get*?" (The answers: about 24 and 29 percent respectively.) Some of the biggest men have offices abroad, in Antwerp or New York, generally operated for them by family members. In addition to allowing for better customer service, it also allows for greater finagling flexibility.

In addition to the difficulties confronting government tax auditors everywhere in their approach to the diamond business, the Indian IRS man is hampered by the fact that in India the computer is a century away, and the telephone barely pretends to work. His better course is simply to give up, which is pretty much what he has done. When his frustration mounts past endurable levels, he stages a batch of raids on diamantaires' offices. A series of raids in 1979 directed against both diamond and "colored-stone" people (dealers in rubies, emeralds, and the like) yielded large amounts of unaccounted-for cash and diamonds as well as interests in previously undisclosed foreign real estate and bank accounts.

India's greater concern is not whether the diamantaires pay their full income tax, but rather, ensuring that Indian capital is used to develop India, and is not siphoned away from that task. Government policy is that Indian capital flowing abroad must be restricted to the acquisition of necessities or of items desirable for the national economy—machinery, foodstuffs, petroleum. It is not supposed to be sent abroad and removed from the Indian economy, or spent abroad for luxury items—gold or diamonds—that, even if physically situated within India, will make no contribution either to the country's survival or to its development. The government's interest in the diamond business has been two-sided: to develop it as a source of employment and as a winner of foreign capital for India; and to police it to ensure that Indian capital is not drained away from socially desirable uses, either by the diamond merchants or by its citizens at large who might buy diamonds. The two concerns have been competing.

The government has devised an intricate import licensing system to control the flow of both stones and currencies, but smuggling is the way around it, smuggling of the world's most smuggleable commodity.

India is one of the world's biggest consumers of gold, though it produces virtually none itself and virtually none can legally be imported. Diamonds is an easy sideline for the well-developed smuggling industry that caters to the Indian gold market. Timothy Green, an expert on the gold trade, quotes a Bombay customs official as saying, "There was a time when we knew A, B, C, and D were smuggling. Now it's only A, B, C, and D who are not smuggling." Imports are smuggled in to evade the import restrictions. Some manufacturers have preferred buying rough in Antwerp at premiums to buying for less from the DTC: DTC goods can enter India only via official channels, with proper import licenses, whereas Antwerp goods can travel more informally. Exports are smuggled out both to profit from the 25 percent disparity between official and black market rates on the rupee, and to spirit capital away to healthier repositories like Lucerne. The important Siamese jewelry-manufacturing industry depends largely on diamonds imported from India, though these stones appear on the export-import statistics of neither country.

The government of India well understands the ways of the diamantaires and appreciates the adverse effects that they and their diamonds have visited upon India. Still, it wants what benefits come along with the industry. In terms of gross exports, diamonds are probably India's biggest export item, and even in terms of value added on stones handled through official channels, diamonds are an important foreign currency generator. However much of that value added remains in India to be invested for the country's further development is all to the better. A country with massive unemployment (unlike Belgium or Israel), India wants the jobs. For India the answer to the question "What price diamonds?" is: "Not too much."

26

47TH: THE STREET
WITHOUT CASH REGISTERS

◆

"The street gives the whole industry a bad name," one dealer on 47th said. The street is 47th Street, but not all of it, only the one short block between Fifth and Sixth avenues. Close to half of the whole world's output of polished diamonds flows through the street en route to the American consumers.

The dealer went on: "The steerers, grabbing people, dragging people into their concessions, they make my skin crawl. The huckstering, the hard sell—telling people 'This is a two-thousand dollar stone but I can let you have it for twelve hundred'—that's only going to make the public lose confidence in the stability of diamond values. It's vulgar, it's sleazy."

It is. But the street is also vibrant, earthy, electric, colorful, charming. You have to love it (if you will) in the same way that people love London's Petticoat Lane, or the Paris Flea Market. Forty-seventh Street is one of the great American bazaars.

There are literally hundreds of small jewelers located on the ground level of the street. Some few have their own storefronts, the windows mostly crammed with the gaudiest diamond "creations" ever imagined, each item labeled "Sale!"; "Today's Special!"; or "Bargain!" Many more work from small stalls in the series of jewelry arcades that line the street, each one an exotic market complete unto itself. Mixed in with the jewelry sellers in the arcades are the jewelry industry service people, the men who sell "findings," very small component parts for rings and earrings at maybe eighty cents a part; pearl stringers; stone setters; free-lance cutters who will polish away the chip in your diamond ring; watchmakers and others who do highly specialized repairs; and dealers who sell only small supporting stones, the tiny Israeli or Indian diamonds that will ring the more important stone in a piece of jewelry.

When they speak English on 47th it is highly colorful—and occasionally dramatic—dialogue, and anyone who wanders through the arcades can pick up snatches of it: "At twelve I will not make any profit at all, as sure as I am standing here!" Elsewhere: "Don't tell me how big it is! Any *schmuck* on the street can figure a twenty-pointer!" Elsewhere: "He is worse than any of the guards at Auschwitz, and I know what I am talking about"—said as the speaker rolled up his sleeve, revealing a tattooed number. A surprising lot of the industry mechanics are Christians, including many Italian-Americans and Puerto Ricans. Still, Yiddish vies with English as the first language among the babel of tongues heard on the street.

Much of the ground floor traffic is between the dealers themselves, as they buy and sell the same goods back and forth along the arcades and with dealers across the street. With a little prodding everyone will tell you a variation of the story of Jake and Izzy, who sold the same stone back and forth between themselves. First Jake sold it to Izzy for $750 a carat. Then Izzy sold it back to Jake for $800; it went back to Izzy at $900. Finally Jake called Izzy and said, "I'll give you an even thousand a carat for the stone!" only to be told, "Sorry, Jake, I sold it." "What? You sold it? You moron! We were making a living on that stone!"

"We never let any of the goods off the street," one arcade concessionaire told me with a good-natured wink. It isn't really true—they will sell to outside buyers, oh boy will they—but it is true that the big boys who supply the nation's retailers are not on the ground floor in any of the arcades. They are upstairs. The shopper will not get to see any of them.

Much of the street-level traffic is with out-of-town jewelers who come to the street every so often to visit their repairmen, to pick up supplies, or to take a couple of pieces of jewelry from a stallholder on "memo." You can spot the out-of-town jeweler easily enough: When he plunks his briefcase down on a counter and opens it, a batch of manila envelopes will spill out. Jewelers all use the same envelopes. Each envelope contains a ring requiring a stone, or a stone requiring a ring, or a handful of pearls to be strung, or a small part that broke off.

One jeweler permitted me to tag along with him from arcade to arcade as he visited the findings sellers and the stone setters, leaving a few envelopes here and a few there, and returning for pickups later. He stopped at a booth and showed a small supporting-stone dealer a ring set with eight garnets. The jeweler's customer wanted the garnets replaced with diamonds. Did the dealer think that it required 8-point diamonds? They both studied the ring through their loupes and then finally the *maven* ruled that smaller 6-point diamonds would do—at $450 a carat or $216 for eight 6-point stones. "Nice goods?" the out-of-towner asked. "What do I ever give you? You want better, I sell you better, you want cheaper, I sell you cheaper." The visitor did not look at the flakes of stone but said he would call his customer and might be back. He disappeared, then returned; the customer had said that the $216 price would be all right. He paid by reeling off bills from a fat wad of currency. On the street everyone prefers cash, just cash will be perfectly fine, but there are no cash registers on 47th Street. The money gets stuffed into pockets.

Everyone rushes on 47th Street, everyone is in a hurry. The frenzy that characterizes the street is at its height on Wednesdays. Wednesdays the theater matinees attract people—mainly women—to their neighborhood, and the doctors don't work on Wednesdays. Theatergoers and doctors are popular on 47th Street. The hectic pace slows down after noon hour on Friday to a crawl, when stall owners close up and the cutters who work "upstairs" drift off early to ready theselves for *shabbes*, the Jewish day of rest that begins at Friday sundown.

People on the street are brisk, sometimes to the point of rudeness, as they jostle each other for places at the luncheonette counters and push each other while stepping off the curb to go around a slow-moving pair of *schmoozers*. At the same time, 47th is a friendly street for those who are a part of it. After a few days on the street you begin to notice the same faces repeatedly, then begin nodding at familiar ones and exchanging hellos.

The Hasids (or Hasidim) are the most prominent feature of the street. They are easily identified by their costume: long black coat, wide-brimmed hat, full beard, and *payess*, the long strands of head and sideburn hair alongside the ears which, in accord with biblical commandment, are never cut but which they often curl around the ears or stuff under their hats. (Insiders sometimes call 47th the Rue de la Paix-ess.) These are the superpious most-Orthodox Jews. Their garb serves as a reminder to themselves of their identities as Jews, and simultaneously as a protection against the temptations of the outside world.

The Hasidim are a bulwark against the assimilation and intermarriage that has threatened the continuity of the Jewish peoples since long before Shylock's daughter, but never and nowhere more so than in present-day America. They segregate themselves not so much from the Gentile as from the much greater threat of the assimilated Jew, and live together in enclaves, principally in Brooklyn's Williamsburg section, much as they did in the *shtetlach*, the Jewish villages of eastern Europe before the war—to a great extent before the First World War. In Williamsburg, it is the visitor that is the stranger in a strange land. Most of New York's diamantaires have considerable affection for the Hasidim, and will react strongly to unintended slights towards their "funny" brothers. "Why do you guys [journalists] always treat them like freaks?" one challenged me. ". . . Why are they any more freaks than the Hare Krishnas?"

Because the Hasidim are so numerous and so easily recognized on the street most outsiders believe that their importance in the trade looms very large. It doesn't. They are "little guys"in the diamond world, mostly cutters or brokers or at most small dealers. No one that I asked either at the DTC or on the street could bring to mind any Hasidic sightholder. The Hasidim are interested in God, not in temporal empire building. (Several score of bacon-eating sightholders will claim to be Hasidim on the theory that their roots trace back to one of the great Hasidic communities of eastern Europe. *Bubkes!*)

In the old days, before the Great Depression, the diamond and jewelry trade people were all located far downtown, on Maiden Lane, John Street, Nassau Street, the Bowery, Canal Street. The City Hall bus, lumbering up the Bowery, was always crowded with diamond men. The Diamond Dealers Club was founded at 80 Nassau Street in 1931.

"We didn't have a nickel," recalls Al Lubin, the young lawyer who incorporated the group and who remains today, an old lawyer, as the club's executive secretary. Lubin is the last of the "old crowd." When they had a few more members and a little more money, they moved to a "fancier" address at 95 Nassau Street. But by then the trade was already beginning to move north, attracted by the flurry of activity in midtown Manhattan that was stimulated by the construction during the Great Depression of Rockefeller Center. One by one the jewelers and the diamond people settled in on 47th, the jewelers on street level, the diamond wholesalers on the floors above. The club joined them in 1941, serving as a further impetus to the centralization of the trade. World War II brought a huge influx of Antwerp and Amsterdam diamantaires into the American diamond community, and the burgeoning of the American cutting industry. After the war, displaced refugees from eastern Europe, largely but not exclusively Hasidim, began learning the cutting trade and taking their place in the scenario of the street.

The centralization of the diamond wholesalers all on one short stretch of street was a magnet for the nation's retail jewelers in the fifties and sixties, before wholesalers sent legions of salesmen on the road and before matured diamond-classification systems enabled telephone ordering. The retailer from the hinterlands would come to the street maybe three times a year, visit his contacts, and do his ordering. Close proximity of the wholesalers brought them all more business.

The proximity is no longer so important for the diamond wholesalers, but the trade remains clustered out of force of habit. There are rarely vacancies in most of the buildings on the block; as soon as one tenant moves there is another ready to take his space—"paying rent from yesterday," says Lubin. The landlords are not diamond people. Spillover diamond businesses have located on the upper floors of 46th and 48th streets, and adjacent portions of Fifth Avenue. These locations, one street away, are temperamentally worlds distant, quite lacking the brusqueness, the fear, and the grubbiness that permeate the buildings of 47th Street. Much smaller colonies of diamantaires still operate in the long-ago locations, principally on Canal Street, which has arcades similar to those on 47th Street. Canal Street diamond merchants are colorful and abrupt.

As in the rest of the diamond world, 47th Street is losing the rich and special character of the diamond trade with the influx of more and more people, the decreasing significance of the father-to-son tradition, and the increased mechanization of the cutting process.

All the old-timers detect the change. Mostly it is attributed to the newcomers—probably more than twice as many people are in the trade on the street as five years ago. Mostly, it is attributed to the Israelis. One street observer said bluntly, "The Israelis have killed the Forty-seventh Street subculture." And they are resented because of it. The owner of a cutting shop will proudly say that all of his employees are "American Jews." American Jews means immigrants from Poland, the Ukraine, Hungary—maybe even someone born in Brooklyn. It is a euphemism for "no Israelis."

The street is flooded with Israelis trained as diamond polishers in Israel who come to ply their trade in better-paying New York. They come on tourist visas (which do not permit them to work), but it is easy for them to get jobs polishing on 47th Street without proper visas or working papers. All of New York's polishers are "independent contractors," so the employer is under no obligation to ask about such matters as Social Security numbers or to take payroll deductions. The employer can always say, "I didn't know." The visas run out but the Israelis stay on at their scaives. Some of them, I am told, are bullied and mistreated by employers who capitalize on their illegal status, just as some Texas canners take merciless advantage of the Mexican wetbacks. But probably far fewer Israelis get kicked around than Mexicans.

In large measure the resentment against the Israelis is a matter of simple economic competition. Israelis work too hard, too long, too cheaply, thereby taking too many of the stones while undercutting the wage level for the less ambitious "American" diamond workers. They also work too fast, with the result that the overall quality of their output is inferior to that of the slower-working Hasidim and Puerto Ricans. The dislike for the Israelis, however, is rarely stated in those terms. It is attributed to their "arrogance" or to other supposed—or maybe real—personality and character traits of the Israeli. "Believe me," says a manufacturer, "it hurts me to say this. I'm a staunch Zionist and a very Orthodox Jew, but the good ones aren't here; the good ones are in Israel. Here they're just money grubbers, rude and pushy."

"Also," interjects a kibitzer, "they kill people." In September of 1977, Pinchos Jaroslawicz, a young super-Orthodox broker known on the street as Mr. PJ, disappeared with $600,000 worth of diamonds. The last man known to be with him, Shlomo Tal, an Israeli cutter, disappeared soon after, but was discovered after several days asleep in his car. Tal told a bizarre story: PJ had been at his office when two masked men had forced their way into the room, had robbed and killed Jaroslawicz, and had threatened Tal with death to himself and his family if he spoke. Days later the men had kidnapped Tal and taken him for a three-day ride to reinforce their threat, before drugging him and abandoning him in his car. Tal led the police to PJ's body, hidden in Tal's workroom, where he had left it upon orders of the assailants. (And where the police had failed to discover it on their earlier search of Tal's tiny room.)

Initial police skepticism about Tal's account was heightened when he described one of the assailants as a black man with a Polish accent. Ultimately Tal and another Israeli cutter were convicted of the murder.

PJ was not the first murder victim in the diamond world. In the couple of years before his death several other diamond people had been murdered, but none on the street. Perhaps they had been murdered by common criminals—outsiders. PJ had been killed by people from within the trade; by "one of our own"; by Jews. It was shattering to everyone on the street. A dealer said, "I can believe that a Jew will steal; I can even imagine a Jew holding a gun on another man. I cannot believe that a Jew will kill another man! . . . Can I?"

Since then there have been other killings. Periodically police handbills are plastered about the diamond district, in hallways and beside elevators: "Information wanted as to whereabouts of Martin Paretzky, Missing Person." "Information wanted as to whereabouts of Satya Gupta, Missing Person." Both were found murdered.

Security is tight everywhere. The street level is crowded with private security men, and the lobbies of the more important buildings bristle with impressive banks of TV screens which monitor everyone entering or leaving the building, and the goings-on in the elevators and main corridors. That's the obvious security, which suffices to scare off some potential criminals. Then there is the secret security: the dozens of other hidden TV cameras; ultrasonic beams that trigger a signal when anything—or anybody—interrupts their path; secret buzzers never more than an arm's length away that will summon a battalion of security men armed like the Haganah.

Upstairs all doors are kept locked until the caller is interrogated through the intercom. "Who's there?" is the first question asked, and if the answer is not immediately forthcoming the demand is made again, this time nervously: *"Who's there!!"* Fear is the emotional constant on the street. "We got the best security in the world," a dealer told me. "You gotta go through three locked doorways and two TV monitors to get to me. All right, so now you're here. You wanna pull a gun and kill me? I'll push a warning button, but by the time they get here, you already killed me—a lot of good it did me."

"Is the security good here?" I asked at my next stop.

"There is no good security anywhere," was the reply. "My brother-in-law, thank God, he wasn't killed. . . ." Everyone has a story.

Thefts and burglaries are commonplace on the street. Some involve acts of engineering brilliance and acrobatic daring. Many more are matters of simple thuggery, accompanied by violence. Virtually all of them have an inside link, something that was unheard of even ten years ago.

No one can really say how many burglaries occur. Officials of the New York City Police Department believe that many incidents go unreported because the victims are afraid that the report of theft of goods beyond the victim's apparent means would alert IRS to their tax evasions or because such a report might implicate the victim himself in fencing operations. On the other hand, police and insurers are invariably suspicious when thefts *are* reported. Nonthefts, perpetrated to swindle insurance companies, are common in the diamond world.

Very few of the thefts are ever solved and very few goods are ever recovered. Both police and private security people agree that the loot is fenced on 47th or perhaps on Canal Street, at about a quarter of wholesale value. An article in *Cosmopolitan* magazine quoted without comment in *Jewelers' Circular–Keystone* says, "Today's fences are generally respected members of the Diamond Exchange who specialize in selling gems. They deal in hot rocks because of the enormous profits involved (quadruple what a normal sale would bring), because of the thrill and often because they simply become charmed and won over by glib thieves." The New York *Daily News* quoted diamond district insurance broker Robert Gordon in 1979 as saying, "A guy who knows where to go can steal diamonds on the second floor of a building and fence them on the third floor. All he needs is some knowledge of the business and the people in it."

Diamantaires everywhere are reticent, but nowhere more so than in New York, largely because of the thefts and violence that have plagued the street. Every mention in print of the violence makes them apoplectic because it invites more, and the journalists who publicize it are regarded as in some way accomplices to the criminals. One who refused to talk to me at least explained why:

> Every time there's any trouble down here, some television newsman stands in the middle of the street and tells the world, "There they are, every one of these people is carrying one million dollars." Then for the next three weeks, every glassy-eyed freak in New York is down here looking us all over and drooling. I was complaining about this the other day to one of my Hasidic associates, and he said, "You? Worried? What about me? The way I look is like carrying a sign on my back, 'Rob me, kill me.'"
>
> I heard some television guy on the news saying, "Those men in the

black robes are the Hasidim, the wealthy Orthodox Jewish diamond dealers. Why do you suppose their robes are so bulky?"

Now please excuse me, mister, I'm busy.

The American diamond manufacturing business, like Antwerp's, has two branches, a *grof* branch processing the choicer stones in New York, and a *klein* branch working the more routine diamonds in Puerto Rico. For both, however, greater labor costs have generally restricted the American manufacturer to handling larger stones, in which labor costs are a less significant factor in the eventual wholesale price of the finished stones. What is the smallest size stone that you can economically process? I asked "Max," a major 47th Street manufacturer. He answered Jewish style, with a question: "Do you know that in Bombay a street sweeper gets nine dollars a month?"

"That was a *long* time ago, Max!" interjected a kibitzer. (There is always a kibitzer in the diamond world.)

Max didn't argue the point: "All right, so maybe a street sweeper in Bombay gets twelve dollars a month."

Well, does a Bombay diamond cutter get more or less than the street sweeper? "I dunno," Max replied, "but if he gets a penny more than the twelve dollars—it's *gra*-vy! How you gunna compete with that? I can't handle anything less than two carats rough; maybe from that I'll get a carat of polished. On little stones? Forget it!"

Because the efficiencies of each operation differ, other manufacturers told me that they could profitably work stones half that size—and another said that he could not economically handle rough smaller than four carats, which might yield two stones totaling two carats in weight. Even in Puerto Rico it is usually unfeasible to process typical Israeli goods, let alone Indian goods.

The larger manufacturers work out of both locations. The more important stones are worked in New York principally so that the manufacturer himself can supervise the processing of them. These are cut in ateliers or in small manufacturer-owned factories. In either case they will be worked by "independent contractors." The New York cutting industry is a "cottage industry" that has been moved to a centralized location. It cuts more of the world's most important stones than any other center (the rest of them being cut in Antwerp).

The lesser stones in the American boxes are shipped to the sizable diamond factories in Puerto Rico, in and around Ponce and Caguas as well as in the San Juan/Santurce metropolis. Lazare Kaplan established the first diamond factory on the island in the 1920s. Molasses, rum, and other sugarcane-related enterprises were the only industries on the island at the time and Kaplan had to train his own work force from scratch, but he found that the Puerto Ricans were "very good pupils, with their delicate hands, so fine for diamond work." Others followed

him there. Kaplan is quick to attribute much of his own success and
the success of Lazare Kaplan & Sons to the cooperation of the government of Puerto Rico. Puerto Rico has been good for diamonds—and
diamonds have been good for Puerto Rico.

Except for Piermatic operators, who are paid hourly, the workers
in Puerto Rico are paid on a piecework basis, but they are regular employees, subject to payroll deductions for income taxes and entitled to unemployment compensation at slow times. The government of Puerto Rico
has refused to suffer the shams that the diamantaires commonly perpetrate elsewhere.

More of the world's polished diamond output is sold in the United
States than anywhere else, and most of that is handled by New York–
based wholesalers. The city also attracts many foreign dealers who come
to New York to buy big stones. Probably most of the carat-plus goods
cut in New York are sold to export buyers.

New York's role in the national diamond trade, however, is no longer
unchallenged: Los Angeles (which will soon have its own eleven-story
diamond center building) and to a lesser extent Miami are both becoming
increasingly important as diamond importing and diamond trading centers. New York's response to the challenge of the newer centers is the
same as Tel Aviv's: build a building. After negotiations that extended
over several years, in the summer of 1980 the New York Diamond Dealers
Club and Korvette's finally reached accord for sale to the club of Korvette's location at the corner of Fifth Avenue and 47th Street. The club
expects to raze the building and erect a thirty-story high-rise which it
will merchandise on a condominium basis. The club envisions a diamond
exchange building similar to that in Ramat Gan—with even better security—which will centralize most of the trade and possibly some of the
cutters as well within a diamond bastille. The price for the land rights
came to something over $18 million—cheap in midtown Manhattan.
One of the club negotiators told me with a twinkle, "Diamond men—
well, we know how to bargain."

The Diamond Dealers Club is the commercially more significant
of the two diamond clubs in New York (the other being the smaller
but highly respected Diamond Trade Association). Perhaps 10 or 15
percent of the national volume passes through its doors. It is a highly
colorful organization. Some three-quarters of the older members are
World War II refugees, and perhaps half of the younger men are Hasidim. Its trading floor and lobby are both usually packed with loitering
Hasidic brokers, hanging around in hopes of smelling out some action.
The club has a long list of people waiting to be admitted to membership,
and who gets in has for a long time been largely a matter of intraclub
political pull.

William Goldberg was elected president of the club in 1978, in the first live election contest that the club had seen in years. The Goldberg forces organized themselves like a political machine and even brought in a part-time political consultant.

After his first election, Goldberg offended some in the trade by being more open with the press than many would have preferred; to Goldberg's view, "We are honorable men and women in this industry. . . . We are not an industry that should behave as though it has something to hide." One important dealer complained to me, "I like Bill Goldberg more than I like anyone else on the street, but . . . well . . . Did you ever know how some guys fall in love with the sound of their own voice?" He proceeded to blame Goldberg for most of what he hasn't liked reading in the newspapers since Goldberg first became president.

In response to this kind of criticism, Goldberg has lowered his profile somewhat in the more recent past, a difficult thing for one of his extraverted temperament to do. Goldberg is irrepressible and flamboyant, and about the only one left on the street since the death of Harry Winston with a sense of showmanship. He is a stocky, full-faced man with shaggy eyebrows, twinkling eyes, and generous chins, with long salt-and-pepper hair that falls to either side of his balding pate. If a movie were to be made about 47th Street, the role of Goldberg would be played by Robert Morley. Goldberg was reelected to his second term as club president in January of 1980.

The tax-evasion techniques used by American diamond dealers depend on the nature of their operations and their relative size.

Many diamond dealers run a "legitimate" business in which they keep auditable books of dubious probity while simultaneously conducting an under-the-table business in which cash is exchanged for unrecorded stones from their private stock. They will deal in and out of either or both. The bigger fellows do relatively little of the cash-money dealings; invoicing strategies give them enough leeway to permit them to remain almost entirely respectable.

The American buyer in Antwerp or Tel Aviv is likely to request and to receive an invoice showing an inflated cost price. This he pays with a check in the exact amount—proof of payment. He is rebated the overpayment by deposit direct to his bank account in Switzerland, or in cash, or in additional "free" diamonds, unrecorded stones that he will use in those aspects of his business that he conducts extra-ledger. When it comes time for the American to compute his income tax, the inflated figure shown on the invoice and confirmed by the canceled check gets added into the "Cost of Goods Sold," thereby reducing his apparent profit and his income tax. His books will come out clean and auditable, even though they bear only a weak link with reality. Until the United States Internal Revenue Service figures out how to audit

Antwerp and Tel Aviv diamond businesses—something that neither Belgian nor Israeli tax collectors have yet learned to do—this modus operandi will be perfectly safe.

Even those who do an entirely domestic trade have opportunities for cheating in excess of those available to other businessmen. Any diamond man, big or small, can switch stones back and forth between his business inventory and his private collection, manipulating both the on-paper and the realistic values of both in the manner most advantageous at tax time. No tax examiner in the world will know what to make of a diamond man's inventory. He is entirely at the diamantaire's mercy.

The cash deals can be made from his private stock, out of view, or can be channeled through the business record as circumstances dictate. To the extent that diamonds in New York is a cash business, it is largely an under-the-table business.

The flexibility of the diamond man's position is such that even the entirely domestic manufacturer or dealer could keep perfectly auditable record books while still paying however much in taxes he wanted to pay. However, most of the smaller men do not keep such records. The typical small cutting shop will have, in lieu of precise books, a shoe box into which are jumbled a mass of crinkled receipts and memos reflecting most of their rough bills and some of their labor expenses, copies of many of their own invoices, an unpaid parking ticket, a scattering of their own and others' business cards, a couple of light bills, a laundry check, and some torn matchbook covers. Such records are, unfortunately, somewhat difficult to audit.

On the lowest level, many small operators will buy and sell entirely or almost entirely under the table, and make either principally fabricated tax returns or none at all. The Hasidim control much of this end of the trade. " 'Piety' and Honesty," a 1980 consideration of the Hasidic ethic by Rabbi Louis Rabinowitz published in *Judaism* magazine, concludes that there is little correlation between piety and honesty. What smuggling survives in the American diamond world today revolves around this quiet-money segment of the business.

Once upon a time diamond smuggling into the United States was undertaken principally to save duties and excise taxes totaling 20 percent on polished and 10 percent on rough. In those days the professional diamond smugglers constituted a great industry, a well-ordered system of transportation operating something like United Parcel, and with the same reliability and regularity—and integrity. Only an infinitesimal percentage of the smuggled goods were detected, and the smuggling rings would make good any losses. Customs couldn't compete.

Then the duties were successively reduced, and abolished entirely on rough, and the excise tax was phased out. One 47th Street leader told me, "When the duty was first dropped a lot of the old-timers were so accustomed to doing it crooked that they couldn't adjust to doing it straight." But with each drop in the duty, smuggling became less and less inviting. With each reduction, the total tariff take on diamonds soared, as more and more stones began to come in legally. Not only does every man have his price, the price is computable on a percentage basis!

Smuggling to avoid the duty practically ceased when the duty was reduced to 5 and 4 percent levels, and in January of 1981, the duty on diamonds was completely abolished. Smuggling has continued in order to avoid records and traces, to supply rough or polished goods for hidden businesses, and to keep quiet money out of the scope of vision of government people. Even when duties on polished stones were assessed at nominal levels, most diamond smuggling involved rough— on which the duty had already been abolished. Duty considerations have long been secondary to American diamond smugglers—except, that is, where Soviet goods are concerned.

When it comes to diamonds polished in Russia, diamantaires large or small, those with seemingly legitimate books and those who do not pretend to have books, are likely to be involved in "soft" smuggling: bringing in goods through official channels but knowingly misdescribing them on their customs declarations. Diamonds polished in the Soviet Union continue to be dutied at the 10 percent level that has been applied for many years. Nobody in the diamond world thinks that this is fair. It is difficult to deal profitably in Soviet goods if you must pay a 10 percent duty on them; the difference between 10 percent and 0 percent is the difference between profit and loss. So what do you do? Refuse to deal in Soviet goods? Well . . . those are good stones. (It makes not the slightest difference to anyone in the trade that world Jewry is calling for a boycott of Soviet products.) You bring them in but call them free-world goods. Official customs reports indicate that in 1980 only one-tenth of 1 percent of the total caratage imported into the United States was of Russian origin. In fact, at least 8 percent of the diamonds imported into the United States are Russian made, maybe very much more than 8 percent. Virtually all of them are imported illicitly, some few by outright smuggling but most of them simply passed off as "other" merchandise, thereby evading the 10 percent duty. Haim Danieli, executive secretary of the Israeli Diamond Manufacturers Association, reported in *Israel Diamonds* that at the 1980 international diamantaires' convention held in Johannesburg, the Americans present had agreed "that it was extremely easy to 'get around' this duty."

Goods made in the Russian style actually are easy to spot: The girdles on them are remarkably even in thickness and often the girdles, as well as the body of the stone, are faceted. The tables on them are always 62–63 percent of the stone's diameter. In all ways they are remarkably regular, and of remarkably fine make. In their original packagings, they are contained in *briefkes* longer than the papers customarily used in Antwerp and Tel Aviv, and each paper commonly contains an even carat of goods.

Customs has encountered some rather crude attempts to ship Soviet goods into the United States as other than Soviet merchandise, one incident involving one of London's most reputable brokers. Someone at the broker's office forgot to remove the original Soviet invoice from the box. When, however, the Soviet goods are spilled from their original wrappers and mixed in small proportions with Israeli, Indian, or Antwerp goods, they are likely to go undetected amidst the great volume of parcels that customs must inspect. One of the world's biggest dealers in Russian polished told me that he regularly ships Russian stones to the United States as parts of mixed lots and that they have regularly slipped through.

No one on the street likes to talk about things like smuggling and tax evasion. US tax collectors are different from their counterparts in Belgium and Israel. They mean business, and tax evasion and smuggling are not things to joke about. American diamantaires are touchy about them. "Listen!" one manufacturer exploded at a delicately raised question about income taxes. "I pay my fair share—we [the industry] pay our fair share! I'm supportin' ten welfare families! Hey, Sarah!" he yelled to the secretary in the next room, ". . . how much taxes did I pay this week?" After a pause to check the ledgers, Sarah yelled back, "Seven thousand dollars, Jake."

"I dunno where you guys get this stuff," the manufacturer trailed off into a grumble.

PART IV

MOVING OUT THE GOODS

◆

Before primitive people really want good housing they want beads, they want decorations, they want romance and this is absolutely fundamental to the human being.

> —Harry F. Oppenheimer,
> Chairman of the Board,
> De Beers Consolidated Mines, Limited

27

SELLING A TRADITION

◆

The retail demand for diamonds turns to some extent on the beauty of the diamond, and to a greater extent on its mystique and symbolism. We will not dwell on the beauty of the diamond. A loose diamond is an item of trade or investment in which beauty is a very secondary consideration. Mounted as a solitaire (a ring containing a single gem) the diamond may be beautiful or, if big enough, it may be transparent ostentation, depending on the viewer's tastes and values; but if it is beautiful, it is surely no more so than an equivalent-sized chunk of cubic zirconium, the budget-priced fake good enough to have fooled most of the members of the New York Diamond Dealers Club when it was first introduced. Or are diamonds more beautiful than aquamarines, the blue-green "semiprecious" stones that sell for a minuscule fraction of diamond prices?

These are arguable questions, matters for the subjective. What is not arguable is that diamonds have a mystique while aquamarines do not, a mystique that turns partly on the greater rarity of diamonds, partly on the mystery of the famous diamonds, partly on the glamour that surrounds the "fabulous" people who wear them—and perhaps most, on the traditions that accompany diamond, traditions that have been popularized through advertising.

Most of the mystique of the diamond is pap.

The rarity of diamonds is much overstated. Every year almost ten tons of diamond are mined, 45 million carats in the form probably of several hundred million separate stones. The production is probably vastly greater than that of most other gems and semiprecious stones. Yet diamonds are "rare" in the economic sense (valuable) because demand outstrips supply. Sir Ernest said, "Common sense tells us that the only way to increase the value of diamonds is to make them scarce, that is, to reduce the production." Control of production has always been the foundation of the value of diamond, first controlled by the ancient rulers of India, then by the Portuguese overlords of Brazil, and now by De Beers.

Harry Oppenheimer is usually credited with appreciating the other route to increasing the value of the diamond: augmenting demand through advertising, which De Beers first undertook in 1939. Supply is increased or decreased by the producing contributors to the CSO in accordance with demand, while demand is augmented by advertising. Both sides of the equation are manipulable and manipulated to keep diamonds "rare" in the meaningful sense: valuable. According to *Israel Diamonds,* the bimonthly published in Ramat Gan, "It is, in effect, mostly the worldwide publicity undertaken by De Beers which keeps the wheels turning in the polishing centers." Most diamantaires appreciate that the value of their product is illusory and dependent on the props maintained by De Beers.

Hypothetically, the same could be done for other precious stones. If someone were to establish a cartel to control the output and merchandising of aquamarines, they could come to rival diamonds in price. Theoretically it could be done. But for now, no single mine could afford to begin promoting a stone for all of its competitors. Only De Beers has sufficient interest in the merchandising of all diamonds to be able to afford promotion.

Promotion of the diamond began when the New York advertising agency N. W. Ayer and Son was first hired to sell diamonds in 1939. The near-universal acceptance of the "tradition" of the diamond dates back no further than that.

Prior to the Great Depression, De Beers had no difficulty moving its diamonds; the members of the pre-DTC syndicate eagerly took every stone that De Beers could dig out of the ground. Advertising to further augment demand was deemed vulgar. That all fell apart in the Great Depression, and by the mid-1930s De Beers was holding stocks valued at four times its annual sales. The dealers and manufacturers who had vied for its output in the boom twenties were all overloaded with pebbles that could be sold for little more than pebbles. Demand had to be created and De Beers turned to advertising. It has been advertising ever since, assuming the burden—on behalf not only of itself but of its buyers and their buyers—of preparing the consumer to make the ultimate purchase. Diamonds is probably the only business in the world in which the supplier of the raw material advertises the end product. But then it is the only business in which the supplier of the raw materials has the biggest stake in selling the end product, the only one in which the supplier is in the best position to spread the costs of advertising among almost all of those who ought to be supporting the advertising effort.

Harry Oppenheimer determined that the United States was the biggest potential customer nation and so retained the American firm to inaugurate De Beers' campaign. Ayer sought to establish the diamond as the most sacred symbol of love, or at least the most sacred symbol of it that could be bought over the counter. It came up with a slogan developed from a saying of Solly Joel's, "A diamond is forever," that is still carried in most diamond ads. Ayer aimed principally to develop "the engagement ring tradition," and more particularly, the *diamond* engagement ring tradition.

Wedding rings, if not engagement rings, are quite ancient but the earliest culture in which they appear to have been significant to the prehistoric retailer is that of the ancient Hebrews. According to *International Diamond Annual* (1971), among the Hebrews the wedding ring had to be

> large, heavy and gold. It was expected to be of a specified value and fully paid for! Indeed, in the Hebrew stipulation that the ring must have a stipulated value we see, perhaps, the origins of later customs which laid down that a wedding ring must be durable and of some worth—not a mere trifle.

The basic principle survives today. It is not the thought that counts, it is the money.

The diamond, costing as much as it did and being as durable as it was, was just what such a ring needed. Somehow or another, sometime in the 1400s, the ring, the diamond, and the status of committed-to-be-married got mixed up together and the *diamond* engagement ring tradition was born. However, it didn't really begin to blossom until five hundred years later. Then N. W. Ayer picked it up and began reminding people—and especially the people of marriageable age in whose magazines it advertised—that a diamond, like love, is eternal. By 1950 about half of young Americans appreciated that a diamond engagement ring was just what was needed to "make it official," and by the early 1960s the figure had soared to close to 80 percent of American betrothed who were making it official by the presentation of a diamond engagement ring. A moribund custom had been revived and popularized with remarkable speed—profitably.

Some time in the 1960s the life-styles and status symbols of middle- and upper-middle-class Americans of marriageable age began to change. Before the end of the 1960s the mink coat went by the boards and the last thing that an upper-class, college-educated nonvirgin wanted to see on her finger was a big diamond ring. (Or so she claimed.) Among sophisticated young modern affluents the diamond became as dated as Margaret Dumont, the plump diamond-studded dowager in the Marx Brothers movies.

Then came the live-together life-styles of the 1970s. Between 1970 and 1978, according to *Jewelers' Circular–Keystone (JC–K)*, cohabitation without benefit of marriage increased by 117 percent. People began to marry somewhat later in life, by which time they would, presumably, be less subject to the sentimental appeals of the diamond engagement ring tradition. The feminist movement spelled (or might have been assumed to have spelled) a rebellion against symbols of the traditional man-woman relationship, such as the diamond ring. And liberals began to boycott things South African. It is surprising that the demand for engagement rings sloughed no lower than to 73 percent of engaged couples in the mid-seventies, before the engagement ring tradition regained ground (along with an increased "conservatism" in the American political climate) to 77 percent by 1979. Ayer has managed to maintain the diamond as an elitist product while selling it to pretty much everyone. This is essential to the health of the worldwide diamond trade: It is the blue-collar diamond that pays the rent; the D-flawless traffic is the profit. Without Morris Zale, founder of the Zale chain of lower-middle-class jewelry stores, there could be no Harry Winston.

Not about to put all its diamonds in the same basket, De Beers' foreign advertising, generally handled by local branches of the J. W. Thompson Agency, has brought the engagement ring tradition to other cultures, and most significantly, to Japan. As one major New York diamantaire says, "The Japanese can be advertised into anything."

Though diamonds and engagement rings play no part in traditional Japanese culture, there was room in the traditional culture for them. The families of Japanese couples traditionally acknowledged *yuino*, the exchange of gifts between the families, and here was the cultural niche for J. Walter Thompson to place the diamond ring. Diamonds could be sold in Japan with a tip of the hat to *yuino*. *International Diamond Annual* characterized Thompson's Japanese ad campaign as avoiding

> any suggestion that traditional customs in Japan should be changed or abandoned: what it does suggest is that the diamond ring is something that extends or embellishes the age-old customs and is in full harmony with the spirit of "yuino." This has aroused only approbation in Japan and it is clear that the attitude of women towards this Western element in their social and emotional culture is to welcome it.

Prior to Pearl Harbor Day, something under one percent of Japanese brides-to-be received diamond engagement rings; by 1966 about 5 percent received them; in 1978, according to the figures tabulated by the Diamond Information Center in Tokyo, 54 percent of Japanese brides received a diamond ring to show as a measure of their intended's love; and Japanese retailers estimated to me in the summer of 1979 that the figure had grown to just under 60 percent. Though the percentage is smaller than that in the United States, Japanese will devote three or four months' earnings to the purchase of their symbol, and spend more on average for their engagement ring than do Americans. On a national per capita per annum basis, the Japanese citizen is spending at least as much on diamonds as is the American. This is truly impressive when one considers that until the Thompson campaign almost no one in Japan was the slightest bit interested in owning a diamond. In the sad and indiscriminate rush to westernization that has corrupted much of Japanese culture, the Japanese adopted the diamond along with the golf club and the ski.

Much the same is true in West Germany. Among the primitive Teutons two gold bands were all that it took to symbolize undying love, and this tradition continued until 1967, when De Beers introduced the concept of the *tri*set, with a third band, only this one studded with diamonds. The fräuleins welcomed it, and today West Germany has come out of the dark ages to become the world's third-biggest diamond-consuming nation, after the United States and Japan.

De Beers began advertising in order to create a demand for its unsalable product in the late 1930s, but it came to appreciate that advertising was essential to maintain and increase the demand for diamonds merely in order to sop up the vastly increased diamond output in the postwar world, and then to increase demand sufficiently further to enable the DTC to increase the price of rough. Over the last decade the De Beers ad budget increased from $5.8 million in 1970 to about $50 million worldwide for 1980, or about 2 percent of the DTC's total probable sales. It apportioned that sum between twenty-four diamond-consuming countries, spending most of it (in declining order) in the United States, Japan, West Germany, France, Italy, the United Kingdom, Brazil, Spain, Canada, and Mexico. In some nations like Italy and Spain, where the gem trade is predominantly an under-the-table business, De Beers' ad budget amounts to amusingly high proportions of the total legitimate wholesale traffic.

While engagement rings are still the bread and butter of the diamond world, De Beers also advertises jewelry for other purposes and occasions, varying the ads and the focus of them depending on what class of diamonds is then overstocked on the wholesale market. Several years ago it was large stones, so De Beers spent much of its ad budget on a large stone campaign in magazines catering to the wealthy. In 1979 the smaller melee and Indian goods were drugs on the market, so for 1980 the company targeted two relatively new markets for special emphasis, eternity rings and diamonds for the man. Both the eternity rings and (to a lesser extent) the men's jewelry advertised featured the smaller diamonds then clogging the distribution pipeline.

The eternity ring, for those who are unfamiliar with it, is a ring faced with numerous small diamonds, which De Beers recommends as an anniversary gift. Its lead ad runs: "You know you'd marry her all over again. But does she? The Diamond Eternity Ring. The anniversary gift that says you'd marry her all over again." In 1980 De Beers spent some $1.5 milllion, in *JC–K*'s words, "To build up the eternity tradition." Other eternity ring ads feature a mature but still beautiful woman and a gray but handsome late-fifties man. They are reliving the moment years before when, together, they had honored the diamond engagement ring tradition. Growing old with De Beers.

Since the death of James Buchanan "Diamond Jim" Brady, men have shied away from diamonds for themselves. De Beers' market research indicated, however, that the typical man was not hostile to the idea of wearing diamond jewelry. It was just that he preferred to have a Porsche. The trend to greater male fashion awareness (shaggy is out; the suit is in) has encouraged De Beers to set about to change that with its diamonds-are-for-him campaign. Its series of advertisements are run with the theme and legend, "He knows how to wear his diamonds," and features handsome, impressive-looking middle-aged businessmen who have "made it." In one ad Mr. Successful is wearing a diamond-studded tie clasp; in another, cuff links; in a third, a diamond-adorned male hand curls around the *Wall Street Journal.* They all bear the motto "He knows how to wear his diamonds" (in addition to "A diamond is forever"), but this last ad has an additional slogan: "No matter how you travel, you have a way of making it all look first class." (Generally, however, De Beers avoids such blatant appeals to superficial values in its ads.)

It think it not without significance that in my travels throughout the world of De Beers and my contact with several score of their employees involved in production, management, public relations, and advertising, I never once ran across a De Beers man wearing a diamond. *They* know how to wear their diamonds. Nonetheless, De Beers spent another million and a half in 1980 to sell diamonds for him to the readers of *Playboy, Sports Illustrated, Business Week, Esquire, Texas Monthly, Money,* and a half-dozen other publications. The *Diamond Registry Bulletin* finds it "significant to note that there is still 81 percent of men out there who ought to be demanding 'Equal Rights' to adornment and in receiving an occasional gift of love," and Mort Starrett, president of the Jewelry Industry Council, another "ERA" backer, asks, "Why shouldn't a man have an engagement ring too? If a woman can give a man flowers— why not the pledge of love?" Good question.

De Beers is also spending a lot to promote diamonds for him in Italy. A company spokesman told me that Italy is a good market for that kind of thing.

However, the bulk of De Beers' 1980 ad budget of $14 million for the United States was still spent on the engagement ring, and the biggest single chunk of that went to the *Reader's Digest.* De Beers also advertises engagement rings in such journals as *Teen* and *Coed,* as well as *Bride's, Modern Bride,* and even *Scholastic,* the magazine for high-schoolers. *Scholastic* ads probably encourage premature commitments of varied kinds.

In merchandizing diamond engagement rings, De Beers has been confronted with some very real problems of late, and it is turning increasingly to the level-headed male minds of the readers of *Hot Rod* and *Sporting News* to bail them out. The problem is the shrinking size of the diamond component in the engagement ring.

The typical engagement ring buyer has a budget for his ring. A skillful salesman can jockey him up a few hundred dollars, but most are afraid to appear "greedy" for fear of running the buyer off. The retailer's clerk would rather undersell and secure his small commission on a lesser amount than risk losing the customer. He will take the couple for what they say they can spend, maybe a little bit more, and be satisfied.

The greatly increased price of rough over the past four years has not reduced the number of buyers of engagement rings, or the total dollar (or yen) amounts spent. But the price rises have forced the typical couple to settle for a lesser stone in their ring than that sold to the eternal lovers of yesterday. *JC–K* studies indicate that the typical engagement ring diamond has shrunk in size from 33 points in 1973 to about 15 points in 1980 (and 6 points in England). According to its editor Mitchell Gilbert, "The average couple today actually spends 10 percent *less* of their real discretionary income (after discounting for inflation) than the average couple spent in 1973." The average amount spent by the typical American betrothed for their symbol in 1979: $585.

The retailer's problem, and De Beers' problem, is to convince the buyer that "more" really is sounder. Here De Beers has begun to turn to the men. The truth of the matter is that the women really want a symbol of their love. They are not, fundamentally, the ones that are interested in the ostentation. The men are more easily convinced of the "wisdom" of spending more than are the women. De Beers aims at the "practical" in the man with ads that lead, "Why she's too shy to tell you to 'think big.' " The reason: She is too worried about you, too worried about your expenses and your budget. She wants to save you money. Sweet thing. But come now, we all know about penny wise and pound foolish, eh? The ad says, "Since you are the one who makes the final financial decision [an appeal to the macho image] you should know why 'thinking big' is important." The point is, as a practical matter, and let us be ruthlessly practical now, you really ought to

OWN THE LARGEST DIAMOND YOU CAN AFFORD

the ad says in bold type. In fact, it really isn't difficult to tell forests from trees: "In fact, if you take it slow and don't think 'small,' you'll feel secure that you have given her the one gift that can stand up to the toughest test of all. The test of time." De Beers doesn't bother to tell the readers of *Hot Rod* why they should give the maiden a diamond; it knows that the readers of *Teen* and *Coed* will take care of that. Instead it tells the fellows why the bigger diamonds, the more expensive diamonds, the stones that De Beers has forced to be priced at higher than traditionally reasonable levels, are really the sounder symbols of love.

Its advice to the man is not entirely bad advice. One can purchase a diamond engagement ring for as little as a hundred dollars. Such a symbol will contain a diamond of something less than 10 points, with only the smallest defect visible to the naked eye, the rough cost for which to the Bombay manufacturer came to perhaps $6. The stone was polished in a Surat cottage for a dollar, and then the end product was mounted in a gold-filled mounting with a gold value of maybe another dollar or two. All the rest of the hundred-dollar sale price is markups. The thousand-dollar engagement ring, while also a bad buy, still has an "intrinsic worth" (whatever that may mean) that amounts to a much higher percentage of the total purchase price, and the markups, percentagewise, will be very much smaller. Something over 99 percent of engagement rings, however, cannot under any stretch of the concept be considered as an "investment."

De Beers' ads have also begun to address the question, at long last, "How much should you pay for that engagement ring?" Young couples embarking on a new life together are told by the Sylvia Porters that they might wisely budget thus-a-percent for housing and so much for food, but Ms. Porter and her ilk totally neglect to advise how much the couple "should" spend for their engagement ring. Fortunately, N. W. Ayer has filled the gap. A De Beers ad run in the United States asks and answers the question: "How much should you spend? A good guideline is about a month's salary." Good for whom? If the 77 percent of American newlyweds who buy the De Beers product spent, on the average, one month's salary, a significant proportion of the total American payroll would be going into diamond engagement rings and that would be very good indeed. For someone.

28

THE FOUR C'S

◆

The wholesale diamond market is very much an informed market in which buyers understand the qualities of the goods. In the wholesale world the goods must sell themselves or remain unsold. The retail diamond market, on the other hand, is what economists call an "uninformed market," one in which the average buyer has an incomplete idea of the nature of the goods he is buying and judges their qualities not by any really understood standards, but on the basis of advertising, reputation, eye- and ear-catching features. The uninformed buyer, the typical retail diamond customer, is at the mercy of his retailer.

Everyone who buys a diamond, however, should at least understand the fundamentals of diamond grading. Those aspects of the diamond that the reasonably intelligent layman can most easily appreciate—the apparent quality of the finish workmanship—are not particularly important to determining the stone's value. Occasional facets that don't quite join or slight off-centering of the table (the top facet) or an extra facet, nicks and surface scratches, roughness around the girdle (rim) or obvious grinding wheel abrasions just do not affect the value of a diamond very much. Much more significant are the differences between seemingly imperceptible and maddening shades of whiteness, and internal structural flaws that would be invisible even to a watchmaker with his three-powered eyepiece and almost invisible even to the trained eye using a jeweler's ten-powered loupe. The buyer should concentrate on the qualities that make for important price differences in the trade, usually known as the 4 Cs: carat weight, color, clarity, and cut.

Carat weight. Bigger stones do not simply cost more than smaller stones; they cost more on a per-point basis. There is a good reason why: Bigger stones are geometrically rarer than smaller ones. Though diamonds are not, geologically speaking, particularly rare, the bigger diamonds are more nearly rare, and really big diamonds really are rare. As of June 1, 1981, the Diamond Registry was offering fifth-of-a-carat stones that it classed as "White VS2"—typical American engagement ring stones—to wholesale buyers at $725 per carat, or about $145 per stone. For its one-carat stones of similar quality, five times as heavy, it was asking not five times as much but 16.8 times as much, or $2,440 per carat. Differences in price per carat continue on upward: If a one-carat superfine quality stone ("D-flawless") is worth, call it, 100 units *per carat,* the two-carat superfine will likely cost 177 *per carat;* the three-carat piece, 235 *per carat.*

There is a surviving principle: The stone that is twice as heavy will cost significantly more than twice as much. It will not, however, *look* twice as big when viewed in the ring setting. A well-proportioned one-carat round brilliant will have a surface area of about 32 square millimeters, while a half-carat stone will have a surface area of about 21 square millimeters. To get half as much again in apparent size you will have to pay from five to eight times as much (depending on the qualities involved).

The buyer should also be aware of the "critical weights." Diamonds of just over one carat are likely to cost disproportionately more than those of just under a carat. One carat is a "critical weight," a weight buyers look for. The price differential between a 99-point stone and a 101-point stone (one carat plus one point) will probably be at least 10 percent, probably more.

The buyer with his druthers should opt for the 99-point stone not only to save the 10 percent but also because the 99-point stone is apt to be a better-made product. The stone that is just over the critical weight, 101 to 105 points, has probably been finagle-cut in order to push it over the critical level. In the trade such pieces are known as "cheated" or "swindled" stones, depending on the type of finagling with proportions that has been done in order to push up their weight. Whatever they are called, they have been cheated or swindled out of their proper optical properties. Many of the stones that weigh in at 101 points would have made "honest" 96-pointers, but any manufacturer in a position to push a 96-pointer into a 101 is going to do so in order to get it over the critical level. One sightholder told me that "in this business you don't get rich by giving good make; you get rich by swindling [stones]." On the other hand, a stone that weighs 97 points, while probably also poorly made, is less likely to have been subject to heroic swindling.

Color. There are colored diamonds known as fancy colors, but when diamond graders talk about color they are talking about the relative color of "white" stones, or more accurately, of "colorless" stones. A vast majority of diamonds are basically colorless but tinged, most commonly with yellow, less commonly with a brownish or grayish cast. The more nearly colorless a stone is, the less of a cast to it, the rarer and more costly it will be. The Gemological Institute of America (GIA) recognizes twenty-three grades of color in a "white" diamond, ranging from

D, which is colorless, down through the K, L, M, N colors which become increasingly yellowish, on to the W, X, Y, Zs, which are decidedly yellow. The lower the letter, the less the price. The most desired color is called D rather than A because at the time that the GIA devised its scale, the As and the Bs had already been hopelessly confused by earlier grading systems.

The color grade of a white diamond is most commonly determined by comparing it with the colors of the white diamonds in a "master set," a set of diamonds of about the same size and quality that represent the full range of colors and are arranged in alphabetical order. Many novices will find it easy enough to place the stone to be graded in the proper range on the master set but then, determining whether the stone is an L or the ever-so-slightly yellower M is a highly subjective matter. Reasonable eyes can reasonably differ, and it is common for equally competent GIA graders to differ by a color grade. However, a one-letter difference on a one-carat stone will spell the difference of one or many thousand dollars in its "value," depending on the qualities.

Although better colors are rarer and cost more, minor shading differences that will spell a two-letter grade spread will be indistinguishable once the stone has been set. A one-carat H or I stone will have a slight trace of color when loose, but once it is mounted in a platinum-colored setting, it will "face up" colorless to anyone other than a jeweler. A one-carat D-flawless that really is colorless will cost about six times as much as a one-carat I-flawless that only looks to be colorless in the ring. Smaller stones will face up colorless in the still less expensive J, K, and L ranges. Those who determine to get away with a mid-alphabet stone, however, should be certain not to mount their diamond in a gold setting. The yellow of the gold will bring out the yellow in the stone and give it all away, which is the bigger part of the reason why platinum has become a part of the diamond engagement ring tradition.

Stones farther down the color scale, in the M to W range, have been just about impossible to sell in the United States despite retailers' efforts to move them as "champagne-hued" or "honey-colored," and De Beers is attempting in subtle ways to stimulate more consumer interest in these less salable goods. If demand could be boosted, prices could be boosted. In its widely circulated little pamphlet "Diamonds: Buying and Care Guide," distributed through retailers, De Beers tells the consumer that "a diamond with a hint of color seems to have more fire, a warmer beauty." Seems to whom? Not to the market. The company's objective is simply to move the merchandise that is overcrowding the stockrooms, just as the haberdasher will push the goods that he wants to get sold.

Fancies—the blue, orange, amber, green, violet, rust-colored, pink, and intense yellow diamonds—constitute the arena for the connoisseurs, though they are not invariably more expensive than whites. Blues, violets, and intense pink stones will cost more than D-ranked white stones, but the other colors will generally cost something less than E–F whites, and the buyer might consider them as an alternative to the routine white stone. Unless purchased from an honorable expert in fancies, the buyer should have any fancy stone lab-tested to ensure that its apparent color is indeed natural. White diamonds of undistinguished color can be transformed into a dazzling blue, green, or yellow by irradiation. George R. Rossman, associate professor of mineralogy at California Institute of Technology, estimates that "anywhere from a quarter to a half of the colored diamonds on the market are irradiated." No less a seller than Christie's and no less a buyer than Van Cleef & Arpels bought and sold a huge irradiated yellow stone in 1971 for 1.2 million Swiss francs. Neither knew. (Christie's took it back.)

Clarity. Clarity refers to the internal qualities of the stone: the number, kind, size, location, and overall significance of the flaws and imperfections within it. Except on stones that might otherwise be graded as "flawless," surface blemishes will count for very little in clarity grading: Clarity is concerned almost exclusively with the inside. These internal flaws, though generally invisible to the naked eye, will affect a stone's light-reflecting ability and therefore the beauty of the stone and therefore its cost. A stone will be graded as "flawless" only if an expert eye can find no flaws after studying the stone under the ten-power magnification of a jeweler's loupe. Only very rarely will a stone meet that standard. Diamantaires commonly use the phrase "loupe clean" in place of flawless, perhaps a recognition of the fact that under a high-enough magnification, no diamond will actually be without flaws.

Sellers' talk is the international language of the jewelry trade, and clarity grades are designated in that tongue. The consumer might reasonably assume that a diamond graded as SI1, which means "Slightly imperfect but still first ranked in its class," is the next grade down from perfect or flawless. What else could be next to "perfect" but "slightly imperfect"? But between flawless and SI1 come "internally flawless," "very very slightly imperfect 1," "very very slightly imperfect 2," "very slightly imperfect 1," and "very slightly imperfect 2."

The determination of clarity grades is again a highly subjective matter in which opinions reasonably differ. A one-step change in clarity grade makes about as much (actually a little bit less) of a difference in price as one difference in color grade.

Because the SI (slightly imperfect) qualities will still be "eye clean" (appear flawless to the naked eye) and are ever so much less expensive than the grades whose defects are apparent only with study and under magnification, they make the most sense for the typical couple. Here, for a change, my opinion is consistent with what De Beers would really *like* you to buy. The less desirable and less desired SI clarities, like the more tinted colors, are just not moving and De Beers would like to turn that around. In its "Diamonds: Buying and Care Guide" pamphlet, De Beers includes line drawings of the most popular shapes: the round brilliant, the pear, oval, marquise, and emerald, but its sketch of the round brilliant shows an obvious "feather"—a flaw—right under the table. It is showing an SI stone in its example of the most popular engagement ring stone—preparing the buyer to accept a lesser clarity grade.

When you inspect the diamond at the retailer's you should expect that the stone displayed mounted in a ring will almost certainly have a flaw hidden beneath one or more of the prongs. This is perfectly all right, provided that the buyer is not misled into thinking that he is buying something that is "cleaner" than it is.

Putting together carat weight, color, and clarity, it will be seen that a half-carat, I-colored, SI1 stone will look to the naked and untrained eye to be almost as big, almost as white, and almost as perfect as a one-carat D-flawless. At the wholesale level on June 1, 1981, the somewhat less desirable piece cost $492.50, while the somewhat more desirable one cost $40,000. The cheaper one may seem the wiser purchase, and especially if the buyer can find a half-carat I SI1 of excellent cut. That is easier said than done.

Cut. Orin Terry, president of the Scientific Gemological Laboratories of Huntington Beach, California, calls cut the neglected C. Cut pertains to the proportions of the stone: the angle between the girdle and the crown, the angle between the girdle and the pavilion, the size of the table relative to the stone's diameter, the height of the crown and the depth of the pavilion, and the thickness of the girdle. In one respect proportions are a matter of taste: Do you prefer a larger table or a smaller table? A stone that is otherwise well proportioned will gain or lose brilliance and inversely, gain or lose "fire," depending on whether it has a bigger or smaller table. Which you prefer is a matter of taste, and tastes and the cultural concepts of desirable proportions can evolve.

Other aspects of proportions are not matters of taste: the deviations from these proportions will adversely affect the optical properties of the stone with only one countervailing advantage: deviations can produce a heavier, larger piece of polished even if it is a less attractive one.

On balance, both the manufacturer and the retailer will usually make more money selling poorly proportioned but bigger stones than they will make selling smaller, well-proportioned ones. The simple fact is that most diamonds sold today are poorly proportioned, and in a *JC–K* survey published in September 1979, fewer than 10 percent of retailers reported that fine make was important to them. In all but the highest qualities, wholesale prices for polished have not kept pace in the past few years with increases in the price of rough, and this has served as an increased incentive to manufacturers to preserve rough weight through cheating. "Cheating" is a term of art in the diamond industry.

To cheat a stone is not—in and of itself—immoral; diamond planners cheat in response to market dictates.

Innumerable tricks of the cutting trade enable a cutter to retain greater weight at the expense of proper stone proportions, and the diamond planner will use the one or the other depending on the basic shape of the piece of rough. Simply thickening the girdle beyond acceptable standards can add several points to a stone's weight. Crown angles and pavilion angles can be widened or narrowed, the polished as conceptualized being pushed upward or downward within the rough, and boxed out or narrowed up in order to preserve more of the rough in the polished. This kind of cheating can often be disguised to all but the mostly highly sophisticated eye.

A competent GIA-trained diamond appraiser will discount a stone for its bad proportions, determine a "corrected weight," and then value the stone on the basis of whatever color and clarity characterize it, but at its corrected weight rather than on its actual weight.

Only an expert can determine the various degrees and percentages and make the proper deductions, and most jewelers never develop more than a passing feel for cut evaluation and corrected weight. Many sellers will discount the corrected-weight approach with the simple assertion that "the real market does not operate that way; in fact, it does not consider cut," and indeed, probably most retail buyers do not consider cut because they do not know how to handle it. If, however, you have two stones of equal size and similar qualities, one well-proportioned and the other not, the one will definitely be worth more than the other— and will bring more within the trade. About the best that the prospective retail buyer can do is to ask the jeweler, "How's it cut?" and let it go at that.

29

THE RETAIL WORLD

◆

Engagements are indeed joyous occasions—for the jewelers. The retail jeweler's markup is one of the fattest in the business world. The trade measures its markups in "keystones": to mark up by one keystone is to double wholesale price. On inexpensive jewelry items, triple and quadruple keystone markups are not uncommon, meaning that such wares are sold at four or five times wholesale.

Diamonds, according to one of the nation's leading diamond appraisal services, will be marked up in excess of one keystone up to the $5,000 wholesale level; at the $5,000 wholesale level, the retailer will still ask for a full keystone markup and charge $10,000 for the stone. Thereafter the markup tapers downward until at around the $100,000 wholesale level it levels out at a 20 percent markup over wholesale. For a storewide indication, *JC–K* reported in its September 1979 issue that in a robbery of a Rockford, Illinois, mall store, the victim lost goods worth approximately $400,000 wholesale, which the store owner estimated to be worth $900,000 retail.

Staggering as the markups may seem, there isn't much the typical retailer can do about it. The jewelry retailers' overhead expense for rent, interest expense on their inventories, and advertising are enormous, almost always greater than those of retailers in other lines, which is why their markups must be greater than those of retailers in other lines. High overheads lock them into high markups. For most goods, simply doubling up wholesale to reach retail would be a loser for the retailer. On the typical engagement ring, the retailer has to charge more than a 100 percent markup.

Keystone pricing is not new to the jewelry trade. The *Arthasâstra* of the third or fourth century BC reported that the diamond merchants "live by making a hundred percent profit in panas or kumbhas." Or dollars or yen. At the same time the jewelers have always been touchy about their margins of profit. In *The History of Diamond Production and the Diamond Trade,* Godehard Lenzen quotes medieval texts that say that the Hirschvogels of Nuremberg and the Herwarts of Augsburg in the 1500s feared that the disclosure of their profits might visit upon them and their cities "all manner of inconvenience and disadvantage at the hands of the emperor, kings, electors, princes and others to whom stones were sold." More recently the people at NYDEX (formerly New York Diamond Exchange, until New York law forced them to drop the word "Exchange" from their name) became the most unpopular people in the diamond world when they began publishing wholesale prices in the *Wall Street Journal*—almost realistic wholesale prices—for "certificate diamonds," those sold principally to investors. Much of the June 1980 trade conference on investment diamonds held in Los Angeles was taken up with bad-mouthing NYDEX for "telling too much." The jewelry trade, like any other, universally believes that the less the public knows about wholesale prices the better.

Occasionally the diamond market has one of its periodic recessions and wholesale prices drop by 10, 15, or even as much as 20 percent. These drops never filter down to the retail customer the way that down prices in the wholesale beef market are reflected in butcher shops. Dealers in a position to stock the goods pick up the bargains and then sit on them until sales prices are healthy in the market in which each dealer will sell. Even if the retailer should benefit by the price drops, there is never any reason why he should pass the bargains along to his customer, and he is not going to do so. Diamonds are a "blind item": the retail buyer does not know how much they *should* cost, and the retailer is unlikely to sell one more diamond by cutting his prices.

The alternative to buying at retail is to buy "wholesale." When the retail buyer thinks of buying wholesale he does not mean that he wants to buy in wholesale quantities, he means that he wants to buy in retail quantities—one—but that he wants to pay wholesale price. He wants to pay for one routine stone what the retailer who buys them by the dozen would pay for one. He wants a bargain. Very well. But there is no reason why the wholesaler should give the unsophisticated one-item buyer a single stone at the price that he would charge a retailer to whom he sells a great many, and he is not going to.

In diamonds, shades of wholesale are as many as the shades of whiteness. There is wholesale and then there is wholesale. M. Fabrikant, the major American wholesaler, for example, buys diamonds by the kilo in Bombay and Tel Aviv at a price that is certainly "wholesale." Fabrikant sells to other wholesalers by the pound at what could fairly be regarded as "wholesale." Some of these wholesalers will sell to lesser wholesalers by the ounce at wholesale, who sell to retailers by the carat— at wholesale. Many of those retailers then sell to the general public at what they call "wholesale," a wholesale which by then has had two, three, or more middlemen's markups tacked on, all capped by a final keystone. The point is, access to the market in which Fabrikant sells is closed to the typical buyer, let alone the market in which it buys, because the typical buyer is not buying wholesale quantities in the ordinary course of a wholesaler's business.

There are few bargains in the diamond world, but there is such a thing as more expensive and less expensive. I believe that New York City is the cheapest place in the world (possibly excepting Hong Kong) for the typical retail customer to buy a diamond. New York retailers, unlike those in Wichita, are in a position to shop among wholesalers, and so the wholesalers—though they won't admit it—commonly have a different and lower price for New Yorkers than they have for out-of-town retailers. Besides having a somewhat lower "in" cost, the New York retailers also must face the fierce competition of the 47th Street arena where almost every Manhattan retail customer "shops"—and the scrutiny of America's most nearly sophisticated diamond-buying consumers. If keystone weakens anywhere it is in New York, and especially right after New Year's, when the diamond retailer must look forward to several bleak months without significant sales—until the spring engagements bring respite from the drought. That does not mean, however, that you are going to get a bargain on 47th Street.

The real wholesalers on 47th Street are upstairs, but unless you come well introduced, you won't be able to get in to see one of them. They view the stranger as a likely thief/murderer, an understandable reaction when one considers the 47th Street record. If you haven't come to rob him today, you have come to "case" him for tomorrow's robbery. He is not going to take risks in order, maybe, to sell one stone to someone who is probably only wasting his time anyway. The average retail buyer will be limited to buying from one of the self-proclaimed "wholesalers" on the ground floor.

Forty-seventh Street is no place for the unobtrusive browser. Step foot in an arcade and you are set upon: "Can I help you?" "Yes, sir, what is it you are looking for?" Others, out on the street, are equally willing to serve if you will "just step into my shop." The stands closest to the door pay the highest rent and have the most persistent salespeople. Friendly, helpful, best prices and all, but they get pretty curt when they think you are wasting their time, and if you are really just browsing—or if you are comparison shopping—you are wasting their time. "I'm not here to teach, mister," one told me.

The typical 47th Street seller will vastly overstate the quality of what he shows you, and why not? You are not going to know the difference. "Perfect" diamonds are as common as SI2s. (Caveat: The jeweler who tells you that the diamond he is showing you is "perfect" is a scoundrel and very likely a thief as well.) You want an appraisal? By all means, the seller will get you an appraisal, very competent appraiser. A certificate of the stone's qualities? Of course. No, not from the GIA because the GIA won't touch a stone under one carat (which is true), but they will get you a certificate from a lab, very reputable.

Big and little buyers get taken on 47th Street by the droves daily. In 1971 a midwestern executive—they just love midwestern executives on 47th Street—bought a diamond bracelet for $60,000 from a major 47th Street dealer, with 203 half-carat diamonds and a guarantee that the seller would repurchase if it were not as represented. Six years later an auction house turned its nose up at the bracelet with a $25,000 appraisal. Well, there were only 202 diamonds, none of them as large as a half carat, and many of them were chipped, but mounted with the chipped side down. The executive demanded that the seller take the bracelet back and refund the $60,000, but even though six years of inflation had been very healthy for the price of diamonds in the interim, the seller refused. There were many keystones in that bracelet. At trial, the executive won his case, but most cannot afford to go through that kind of hassle. The seller, bear in mind, was a thoroughly honorable man within the trade, still a leader on "the street," and he fully adheres to the high ethical standards of the trade. It's just that those standards do not apply to the outside world. To you. After shopping eleven 47th Street diamond retailers for *New York* magazine in 1978, Peter D. Lawrence concluded that he could consider patronizing only two of the eleven. At most stalls he was confronted with color-distorting lights, intentionally fuzzy terminology, and high-pressure tactics that at places became bullying and insulting. If you think that that's not for you, you might consider one of the alternatives.

Buying at auction makes sense for those in the market for diamond necklaces, bracelets, and the like. Dennis Scioli, head of the jewelry department at the New York branch of Sotheby, which does the world's biggest auction house gross in jewelry, estimates that 75 percent of the goods sold in one of their "fine jewelry" sales will be sold to dealers. ("Fine" at Sotheby is a lesser grade than "important," "highly important," or "magnificent" jewelry. Sotheby speaks the jeweler's language.) On most routine pieces the "other" bidder will be a dealer, and probably a competent dealer, and for most items he will not pay more than what he thinks to be the wholesale value of the diamonds that go to make up the piece. The nontrade buyer can afford to pay a little more than the dealer and know that he will still be getting the piece for very much less than "retail."

Sotheby and most of the other leading New York auction houses publish presale estimates of what they expect each item to bring, thereby giving the novice advance indication of what he can and cannot afford and enabling him to spend his time at the presale inspection studying those pieces that are within his price range. The beginner will usually rely on the estimates as a guide to how much he can safely pay for a piece. Those who do so should be aware of the little biases of auction-house presale estimates: At Sotheby, the poorer-quality merchandise is likely to have been estimated on the optimistic side, and for such items the novice buyer should not pay more than a figure on the low side of the house estimate. Sotheby's estimates on routine items valued at $1,000 to $1,500 are likely to be remarkably accurate, and if you like the piece you can safely bid on the high side of its estimate. The buyer of the $1,250 item at Sotheby is likely to have saved himself the retailer's keystone. On the best-quality goods, Sotheby's estimates are likely to be on the conservative side. Such wares are worth—or in any case, they are likely to fetch—somewhat more than the house estimate. The "magnificent" pieces usually sell to private buyers, not to dealers, and bring "retail" or very close thereto.

An elaborately worked piece will sometimes bring a price in excess of intrinsic value of the stones, particularly if its styling is consistent with current tastes, and pieces signed by one of the prestige jewelers will also bring a premium over raw material value. A Cartier-signed piece or a Tiffany art nouveau item generally will bring the healthiest premium; Van Cleef & Arpels or David Webb work may do a little less well, and, still in the prestige class, a nondescript Tiffany or Harry Winston item will sparkle least on the auction market. These matters are taken into consideration by the house in arriving at the presale estimate.

Those interested in diamonds or in jewelry should go to the auction houses whether or not they intend to buy if only to be able to inspect at close range a wide variety of items, including some truly staggering gems far outside the reach of any but the super rich. After Cartier bought the Elizabeth Taylor diamond at Parke-Bernet (as Sotheby's New York branch was then known) in 1969, people stood in block-long queues outside Cartier's New York store for a chance to view the big piece of stone, separated from it by two armed guards and a thick glass case. Any hausfrau could have gone into Parke-Bernet a week earlier, tried it on, and fondled it. Very little makes sense in the diamond world.

Buying a fake is also an alternative, and buying a synthetic diamond may become a live alternative. There is an important difference between fakes and synthetics:

By "synthetic diamonds" we mean diamonds that actually are diamonds, chemically and structurally, with all of the properties of diamond, but which are man-made rather than a product of nature. By "imitation" we mean that the diamondlike substance is not diamond and does not have the properties of diamond, but might be mistaken for diamond and substituted for it for decorative purposes—a fake.

It is easy to make diamonds, real diamonds: All you need is a good grade of pencil lead, 1400° Centigrade, and the pressure of sixty thousand atmospheres—about the pressure that would be exerted if you were to invert the Eiffel Tower and place it on the palm of your hand. Put them all together and, presto!—you have diamonds!

Adequate supply of pencil leads has never been the problem, and for decades scientists have been able to generate degrees of heat well in excess of the required temperature. The same is true with the pressure. The trick has been to create both the sufficient heat and the sufficient pressure at the same time and place; to make dies and instruments and housings that could withstand both the heat and the pressure. That has been the rub. General Electric claims to have first performed the alchemy in 1955, and patent courts have agreed with it. De Beers and a Japanese concern followed shortly after GE and today there are synthetic diamond plants in numerous countries, all turning out tiny industrial-quality stones. Their total annual output exceeds the total caratage of diamonds mined worldwide.

Synthetic gemstones is another story. GE has manufactured synthetic gem diamonds for experimental purposes only (its scientists deny any interest in entering the gem market) and had them polished by Lazare Kaplan with wide publicity. De Beers has surely done as much, but as De Beers has no incentive to publicize the synthesis of the symbol of love, it has kept its accomplishments quiet. For the moment, however, the costs of producing gem diamonds are prohibitive, and given the current state of the art, it does not seem likely that it will be possible to make gem diamonds commercially for a long time to come.* Until the synthetic gem diamonds are available, the cheapskate will have to content himself (or herself) with fakes.

Imitations of diamonds are both old and respectable. In medieval times it was accepted without embarrassment that many or most royal "jewels" were paste, lead-based glass, that had been acquired as glass without pretense that they were anything but attractive pieces of glass.

Over the centuries as the art of diamond cutting matured, so too did the art of making paste diamonds. The latter perhaps reached its pinnacle in the rhinestone, though this assertion is admittedly a matter of taste and values. In any case, the technological revolution of the twentieth century did not neglect diamond substitutes, and modern developments have left the rhinestone looking like a pale imitation. There came a wide offering of imitation diamonds, usually known either by abbreviations of their chemical designations—e.g., YAG and GGG—or by the brand names under which they were merchandised, such as Fabulite, Diamond-ite, or Madame Wellington's Counterfeit Diamonds.

* When the breakthrough occurs, the effects on natural diamond prices and on the diamond industry are likely to be more muted than one might expect. The "Chatham" emerald is in all respects a genuine emerald, though it is man-made and can be distinguished from a natural emerald. When it was first introduced, the Chatham shook the emerald market, but after a period of readjustment, the natural revived and with time the natural and the Chatham learned to live nicely together.

Many of the substitutes approached the qualities of the diamond so closely that even an expert had to perform simple tests, or compare the stone with a real diamond, in order to detect the fake. The super rich began to have copies made of their masterpiece jewels, which they might wear in place of the real ones, thereby saving themselves from having to go over to the bank to remove their showpiece from its vault, and the burden of wiring Lloyd's of London—and the expense of paying the additional premium—for each wearing. The super rich were the first to appreciate that fake may really be better than real.

The fake then started to win the acceptance of the upper middle class, principally due to the profit-motivated efforts of Helen Ver Standig, alias Madame Wellington. Madame Wellington, purveyor of the Counterfeit Diamond, a trademarked phrase, opened shops in fashionable places like Palm Beach, each decorated something like a small Van Cleef & Arpels, and began running ads in prestige magazines. Her ads were designed to appeal, wrote Bernard Collier in "The Psychology of Fake" (*Washington Post Magazine,* April 9, 1972), "to every money-loving, status conscious and secretly fraud-minded bone in the human body." Each ad featured the caricature of Madame Wellington drawn by the famous caricaturist Al Hirschfeld, portraying Mme W as she intentionally projects herself—a rakish old broad. An effervescent, likable publicity seeker, Madame Wellington did for fakes what Harry Winston did for diamonds. They became common and then fashionable among "respectable" people.

Then, in 1977, came what might have seemed the death blow to De Beers, not to mention Madame Wellington: the invention of CZ, cubic zirconium. At first CZs fooled virtually everyone in the trade. Even today, when diamond people are on the lookout, if you were to put one CZ in a paper with a dozen diamonds, the professional diamond dealer would spot it only if he were looking for it—and then he would have to look to pick it out. The Ceres Corporation of Waltham, Massachusetts, manufactures mechanical equipment to enable the professional jeweler to do scientific tests to satisfy himself, and trade publications regularly include tips on how the jeweler can tell the difference. If the professional jeweler with years of experience handling diamonds needs tips and gadgets to tell a diamond from a CZ, neither you nor the lady next door is going to be able to detect the difference: The decorative value of a CZ must be reckoned at precisely the same as that of the diamond. Its "sentimental" value, of course, is close to zero, but, Madame Wellington asks in her ad, "Is the price of illusion too high? No doubt about it!" CZs have no investment value, but then . . . well, we are getting ahead of ourselves.

If you want one, the influx of Taiwanese and Korean CZs has caused the price of CZs to tumble on the wholesale market to under $10 a carat, but they are quadruple keystone items. Bear in mind in buying your CZ that if the stone looks to be more expensive than you could conceivably afford, you will give the whole thing away, so avoid ostentation in picking a CZ. To take a phrase from Madame Wellington's ads, "It makes sense in this senseless world."

Four years after the introduction of CZs, diamonds are still going strong, to the pleasant surprise of around half of those in the trade, and so, for that matter, is the redoubtable Madame Wellington. She is still probably doing the biggest gross in fakes, though almost everyone in the diamond world regards her product as decidedly inferior to the less expensive CZ. Madame Wellington stays on top for the same reason that more diamonds sell, and sell for more, than rubies or emeralds: The CZ producers are not in a position to publicize and merchandise CZs. Only Madame Wellington sells genuine Counterfeit Diamonds, and she keeps selling them the same way that the competition, De Beers, keeps selling diamonds: advertising. There is no substitute for the real thing, not even in fakes. Madame Wellington may sell counterfeit diamonds, but she is a genuine diamantaire.

30

THE SUPER-ELEGANTS

◆

Just around the corner from the cacophony that characterizes 47th Street is the elegance of the world's most elegant retailers—the world's, not just the diamond world's. Clustered on Fifth Avenue within a half mile of the high-pressure hucksters on 47th Street are the houses of Van Cleef & Arpels; Cartier; Bulgari of Rome (lesser known in the United States but probably the biggest international top-quality jewelry retailer); Gübelin, the Swiss firm; and the two truly great top-quality American-based jewelry retailers, Tiffany and Harry Winston. In this very different world, Annalee Gold writes in *Jewelers' Circular-Keystone,*

> The atmosphere is always cool, and the very language of selling changes at the top. A woman is never told a style is "hot," and even in private, terms like "closing the sale" are suppressed. Customers are called clients, a word that implies a continuing relationship of mutual esteem, one in which service, as well as merchandise, is exchanged for money.

Yes, they are selling diamonds and high-priced diamonds, but more, they are selling a way of life.

Except perhaps for Van Cleef, the most expensive of the pack, most of the super-elegant jewelers will have a number of modestly priced stones on hand (modest for them: in the $5,000 to $10,000 range), but they make their real money on the truly great stones, the rare stones, the stones for which price really does not matter. Such stones are valued in terms of emotion rather than more nearly objective criteria; their value is in the values of the beholder. The effect of price in this very different arena is never exactly clear. An item may sell more easily if it is priced higher than if it is priced lower.

Lately there just have not been enough truly staggering gems to go around, and the super-elegant retailers are doing more of their traffic in the fabulously expensive wristwatch, made fabulously expensive by the use of more and/or bigger diamonds to ornament respectable time-keeping innards. Jacqueline Onassis owns a $20,000 LeCoultre, but Le-

Coultre doesn't "push" that top-of-their-line model. "It's a status thing," LeCoultre's Max Naefeli told *JC–K*. That's just a Timex cheapie when compared with some of the Piaget timepieces. When *JC–K* asked Gedalio Grinberg of Piaget's North American distributors, he just happened to have a serviceable timepiece on hand that he could let go at $450,000. If you can wait, though, you can order one studded to whatever extent you want to spend. The big volume in this class of item comes from Americans with what Grinberg characterized as "new money." Good old-fashioned big rocks go to the Arabs. By a curious alchemy of their own, the Arabs are converting oil to diamonds.

According to *Diamond World Review* (Winter, 1978–79), the annual diamond turnover of the retailers based within the Arabian peninsula comes to about $600 million—about 20 percent of the US volume in a region with less than 5 percent of the American population. The biggest of the Arab purchases, however, are made abroad from the prestige European and American jewelers who vie for their trade. Just a phone call will send any of the jewelers scurrying down to the Saudiair ticket counter clutching an attaché case chock full of goodies and a change of underwear, for a seat on the next flight to Riyadh, Jedda, or Kuwait.

The mere mention of Arabs brought a smile to the face of the late Pierre Arpels, of Van Cleef & Arpels. More than 35 percent of the firm's European business goes to the Saudis. The Arabs prefer diamonds, Arpels told the *New York Times* in a 1978 interview, "because diamonds are the most basic of all and the Arabs are beginning on page one. You have to be more of a connoisseur to like a ruby better than a diamond." His partner, Van Cleef, told *Diamant* that the Arabs are exacting and knowledgeable; they go around to all the jewelers, haggle a little, but invariably they buy, and buy complete sets of jewelry by the half dozen—one for each wife.

In a 1975 interview, Harry Winston told *Women's Wear Daily*, "The Arabs are buying everything, money means nothing to them." He was not complaining. Winston sold the sheikhs diamond bracelets by the dozens, one each concubine (a more numerous class than wives). Sometimes the peculiarities of a sheikh's domestic situation take him out of the market for the truly unique piece. Winston enjoyed telling the story of the sale and repurchase of the Winston Diamond. As he told it to A. N. Wilson for the *International Diamond Annual*, Winston sold the 62.5-carat pear-shaped to a sheikh who "had a very large court—four wives and something like eighty concubines. He was a considerable exponent of the art of love." Months later, after buying another couple of million in gems, the sheikh pushed a wrapped stone toward Winston and asked the jeweler to take a "trade-in." As Winston unwrapped the paper he realized it contained the Winston Diamond:

> I was astonished "But you can't give this back," I said in my amazement. "It is *the* most beautiful diamond." The king looked at me quizzically.

"Harry," he said, "I'm fond of living, just as you are. I want to go on living. If I gave this stone to one of my four wives, well, my life would not be worth a moment's purchase."

As I was taking my leave, the king asked: "By the way, Harry, if you have three other gems just like that, let me know."

Was it true, I asked Richard Winston, Harry's nephew and confidant, that during the Arab boycott of "Zionist" businesses, the sheikhs sneaked in Winston's back door anyway, to bid for his treasures? "No, it is not true," he responded with a bit of impatience. Then, with subdued pride, " . . . they came in the front door. They are not," he added, "anti-Semitic."

If what you want is diamonds, big diamonds, Winston must be regarded as "the source." I asked Richard Winston to compare the Winston enterprise with its competitors, Van Cleef, Cartier, Bulgari, and he answered, "Well, let me say that the stores that you mention are fine establishments and I'm sure that they might disagree with me, but . . . well . . . we have the stones, the finest, the biggest, the rarest stones. They just don't have them." By training and habit he has learned not to mention the names of the competitors—and not to use the word "competitors." Winston does not acknowledge that it has any competitors. Still, there was no urgency in his tone as he spoke. He was making a simple statement of fact.

Over the years, the Winston name has been associated with more famous diamonds than that of any other jeweler in the world, and the Winston salon has never been surpassed for simple elegance. In 1954 Winston's aide Count Adlerberg told *The New Yorker,* "When people come into this room they will feel able, they will feel willing, they will feel *eager* to pay two or three hundred thousand dollars for a diamond." In those days, that was money.

Winston, however, is not only the fancy showplace on Fifth Avenue. The Winston enterprise is probably the only wholly verticalized diamond business in the world, and a giant in every aspect of the world diamond trade. Winston has interests in diamond-mining ventures; it buys rough in the trading centers of West Africa and probably South America as well (company spokesmen are fuzzy about those kinds of details); at most sights Winston will be the biggest buyer; it has polishing plants of its own and contracting plants doing only Winston work which together employ perhaps 3,500 polishers in several countries; it buys the polisheds of other manufacturers; it is, depending on the state of the market, sometimes the biggest and always one of the biggest wholesale diamond dealers in the United States, selling bread-and-butter diamonds to retailers across the country with the understanding that they *not* be merchandised as Harry Winston diamonds. Winston told the New York *Daily News* in 1968, "The masses are our major outlet. We have every chain, every catalog house." And best known, it has its own retail outlets, selling only the very best of what passes through the corporate hands, and only to the super rich. Since the death of the founder in December of 1978, the firm is beginning to become more "democratic" in its own retail shops, but the stones of choke-a-horse size are still what Harry Winston is best known for. Who buys them? I suppose, I suggested to Richard, that you have a small number of highly important clients who— He corrected me with an interjection: "A large number."

Harry Winston, who created the largest satrapy within the De Beers empire, did for diamonds what Lord Duveen did for old masters: He taught the very wealthy to appreciate them; to associate his name with the very finest; to buy them; to buy them from him; and to buy them at prices that they would never have dreamed of paying—until they met Harry Winston. Winston never had any cutting experience himself, and his mind was not bedeviled by the considerations of small percentages that dominate the waking thoughts of the typical cutting-trained diamantaire. He could think in terms of big percentages and more: He could escape the profit-restraining trap of percentage-bound thinking. He challenged all the old diamond-pricing concepts, appreciating that for the truly unique stone the market would bear very much more than it had ever been asked to bear if the merchandise was properly presented—if it was presented as other than merchandise; if it was presented as a symbol, as a platonic ideal.

When one of Winston's salesmen told him that he thought a Winston stone was worth $750,000, the salesman later recalled, "He turned to me and said, 'Why not a million?' And why not? Only a genius can think like that." A lot of people in the diamond world described Winston to me as a genius, but the examples cited of his genius were always of that kind: He had the vision to ask a million for what lesser men would have priced at $750,000. It was the "genius" of the diamond world. By those standards, Winston was probably the fourth greatest genius in the history of the diamond, after Rhodes, Sir Ernest, and Harry Oppenheimer. Diamonds is a turnover trade, in which Winston, Goldfinger of Tel Aviv, and only a very few others have ever become fabulously wealthy.

The important elements of Winston's success were his access to financing in his early days, his instinct and timing, his flair for personal publicity, and his understanding of the psychology of salesmanship. He would show his great stone of the month—he always had a couple of peach pits kicking around—to the sheikhs or to King Farouk, not to sell it to them, but only as fellow connoisseurs. It was not for sale. They were never for sale—until, that is, Winston found the connoisseur who could not live without the finest stone ever cut. That month. Then he would part with it; no, not for the money, but as a gesture of friendship, as a sign of appreciation for previously loyal patronage. An old ruse, but no one ever pulled it off better than Harry Winston. Mostly, however, his success was attributable to a dynamism, a force of personality, that made him the master of whatever situation. Selection Trust's John Dimond says that "you could feel Harry Winston's presence from the other side of a crowded room." No, not a genius or a great man, but a tremendous, driving personality.

There are literally hundreds of Harry Winston "graduates," former employees who got their start with the giant, working in every aspect of the diamond business in New York and abroad. A surprising number of them, especially among production line and lower echelon white-collar people, remember him with genuine affection, and even those who were exposed to his often difficult, distant, and sometimes supercilious side left the firm with tremendous respect for Winston as a man. Everyone on "the street" is grateful to him for having glamorized their industry. One of the little guys told me, "He hyped diamonds, not just for Harry Winston; he was hyping diamonds for me."

Harry Winston was born in 1896, son of a small-time jeweler on the Upper West Side of Manhattan. Though no one that I spoke to directly knocked Winston, nearly everyone found it necessary sooner or later to tell me, invariably as a by-the-way, that his real name was Weinstein, or some said Weinberg. His mother died when Harry was seven, and for health reasons his father moved the family to Los Angeles soon after. Harry attended public school there, but from his earliest moments he was "in the trade," and dropped out of school at fifteen to enter his father's store full time. In the tradition of the new immigrant peddler, Harry would sometimes take a satchel of his father's wares on the road to sell to oil prospectors in the boom towns of the Southwest.

Around the time of the First World War the family returned to New York and Harry set out on his own, diamond dealing in the Lower East Side of New York, the predecessor to the 47th Street jungle, strictly within the trade, usually on borrowed money, sometimes on kited checks. It was a tough business, he told the New York *Daily News* years later: "I was with a little New York bank at the time. I would buy something, give the bank a check for the next day, and then sell it. You had to know what you were doing."

In his twenties, Winston hit on what was to be the route to his first success: estate jewelry. He began to specialize in hunting out and buying up the jewels of the recently deceased, removing the stones from their settings and having them recut by modern techniques that improved their brilliance and their value, and then reselling the stones. He sent mailings to the names in the *Social Register* and contacted attorneys and bankers who might be administering the estates of bejeweled decedents. By the end of the 1920s he had bought and sold famous collections from the most fashionable of the American Protestant elite.

Like most diamantaires, Winston spent every waking hour in the trade. He took a moment out to marry in 1933, but Mrs. Winston told Lillian Ross of *The New Yorker* that right after the wedding, "He went right straight back to selling jewels. He spent most of our honeymoon talking about the big diamonds he hoped to buy. We've been chasing diamonds ever since."

Winston remained principally what Winston people call "a jeweler's jeweler" (translation: a wholesale diamond dealer dealing to the trade) until 1935, when he bought the famous Jonker diamond to the tune of $700,000 and tremendous press publicity. The *New York Times* began its report on the purchase, "Until a few days ago Harry Winston was just a dealer in precious stones. Today his name is known all over the world." The cutting of the Jonker by Lazare Kaplan established the Kaplan name worldwide as well.

At the time that Winston purchased the Jonker rough, big stones had for many years been regarded as a hazardous field for the diamantaire, and would remain so regarded right up until the oil explosion of the 1970s. The market for a fifty carater was just too thin; better to cut up the big chunk of rough into dozens of two and five caraters that might be peddled to the dozens of upper-echelon executives of General Motors and the Pennsylvania Railroad than to hold out for the one big sale to the Imam of Oman.

Winston and almost no one else appreciated that the big chunks were undersold, and he appreciated how to sell them to the Imam. As each big stone came on the market, Winston bought it, paying more than anyone else and reselling it at a greater profit than the one before. He became a well-established retailer, a diamond manufacturer, a sightholder and an increasingly significant one. Private owners of "important" polished that they wanted to sell were pretty much limited to selling to Winston or to selling for less, and the DTC had only one outlet for its truly impressive pieces of rough: Harry Winston. For those, the DTC needed Winston. Some of his most significant purchases from "the Syndicate" he negotiated directly with Harry Oppenheimer.

Just as it is the DTC's duty to protect the diamond market in general against periodic slumps, it became Harry Winston's special function to protect the big-stone market. When one came on the market, he either bought it or made sure that it didn't go cheap. "I don't want to see great things cheapened," he told Lillian Ross. It was much more than a simple devotion to the ideal: Harry Winston owned more of those "great things" than anyone else.

The rest of the diamond world viewed Winston's plunges on the huge stones as simple gambles, and he encouraged that kind of view with his frequent descriptions of himself to the press as "crazy." But he knew his "gambles" in the big stone market for what they were: sure things, or at least sure things for a salesman with the savoir of

Harry Winston. He was a Jewish high-school dropout but he had the savoir of Prince Michael Romanoff himself.

The series of Winston's great purchases were all detailed in the press. He was probably the first retail jeweler to maintain a full-time public relations person, Jill Ciraldo, who sat in on most of his press interviews. When she participated in the interviews herself, requiring an identification of her in the reportage, her role would be euphemized— as is so much in the jeweler's realm—and she would be identified as "Mr. Winston's personal assistant." (She is now out of the closet and identifies herself as the firm's public relations officer.) When it was a major piece of rough that Winston had bought, there would be a press release at the time of the purchase and, frequently, the press would be invited to the cleaving. If he wasn't the high bidder on a big stone at a Parke-Bernet auction, he got in the press clips anyway, with "the bidding was opened by Harry Winston." It was good for Harry Winston and it was good for Parke-Bernet. When the Elizabeth Taylor diamond was bought by Cartier at Parke-Bernet for $1,050,000 in 1969, Winston admitted to the press that he had processed it from the rough and had sold the stone only a year and a half before for half as much money. There were two lessons for the reader: If it's a famous stone, Winston is in on it someplace; and, if you don't want to overpay, better buy it from Winston.

The publicity was never greater than when Winston acquired the forty-five-carat dark-blue Hope Diamond, with its famous curse, the legend of which was largely the creation of its next prior owner. At the time, *Time* reported that "though Winston laughed at the legend that the Hope Diamond had brought only trouble and tragedy to its owners and wearers, he soon had his press agents grinding out new embellishments of the tale." During the ten years that Winston owned the Hope, he would lend it for display at this or that Junior League Ball or other charitable functions, with, of course, the Harry Winston name attached. He appreciated that in due course some of the Junior League ladies might want to buy some rather expensive jewels themselves. Meanwhile, though, the curse of the Hope visited upon Winston increasingly fiercer bites from the Internal Revenue Service, until he could endure it no longer. He threw off the accursed stone—gave it to the Smithsonian Institution in 1959—and by that act won exorcism from the curse, manifested by a vast charitable deduction from income taxes which, under the tax law of the day, conceivably produced as great a "profit" to the firm as if it had sold the stone—not to mention the publicity value.

Much as he pushed the Winston name, however, Winston refused to publicize his face. It was a matter of personal security: The less his face was recognized, the less likely that he would be the target of criminals. Rather than acknowledge his family's legitimate security concerns, though, he blamed his reticence on the insurance company—"It's the insurance; they'll cancel my insurance instantly if anyone takes my picture," the *New York Times* quoted him as explaining. Articles about him usually included a picture of the *back* of his head along with the explanation, so that everyone who was interested in high-priced gems "knew" that Lloyd's of London had ordered him to avoid the cameras. The more gullible even believed it. It added to the Winston mystique. Only the true elite—those who had bought from Harry Winston—knew what this modern maharajah of Golconda really looked like. In fact, he was a very attractive man, though only five feet four.

In they trooped to see him—the women who devoted the larger part of the day to the management of their personal adornment. Harry did not just sell them jewels, he nurtured their every vanity. He appreciated when a strain of obsequiousness was needed, and he was not above giving the extra deep salaam. But he despised them. Sorting through a batch of stones, he commented to an assistant (as reported in *The New Yorker*):

> "These round stones are good for women over forty or fifty, when women get that hard look from all the smoking and the drinking, they need the softness and roundness of these stones." Suddenly angry, he gave the cardboard square a shove. "Adornment!" he said. "They'd wear diamonds on their ankles if it was stylish! They'd wear them in their noses!"

At the same time, Winston himself became overwhelmed by his customers and by his role. He really was impressed by the kings and the maharajahs. When King Farouk, upon abdication, made the effort of secreting a fabulous unpaid-for emerald to the American consul, entreating the diplomat to return it to Winston, the jeweler told his son, "When dealing with royalty, you must remember you're dealing with people who are brought up with honor." (This before he realized that Farouk had swindled him out of a million on a different gem.) He was even impressed by the meaningless "royal" titles of obscure European houses, whose impoverished members he employed. Maybe they lent stature to the corporate image; they did lend stature to the self-concept of Harry Winston.

"Of course this is a Cinderella world," he commented as he showed a *Daily News* reporter about the premises, and of course it was. Increasingly Harry Winston lived in that Cinderella world in which all values were topsy-turvied; in which dollar figures, like those attached to his gemstones, had no more significance than telephone numbers. It was his world, and he learned to live in it as if he were one of them—one of the kings and maharajahs and society ladies who patronized Harry Winston, Inc. He was Harry Winston, Winston the Magnificent, no longer the son of the Columbus Avenue trinket dealer! The five-foot-four-inch hustler had made it to the top.

Winston is gone now but his legend has changed little since his passing. There wasn't much room for it to grow. The firm is now guided by his son, Ronald, together with nephew Richard. Ronald is attempting to change the firm's super-super-rich image and to attract the mere super rich to Harry Winston, Inc. He aims to capture a larger share of the $10–20,000 "boutique" traffic with the kind of goods that his father would have said were being sold in the "supermarkets." Times have changed, Ronald told the *New York Times* in his first press interview in December of 1979: "The day of the carriage trade, when people drove up in chauffeured cars and spent the entire afternoon sipping tea with my father, is over." Still, he does not intend to overdemocratize: ". . . this is not going to be like Tiffany's, where the door is always revolving." He only wants to double the limited traffic at the Winston retail outlets, while further developing the business's wholesale trade.

But the founder's tradition remains. The main salon of Harry Winston, Inc., on Fifth Avenue, is exquisite. It has the marvelously opulent feeling of the lobbies of the truly great hotels, the Ritz in Paris, or Brown's in London, the places that one can never afford to patronize. Some few, of course, can, and can afford to buy the Harry Winston treasures.

There is very little merchandise on display; too much would only confuse the prospective purchaser, make it harder for him (or her) to decide. More important, too many goods on display would reduce the spectacular impact of any given piece and detract from the "uniqueness" of the jewel. Spectacular impact, uniqueness—those are what Harry Winston, Inc., has to sell. With Richard Winston, a charming, adept, and graceful man, I paused at a showcase containing two fabulous diamond necklaces and a ring mounted with one gigantic solitaire. "What's that?" I asked, pointing to the ring.

"Twenty carats, D-flawless. It is one million dollars."

"I'll take it," I said.

"Sorry." Richard was disappointed to have to disappoint me. ". . . It's sold."

31

THE HARDEST INVESTMENT

◆

The price rise in top-quality diamonds over the last ten or fifteen years is absolutely staggering. In 1966 those in the trade could buy a one carat D-flawless at $1,000 a carat (that is, a 1.17-carat D-flawless would cost $1,170). Ten years later, the value had increased to $8,000 a carat, an appreciation rate of about 25 percent per year, compounded annually. Not bad—but the best was yet to come. The price stood steady for a year and then began to take off. In the closing months of 1977 it jumped from $8,000 to $12,000 a carat. Thereafter it was up and up. The "chart" on wholesale one-carat D-flawless prices would look like this: It began 1978 at $12,000, went up to $17,000 then retreated to $16,500, and then spurted ahead to close the year at $22,500—an 85 percent increase for the year. It opened the next year at $22,500, slid back to $21,000 and then, in the late summer and fall, as gold began its six-month climb from $250 levels, the D-flawless followed along. It closed 1979 at $37,000. In January of 1980, when gold peaked at $850, the D-flawless traded at about $42,000, but then, as gold began its decline, the diamond continued upward, even more strongly than before, peaking two months later in March of 1980 at $63,000. Thereafter the D-flawless also retreated, down to $50,000 levels where it lingered throughout the latter part of 1980, before dropping—along with the price of gold—in the last months of 1980 and in 1981. As of June 1, 1981, D-flawlesses were trading at $40,000.

The reason for the price increases in the D-flawless is the same as the reason for the jump in gold prices from a low of $105 in the mid-seventies to $850: lack of confidence in all paper currencies, encouraging investors to transform money into durable stores of wealth—gold and diamonds. There is nothing new here. In the mid-1700s, the British jeweler David Jefferies was probably the first to sell diamonds as an investment. He wrote in 1750:

> If, for instance, an article which hitherto cost £200 had to be bought for £300 it is clear that the purchasing power of £300 has dropped to £200.

The best safeguard against this calamity is the purchase of jewellery, which, although it earns no interest, is a durable treasure useful in general as well as in special cases of emergency.

Europeans and many Orientals, familiar with runaway inflation and the general worthlessness of money over time, have long viewed diamonds as an investment or at least as a store of value, and have put money into them as such. Many of them have been bitterly disillusioned: Before any French or Italian general election in which the Communists look strong, French and Italians buy diamonds; then, when the Communists fail to win, diamonds slump badly on the local markets. Still, those who have been in D-flawlesses and have held out long enough have realized impressive gains.

Americans were slow to get into diamond investments. Until the 1970s, only "irresponsibles" of far-right political bent seriously believed that the value of the dollar would collapse to the extent that it has; greatly increased rates of inflation throughout the 1970s showed that "the Birchers" were not wrong about everything. US buyers began to get in and to get in big, and Japanese too. Thus, the D-flawless went from $1,000 to $22,000. Then, in the summer of 1979, the same panic flight from currencies that brought havoc to the gold market boosted the D-flawless by almost (but not quite) the same percentage rise as gold. When the panic ebbed, gold dropped back to 60 percent of all-time highs, and the D-flawless dropped by almost (but not) as much. Still, it rests at forty times the price of 1966, four times the price of 1977, twice the price of 1978.

People in the diamond trade never believed that what happened could ever happen, and with rare exceptions—those few who were of the "gold bug" mentality—declined to bet on anticipated price rises. They "invested" in their inventories as they always have, mostly in unimpressive bread-and-butter stones, not in the very finest sizes and qualities, which enjoyed the colossal appreciation. When the D-flawless hit $17,000 in the spring of 1978, the diamantaire thought to himself, "They've more than doubled in the last six months. They can't go much higher." Sure enough, they dropped back and leveled off at $16,500. Except for those with a stake in the D-flawless bren, everyone felt more comfortable with the D-flawless stabilized. And then it spurted to almost three times the price of a year before. Surely, they *couldn't* go much higher. The figures just didn't make any sense. When, finally, in the fall of 1979, I heard that a D-flawless had traded at the New York Diamond Dealers Club at the mind-boggling price of $37,000 a carat, I stopped to see one of the club's executives for confirmation. Was it true? "No, it is not true," he said. "It traded at thirty-five! *Thirty-five thousand dollars a carat!* Can you believe it? Who wants a shiny pebble for thirty-five thousand dollars?" the clubman asked the journalist. Answering the question himself, he went on: "Not me! I wouldn't buy one. I'd rather have a Rolls-Royce. Of course, I said that when they were at a thousand; I said, 'Who wants a shiny pebble for a thousand dollars? I'd rather have a Ford.' I guess I missed the boat." But there was no question in his mind that he wasn't missing any boats in passing up the pebbles at $35,000. Then, within five months, they went to $63,000—Duesenberg levels.

The biggest pitfall in investing in diamonds revolves around the central difference between diamonds and listed securities, or bullion, or commodities. Each share of IBM, each Kruggerrand, each bale of cotton, is exactly the same as every other. They are fungibles. No two diamonds, however, are alike; they are not fungibles and cannot be reduced to fungibles. Principally for that reason diamonds can never have a "market value" in the sense that IBM has a market value: IBM can be bought or sold at exactly the same price, plus or minus a small commission. It is not in the interests of those in the trade that diamonds have that kind of market value. Diamonds are traded in an arcane world in which the investor, the nonexpert dabbler, is an outsider: fair game. There is a price for the savvy and a different price for the uninitiated; the investor must buy in a seller's market and sell in a buyer's market. He must pay a substantial initiation fee.

Notwithstanding the breathtaking rises that the D-flawless experienced, almost nobody in the world diamond community—whatever they may say publicly—really thinks much of diamonds as an investment for the nonexpert. They know how much they will give to the outsider who comes to them with a diamond for sale. The two most significant diamond trade journals have this to say: "Diamonds, however—although they never fall in price—safeguard your wealth, and even increase it, as long as you do not have to sell them. The diamond market is a market which for outsiders is sellers only" (Israel Diamonds); "Large stones have become exceptionally speculative over the past two months. . . . Investors will get the worst of it" (Diamant). In a written response to a query from JC–K, Harry Oppenheimer gave his view of investing in diamonds: "The specialist nature of the business, and the product, requiring expert advice at all times, and the margins [of profit] involved make investment in diamonds less attractive except for those involved in the diamond business." Many investors think they know something that Diamant, Israel Diamonds, and Harry Oppenheimer do not.

Investor interest has been good for the diamond world: It has attracted a new group of buyers for their wares, increased the value of everybody's inventory, made more money for the entire trade. It has permanently raised the price level for the ongoing output from the diamond mines. Nonetheless, the diamond community, and especially De Beers, has a stake in keeping investors out of the diamond market. As is so often the case in the diamond world, what is best for De Beers really is best for the consumer, or in this case, for the investor.

At least since 1934 diamonds have not been a "commodity" in the sense that most other commodities have been: The price of diamonds has not risen and fallen in response to conditions affecting free market prices. Diamonds have gone only up in price, up and up, gradually but steadily (until, that is, the "adjustment" in D-flawlesses from the highs of March 1980). By increasing or curtailing the flow of rough onto the market, or by buying polished on the wholesale level when necessary, De Beers has insulated the diamond market from determinations of price by supply and demand and from the vagaries of general world economic conditions. Its success in doing so has depended on its direct or indirect control over the salable stocks of diamonds, and it is De Beers' success in maintaining the diamond's upward-edging price stability that has attracted the investor.

However good the investor has been for diamonds to date, he is a very different buyer than the sentimentalist. He is potentially very dangerous. When the sentimentalist buys a diamond, he buys it "forever." His diamond is not likely to reappear on the market, or at least significant numbers of them are not likely to reappear on the market at the same time, thereby threatening market prices. Diamonds sold to the affianced have been consumed. The investor, however, buys his diamond expecting to resell it at a later date, when he wants or needs the money—which is likely to be at the same time that other diamond investors also want money. As more and more polished diamonds disappear into investors' portfolios, the investors become a new and increasingly significant source of salable diamonds, a source far removed from De Beers' control, a source that threatens De Beers' control increasingly as investors' stocks mount. De Beers' control is essential to maintaining the upward-edging stability in the future which attracted the investor in the first place. Thus, the very success of the De Beers operation contains the seeds of its possible destruction.

The company has already lost control of the D-flawless market, and the investor can no longer confidently assume an ever-upward trend in D-flawlesses. In the 1960s De Beers still controlled so many D-flawlesses (in rough form) that it could control their price by increasing or decreasing the flow onto the market of rough that would be likely to produce D-flawlesses. At this point, ten years of one-carat D-flawlesses have been funneled almost entirely into investors' portfolios, where they are sitting, waiting to be resold. As a bloc, investors own many times more D-flawlesses than De Beers, and the investors are all subject to similar economic impetuses. If economic conditions—such as a major drop in gold prices making gold a more attractive investment—should impel significant numbers of investors to liquidate their D-flawlesses at about the same time, De Beers would be powerless to stop a plummet of D-flawless prices except through major direct intervention in the market: by buying up polished D-flawlesses in order to keep up the price level. In fact, it has refused to do so, but permitted the D-flawless to drop from its $63,000 high to $40,000, paralleling the drop in gold.

I believe (and this is pure speculation) that the company has determined as a matter of policy not to prop up the D-flawless, but to let it go "free market." It will feed out potential D-flawless rough when prices are high, hold it back when prices are low, but will otherwise let the D-flawlesses go their own way. De Beers could live with a two-tiered market, an investors' market in the top top grades and a sentimentalists' market in the lesser grades, so long as the investment fever does not spread further down from the uppermost levels already controlled by the investors.

If investors began to control other than the uppermost grades—little stones, routine stones, bread-and-butter stones, the backbone of the diamond world—then the whole CSO system, nurtured since 1934 to provide an advantageous price stability to the diamond world, would crumble along with the crumbling of De Beers' control of the significant salable stocks of diamonds. For this reason, De Beers is decidedly opposed to any further spread of the investment fever. Oppenheimer wrote *JC–K,* "The possibility that lower grade goods may be siphoned off for investment purposes is not consistent with price stability, and therefore the interests of the industry and the consumer."

De Beers' attitude is shared by the more farsighted in the community. A leading Antwerp polished dealer told me, "Every diamond that is sold to an investor will come back to haunt us," and Schnitzer, president of the World Federation of Diamond Bourses, in a 1980 address to the assembled diamond world, described the investment sale of diamonds as a "powerful time bomb which may ruin not only those directly involved but also inflict heavy damage upon our trade as a whole." The diamantaires, however, live for today's profits, and almost to a man are doing as much as possible to stimulate investor interest in the goods that each carries. If you insist on investing, Schnitzer, the melee magnate, believes melee to be a promising field, and those who want to sink a million in melee might call him.

Though diamond investors have largely confined their interests to top-quality stones of a carat or larger, others have dabbled in lesser-quality caraters and in smaller goods (and some even in rough or in industrials).

Investments in lesser stones have done markedly less well than those in D-flawlesses. In the long sweep of time from the Great Depression to today, routine diamonds (and for much of the time, even D-flawlesses) have often lagged behind general levels of inflation, and overall have performed unspectacularly. More recently, investor interest in the best-quality diamonds and the trickle-down effect of high D-flawless prices have boosted other prices but on a continually diminishing basis. During the one year when the D-flawless tripled in price from $21,000 to $63,000, the typical bread-and-butter engagement ring stones increased in wholesale price by only 12.5 percent, on average, and that rise was attributable principally to recovery from the post-bren recession in routine stones.

Though many believe that the lesser-quality diamonds will yet go through the same spurts that the D-flawless enjoyed, investor interest has been fairly well confined to "certificate stones," good-grade diamonds of over one carat that come accompanied by a laboratory certificate attesting to the diamond's quality. The intelligent investor understands that diamonds is a matter of considerable expertise; the certificate, as he views it, capsulates the expert's expertise into a format that the investor can manage. It gives him the confidence that he needs to enter an arena that he would otherwise avoid, and the diamond investment market totally depends on the public's confidence in the certificate. We should consider more carefully the fifth C—certificates.

In the United States today there are at least forty gemological laboratories that issue diamond-grading certificates, all but four of which have opened within the past five years. One dealer told me, "The certificate industry is a product of the entrance into the diamond business of people who do not understand diamonds and have no business being in it." The certificate-crazy Japanese support more than fifty diamond grading labs, commonly spending a disproportionate amount of a 15-pointer's wholesale value to have its quality certified. The labs are proliferating in Europe as well. Many of those operating in the United States are run by graduates of the Gemological Institute of America and most of them purport to apply GIA standards. In fact, their degrees of expertise and their standards vary greatly.

Even assuming honorable inspection and certification by each, a stone carrying one lab's grade can never be equated with a stone equivalently graded by a different lab, even though both stones will be described in GIA terminology and both labs will purport to apply GIA standards. As much or more to the point, the ethical standards maintained by the various labs range from "Internally Flawless" to "Imperfect 3."

As certificates go, a GIA certificate, one issued by the GIA's own laboratories in New York and Los Angeles, will be recognized and preferred worldwide, followed by an HRD certificate, one issued by the lab operated by Antwerp's Diamond High Council. While the HRD's published grading standards are more objective and scientific than are GIA standards, even in Antwerp a GIA certificate will be more nearly respected. Anyone buying a multithousand-dollar stone should insist on a GIA certificate, if only because it is more likely to be taken seriously when the time comes to sell. When an "important" stone is sold with other than a GIA certificate, most savvy buyers will assume that the reason is that the GIA would not have rated it as highly; indeed, they will assume that the GIA evaluated the stone and *did* not rate it as highly.

Even a GIA certificate, however, will not be accepted at face value by anyone who understands the vagaries of diamond grading. A certificate of a diamond's qualities is only as reliable as is the art of diamond grading. At its best, which it rarely is, diamond grading is an inexact, subjective art, and never the objective science that most investors comfort themselves in thinking. Which of two borderline grades of color or clarity a stone falls into will often be a close matter of judgment on which two equally competent and honest experts might reasonably disagree. Robert Crowningshield, strongman of the GIA's New York operations, says that if he examined a "borderline" stone twice in the same day he might easily resolve the grade differently each time. In upper-priced certificate stones, remember, the difference of one color grade usually means a price difference of some 20 percent. The same is true of clarity grading. Put color and clarity together and you find that one color grade higher together with one clarity grade higher will mean at least 30 percent more in sales price than a grade lower in each would bring. Whether the stone is given the benefit of the doubt or not depends on which of the GIA's hundred-plus examiners—some more experienced than others—evaluates the stone and how he feels that day.

When stones are regraded a second time by the GIA, often the new certificate will recite different gradings than the stone received when the GIA first examined it. The GIA acknowledges that this happens, but believes that it happens infrequently. Dealers told me that it happens all the time. For a public example: When Richard Burton bought the fabulous bibelot for his wife, Elizabeth, it was accompanied by a GIA certificate grading it as E–F in color and Internally Flawless in clarity. On regrading (one of the less frequent cases in which the GIA was aware that it had previously issued a certificate on the stone) the GIA resolved the color question squarely in favor of the less desirable F color, and it downgraded the clarity rating by two notches, to a VVS2.

I have seen one stone evaluated on three different GIA certificates, once as an F-VVS2, once as a G-VS1, and once as an H-VVS2. As of June 1, 1981, the most valuable of the three certificates would have wholesaled at about $9,750, the least desirable for about $6,000. Which certificate do you suppose the dealer will show to his prospective purchaser?

"Certificate shopping" is standard procedure for many if not most diamond dealers. "Here!" One New York dealer thrust a stone at me as he asked, "Tell me what color this stone is!" I looked at the stone, held it up to the light (which diamond people never do), then held it down and against a white paper (which is what they do do), tried to look contemplative for about four seconds, and then gave my judgment: "G." "No!" he said. ". . . That stone is light pink!" Perhaps it was just a hair pinkish when viewed at just the right angle. The dealer went on, ". . . and I'm gunna get a GIA certificate saying that it's light pink. And if they won't give me one, then I'll send it to the GIA lab in Los Angeles, and they'll give me a certificate saying it's light pink, and if they won't, then I'll send it back to the GIA lab here and they'll give me one saying that it's light pink, and I'll send it here and there and back and forth as long as it takes, but ultimately I am going to get a GIA certificate saying that this stone is light pink! And when I have that GIA certificate"—he paused for dramatic effect, and then completed his sentence with a tone of finality—"this stone *will* be light pink!"

In short, a GIA certificate of a stone's color and clarity, while stated in what investors take to be absolute terms, is not by any means absolute. It is, however, at least an indication; it reduces color and clarity to manageable terms. It fails to do the same for proportions, for cut, the neglected C.

The GIA certificate recites the relevant details of the aspects of cut so that a professional can know what to make of a stone's proportions. From the data given the dealer could arrive at a "corrected weight" for the stone to compensate for deviations from desirable proportions. The certificate does not, however, state what the GIA would compute the stone's corrected weight to be (though corrected weight is a GIA concept), and not one investor in a hundred knows how to figure it out. Instead, the investor will value the stone at whatever weight the scale shows it to be, disregarding proportions. Most of the more severely "cheated" stones will end up in the portfolios of cheated investors.

The simple fact is that no knowledgeable diamond dealer when buying on his own account—as opposed to brokering the sale of a certificate stone to an outsider—will accept a GIA certificate at face value and the certificates of other labs are viewed even more skeptically. "The certificate is just a gimmick to sell diamonds," one of Antwerp's most respected polished dealers told me. "You can't bluff your way [with a certificate] here," said his New York cousin; "the merchandise must sell itself." When the dealer sells, however, then the certificate speaks for itself: "Stones with identical certificates are of identical value," asserts an article in the Fall 1980 issue of *Diaco Report*, published by Diaco International, investment diamond dealers, but the truth of the matter is that stones with identical certificates are quite definitely not of identical value—except when being sold to dentists. Almost every dealer on the street has owned and sold stones he believes to have been overcertified, graded at a higher level than warranted, and most have a couple of overcertified stones in their safes right now. One told me, "I'm waiting for a buyer that wants to buy a certificate, not a diamond."

Notwithstanding all of the above—and further generally adverse comments yet to follow—there is still a large class of buyers for whom diamonds make the very best possible investment: criminals and others with black money. Suppose, just for the moment, that you were a major factor in, say, the cocaine industry. The cocaine executive is just as concerned about protecting his gains from the ravages of inflation as is any other druggist. But he has a harder time finding an appropriate investment vehicle than the Rexall man. If he invests in real estate, the IRS may ask where he got the down payment. And if he has to leave the country on short notice, he will not be able to take his apartment house with him. Where, oh where, can he find the right investment?

Diamonds is a private market. Nobody ever asks for anybody's Social Security number, a matter of some delicacy to cocaine dealers and mafiosi, and of considerable appeal as well to millions of perfectly respectable professionals, possibly including the reader. Respect for confidentiality is the only aspect of the diamantaires' ethic the benefits of which are extended to the outsider as well. Yes, the diamond dealer will take cash money. When it comes time to sell, transactions can be handled with equal circumspection. It would be interesting to know how many people annually declare capital gains on the profitable resale of investment diamonds. Diamonds are forever taxfree.

The extent to which these kinds of "attractions" fuel the investment market can only be speculated. According to *Diamant,* West Germans, big buyers for investment stones, buy largely out of undeclared income and take delivery in Switzerland, Liechtenstein, or Luxembourg. Given the staggering value-added taxes in most European countries, a European would have to be a greater than ordinary fool to invest in diamonds on other than an under-the-table basis. Everyone that I interviewed in Japan told me that there was no interest in Japan in investment diamonds, and foreign investment companies that have opened in Tokyo to sell investment stones have failed. However, everyone that I interviewed outside of Japan told me that the Japanese are big buyers of investment diamonds. Obviously, Japanese are buying their big rocks abroad and then stashing them in safety deposit boxes someplace, almost certainly to evade Japanese income and estate taxes.

The pioneers in selling investment diamonds to Americans were mostly flimflam operators, high-pressure telephone salesmen who made extravagant promises and then sweet-talked the unsophisticated into "investing" in stones at quadruple keystone markups. Their thoroughly dishonest tactics have now largely fallen into disuse, but the investor will still occasionally encounter unarguably fraudulent tactics. The out-of-the-trade swindler may attempt to peddle CZs to the buyer. The in-trade swindler has his own techniques.

Some dealers will show the buyer an inflated invoice—issued by his Antwerp or Tel Aviv source for the purpose of cheating both IRS and the consumer—in order to convince the buyer that he really is getting a good deal.

Certificates are sometimes matched up with stones other than the ones for which they were issued. A larger but lesser-colored flawless can be polished down to fit the weight and dimensions of the D or E or F flawless described on the certificate. As for other than flawless stones, the GIA certificate comes accompanied by a diagram showing the location of the flaws within the stone, but sometimes the GIA will send the certificate ahead of the diagram, permitting the dealer to switch diagrams, so that a lesser stone will be mistaken for the one characterized on the certificate. Riding up in the elevator of the New York Diamond Dealers Club I overheard this conversation:

FIRST MAN: The certificate says one thing, but the stone *seems* to weigh a point less. *Nu?*
SECOND MAN: So you want it for a point less?
FIRST MAN: The question isn't whether it's a point less.

He didn't say what the question was. The second man was mute. He understood the unasked question: Was it the same stone?

To curtail this kind of dishonesty, some labs will customarily encase each stone examined in an untamperable plastic wrapper containing both the stone and a tab that keys the stone to its certificate. Inspection of the wrapper will immediately disclose whether anyone has opened it. This is foolproof protection against stone-and-certificate matching, but only for those who will know the original wrapper from a replacement wrapper.

The first caveat usually given when discussing diamond investing is "Deal with a reputable jeweler." "Reputable jeweler" is often a euphemism referring to the jeweler who tacitly admits to charging such a hefty markup that his incentive to preserve his reputation exceeds his incentive to take the buyer for a still bigger chunk of profit through dishonorable means. His ordinary keystone-gauged markup is such that no smart investor will buy from the reputable jeweler—at least not on his usual basis.

The alternative to buying from the jeweler is to buy "wholesale," discussed previously, or to deal with one of the several diamond investment houses. Diamond investment houses are the principal repositories of overcertified and worse-than-usually-proportioned stones. They give those who want to buy a certificate what they pay for: a certificate. Most of them are brokering operations, buying and selling on commission; but no, not the usual in-trade 2 percent, for they must bear walloping overheads for the fancy addresses and appointments that give their operations an aura of legitimacy.

Selling a diamond is the hard part. People commonly romanticize diamonds into a form of international currency. They are not, and to think of them as such is to invite disaster. Unlike currencies (possibly including Krugerrands and other forms of gold bullion), diamonds are not freely exchangeable at easily ascertained rates of exchange. They are in no way similar to negotiable instruments; they are nigh unto impossible for the outsider to "negotiate" except at substantial discounts. This is especially true for those who find that they must liquidate in a hurry. The extensive list of offerings published by Diamond Listing Corporation of Huntington Beach, California, includes hundreds of lab-graded stones weekly that are being offered at sizable discounts from what could fairly be regarded as wholesale—some at half of wholesale—these being offered by people who have to unload in a pinch. They stand as a first-level caveat: Do not let yourself get in the position of having to sell in a pinch. They also hold the germ of a second-level warning: There will always be someone that has to sell in a pinch, and the presence of these "desperate" sellers of isolated stones operates as a powerful depressant on the market for everyone else who wants to sell stones outside of established wholesaler-retailer relationships.

For a public experience, let us look at that of Security Pacific National Bank, unwitting buyer and unwitting seller of four pounds of fine-make polished diamonds. Security Pacific was the victim of one of the most imaginative heists in banking history, when computer expert Mark Rifkin managed to computer-out $10 million of the bank's money into his own control. He used $8.145 million of that to buy eight-thousand-plus carats of polished from an arm of Almazjuvelirexport, the selling agent of the Soviet polished industry, late in October of 1978. He bought via a knowledgeable diamantaire and at about the most wholesale level (albeit from one of the less flexible sellers). His scheme went awry, and Security Pacific ended up owning four pounds of polished. One year later it sold. In the meantime the DTC had increased the price of rough by 13 percent, and the D-flawless had spurted from $21,000 to $33,000 a carat. Maybe diamonds were the best thing that ever happened to Security Pacific! Well, they weren't.

The bank tried to sell the stones by sealed bid and didn't get anywhere near its own reserve price. Ultimately it accepted an offer of $6.5 million from a New York–Tel Aviv–Swiss combine. As part consideration the buyers wangled unrealistically advantageous terms: no down payment, with payment to be due eighteen months later, with interest in the interim to run at 5 percent per year—this at a time when inflation and the prime rate were running neck and neck at a percent a month. What it meant to the buyers was they could liquidate the stones at their leisure, pay as they want (if they felt that they wanted to pay off a 5 percent per year debt), and pocket the profits without ever having to shell out a dime.

To the bank it meant a real sale price—after discounting for the unrealistic financing—of maybe $6 million, or a loss on its money of more than 25 percent for the one year. The bank was counseled by a reputable firm of West Coast diamantaires, and because of the volume, it was in a position to talk to the world's most powerful and responsible potential buyers. The average investor is most unlikely to do anywhere near that well. Most of the famous collections accumulated by private individuals, including those of "Diamond Jim" Brady and Evelyn Walsh McLean (Hope Diamond and the Star of the East) have ultimately been liquidated by their executors at tremendous losses. The point is: If you are an outsider in the diamond market the diamond market is likely to treat you like an outsider.

If you have a certificate stone to sell, you should try to find someone at the country club who will be willing to buy in reliance on the certificate and the NYDEX price quote in the *Wall Street Journal*. Otherwise, you can place it for sale with an investment house for brokering. Be prepared for the investment broker to tell you that your stone has been overcertified and that—as an honorable and reputable dealer—he can offer it only at a lower grade. Then, when you agree, he will place your listing among his many hundreds of other listings. He can really put on a push to sell your stone; or, instead, he can put a push on to sell the somewhat similar stone offered by one of his in-trade consignors who sends him a lot of business. Unless you price your stone at well below market value, it is likely to be neglected. If you price it "to move," then it will probably be bought by someone in the trade who has a hot prospect (someone just like you used to be) who will pay its realistic market value—probably more.

People trying to sell "jeweler's goods," lesser diamonds than the certificate stones that investors usually buy, have it even harder. The retailer is the most obvious buyer for them.

The simple truth is that your retailer not only cannot afford to pay you retail for your diamond, he cannot even afford to pay you wholesale for it—even if he wanted to. Wholesale is what he pays for stones that he wants or needs, and he buys those from his regular wholesaler who supplies him promptly and efficiently as the needs arise. The wholesaler may also extend him ninety days' credit (you won't) and the wholesaler may give him particularly good service or personal consideration if the retailer should find himself in a bind (you can't). Your particular stone will not fit his precise wants or needs at the moment that you bring it to him, and when the time comes that he does need a stone just like yours, he can call his wholesaler and get it within forty-eight hours. At that time he can afford to pay wholesale. He can afford to tie up his limited capital in your stone only if he thinks he can turn it over quickly at a small profit, perhaps by selling it to *his* wholesaler, or if he can get it for a "steal." How much *will* he pay? One dealer, affecting a fishy eye as he spoke, told me, "Maybe I'd give you sixty percent of wholesale—maybe," with a tone that said that he really wouldn't. This is consistent with a Knight wire service story that appeared in many newspapers in December of 1979, which reported that "brokers and representatives of auction houses say you may get only half to two-thirds of wholesale value from jewelers."

The seller should definitely shop around before selling, as offers for diamonds or for diamond jewelery will vary even more greatly than retailers' selling prices for equivalent goods. A retailer's offer will depend on the regularity with which the particular retailer's clientele demands goods such as yours; the retailer's cash position as of the moment that you approach him, and the extent to which he wants to gouge you. Last and possibly least, different retailers' offers will depend on their differing views of the quality and market value of the stone.

On the basis of an ad in the *New York Times,* I would urge everyone to offer their goods to Siegelson's Jewelers, a 47th Street landmark and a pioneer on the block. They advertise:

There are precisely two possibilities: one is that the Siegelson ad is somewhat less than candid, and the other is that Siegelson's foolhardy buying policy will have led to the failure of their business by the time of publication of this book. This would indeed be sad for a house that has been in business since 1920. Siegelson lists itself in the New York Yellow Pages under jewelry wholesalers. They apparently buy at retail and sell at wholesale, probably working under an ingenious reverse-keystone pricing policy, buying at $1,000 and then reselling at $500. How do they stay in business? Volume! Siegelson's volume is one of the biggest in the city.

THE SPREADING MONOPOLY

◆

My father brought me into this business and his father brought him into diamonds, and his father before him too. . . . But no, my son will not be a diamantaire because in his day, there will be no diamantaires. There will be only De Beers.

—*Antwerp diamantaire*

What a lovely little world diamonds was in the early part of this century. Diamond manufacturing was confined almost exclusively to the Lowlands, and operated there principally as a cottage industry. Most manufacturers were little people from the countryside around Amsterdam and Antwerp, who would come to town once or twice a week to the bourse or, equally common, to one of the flea markets, to buy rough and sell polished. Friday was the busiest day, settling-up day, and countryside diamantaires would come with suitcases of cash to settle up their debts. It was a cloistered, unstructured industry, isolated from time and medieval in organization and texture.

The diamond trade was scarcely more sophisticated. A diamond was a diamond, and it was sold by weight. Few in the business recognized or much cared about subtle differences in color, clarity, or cut. There was virtually no communication between the Lowlands and the almost insignificant diamond centers in London, Paris, Milan, and New York.

Ah, those were great days for diamond world Jewry, the regents of their small world in which everyone knew everyone and their families; in which they could preserve the rich traditions and flavor of eastern European Yiddish culture while enjoying occasional luxuries and a much easier life than that in the countries of their origin. Oblivious to the happenings outside of their diamond ghettos, the great cataclysm took most of them unawares.

Many of them returned to Antwerp and Amsterdam after World War II and attempted to revive the former diamond culture, but it could not survive indefinitely in the postwar world. A new affluence in the United States led to the birth of a genuine mass market for diamonds. Hong Kong woke up the Orient to diamonds, and then, just in the past decade, Japan proved to be a sleeping giant of a market. Mass markets developed in Germany and Italy. Increased diamond production by De Beers, together with the stones from the important new sources in the Soviet Union and Botswana, was necessary to satisfy demand.

Meanwhile, the seeds that the Lowlanders had left behind in the lands of their temporary wartime residence, in Palestine, India, and New York, began to grow, and to grow as tall almost as Antwerp, while Amsterdam died of old age or whatever. Manufacturers began to verticalize, the biggest—Winston and Zale—even to the retail level. Chain-of-six factory organization reduced the cutter's input to purely mechanical levels. More sophisticated grading standards removed a lot of the guesswork from the diamond business—and a lot of the individuality of it—and brought about a narrowing of price spreads. The jet and the telex both expanded and shrank the diamond world, and the computer found a place in the business, monitoring the inventories of major diamantaires. The new people came into the business, tripling or quadrupling the population of the diamond world, bringing with them more frenzy and larceny, and more competition, forcing the diamantaires to work on still lesser margins of profit.

Diamonds is no longer a cottage industry, and the *tamm,* the flavor of the old days and ways, has largely evaporated with the change in the industry's organizational structure. A number of steps are still left, however, before the structure of the industry is fully matured.

The most significant ongoing changes result from the increased control by the DTC and by verticalization of its efforts. These, in turn, are responses to threats against that control from the CSO's producing participants, and particularly the Soviet Union.

To a great extent, De Beers' continued control exists at the behest of the Soviets. Not less than 20 percent of the stones in the typical DTC rough box are of Siberian origin; one responsible source told me that Soviet goods account for close to half of the DTC's wares. The Russian share of the rough sold by the DTC (however much it is) plus Russian sales of polished diamonds totaling about $500 million a year (or a fifth of the DTC's rough sales) must mean that something more than 40 percent of the diamonds entering the market every year are of Russian origin. In terms of control of production, the Soviet Union is already the dominant partner in the cartel.

Whatever its real production is, Russia introduces to the rough market as much rough as it can sell to the CSO pursuant to its understanding with the Diamond Corporation; it introduces to the polished market as many stones as it can without oversupplying and upsetting that market. It mines, however, in quantities that are economical for it to mine and process—probably more than it sells. *Diamant* and most other sources believe that in addition to reserves in the ground, the Soviets have significant stockpiles of both rough and polished goods. More important for the future, Soviet production capabilities seem sufficient to satisfy total world diamond demand indefinitely. Russia's relative position must annually grow stronger. As production control shifts increasingly to the Soviets, many diamantaires foresee the Russians breaking away, and a diamond war between the DTC and the USSR.

As production from De Beers' own mines becomes less significant in world totals, the company's influence elsewhere along the line will become increasingly vital both to maintenance of its own position and to maintenance of price stability in the diamond market. Thus, its stepped-up efforts to control in the western world, and its verticalization. Paul Gibson, writing in *Forbes* in 1978, quoted Hubert Dagnall, then of the DTC's public relations department, as venturing that the company's forward integration was the most important shift for De Beers since Sir Ernest's time. "The industry is at a crossroads," according to Dagnall.

There has been a significant decline in the number of important rough dealers over the past decade. Many have simply lost their sights. Some, such as the Tel Aviv and Bombay affiliates of London Star, the world's biggest rough dealer, have gone into manufacturing themselves. Some outside rough dealers have had their supplies competed away from them by Diamond Corporation buyers in the countries with outside production. Other rough dealers have lost their biggest customers when the DTC awarded sights direct to their buyers.

Perhaps most important in this context, however, rough dealers have had their customers usurped by important new entrants to the business—rough-dealing DTC "affiliates." Diamdel (*Diamond Development*), the most powerful rough dealer in Antwerp; Diamdel of Tel Aviv, second or third in its market; and Hindustan Diamond Company (HDC), the only legitimate rough dealer operating in India, are all DTC affiliates. The legal relationships between them and the DTC are shrouded in secrecy. While they function as subsidiaries of the DTC, other Oppenheimer interests are probably their controlling stockholders and everyone involved is careful to avoid the use of the word "subsidiary" in describing the relationships. (This is not a matter of fooling anyone in the trade—or if it is, no one is fooled—but almost certainly a matter of avoiding presumptions that arise in antitrust law when one of many buyers from a dominant seller is a subsidiary of that seller.)

HDC is too new to have a matured business style, but the Diamdels have a track record. They operate like any other rough dealer, but with an important exception: Other rough dealers will usually sell to the highest bidder for whatever he will pay, while the Diamdels give preference to nonsightholders and limit their overall margins to modest proportions—not because they are "nicer" than other rough dealers, but because they exist as much to serve the policy objectives of the DTC as to generate short-term profits. In accord with DTC policy, they view their role as a service to the manufacturer too small to have a sight in his own right, and insufficiently capitalized to pay top dollar for rough in bren periods. During the bren of 1978, when other rough dealers demanded astronomical premiums, Diamdel limited itself to profits of 5 and 10 percent and, by so doing, may well have been responsible for the very survival of the cutting industry in Antwerp's *kempen.*

Diamdel officials insist that they are treated just like any other sightholder, and receive no preferential treatment because they are affiliates. Any other course of conduct on the part of the DTC might have nasty antitrust implications, affiliate or no. Because, however, one of the standards by which the DTC evaluates all sightholders is the degree of consonance of the sightholder's operations with overall DTC policy, and because the Diamdels conform much more closely to it than do the exclusively profit-motivated rough dealers, the Diamdels score extremely well when measured by the same standards applied equally to all sightholding rough dealers. For that, they might be rewarded. The prognosis for the other rough dealers has been clear since Diamdel first opened its doors. For all manufacturers, big or small, it means still greater dependence for rough supply on De Beers.

Lens Diamond Industries, the vast diamond-sawing factory in Antwerp's *kempen,* is another of the DTC's affiliates, and the earliest of them to enter the field of diamond processing. Threatened diamantaires regard it as the thin edge of wedge.

Relatively few diamond manufacturers do initial division of the rough. Most of them farm out the sawing (or the cleaving, which is commercially less significant) to shops that do only that on contract for manufacturers. The economics of the diamond business is such that most manufacturers will slow down at about the same time, and when manufacturers slow down or suspend operations, they send fewer stones to the sawyer to be sawed and the sawing work force is out of work. The sawyer is always the first to be laid off in one of the diamond world's periodic recessions. Then, when busy times return to the business, the sawing facilities become hopelessly backlogged with work, delaying manufacturers in their processing schedules and interrupting the flow of work to the brutting and polishing labor forces. The problem became particularly acute in Antwerp in the mid-1970s, when manufacturers had to anticipate tie-ups at the sawyers' of five or six weeks. Five or six weeks is money.

Jan Lens (d. 1978) approached the DTC with a solution to the problems of the Antwerp sawing industry. Lens proposed to open a huge sawing factory that would offer permanent, steady employment to sawyers by sawing goods for the DTC in slow times and good. The DTC could then offer its sightholders pre-sawn goods. If it had to stockpile sawn goods in the slow periods, that was little worse than its burden of stockpiling rough in slow times; in the bren periods, the manufacturers would be able to order goods already sawn and save themselves the delays at the sawyers'. His proposal would be good for the industry, the work force, and for the DTC. Oppenheimer interests took a majority stock interest in his proposed Lens Diamond Industries, and backed the business with loans. Today LDI (also known as Belsaw, *Bel*gium *Saw*ing) operates the world's largest diamond sawing plant. It saws only DTC-owned rough on contract for the DTC, after which the goods are moved out into sightholders' boxes as they may be requested. DTC assignments keep LDI working continually so that Lens and Lens alone is able to keep its men employed without layoffs.

However desirable LDI might have seemed to the diamond world in the mid-1970s, today not one manufacturer anywhere welcomes the LDI-sawn goods. Where to divide the stone is the most important planning decision in the entire manufacturing process; it is an irrevocable decision that determines what final stones will ultimately come out of a piece of rough. It is in his planning ability—and especially his approach to division—that the diamond manufacturer's experience, flexibility, and ingenuity contribute most to his profit. When, however, the goods arrive at his office already sawed, he is deprived of the most important arena in which his own skills might operate, and he loses the opportunity for a profit commensurate with his skills.

LDI also has a cleaving division, cleaving more expensive stones in Antwerp and lesser ones in Tel Aviv, where LDI operates through its subsidiary Valdiam. More and more of the abler workers are opting for the regularity that Lens provides. The independent sawing and cleaving firms find it increasingly difficult to compete, and they are leaving the market, making it more difficult for manufacturers to obtain outside division services. *Diamant* reports that at the start of 1978 there were forty-seven independent cleaving firms in Antwerp employing three hundred cleavers. At the end of the year only thirty-five firms were left, employing two hundred people—a third of the independent cleavers had vanished from the market. One rough dealer told me that it is extremely difficult for him to sell stones that will have to be cleaved in Antwerp because LDI has "monopolized" the cleavers, and it cleaves only for the DTC. The situation is increasingly the same with sawyers both in Antwerp and Tel Aviv. As manufacturers find it more difficult to have their stones sawn or cleaved, they will be prompted to request and accept more predivided stones from the DTC, thereby further discouraging the independent sawyers and cleavers from remaining in the market. Always dependent on the DTC for rough, the manufacturers are becoming increasingly dependent on it for division services as LDI takes increasing control of the first step in processing.

After division of the rough, the two portions of the stone are brutted: the girdle is cut onto each. Some sightholders' boxes have already included brutted goods—very badly brutted, says one. These stones, already sawn and brutted by DTC agencies, are ready to be plunked into the DTC's Piermatic for finishing off. In meetings with Antwerp's Diamond High Council, De Beers has acknowledged that it intends to become more deeply involved in brutting, though it anticipates that it will be several years before it is a significant factor in this end of the business. Unlike sawing and cleaving, which manufacturers have customarily farmed out, brutting is fully a part of most manufacturers' factory operations, something they do "in house." Little by little the role of the manufacturer is being reduced, and the individuality of each manufacturer's operation is being stripped away. This affects both his profits and his self-image.

Sawing and brutting are all well and bad, but still worse for the manufacturers, De Beers "affiliates" are now performing the complete polishing process at plants in Portugal and, to a very small extent, in Antwerp as well. The extent of its polishing is small, approaching insignificance, but it poses an alarming specter for all diamond manufacturers. Sightholders notice fewer and fewer of the bigger and better stones in their boxes—the stones that are most salable—and suspect that the DTC is stockpiling them, perhaps for processing by the company's polishing affiliates.

The biggest importers of polished diamonds into Antwerp are now the DTC affiliates. Diatrada, Throgmorton Gems, and Chichester are all polished-dealing arms of the Oppenheimer group, and they are taking over more and more of the market for polished diamonds, which they buy from diamond manufacturers and sell to important wholesalers. Diatrada, based in Antwerp and owned directly by the DTC, does most or all of the buying of polished stones purchased by the Oppenheimer group, buying in both Antwerp and Tel Aviv. Most of Diatrada's purchases are ultimately sold by Throgmorton, sometimes identified as Diatrada's subsidiary, which offers goods only to a few dozen of the world's very biggest buyers in Lucerne. The trade calls Throgmorton's offerings "sights," but they are not sights in the sense that the DTC offers rough: A favored buyer merely calls Throgmorton and arranges to come to Throgmorton's Lucerne office to inspect merchandise in huge lots, which goods can be accepted or not, and even bargained a little, on a no-hard-feelings basis. Smaller polished buyers, people in the $100,000-plus class, can talk to Chichester on the same basis in London.

De Beers has used its polished dealing arms as market-stabilizing vehicles operating in the polished market, buying up excess polished production rather than risking having too much polished on the market. They operate as a buffer against vagaries in the polished market, just as the CSO operation acts as the buffer in the rough world. In 1978 the group unfroze vast resources for the purchase of cut stones, and in the waning months of the year, when no one else was buying, Diatrada made regular purchases at what *Diamant* described as fair prices. Everyone in the trade likes that. What they don't like is that the polished arms then sell the polished, and sell it to customers who would otherwise be buying from them.

The DTC explains that its ventures into selling are only for the purpose of testing the market and having a more direct feel on the pulse of the business. No one in the trade believes it. Diatrada and Throgmorton have gone far beyond pulse feeling. Already they probably account for upward of 10 percent of total DTC volume, and both their dollar volume and their total share of the world polished trade are growing annually. DTC sightholders and major polished dealers see themselves being competed out of business by the supplier of their raw materials.

The DTC's polished dealing entities have now opened a wholesale outlet in Hong Kong, to be operated on the same basis as Throgmorton's Lucerne operations. Hong Kong is attractive to the DTC as the center of the Oriental trade; as a bridge to mainland Chinese doings (which may become increasingly important with the development of both the Chinese diamond mines and the Chinese diamond-processing industry); as a general Oriental "listening post"; and as a tax haven. The Hong Kong corporate income tax is limited to 17 percent, and it is advantageous to the DTC to channel some of its earnings to that city to escape vastly higher taxes elsewhere. The DTC's arrival in the crown colony foreshadows an increasing role for Hong Kong in the world diamond trade. *Jewelers' Circular–Keystone* quoted a Hong Kong dealer in 1979 as boasting, "We will be the Antwerp of 1985."

Verticalization of the Oppenheimer group interests throughout the diamond pipeline raises potential antitrust problems for the giant that are probably more apparent than real.

Anticompetitive agreements to control prices in the diamond market are as old as the diamond itself. The *Arthasâstra* reports that "the [diamond] merchants . . . combine in order to determine the rise and fall of prices." The government of that day fixed maximum prices. Since ancient times, however, regulation of trade-restraining combinations in the diamond world has not been effectively brought to bear.

More recently, the United States was the first and to date the only country to give serious attention to the antitrust implications of the CSO's modus operandi. The CSO operation—admittedly—is a concerted action by diamond producers to restrain trade, resulting in higher prices to the consumers. Undeniably, it operates in violation of the United States antitrust laws, to the extent that those laws apply to it.

De Beers has been reasonably careful to avoid having any corporate presence (within the meaning of US law) in the United States so as to keep outside American jurisdiction. It sells *to* the United States but not *in* the United States; it maintains no office or bank account in the United States; insulates itself from the operations of "its" Diamond Information

Center in New York; places its American advertisements in London, not in the United States; and otherwise keeps out of the country.

In one backwater area of the business, however, someone let down the guard. Industrial grit, the minuscule particles of diamond used principally in grinding wheels, is sold in the United States by both General Electric and by De Beers' Irish subsidiary. De Beers' sales of grit are made within the United States by two (formerly three) distributors. When the distributors were reduced from three to two, someone was left disgruntled and began talking to the government. Grand jury investigations were held in New York in 1973–74; upward of two hundred subpoenas were issued, demanding evidence from everyone of note in the American diamond community. To have been subpoenaed became a status symbol on "the street." At the grand jury inquiries, the government investigators asked not just about grit but about every aspect of the organization and operation of the diamond world.

Grand jury records are never opened to the public (regrettably for the historian) and so we can only speculate about such matters, but apparently the vital jurisdictional handle could be maintained only with regard to the distribution of grit; only as to that could the Justice Department make out a color of a claim that De Beers was actually dealing in the United States. The company had sent the grit to the United States on consignment; the sales of the goods were actually completed within the United States. That fact made for sufficient nexus to establish that De Beers really was in the grit business in the United States! Had it been an important aspect of De Beers' business, company lawyers would have seen to it that the sales were completed abroad, as DTC sales of gem rough are completed abroad, but US grit sales were among the least important aspects of De Beers' business, amounting at most to an insignificant $15 million-or-so a year, and so no one really paid much attention.

A fine jurisdictional question, however, remained: Was it the giant, De Beers of South Africa, that was dealing in the United States, or was it its subsidiary, De Beers of Ireland, that might be held? Could the sins of the corporate progeny be visited upon the corporate parent?

For whatever they were worth, criminal indictments were handed down as to the trade in grit against the ultimate target, the South African corporation (actually its South African industrials division), and against the two American distributors of De Beers' grit. Simultaneously, the government instituted a civil action against all three, seeking permanent injunctive relief against the continuation of clear abuses in the distribution of De Beers' diamond grit within the United States: division of territories between the De Beers distributors, a refusal of the distributors to compete with one another, and retribution from above for anyone who introduced an element of competition into the distribution of De Beers' diamond grit. These are classical antitrust violations, ones that typify the business giant that tries to keep up prices in violation of US antitrust laws. The local distributors were clearly guilty of them and quickly submitted to both criminal court and civil court judgments against themselves.

De Beers, however, remained elusive. It refused to acknowledge that the court had jurisdiction. It appreciated that much more was involved in the grit case than grit; that the Justice Department was using the case as an investigative tool that might enable it to bust up more important aspects of the diamond trade—the trade in industrials used in drill bits or even the gem business.

De Beers approached the case with a grim concern. The company's usual preoccupation with secrecy became paranoiac. Its American lawyers were told only so much as the company thought it essential for them to know; the company had all rooms electronically debugged before holding conferences, and had its lawyers fly from New York to Canada to place important phone calls. On De Beers' behalf, South Africa passed a law making it an offense for South African citizens at home or abroad to reveal the type of information customarily required by American grand juries, and to be on the safe side, De Beers kept its officials from passing through the United States even on holiday.

In fact, though, the government had no case other than the surface case—the case involving industrial grit—and then, not against the foreign defendant that it had sued, De Beers' industrials division in South Africa, but only against the Irish subsidiary, De Beers Industrial Diamond Division (Ireland) Ltd., the marketing organization for De Beers' grit. As a negotiated matter, the Irish subsidiary was substituted for the giant of the gemstone business, and stipulated that a judgment might enter against itself that involved only it—not De Beers Consolidated or any other agency of the CSO. On the face of things, De Beers—or at least a direct subsidiary of it—"lost" the US antitrust case, but the loss constituted a real victory for De Beers in its implications: In agreeing to the settlement, the government implicitly acknowledged that De Beers Consolidated does not do business within the United States; that it—and almost certainly the DTC as well—are beyond the reach of the US antitrust laws. A judgment against the giant itself would have had wide repercussions throughout the industry, and the *Jerusalem Post* reported that the outcome was greeted with relief in Israel and Antwerp. De Beers weathered the storm; its antitrust problems in the United States are almost certainly behind it.

De Beers, however, must still face the emerging antitrust law of the European Common Market, to which both Britain and Belgium and most other European nations belong. The Common Market lacks the body of precedents that the United States has evolved in almost a century of antitrust vigilance; both interpretation and enforcement of its antitrust law are still very much in the evolutionary stage. Ultimately, De Beers will be confronted with problems arising from it. The Common Market law, however, is relatively docile when compared with the stringent American statutes. Dominant elements in any industry are likely to be left alone so long as they do not abuse their positions of power.

For the moment De Beers is keeping its nose clean, as best it can, and is otherwise adopting a wait-and-see attitude. It will closely monitor the fleshing-out of the Common Market law, and if and when the precedents begin appearing too threatening, the DTC, like its wares and its customers, is portable. It is ready to flee both Britain and Belgium and to move to the land of freedom, privacy, and hospitality for ruggedly individual money and ruggedly individual businesses: to Switzerland. Switzerland does not belong to the Common Market. The company's existing Lucerne operations, distributing both melee rough through the Diamond Trading Company and polished diamonds through Throgmorton Gems, constitute its beachhead for if and when. De Beers, however, thinks that it will be able to live within the strictures of the law. It recently spent many millions in refurbishing No. 17 Charterhouse, across the street from its longtime headquarters at No. 2, tangible evidence that it does not contemplate flight in the foreseeable future.

Diamantaires foresee a world a couple of decades hence in which DTC affiliates are performing the complete polishing process on most stones that pass through the CSO, and are sawing and brutting what they don't actually polish. That is not De Beers' wish. Big businesses are unsuited for diamond polishing.

In any manufacturing line, a factory sooner or later gets so big that it cannot practicably be overseen, but in diamonds the maximum size is reached rather sooner than later. According to Raoul Delveaux of Antwerp's Diamond High Council, the *kempen*'s smallest cottages have better yields than Antwerp's middling factories, but they in turn have better yields than the larger factories. "It's an economic law in the diamond business: small can do it cheaper and better than big." Diamond enterprises require close planning of stones and constant supervision to maximize profits, and both become progressively less effective the larger the factory.

De Beers' experience with large factories has been consistent with the general rule. Manufacturers point to Lens Diamond Industries. Arieh Ketsef of the Israeli Diamond Manufacturers Association insists that the overall weight yield of LDI-sawn goods is 5 to 7 percent less than the yields he and other Israeli manufacturers retrieve from similar rough that they plan and have sawn themselves. No, LDI's work will not improve with time; it is too big to be able to operate efficiently in the diamond business. And its errors are costing everyone along the way money.

If De Beers should seriously expand its polishing efforts, lapses in planning and supervision that are inherent in size would whittle down the per unit profit that its sightholders are earning on the same goods. What was left of that profit would be eaten by increased cost factors affecting the company. It would face much greater militance from organized labor than has confronted the diamantaires with their family-atmosphere factories, with the almost certain result of increased labor costs. And like any other big business—but unlike the diamantaires—De Beers would have to pay a full tax bill. As things stand, the company is a substantial beneficiary of the diamantaires' efficiencies, of their happy labor relations, and of their tax evasions, by virtue of all of which it is able to charge and the manufacturers are able to pay significantly more for rough than would otherwise be the case. It is almost certainly making more after-tax money selling rough to efficient tax-evading businesses with contented personnel than it could make if it were to polish the diamonds itself. De Beers understands all of this, but it may have no choice; it may have to verticalize to an even greater extent if it is to continue to exercise determinative control over the diamond market. Its steps to forward integration accomplished to date give it the flexibility that it may need to handle whatever it may be called upon to handle.

The war that the diamantaires expect between the Russians and De Beers will not materialize. De Beers' increasing preparedness will avert any open confrontations and will ensure a continuation of the modus vivendi. The Soviets will continue to sell as much rough to the CSO as they can, while selling as much polished outside as they can without upsetting the market. Antwerp's important polished dealer V. Barsamian says, "Wolves do not eat each other." The frightful preparedness, however, will have one important casualty: the smaller man. As De Beers increasingly verticalizes, it will take more and more business away from those least financially able to keep up—the most efficient operators in the diamond world.

The trend against the little man in the diamond world has been apparent for only about a decade, and circumstances did not begin to bear down powerfully upon him until the bren of 1978 and its aftermath.

Until the mid-1970s, diamond manufacturing was an easy-entrance business. The little man could start up on a very small scale with inexpensive equipment and inexpensive rough, especially if he worked smalls and melee. There was a vigorous rough market to serve the nonsightholder, fueled both by dealers' boxes and by the infusion of rough from outside markets. The little man could often buy rough at discounts from DTC prices, but when he had to pay a premium, it was usually modest enough not to be an insurmountable burden and the economies of small enabled him to overcome the premium. With talent and ingenuity he could make a success of himself in diamond manufacturing.

Today more and more of the outside rough is acquired in its markets by Diamond Corporation buyers and becomes inside rough, available principally to the sightholders, the big boys. What the CSO buyers do not buy on the outside market others buy, but at such prices as to be too expensive for economical processing. Rough dealers everywhere have been squeezed out, and DTC control over the non-Soviet market has been increased. From 1976 to late 1978, almost no goods sold at discount. Since then, many classes and qualities of rough have been discounted, but the market in melee and smalls has been so slow that it has not paid the little man to work them, while bigger goods have been too expensive to be within his means. The premium on "premium stones" has usually been too great to be overcome by close planning. The smaller manufacturer is increasingly limited to buying sightholders' castoffs or to buying from the Diamdels. The Diamdels have been god-sends to the little man, and will continue to be—so long as the little man has a place in the DTC's picture.

A doubling of DTC prices since 1976, however, has scared off many of the little men, even those with access to Diamdel. Price rises have increased the risks of the business; the stakes are higher now than for-merly. If a stone turns out to be less desirable than it might have seemed in the rough, as is often the case, or produces a lower yield than the small manufacturer expected, the repercussions are more serious than they were in the days when rough cost half as much, and they may be grave in the case of large pieces of rough.

The bren was disastrous for the little men. Big boys bid them out of the rough market altogether. In the recession that followed, only those who had the capital to suffer through the hard times could continue polishing. Throughout the diamond world, the small entrepreneurs folded their tents. According to S. G. Jhaveri, chairman of the Indian Gem and Jewellery Export Promotion Council, in 1974–75 there were almost seven hundred Indian diamond exporters; by 1978–79, India's total exports had expanded greatly, but the number of exporters had shrunk to below three hundred. The little man had been shuffled out. Kantilal Chhotalal says that "the afflicted factories [in India] are without exception firms that do not obtain their supply of raw materials direct from the syndicate. Conversely, not a single firm that holds a sight has curtailed production, let alone closed down." The situation was much the same in Israel. Everywhere the sightholders—the monopoly within the monopoly—tightened their grip on diamond manufacturing.

Increased acceptance in the future of both the Piermatic and of LDI-sawn goods will hasten the exit of the remaining small men in dia-mond manufacturing. Because one employee can operate six Piermatics, it is most efficient to use them in banks. Bonas, the Piermatic distributor, likes to sell them in units of forty. That demands volume. As the Piermatic continues to win an increasing share of the market, diamond shops will become fewer in number, each handling stepped-up volume. The small melee man will therefore be automated out of business in the 1980s along with his employees.

The effect of presawn goods will be much the same. By reducing the role of individual skill in processing, presawn goods make it much harder for the agile small manufacturer to overcome the premiums that he must pay for rough. The sightholding dullard will make about as much from a presawn stone as will a nonsightholding genius, so that the latter will no longer be able to compensate for the former's purchasing advantage by getting more out of the stone.

The trend against the little man is even stronger in the diamond trade than it is in diamond processing. Polished dealing has not been an arena for the little man for over a decade, but things are getting worse for those of modest size. Prior to the impressive price rises of the late 1970s retailers would buy for stock, but the increased prices have forced retailers to trim their inventories, requiring that polished dealers carry more of the financial burdens of stocking than formerly. That requires capital; to be most effective, capital of the proportions available to Diatrada, Throgmorton—and Almazjuvelirexport—and not too many others.

The international credit crunch has significantly affected both the American and the Japanese wholesale buyer; it has worked to the advantage of those dealers who can make credit facilities available to their customers, and to the disadvantage of those dealers—mostly the smaller men—who cannot. One polished dealer told me that he has lost half his customers since the bren because he is not in a position to arrange financing for his buyers. The capital requirements that polished dealers have faced in the last few years have led to the departure of the smaller dealers and to increased dominance of the market by the major wholesalers.

Consolidation of the trade into bigger units will spell a continued decline in the significance of the clubs. Even the highly personalized art of the diamond broker is becoming "modernized." In New York, broker Joseph Schlussel has computerized the stocks of the sellers whom he represents, and can match buyers and sellers with a flick of the finger. Schlussel's computer requires a capital investment beyond that available to the old-style broker, but he represents the future.

The chain of six meant the beginning of the end to the craft of diamond polishing, and the Piermatic eliminates any remaining aspect of craftsmanship to the processing of diamond rough. The changes in the organization of the diamond world currently under way make the extinction of the small manufacturer and dealer and their brokers seem certain. The exit of these little men, the dominant elements of diamond manufacturing and trade throughout history, will complete the transformation of diamonds from a cottage industry to an up-to-date business. The passing of these flavorful fixtures will also represent a tremendous loss to the cultural heritage of the diamond world. About all that will survive from the arcane and colorful circle of the diamantaires will be De Beers. Some things really are forever.

GLOSSARY

◆

ALMAZJUVELIREXPORT The arm of the Soviet government that sells diamonds polished in Russia.

ANAMINT Short for Anglo American Investment Trust, a publicly traded corporation that holds important interests in De Beers and in the Diamond Trading Company, and which, in turn, is majority owned by Anglo.

ANGLO Anglo American Corporation of South Africa, Limited, the great South African mining and industrial entity founded by Sir Ernest Oppenheimer, which is the sister company of De Beers.

BREN Yiddish for "fire"; used as the diamond-world equivalent of a bull market.

BRIEFKE A small rectangular sheet of white paper folded like a blintz, used to store diamonds.

BRILLIANT Short for round, brilliant-cut diamond, the most popular form for polished diamonds.

BRUTTING The process of applying the girdle to a brilliant.

CAST Consolidated African Selection Trust, a Ghana-based diamond mining company which was the corporate parent of SLST.

CDM Originally an abbreviation for Consolidated Diamond Mines, Ltd., the diamond-mining entity of South West Africa/Namibia founded by Sir Ernest Oppenheimer. Now a wholly-owned De Beers subsidiary, the official name of the company has been changed to CDM.

CENTRAL SELLING ORGANISATION The collection of Oppenheimer-related diamond-buying and -selling companies that together constitute a central selling organization for all of the world's most substantial diamond producers.

CLARITY Diamond graders' term to refer to the structural quality of a diamond.

CLARITY GRADES A stone that appears to be without flaws when viewed under ten-power magnification by an experienced eye is graded Flawless. A stone is IF (internally flawless) if it would be graded as flawless except for minor surface blemishes that can be removed with repair polishing.

Stones that have only one or a very few flaws, all of which are difficult to detect even under ten-power magnification, are graded VVS1 or VVS2, "very very slightly imperfect." Stones whose flaws are somewhat more prominent are still graded VS1 or VS2, "very slightly imperfect."

Slightly imperfect stones, SI1 and SI2, are obviously included (flawed) under magnification, but should still be "eye clean," should still appear flawless to the naked eye of a trained viewer, at least when viewed from the top. Around SI2 we begin to approach the grades of stones that are obviously flawed, even to the naked eye. An SI2 stone may appear flawed to the naked eye of a trained diamond grader when viewed from just the right perspective.

I stones, imperfect ones, are divided into three classes, I1, I2, and I3. They admit to being imperfect to the naked eye. I3 is the lowest grade for a "gem" diamond, and identifies stones that might alternately have been classed as industrials.

CROWN   The "upper" side of a brilliant, the portion of it above the girdle.

CSO   *See* Central Selling Organization.

CUT   Cut may refer either to the shape of a polished diamond or to the quality of its proportions.

CZ   Cubic zirconium, the most convincing fake diamond devised to date.

D   The rarest and most desired shade of "white" diamond. A D stone will be completely devoid of color.

D-FLAWLESS   The very best grade of diamond, D in color and free from internal flaws or surface blemishes of any kind.

DIAMANG   Companhia de Diamantes de Angola, the diamond mining company that exploits the diamond deposits of Angola, now majority owned by the government of Angola, with a small minority interest owned by De Beers.

DIAMANTAIRE   Anyone involved in one or more aspects of diamond manufacturing or the diamond trade.

DIAMOND CORPORATION   A wholly-owned De Beers subsidiary that purchases the diamond production of non-De Beers diamond-mining entities for resale through the Diamond Trading Company.

DIAMOND TRADING COMPANY   The selling arm of the CSO, commonly known as the DTC.

DIMINCO   Acronym for National Diamond Mining Company, the principal diamond-mining entity of Sierra Leone.

DMC   Diamond Marketing Corporation, an agency of the government of Ghana that merchandises all of the country's legitimate diamond production.

DTC   *See* the Diamond Trading Company.

EIGHT-CUT (or ACHTKANT)   A round brilliant with seventeen or eighteen facets that is not further processed into a fully finished brilliant with fifty-eight facets.

"FANCIES"   "Fancies" generally refers to diamonds cut in one of the so-called fancy shapes, illustrated on page 168 of the text. In the appropriate context, however, "fancies" may also refer to fancy-colored diamonds.

FANCY COLORS   Naturally colored diamonds. Yellows and browns must be intensely yellow or intensely brown to be regarded as fancies. Yellowish and brownish stones are not "fancy colors," but are discolored "white" stones.

FANCY SHAPES   Any of the shapes into which diamonds may be cut other than the round brilliant. See page 168.

FOUR Cs   Carat weight, color, clarity, and cut, the criteria by which diamonds are evaluated.

GCD   Ghana Consolidated Diamonds, the only significant diamond producer in Ghana, majority owned by the government, minority owned by CAST.

GDO   The Government Diamond Office of Sierra Leone, managed for the government by De Beers' Diamond Corporation.

GE   General Electric, the villain that invented the process for synthesizing diamond.

GIA   The Gemological Institute of America, an educational institution serving the jewelry trade, one of whose arms operates the most nearly respected diamond-grading lab.

GIRDLE   The circular rim or equator around the midsection of a round brilliant.

HDC   Hindustan Diamond Company, a joint venture of the government of India and the DTC, and the only dealing sightholder in India.

HRD   Hoge Raad Voor Diamant, or Diamond High Council, the parliament of the Antwerp diamond community.

I (Imperfect)   Diamond graders' term to characterize a stone that is plainly flawed. *See* Clarity Grades.

IDB   Illicit diamond buying.

IDM   Illicit diamond mining.

IF   Internally flawless. *See* Clarity Grades.

JC–K   Jewelers' Circular–Keystone, the leading American jewelry trade periodical.

KEMPEN   The countryside outside and easterly of Antwerp. Much of Antwerp's cutting is actually done in the *kempen.*

KIMBERLITE   The igneous rock that is the natural matrix of diamond.

KIMBERLITE PIPE   A volcanic plug hole composed of kimberlite.

LDI   Lens Diamond Industries, a large diamond-sawing enterprise in Antwerp's *kempen,* principally owned by Oppenheimer entities.

LOUPE   The jeweler's ten-powered eyepiece.

MAKE   Term by which diamantaires refer to the proportions and finish of a diamond.

MELANGE   A mixed parcel of diamonds of varying qualities and sizes.

MELEE   Smallish diamonds. At the moment, polished diamonds from about 8 points to around 20 points are regarded as melee. Whether a particular stone is classed as a "size" (largish), melee (smallish), or a "small" is constantly changing, depending on conditions and trends within the trade.

MELEE ROUGH   Small rough diamonds that will be manufactured into melee.

MIBA   Société Minière de Bakwanga, the principal diamond-mining company operating in Zaire, majority owned by the government of Zaire.

NMDC   National Mineral Development Corporation, a government of India entity that operates the diamond mine at Panna, India, the country's only organized diamond mine.

PAVILION   The underside of a brilliant, the portion of it below the girdle.

PIERMATIC   The Piermatic Automatic Diamond Polishing Machine.

POLISHED   Diamond trade shorthand for a finished diamond. The plural of "polished" is "polished."

PREMIUM STONES   Rough stones that will bring a premium in the open market over the price for which the DTC is currently selling similar goods.

ROUGH   A diamond in its natural state, prior to processing. The plural of "rough" is "rough."

SI   Slightly imperfect. *See* Clarity Grades.

SIBEKA (Société d'Enterprise et d'Investissements du Bécéka)   The major Belgian diamond-mining company that operates MIBA for the government of Zaire and also engages in diamond mining in South America. Sibeka is minority owned by De Beers and other Oppenheimer family interests.

SIGHTHOLDER   One who buys direct from the DTC.

SLST   Sierra Leone Selection Trust, the original diamond-mining entity operating within Sierra Leone, which manages Diminco for the government.

SYNDICATE   In-trade reference to either the CSO or the DTC. The term is a holdover from the days when diamond distribution was in fact controlled by a syndicate of buyers. Neither the CSO nor the DTC is a "syndicate" operation, but the term lingers.

TABLE   The flat uppermost facet of a brilliant.

VSI   Very slightly imperfect. *See* Clarity Grades.

VVSI   Very very slightly imperfect. *See* Clarity Grades.

ACKNOWLEDGMENTS AND BIBLIOGRAPHICAL NOTES

De Beers can open most of the doors in the diamond world for the journalist. Or it can keep most of the doors closed. In that sense De Beers has a monopoly on diamond information, as well as on diamond rough, and decisions at the DTC can make things ever so much easier or almost impossible for the diamond writer, just as they can for the diamond manufacturer. There is nothing mysterious or clandestine about this: because diamond people's livelihoods depend on the DTC, nobody wants to risk incurring its wrath. That is not De Beers' "fault."

My impression is that De Beers gives some cooperation to every writer—even those who are obviously hostile—and that the company gives more or less cooperation depending upon how it gauges the journalist's "slant" and the significance of his project to the Oppenheimer group and to the diamond world. In determining its attitude toward any particular writer, the company scrutinizes his background as thoroughly as it scrutinizes that of a prospective diamond sorter.

At least in my own case I would not say that the company had abused its monopoly of information. It opened the doors for me worldwide, and everywhere I went I found the De Beers, DTC, and Diamond Corporation people uniformly helpful and gracious. This book could not have been written without their cooperation and assistance, which is gratefully acknowledged. Within the spheres of their influence, Selection Trust and Sibeka people were every bit as kind.

Fear of commercial retribution, both up and down the diamond distribution pipeline, is a constant in the diamond world, and inasmuch as this book may not be well received there, I express my thanks to the dozens of diamantaires who gave me their time and thoughts in the way that most of them would want: by leaving them unnamed. For the same reason I have generally avoided identifying informants in the text. Though they remain mostly anonymous, I am grateful to them all.

Despite the lumps that the diamantaires have taken throughout this book, I leave this project with considerable affection and some admiration for them as a group, and I hope that some of the relationships established during the research for it can survive the book's publication.

The manuscript was typed, much of it more than once, by Carol Terry. I hope *she* will not be too embarrassed by being named here.

Though this book has been written principally from interviews, it has been influenced by and checked against hundreds of published sources, the most significant of which should make useful further reading for anyone still interested. Of the general works, the standard in-trade text, *Diamonds,* by Eric Bruton (2d edition; Radnor, Pa.: Chilton Book Company, 1978), is authoritative, well written, and gives the best overview. Two superb volumes, *International Diamond Annual* (Johannesburg: Diamond Annual Ltd., 1971) and *International Diamonds No. 2* (Johannesburg: Diamond Annual Ltd., 1972), both edited by A. Wilson, once chief public relations officer of De Beers, were more useful for my purposes because they include in-depth articles about every facet of the diamond world.

Notwithstanding its title, *The Sierra Leone Diamonds,* by H. L. van der Laan (London: Oxford University Press, 1965), is not simply a monograph on its topic, but gives an excellent introduction by a Dutch economist to the workings of the CSO and the entire diamond world, inside and outside. To a lesser extent the same is true of Michael Szenberg, *The Economics of the Israeli Diamond Industry* (New York: Basic Books, 1971). Godehard Lenzen, *The History of Diamond Production and the Diamond Trade* (New York: Praeger Publishers, 1970) and S. Tolansky, *The History and Use of Diamond* (London: Methuen, 1962), are both useful on broader ranges than their titles might indicate. For the current state of the business in the various diamond countries, *Diamonds: Myth, Magic, and Reality,* ed. Jacques Legrand (New York: Crown Publishers, 1980) is worth consulting. To check specifics, I have constantly referred to *The Diamond Dictionary,* by Robert A. P. Gaal (2d edition; Santa Monica, Calif.: Gemological Institute of America, 1977).

Of the diamond books aimed at the general public, two recent entries are the most respectable: *The World of Diamonds* by Timothy S. Green (New York: William Morrow, 1981); and *The Diamond People* by Murray Schumach (New York: W. W. Norton, 1981). Schumach is the more insightful; Green the more comprehensive. These, as well as this book, are to be followed shortly by Edward J. Epstein, *The Diamond Invention* (New York: Simon & Schuster, 1981), not yet seen by this author. Best of the older works, all of them relatively superficial, would be Victor Argenzio, *Diamonds Eternal* (New York: David McKay, 1974); George G. Blakey, *The Diamond* (New York: Paddington Press, 1977); and *Diamond* by Emily Hahn (New York: Doubleday, 1957).

Every few months a major American periodical features a spread on the diamond world. A few of these may be of lasting interest, and particularly Paul Gibson in *Forbes,* May 28, 1979, and other *Forbes* pieces in issues dated February 1, 1970, and June 15, 1973. Others in *Newsweek,* September 25, 1978, and *Dun's,* September 1973 and October 1980, should also be worth consulting for many years in the future. Everyone in the diamond world liked the piece by Fred Ward in *National Geographic,* January 1979, which is also useful. Major diamond reviews in *Jeweler's Circular–Keystone (JC–K),* September 1978, September 1979, and September 1980, featured articles by the talented people now or formerly on its staff, David Federman, Ettagale Lauré, Mitchell Gilbert, and Annalee Gold, all of which were indispensable for my purposes. Reportage of more transitory interest can be picked out of the *Reader's Guide to Periodical Literature.* While *Business Week* has never given close focus to the diamond world as such, its shorter pieces on aspects of the diamond business are usually meatier than most.

The diamond world is fortunate to be served by several very fine trade publications. I have constantly relied upond *Diamant* (Antwerp), *Israel Diamonds* (Tel Aviv), *Gems & Jewellery* (Bombay), and to a lesser extent *Diamond News and SA Jeweller* (Johannesburg). Other diamond trade journals that I sporadically consulted include *Diamond World Review*, which sometimes overlaps with *Israel Diamonds* (both are edited by the insightful Theodore Loevy); *Indiaqua* (*Industrial Diamond Quarterly*), which despite its name is not narrowly focused and which is lively and well done; and *Industrial Diamond Review*, which *is* narrowly focused and (for other than the engineer or scientist) dull.

While not strictly speaking a diamond-trade journal, *JC–K,* the leading American jewelers' magazine, spends more of its space on diamond-trade happenings than on anything else. *JC–K* is very likely the best trade magazine serving any trade anywhere in the world, and is as readable as *Time, Esquire,* you name it—top-notch. *National Jeweler,* the "other" American jewelers' magazine, is also a very fine publication.

Those who are hell-bent on investing in diamonds should probably subscribe to *JC–K* and, perhaps to *PreciouStones Newsletter,* a monthly with informative articles on diamonds, rubies, and emeralds geared to investors. *PreciouStones Newsletter* is devoid of the huckstering quality that too often characterizes "gold-bug" literature. Its monthly tables of representative "wholesale" prices, however, are very much on the high side, as are the "wholesale" prices published by NYDEX in the *Wall Street Journal.* Pretty much everyone on the inside has a stake in keeping the ultimate consumer ignorant as to realistic diamond club prices, so that things that are not bargains will appear to be bargains. For more realistic prices, *The Diamond Registry Bulletin,* a little monthly for the trade published by the Diamond Registry, 30 West 47th Street, is the most reliable I have found, and includes valuable notes on happenings in the diamond world.

The Oppenheimer companies have their own organ, *Optima,* free to stockholders of Anglo American, De Beers, or Charter Consolidated, which frequently carries diamond-related articles. *Optima* puts the in-house periodicals issued by the major American corporations to shame. More first-class journalism.

Some of the other published sources that were useful to me for specific aspects of this book are listed below.

Burgess, P. H. E. *Diamonds Unlimited.* London: The Adventurers Club, 1960. (Candid biography of Williamson.)

Carstens, Jack. *A Fortune Through My Fingers.* Cape Town: Howard Timmins, 1962. (On Namaqualand's diamond riches by the man who discovered them, only to have the fortune run though his fingers.)

Chilvers, H. A. *The Story of De Beers.* London: Cassell, 1939. (Typical in-house company history, long on trivia, short on insight.)

Collier, Barnard. "The Psychology of Fake." *Washington Post Magazine,* April 9, 1972. (Delicious history/biog of Madame Wellington and the Counterfeit Diamond.)

Cox, Keith G. "Kimberlite Pipes." *Scientific American,* April 1978. (Most nearly comprehensible introduction to the geology of it all.)

Cronje, Gillian and Suzanne. *The Workers of Namibia.* London: International Defence and Aid Fund for Southern Africa, 1979. (Finds CDM to be the best of a bad lot of enslavers.)

Fleming, Ian. *The Diamond Smugglers.* New York: Macmillan, 1958. (On De Beers' battle against thievery.)

Flint, John. *Cecil Rhodes.* Boston: Little, Brown, 1974. (Excellent short biography.)

Geological Survey of India, Miscellaneous Publication No. 19, Diamond. Delhi: The Government of India, 1971.

Greenhalgh, Peter. "An Economic History of the Ghanaian Diamond Industry, 1919–1973." Unpublished Ph.D. thesis, University of Birmingham, England, 1975.

Gregory, Theodore. *Ernest Oppenheimer and the Economic Development of Southern Africa.* Cape Town: Oxford University Press, 1962. (Earliest and still the fullest biography of Sir Ernest, by a celebrated English economist—who is not, however, celebrated for this obtuse and unrevealing volume.)

Haberfeld, Cyril B. *A Hundred Years of Kimberley Jewry.* Kimberley: Griqualand West Hebrew Congregation, 1973.

Harbottle, Michael. *The Knaves of Diamonds.* London: Seeley Service & Co., 1976. (The Hastings Airport heist and other skullduggery in Sierra Leone.)

Hocking, Anthony. *Oppenheimer and Son.* Johannesburg: McGraw-Hill, 1973. (Best all-around source on Sir E. and Harry.)

Jessup, Edward. *Ernest Oppenheimer: A Study in Power.* London: Rex Collings, 1979. (Alternates between hagiography and hatchet job; based principally on Gregory and Hocking, *supra,* supplemented by interviews with people who really did not know Sir Ernest very well.)

Lanning, Greg, with Marti Mueller. *Africa Undermined: Mining Companies and the Underdevelopment of Africa.* London: Penguin Books, 1979. (Left-wing criticism of Anglo, De Beers, et al.)

Lawrence, Petcr D. "A Street-Wise Guide to Diamond Buying." *New York,* November 27, 1978. (Good stuff.)

Lewinsohn, Richard. *Barney Barnato.* New York: Dutton, 1938. (Evocative and moving portrait.)

Linari-Linholm, A. A. *Occurrence, Mining and Recovery of Diamonds.* Johannesburg: De Beers Consolidated Mines, Ltd., 1973. (An obscure but useful booklet on its subject.)

Morgan, James. "A Guaniamo Diamond Miner Is Nobody's Best Friend." *Atlantic Monthly,* April 1971. (Adventures in Venezuela.)

Nassau, Kurt. *Gems Made by Man.* Radnor, Pa.: Chilton Book Company, 1980. (On synthetics.)

Nkrumah, Kwame. *Neo-Colonialism: The Last Stages of Imperialism.* London: Thomas Nelson & Sons, 1965. (Devotes considerable space to the diamond world, regrettably without real analysis.)

Poll, Solomon. *The Hasidic Community of Williamsburg.* New York: Schocken Books, 1969. (Engrossing sociological study.)

Rabinowitz, Louis Isaac. " 'Piety' and Honesty." *Judaism,* 1980.

Roberts, Brian. *Cecil Rhodes and the Princess.* Philadelphia: Lippincott, 1969.

———. *The Diamond Magnates.* New York: Charles Scribner's Sons, 1972.

———. *Kimberley: Turbulent City.* Cape Town: D. Philip, 1976. (Anyone interested in the history or personalities of the South African diamond rush should reach for a Roberts book.)

Ross, Lillian. "Profile: The Big Stone." *The New Yorker,* May 8 and May 15, 1954. (Best introduction to what made Harry Winston run.)

Saron, Gustav, and Louis Hotz, editors. *The Jews of South Africa.* Cape Town: Oxford University Press, 1955.

Smith, Douglas W. "Conflict and Change in the Socioeconomic Organization of Diamond Production in Guyana." Unpublished master's thesis. McGill University, 1968. (Valuable insights into the "organization" of disorganized diamond production everywhere, not simply in South America.)

Sunday Times (Johannesburg), May 31, 1936. (Gripping reportage on the conditions of the South African diamond diggers during the Great Depression.)

Tolansky, S. *Strategic Diamond.* Edinburgh: Oliver & Boyd, 1968.

van der Laan, H. L. *The Lebanese Traders in Sierra Leone.* The Hague: Mouton, 1975. (Sociological "sequel" to his *The Sierra Leone Diamonds,* op cit.)

Williams, Eric Lloyd. "Diamond Harvest of the Namib Surf: The Story of CDM." *Optima,* Two, 1978.

Yogev, Gedalia. *Diamonds and Coral: Anglo-Dutch Jews and Eighteenth-Century Trade.* Leicester, England: Leicester University Press, 1978. (Scholastic but interesting.)

INDEX

◆

India *(cont'd)*
  history of diamond-processing
    industry in, 239–41
  importance of diamond-processing
    industry to, 253–54
  labor supply in, 241
  manufacturing in, 241–46
  modern diamond-mining industry
    in, 119–20
  prognosis for industry in, 238–39
  quality of diamond workmanship in,
    210, 241, 246
  revolt of Indian diamantaires, 136,
    142, 248
  significance of in world processing
    industry, 238
  social influence of DTC in, 247
  tax evasions in, 252–53
  trade in, 250–52
  yields of diamond manufacturers in,
    172, 252
Indiaqua, 337
Industrial Diamonds, Ltd., 81, 82, 85,
  161
Industrial Distributors, 70
Industrial Investment Trust Limited
  (India), 249
Ingber, Charles, 186, 206, 211
International Diamond Annual (1971),
  cited or quoted, 96, 233, 273,
  274, 294
Ipopeng, South Africa, 59
Isaacs, Barnett. *See* Barnato, Barney
Isaacs, Harry. *See* Barnato, Harry
Israel, 222–36
  access of diamantaires to financing
    in, 144, 227–28
  and the bren of 1978, 144–47, 229
  citizens of in New York, 259
  costs of rough to manufacturers in,
    172
  criminals in and their relations with
    the diamond community, 223
  currency controls in, 222
  Diamond Controller, officer of, 228
  effect of Piermatic upon industry in,
    230
  export subsidies in, 223
  financing by for its diamond
    community, 223
  frictions between its diamantaires
    and other citizens, 222–25
  history of diamond manufacturing
    in, 211, 226–27

  importance of industry to, 222,
    225
  manufacturing in, 228–30
  political influence of diamantaires in,
    224–25
  quality of diamond workmanship in,
    210
  role of in world diamond industry,
    225–26
  South African competition for, 230
  Soviet competition for, 229
  spawns chain-of-six processing, 182
  tax evasions in, 224, 233–36
  as threat to Antwerp, 215
  use of Piermatic in, 184
  yields of manufacturers in, 172
Israel Diamond Exchange, 206, 207,
  222, 232
  buildings of, 231–32
  and women, 188
Israel Diamonds, cited or quoted, 266,
  272, 304
Israelis
  in New York, 259
  in South Africa, 230
Ivory Coast, diggers in, 65, 66

Jacobs, Erasmus Stephanus, 15, 16
Jagersfontein Mine, 16, 21, 27
Jains, 239, 240
Jamil (Jamil Said Mohamed), 73, 81–
  82, 85, 89–90, 160
Japan, 274–75, 307, 310, 317
Jaroslawicz, Pinchos "PJ," 259–60
JC–K. See Jewelers' Circular/Keystone
JDR Diamonds, Inc. (New York), 177
Jefferies, David, 302
Jerusalem Post (Israel), cited, 224, 227,
  325
Jewelers' Circular/Keystone (JC–K), cited
  or quoted, 49, 147, 273, 275,
  277, 283, 285, 293, 294, 304,
  306, 323, 333, 336, 337
Jews
  in Antwerp, 214
  Ashkenazim vs. Sephardim, 187
  attitude of toward Ernest
    Oppenheimer's religious
    peregrinations, 28
  attitude toward women, 187–88
  and De Beers' personnel policies,
    27–28, 29, 187
  in the early diamond trade, 14, 185,
    186–87